U.S. Foreign Policy and Muslim Women's Human Rights

Kelly J. Shannon

PENN

UNIVERSITY OF PENNSYLVANIA PRESS

PHILADELPHIA

Published by
University of Pennsylvania Press
Philadelphia, Pennsylvania 19104-4112
www.upenn.edu/pennpress

Printed in the United States of America on acid-free paper
10 9 8 7 6 5 4 3 2 1

Library of Congress Cataloging-in-Publication Data
Names: Shannon, Kelly J., author
Title: U.S. foreign policy and Muslim women's human rights / Kelly J. Shannon.
Other titles: United States foreign policy and Muslim women's human rights |
    Pennsylvania studies in human rights.
Description: 1st edition. | Philadelphia : University of Pennsylvania Press, [2017] |
    Series: Pennsylvania studies in human rights
Identifiers: LCCN 2017016758 | ISBN 9780812249675 (hardcover)
Subjects: LCSH: United States—Foreign relations—Islamic countries—History—
    20th century. | United States—Foreign relations—20th century—Social aspects. |
    Muslim women—Civil rights—Islamic countries—History—20th century. |
    Muslim women—Islamic countries—Social conditions—20th century. |
    Women's rights—Islamic countries—History—20th century.
Classification: LCC JZ1480.A55 S43 2017 | DDC 323.3/4088297—dc23
LC record available at https://lccn.loc.gov/2017016758

For Jay,
and in the spirit of Lucy Maynard Salmon

Contents

Abbreviations

AAWORD	Association of African Women for Research and Development
AWN	Afghan Women's Network
BIA	Board of Immigration Appeals
CEDAW	Convention on the Elimination of All Forms of Discrimination Against Women
CSW	Commission on the Status of Women
CWGL	Center for Women's Global Leadership
FGM	female genital mutilation
FMF	Feminist Majority Foundation (a.k.a. the Feminist Majority)
ICPD	International Conference on Population and Development
INSTRAW	International Center for Training and Research on Women
ISNA	Islamic Society of North America
IWTC	International Women's Tribune Centre
NOW	National Organization for Women
OGWI	Office of Global Women's Issues, State Department
OIWI	Office of International Women's Issues, State Department
PICW	President's Interagency Council on Women

RAWA	Revolutionary Association of the Women of Afghanistan
SCIWI	Senior Coordinator for International Women's Issues
SIGI	Sisterhood Is Global Institute
SIGN	Sisterhood Is Global Network
UDHR	Universal Declaration of Human Rights
UNICEF	United Nations International Children's Emergency Fund
UNIFEM	United Nations Development Fund for Women
USAID	United States Agency for International Development
VAWA	Violence Against Women Act
WHO	World Health Organization
WID	women in development
WINN	Women's International Network News
WLP	Women's Learning Partnership for Rights, Development, and Peace
WLUML	Women Living Under Muslim Laws
WOI	Women's Organization of Iran

Introduction

This book traces a quiet revolution in U.S. foreign policy over the last few decades: the rise of women's human rights as a central concern in American relations with the Islamic world. As the United States went to war in Afghanistan in 2001, the George W. Bush administration explained its war goals in striking terms. The United States fought to avenge 9/11 and remove the Taliban from power, they claimed, but an important aim—the press called it a "collateral benefit"—was the liberation of Afghan women.[1] President Bush connected Islamic radicalism with women's subjugation. Even before the war began, he had condemned the oppression of Afghan women in an address to a joint session of Congress, describing it as part of "al Qaeda's vision for the world."[2] After commencing the U.S. invasion a few weeks later, the administration emphasized women's rights as an important objective that went hand in hand with combating terrorism. As First Lady Laura Bush explained that November, "The fight against terrorism is also a fight for the rights and dignity of women."[3]

Regardless of political affiliation, the vast majority of Americans supported the war in Afghanistan that fall.[4] Echoing the administration, the U.S. media increasingly focused on the need to restore Afghan women's human rights. The Taliban forcing women to wear the burqa symbolized their oppression for the American public and policymakers alike.[5] By November, as the Taliban appeared to be on the verge of defeat, discussions about Afghan women nearly eclipsed other coverage of the war.[6] *Democracy Now* observed in December, "As the US-led war in Afghanistan has escalated, the situation of Muslim women has taken the world's center stage."[7] Journalists, women's rights activists, policymakers, and the American public welcomed the liberation of Afghan women.

Women's rights were not traditionally a priority for American policy-makers. Many feminists, scholars, and political commentators found the Bush administration's focus surprising, especially given its adversarial relationship with American feminists before 9/11. They saw Bush's focus on Afghan women as politically opportunistic, designed to elicit public support for the war, and emphasized how the administration's rhetoric resurrected an imperial logic of "saving brown women from brown men," in the famous words of Gayatri Spivak.[8] While these criticisms had merit, they overlooked an important part of the story. Given the geopolitical, economic, and security stakes of the "War on Terror," as well as the Republican Party's record on gender issues, the Bush administration's central positioning of women's human rights in its Afghanistan policy must also be understood in another context: the history of U.S.-Islamic relations during the previous two decades.

The administration's condemnations of the Taliban spoke to a deep-seated American concern about women's human rights in Islamic societies that had become a prominent feature of U.S. discourse about Islam since the 1970s. The "rights revolution" in the United States—inclusive of civil rights, women's liberation, human rights, and other movements—had increased Americans' sensitivity to social injustice, inequality, and oppression, both at home and abroad. Bush's connecting the War on Terror with protecting Afghan women from oppression reflected how much Muslim women's rights resonated with the American public, as indicated by the acclaim for the U.S. military when it supported Afghan women.[9]

In the years before Bush took office, as American public opinion increasingly favored women's equality in the Islamic world, feminists launched effective campaigns to change U.S. policy imperatives to include women's human rights. Feminists had been so successful that, far from being simply politically opportunistic, the Bush administration's attention to Afghan women also spoke powerfully to the effectiveness of the women's human rights movement in making Islamic women's rights a visible policy issue before Bush assumed office. In many ways, Bush was following precedent: women's human rights had become so salient that policymakers *had* to consider them when dealing with Muslim countries.

American leaders also reevaluated the U.S. global mission as the Cold War ended. In the shifting international landscape of the late twentieth century, the Muslim world emerged as a crucially important region for U.S. interests. Liberals and conservatives passionately debated abortion and the role of government but were largely in agreement in their views about the status of Muslim women. American liberals and feminists promoted universal human rights, democracy, and equality, while many conservatives renewed their emphasis on freedom, U.S. values, and the American way of life. Freeing Muslim women from oppression and promoting their human rights served both agendas.

Understood in this context, Bush's emphasis on Muslim women's human rights emerged out of a significant shift in how the United States had approached the Islamic world over the previous two decades. Public support for the transnational human rights movement and the notion of universal human rights meshed with U.S. principles of pluralism and democracy, which allowed activists and policymakers to situate human rights as a meaningful policy issue.[10] American public concern and feminists' lobbying efforts regarding Muslim women in particular drove this shift. They pushed the United States to embrace a more expansive and serious definition of human rights in its foreign policy toward Islamic countries, one that condemned not only public human rights abuses, such as state-sponsored genocide, but also those that transpired in the "private" sphere, the site for much of women's oppression. This initiated a new phase of U.S. human rights policy in which women's rights became a driver and a target of American policy.

This book seeks to understand how American discourse about Muslim women's human rights took shape in the years after the Iranian Revolution and how that discourse, along with feminist activism, affected U.S. foreign policy. Gail Bederman has defined discourse as a "set of ideas and practices" that organize "the way a society defines certain truths." Discourse analysis reveals the ways in which knowledge and power are entwined, particularly how "ideas widely accepted as true determine what sorts of power relations people believe are desirable, and what sorts of political aims and strategies they can imagine."[11] Understanding how the United States deployed state power on behalf of women's human rights in Islamic countries requires that we understand how Americans perceived and understood Muslim women. Public and political discourses often reflect these perceptions and offer a window into the meaning Americans ascribed to Muslim women's rights.

A major element of U.S. discourse was the idea of human rights. Americans came to understand the place of women in Islamic societies largely through the language of universal human rights that emerged from global grassroots activism in the 1970s, which was in turn central to feminist activism. Human rights sometimes competed with and sometimes reinforced older, more imperial discourses that had shaped earlier U.S. understandings of the Islamic world.

To understand the transition, this book engages with the scholarly literature on the history of human rights. The field of human rights history is relatively young, but it has grown exponentially over the last decade. Historical scholarship has focused primarily on how people have defined human rights over time and on the origins of the contemporary human rights movement.[12] Some recent studies, however, have expanded the debate to examine what influential human rights historian Samuel Moyn has called the "salience" of human rights. They investigate why human rights, and not other concepts, "came to fit the imagination and reorient the actions of large swathes of people."[13] Scholarship on U.S. foreign policy also has explored how human rights NGOs and transnational activists influenced and were influenced by U.S. policy, how Americans defined human rights, and why U.S. policymakers and the American public embraced human rights at particular moments but not others.[14] These kinds of questions are central to this book, although the origins of the modern human rights movement are beyond its scope.

This book adds to historical understanding of how the global human rights movement evolved in the 1980s and 1990s by examining public and feminist discourses and campaigns about Muslim women. By the time of the Iranian Revolution, the "human rights revolution" was already well underway as a global, grassroots movement. Because Americans historically privileged civil and political rights over other human rights conceptions, human rights had become a Cold War tool: American policymakers and human rights activists primarily focused on the lack of individual political and religious freedoms in the Soviet Union and Eastern Europe.[15] Many Americans thus emphasized a narrow conception of human rights in the 1980s, but women's rights activists from the United States and Muslim countries debated the concept and ultimately expanded the definition of human rights to include social, economic, and cultural rights.

Women's rights activists urged the international community to embrace a more capacious definition of who was human that included women and girls in order to counter engrained notions in many cultures—including in the United States—that women are inferior to men. In pressuring the United Nations, the U.S. government, and global civil society to declare that women's rights *are* human rights, by the 1990s feminists, especially those who focused on Muslim women, effectively expanded human rights law to include gender issues, such as women's education, bodily integrity, marriage and family rights, freedom of dress and movement, and reproductive rights, as well as violence against women.

Feminist activists concerned about women in Islamic societies logically embraced a human rights discourse. Women's rights had been marginalized internationally for most of the twentieth century, as demonstrated by the ghettoization of women's issues within the UN system from the 1940s through the 1960s.[16] Quarantining women's rights from the broader human rights movement likely would have continued this trend, while adopting a human rights framework offered feminists an effective way to appeal to governments and global civil society.

The transnational human rights and feminist movements also shared many tactics and goals. Both were universalist grassroots movements that sought political, social, and cultural transformation based on human dignity and equality. Human rights have been enshrined in international law since the late 1940s, so feminists used the power of law and human rights norms to support campaigns for women's equality worldwide. Universal human rights discourse and law allowed women's rights activists to rise above cultural relativism and to counter arguments by male cultural and religious authorities who defended women's subordination as culturally authentic. In other words, feminists could use human rights' claim to universal and transcendent rights to counter relativistic arguments that women's rights derived from religion and culture.[17]

Beyond their appeal to transnational feminists, human rights were also salient for Americans generally from the 1970s onward. In his seminal 1999 article, Kenneth Cmiel explained the rise of "human rights politics" in the United States in the 1970s, as Congress, President Jimmy Carter, and individual Americans took up human rights issues and participated in transnational human rights networks. Cmiel argued that Americans began to take human rights seriously because "for many activists in the United States, a commitment to human rights was a form of patriotism, reaffirming the best ideals of the American nation."[18]

Other historians have built upon this claim to explain the human rights consensus, as many Americans embraced human rights as a central component of U.S. foreign policy by the 1970s. One historian has argued that supporting human rights allowed Americans to recover from the trauma of the

Vietnam War. Liberals could deploy human rights to distance the United States from what they saw as immoral Cold War policies that led to American support for undemocratic regimes. Conservatives meanwhile used human rights to reassert U.S. moral leadership and to attack communism. Thus, human rights "helped redefine America to Americans, for they were about American identity even more than they were about foreign policy," and they "shifted the focus from problems at home to problems abroad."[19]

Implicitly, this interpretation suggests that American human rights activism was another form of U.S. imperialism. However, as this book argues, American support for human rights was often more complex than that. Certainly, calls to advance women's rights in Islamic societies could be used to support an imperialist agenda, but the salience of Muslim women's human rights was not just about American self-absorption or empire building. Many Americans were genuinely motivated by universal concepts of rights that did not always overlay neatly onto preexisting U.S. ideals. While they did not abandon national identity, many American activists sought to build alternate communities that minimized nationalism in favor of other solidarities. The global feminist movement was one such attempt to build transnational community, and U.S. feminists' calls for greater attention to women's human rights abroad went hand in hand with their battle for gender equality at home. Americans' human rights activism was thus simultaneously a project to transform U.S. identity and to build a truly universal system of rights. These two impulses sometimes competed with and sometimes reinforced one another, but, in both cases, feminists redefined human rights as women's rights, and this made U.S. foreign policymakers take notice after having ignored women's rights for decades.

Drawing on the human rights movement's example of lobbying governments and exerting "third-party influence," women's rights activists mobilized public opinion on behalf of Muslim women and ultimately succeeded by the 1990s in getting U.S. policymakers to take women's human rights seriously when formulating policy toward Islamic countries.[20] Consequently, women's rights became a key point of contention between the United States and governments of Islamic countries, such as Saudi Arabia and Afghanistan. This revolutionary policy shift has had a complex impact. U.S. policymakers often adopted feminists' language and human rights concepts and included women's rights in policies meant to advance democracy, pluralism, human rights, and prosperity worldwide. However, they also often combined women's human rights discourses with neoimperialist ones that cast Muslims as backward and in need of Western enlightenment. U.S. policies often assisted women's rights activists in Muslim countries by providing crucial development aid and moral support, but when those policies accompanied military intervention, as in Afghanistan and Iraq after 9/11, they also engendered fierce resistance, as many Muslims came to equate women's equality with U.S. imperialism. This book seeks to decipher the complicated relationship between transnational feminism, human rights, imperialism, and U.S. foreign policy regarding women in Islamic societies.

Beyond contributing to scholarly debates about the history of human rights, this book also touches upon fierce debates within U.S. foreign relations history over the relationship between culture and power. Conventional diplomatic histories focus on policy elites and official state-to-state interactions as drivers of U.S. policy. Their analyses privilege the influence of "hard power" concerns, such as economics, geopolitics, security, and strategy, on U.S. policy decisions. In the last few decades, however, historians have challenged this approach by using cultural and gender analysis to expand the field of diplomatic history into the history of U.S. "foreign relations" broadly defined, which encompass any interaction between Americans and people from other countries. These studies include "soft power" in their analyses of U.S. behavior and seek to understand American foreign relations in a new light, whether by tracing how cultural assumptions influenced policy or by highlighting the influence of non-state actors.[21]

The result has been a division between traditional and nontraditional methodological approaches and an ongoing—although by now fairly stale—debate over the utility of cultural and gender analysis for understanding U.S. behavior. Many excellent traditional studies of American policy shunt culture and gender aside, leaving potentially important factors in policymaking unexamined. On the other hand, because culture is a slippery concept, cultural and gender analyses of U.S. foreign policy often fail to provide concrete evidence that culture had a measurable impact on specific policies. While thought-provoking and engaging, these books often leave traditionalists unsatisfied in their treatment of causation.[22]

The culturalist-traditionalist divide certainly characterizes, and persists in, studies of U.S.-Islamic relations.[23] Those historians who do incorporate cultural analysis often dissect U.S. leaders' cultural stereotypes of Arabs or Muslims, but they tend to focus on the policymaking elite or neglect to examine how human rights influenced American relations with Muslim peoples.[24] Moreover, no history of U.S. policy toward the Islamic world includes women as its central focus. The field—and even those studies that utilize gender analysis—often focuses exclusively upon male historical actors.[25] The relationship between women and U.S. foreign policy remains underexplored.[26] This project therefore examines women as both objects and creators of U.S. foreign policy. Several studies have illustrated the importance of culture, and of gender in particular, in Western or American thought and rhetoric about the Islamic world, but few connect this issue directly to U.S. policy decisions beyond the level of rhetoric.[27] This book, however, makes those connections.

The boundary between traditional and cultural methods is artificial, at least in this instance. This book demonstrates how American cultural attitudes about Muslim women have been absorbed fully into U.S. policy, effectively dissolving the boundary between hard and soft power. Protecting Muslim women's human rights has become an essential part of U.S. policy, and only by transcending the methodological divide between culture and hard power can historians understand how this occurred.

Based solely on traditional approaches, the story this book tells would be inexplicable. In this case, non-state actors, including feminist scholars, activists, and journalists, often spoke directly to American policymakers, and policymakers' language frequently mimicked or reflected the discourses of women's human rights activists and the U.S. public. American cultural perceptions about Muslim women had a specific, measurable impact on U.S. policy, in some cases even trumping hard power concerns. This book, in short, turns conventional wisdom about the drivers of U.S. foreign policy on its head.

Most Americans gave little thought to women living in Muslim countries prior to the late 1970s. Those who did tended to deploy Orientalist stereotypes of Muslim women as belly dancers, harem girls, and symbols of Muslim backwardness—not unlike centuries-old European representations of Muslims. With few exceptions, there was little indication before the 1970s that Americans believed they should help Muslim women claim their human rights.

Edward Said famously argued that Western scholars, novelists, artists, and politicians constructed a binary "style of thought" called Orientalism that cast the Muslim world as the "Other" in order to dominate it.[28] Orientalism therefore worked in the service of the colonial state. Through this discursive construction, the Muslim world was the home of a backward culture that was the mirror opposite of the "modern" West. Scholarship inspired by Said has demonstrated how Western discourse historically cast Muslim women as sexualized objects of fetish or as silent symbols of Muslim despotism and inferiority.[29]

American discourse about Muslim women after the Iranian Revolution certainly contained these elements, but it was not strictly Orientalist in nature. Orientalist stereotyping now competed with other frameworks, such as universal human rights. While many scholars have pointed out the shortcomings of Said's theory, particularly when applied to the post-1945 United States, Melani McAlister's "post-Orientalist" model is particularly useful for explaining American characterizations of Muslims since 1979.[30] McAlister argued that Said's paradigm assumes a homogeneous "West," but in reality the United States differed from European nations, and Americans themselves were never homogeneous. She explained, "Political and cultural conditions in the United States produced a post-Orientalist model. . . . These representational dynamics were not always in the service of U.S. state power; in certain cases, they explicitly contested the presumptions of official U.S. policies. But even the official rhetoric of nationalist expansionism worked to establish the United States as different from the old colonial powers, and it did so in part by fracturing the East-West binary on which traditional Orientalism had depended."[31] Moreover, not all stereotypes of Muslims are Orientalist; "they might be racist, imperialist, and exoticizing without engaging in the particular logic of Orientalism: binary, feminizing [regarding Muslim men], and citational."[32]

In this book, I follow McAlister's lead and characterize American attitudes as post-Orientalist. American public discourse from 1979 onward incorporated new frameworks that sometimes competed with and sometimes reinforced Orientalist understandings. Islamophobia, for instance, was a relatively new discourse after the Iranian Revolution. Scholars have defined Islamophobia variously as "moral panic," "anti-Muslim prejudice," or an anti-Muslim "ideological formation," but these definitions are too vague.[33] The primary, defining characteristic of Islamophobia is fear. Islamophobia casts Muslims, especially men, as dangerous to Americans, the United States, and Western values. Not since the Barbary Wars centuries before had Americans feared Muslims, but because of the Iranian Revolution, Americans began to combine Islamophobic and Orientalist frameworks to understand Muslim men. They also went from seeing Muslim women simply as exotic to seeing them as victims of dangerous Islamic men in need of U.S. support.

Post-1979 U.S. discourse about Muslim women thus incorporated Islamophobia but also placed their oppression within the universalist framework of women's human rights. Muslim women ceased to be silent symbols. Women from Islamic countries increasingly participated in U.S. public debates by giving speeches, authoring publications, appearing on television, and actively participating in NGOs. These women most often were middle or upper class, educated, and secular, rather than conservative or poor. Nevertheless, when Muslim women participated in U.S. public debates, they seemed less like the inferior Other and more like people who cherished the same universal freedoms and rights as Americans did.

The conversation about Muslim women was therefore not an American monologue, nor was it driven simply by Orientalist logic. Universal human rights and women's rights frameworks competed with Orientalism, imperialism, and Islamophobia as Americans sought to understand the place of women in Islamic societies. Much as Bederman described, this discourse was "multiple, inconsistent, and contradictory."[34] Such frameworks allowed Americans to pursue the simultaneous and sometimes opposing goals of fostering an equitable world based on universal human rights and seeking to dominate the Islamic world.

For example, in the late twentieth century, women's rights were one barometer by which Americans judged social progress in Islamic societies. This was not entirely new: since at least the eighteenth century, Westerners generally identified certain freedoms for women—specifically those that Western women enjoyed—as markers of modernity.[35] As Europeans colonized Africa and Asia, they had often pointed to the oppression of women in those regions as justification. The British claimed to defend women from "backward" men in places like India and Egypt.[36] Part of the imperial project was to remake the cultures of the colonized, and women's roles were central to this effort because women symbolized tradition and raised the next generation. Even Westerners who opposed feminist advances at home, such as women's suffrage, condemned non-Western societies for oppressing women in order to validate the Western "civilizing mission."[37] Meanwhile, Western feminists became complicit in imperialism by seeking to uplift their more oppressed "sisters" in the colonized world. Scholars refer to this phenomenon as "colonial feminism."[38] During the Algerian War, for example, French feminists staged a public unveiling of Muslim women in Algeria to demonstrate that only continued French rule could ensure rights for Algerian women.[39]

Late twentieth-century American understandings about Islam were influenced by this history. Conservatives in the United States who sought to limit reproductive rights and opposed the Equal Rights Amendment nevertheless condemned gender practices in Muslim countries. They disagreed with feminists and liberals about many issues, but they did not push for American women to be stripped of the right to vote, deprived of education, subjected to mandatory dress codes, forced to marry at a young age, or forced to undergo female genital mutilation, as women were in some Islamic countries. At the same time, however, many liberals and feminists in the United States characterized Islamic practices that they believed oppressed women as violations of universal human rights. By the 1970s, the impetus to protect Muslim women's human rights came not just from elites, traditionally the shapers of U.S. policy, but also increasingly from nongovernmental organizations (NGOs), the media, scholars, and the general public. While Americans often disagreed sharply about the meaning of concepts like "liberty," "freedom," and "rights," many nevertheless agreed upon the basic desirability of promoting such values on a global scale.[40] By advocating for expanded rights for Muslim women, many Americans sought to bring about a world based upon universal rights and freedoms as they defined them.

While feminists, scholars, and NGOs may not always have dominated public discussions of Islam, they played vitally important roles in the construction of U.S. foreign policy regarding Muslim women. These actors, particularly members of the Sisterhood Is Global Institute, Women Living Under Muslim Laws, and the Feminist Majority, lobbied the U.S. government, publicized violations of women's human rights in Islamic countries, and led campaigns to put international pressure on governments that oppressed women. Ultimately, public opinion and feminists' campaigns had a powerful effect on policymakers, and they competed against the older historical discourses of Orientalism and "rescue" narratives. By the 1990s, concerns about Muslim women sometimes drove U.S. policy, as when the Clinton administration refused to recognize the Taliban regime in Afghanistan, a situation no conventional understanding of foreign policy could have predicted. In this instance, women's human rights concerns surpassed substantial hard power ones. At other times, rhetoric about the oppression of Muslim women was a tool to legitimize U.S. interventions in the Islamic world that were driven initially by quite different concerns. Bush's criticism of the Taliban's treatment of women exemplifies the latter.

That U.S. policy imperatives came to include the protection of Muslim women's human rights at the turn of the twenty-first century says something important about how Americans saw their role in the post–Cold War world. By arguing that U.S. concerns about Muslim women reflected U.S. culture and values, however, this book does not suggest that such concerns were therefore illegitimate or spurious. This book is not an exercise in cultural relativism; many customs and laws in Muslim countries do harm women and should be condemned, as should violations of human rights everywhere.[41] That said, this book's goal is to explain the roots and political instrumentality of U.S. opposition to Muslim practices that subordinate women. Historians of U.S. foreign relations often portray Americans' interactions with non-Western peoples as a zero-sum game, wherein criticism of American policies, attitudes, and actions involves lionizing the "Other" while casting the United States as the villain.[42] Other scholars reverse the roles but use the same framework, pitting the benevolent United States against evildoers.[43] This study seeks to transcend the good/evil binary and demonstrate in all its complexity the influence of Americans' concerns about women's human rights on their interactions with Muslim peoples.

A Note on Terminology: In discussing a topic as broad as the "Muslim world" or "Islamic world," there are limitations in terminology. There are many differences among Islamic societies, and Islam is practiced in multiple ways by groups who hold differing levels of religiosity and myriad political views. Muslim-majority countries stretch from Africa across the Middle East and into Central and Southeast Asia, but Muslims live around the globe, including in Europe and the Americas. At the same time, many non-Muslims live in Muslim-majority regions. Without implying that I see Islam as monolithic and with the knowledge that there are Muslims worldwide, I use the terms "Muslim world" and "Islamic world" as a necessary if flawed shorthand to refer to those countries in Africa, the Middle East, and Asia with Muslim-majority populations.[44] Similarly, when I use terms like "Americans," "American," and "U.S. feminists," I necessarily refer to non-Muslim people in the United States and characterize the United States as a non-Islamic country. Although the population of American Muslims is growing, they still make up only about 1 percent of the U.S. population.[45] When I do discuss Muslim Americans, I indicate that explicitly.

Many people in the United States equate the "Islamic world" with the Middle East and assume that most Muslims are Arab. The majority of the world's Muslims actually live in Asia, and not all Arabs are Muslim. The American conflation of Islam with the Arab Middle East most likely stems from recent foreign policy; older missionary, tourism, and trade activity; and the longer tradition of contact between the Middle or "Near" East and Western Europe. This conflation may also stem from demographics. While the majority of the world's Muslims live in Asia, Muslims make up a supermajority in Middle Eastern and North African countries. Less than 20 percent of the world's Muslims live in the Middle East and North Africa, but over 91 percent of people living in this region identify as Muslim. In contrast, 62 percent of all Muslims live in Asia, but they comprise just under a quarter of the continent's population.[46] This may explain why U.S. understandings of Islam derive largely from the Arab Middle East.

Just as the "Islamic world" is not a monolith, there is no single Muslim gender system. Again, I necessarily refer to this as a shorthand, but I use such terms with the acknowledgment that they obscure complexity. Women's rights, roles, and status vary greatly across Muslim societies. The Iranian and Saudi governments legally subordinate women and restrict their dress and behavior, but in different ways. In other Islamic countries, such as Turkey, and among Muslim communities in the West, women are relatively free and enjoy more legal equality. Within many Islamic societies, some women choose to veil, while others do not. Many Americans assume that all Muslim women veil, but veiling practices encompass a variety of hijab styles and degrees of covering, from women who do not veil at all to women who wear simple headscarves to those who wear the blue burqa of Afghanistan or black abaya and niqab (face veil) of Saudi Arabia.

Beyond geography, women's rights are also influenced by class. As is also the case in the West and other regions, women from wealthy families benefit from higher education and greater resources and consequently often live freer lives than do women from poor families. However, the conventional wisdom in the United States has been that women ubiquitously have significantly lower status and fewer rights than men in Islamic gender systems. While the reality is more complex and women in the United States have yet to enjoy full equality with men, I am referring to this general understanding of Muslim gender relations when I use such terms.

Each chapter in this book focuses upon a key moment that demonstrates the gradual integration of Muslim women's human rights into U.S. foreign policy. This policy issue was mainstreamed slowly, but the process cumulatively created substantial pressure for U.S. policymakers to take women's human rights seriously by the 1990s and 2000s. Chapter 1 identifies the Iranian Revolution as the catalyst for intense U.S. public attention to Muslim women's rights, a conceptual precursor for Americans' later understanding of women's human rights in the Islamic world. Because of the Iranian Revolution, Americans from across the political spectrum began to characterize the harsh repression of women as a key—and reprehensible—characteristic of Islamic fundamentalism.[47]

Throughout the 1980s, the notion that Muslim men in general oppressed women became firmly entrenched in U.S. public discourse, and some Americans began to advocate for the United States to take action on behalf of Muslim women's human rights. Chapter 2 examines the growing concern for Muslim women throughout the U.S. public sphere, from the news media to scholarly studies to popular culture. Public receptivity to the integration of women's rights into foreign policy incubated and solidified in the years between the Iranian Revolution and early 1990s. Feminists later mobilized this public opinion to campaign for women's human rights in the Islamic world.

Chapter 3 traces the development of feminist NGOs and feminist concepts that played an important role in later U.S. policy decisions. The UN world conferences on women during the UN Decade for Women—in Mexico City in 1975, Copenhagen in 1980, and Nairobi in 1985—provided a forum for American feminists and their Muslim counterparts to discuss the problems women faced in Islamic countries and to create networks of information and support. Through these international networks, American and Muslim women allied in the 1980s to form NGOs, such as the Sisterhood Is Global Institute and Women Living Under Muslim Laws, that publicized the plight of Muslim women and later lobbied the U.S. government to prioritize women's rights in U.S. foreign policy. The lively debates between U.S. and Muslim feminists about how to define women's human rights during the Decade also influenced how Americans later defined policy. While the U.S. public and policymakers continued to draw upon older stereotypes about Muslim women, feminist NGOs most forcefully worked to reconceptualize Muslim women's situations as a matter of universal human rights rather than Islamic backwardness.

Chapter 4 centers on the first Gulf War of 1990–91. As the Cold War ended and the Soviet Union dissolved, the Gulf War gave Americans a new enemy: Iraq's Saddam Hussein. However, the war caused some Americans to question the U.S. alliance with Saudi Arabia because of what they referred to as Saudi "gender apartheid." Women's legal subordination in Saudi Arabia caused feminist organizations and a vocal minority of the U.S. public—mainly women—to oppose American involvement in the war. By questioning the U.S. alliance with Saudi Arabia because of Saudis' treatment of women, these Americans suggested for the first time that concern for Muslim women's human rights should be integral to U.S. foreign policy.

Chapter 5 investigates the moment when public and feminist concern for Muslim women's rights first found its way into U.S. policy. American foreign policy priorities began to shift in the 1990s. As part of a transnational movement, American activists tried to eradicate the African practice of female genital mutilation, or FGM, which Americans characterized as an Islamic custom (although the reality is more complex). American activists situated their arguments against FGM within the larger U.S. discourse that linked Islam with the oppression of women. As a sensational issue that garnered much publicity, FGM became for many Americans the touchstone example of the Islamic abuse of women. On a tide of public outrage, Congress outlawed the practice in 1996 and tied U.S. foreign aid to efforts to eradicate the custom abroad. Simultaneously, U.S. asylum courts ruled that fear of FGM for oneself or one's children was sufficient grounds for granting political asylum to women from FGM-practicing societies. These groundbreaking legislative and judicial efforts initiated the institutionalization of women's human rights into U.S. foreign policy toward the Islamic world.

Chapter 6 identifies and analyzes the moment when the U.S. policy establishment fully embraced putting women's human rights at the center of policy toward an Islamic country. Largely due to public opinion and feminist lobbying, the Clinton administration refused to recognize the Taliban regime as a legitimate government owing to its deplorable treatment of women. Because of U.S. interest in running an oil pipeline across Afghanistan and the Taliban's connections to terrorist groups, Clinton's decision had tangible economic and political consequences. Here, human rights trumped economic and strategic considerations. Soft power prevailed over hard power issues in this instance, representing a major shift in U.S. policy imperatives. The chapter traces this historic decision and analyzes its consequences.

Finally, Chapter 7 analyzes continued U.S. attention to women's human rights in the Islamic world since 9/11, when projects to defend Muslim women's human rights accompanied U.S. military intervention in Afghanistan and Iraq. An imperialist, Orientalist framework also prevailed in Bush administration rhetoric and the discourse of some U.S. feminist organizations that supported warfare. The Obama administration, meanwhile, worked to distance itself from Orientalism and imperialism. However, in its haste to withdraw from unpopular wars in Iraq and Afghanistan, it left the place of women's human rights in U.S. foreign policy uncertain.

As the United States deepens its involvement in the affairs of Islamic countries, Americans' relationship with Muslim peoples has become increasingly fraught. The development of U.S. policies regarding Muslim women demonstrates how cultural issues and debates about human rights have become entwined with hard power concerns. Events like the 9/11 attacks, the U.S. wars in Afghanistan and Iraq, the Arab Spring, and the rise of groups like Boko Haram and the so-called Islamic State underscore the high stakes of tensions over culture and women's rights that have developed between East and West during the last several decades.

Chapter 1

Battling the Veil:
American Reactions to the Iranian Revolution

In October 1979, Ayatollah Khomeini gave a rare interview to a Western woman, Italian journalist and famous political interviewer Oriana Fallaci. Both *Time* and the *New York Times* published the interview, which was fraught with tension between the Supreme Leader and the outspoken reporter. The most contentious moment came when Fallaci challenged Khomeini about his fundamentalist agenda for women, symbolized by his insistence that all Iranian women wear the chador.[1] *Time* reported, "Fallaci charged that the chador was symbolic of the segregation into which women have been cast by the revolution.... 'Our customs are none of your business,' Khomeini answered. 'If you do not like Islamic dress, you're not obliged to wear it because Islamic dress is for good and proper young women.' 'That's very kind of you,' said Fallaci. 'And since you said so, I'm going to take off this stupid, medieval rag right now.'" Fallaci immediately removed her chador, which she had been required to wear, and the offended Ayatollah got up and "left the room without saying a word."[2]

Women's rights emerged as a crucial point of contention between Westerners and Khomeini after he assumed power in 1979 and only intensified in the ensuing years. This chapter examines how American discourse about Muslim women's human rights developed in reaction to the Iranian Revolution. By 1979, Americans already had a long history of characterizing Muslim gender practices as inferior. Since at least the mid-nineteenth century, American discourse negatively compared the status of women in Islamic societies to that of women in the United States. After the revolution, however, that discourse became more complex. While older stereotypes persisted, other conceptual frameworks developed that cast Muslim women as fellow human beings who desired the same rights and freedoms cherished by Americans. At the same time, U.S. discourse increasingly combined Orientalist stereotypes with Islamophobia to characterize fundamentalist Muslim men as hyperpatriarchal oppressors of women and anti-American fanatics. Based on these understandings, many Americans began to argue that the United States should promote and defend women's human rights in the Islamic world.

The Iranian Revolution was critical to this shift. Its novelty was that Iran's women *lost* rights and freedoms they had previously. Iran therefore was not simply a case of cultural difference. Iranian women faced new forms of oppression and a loss of rights because of the sudden rise to power of Islamic fundamentalists in their country, who offered a vision of Islamic society that diverged sharply not only from that of the United States but also from Iran's own recent past. What happened to Iranian women also challenged U.S. notions of progress, particularly because Americans had seen Iran as the epitome of Third World modernization since the early 1960s.[3] Khomeini's gender policies came to symbolize the general Islamic oppression of women for many in the United States. Yet Iranian women's resistance to such policies also helped American audiences see Muslim women as less foreign and male fundamentalists as a threat, not only to women's rights but also to democracy, freedom, and U.S. interests.

This discursive shift is significant because it contributed to an eventual—albeit slow—shift in U.S. foreign policy. Many Americans came to judge Muslim societies largely by their treatment of women. The dominant public perception that developed in the United States after the Iranian Revolution was that women in Muslim countries were horribly oppressed; this quickly became conventional wisdom. Over the next three decades, this notion became entrenched in U.S. public discourse, as an avalanche of books, newspaper and magazine articles, television programs, films, and conferences drew attention to the apparent lack of women's human rights in the Islamic world.

In the years following the Iranian Revolution, scholars, journalists, transnational feminists, and the general public pushed U.S. policymakers to declare the attainment of rights for women in Islamic countries a legitimate and important foreign policy goal. American policymakers also operated in the context of U.S. cultural representations that cast Islamic women as oppressed and in need of American assistance. By the 1990s, because of public opinion in favor of Muslim women's human rights and lobbying efforts by feminist activists, policymakers began to integrate concern for women's human rights into U.S. foreign policy. The Iranian Revolution's effect on women set this policy shift in motion.

Historically, U.S. cultural attitudes influenced how Americans interacted with Islamic peoples. Ever since the Barbary Wars, Americans represented the Islamic world in news reports, travel narratives, novels, scholarly studies, paintings, and films. These texts reflected and shaped how Americans understood Islamic cultures and societies.[4] An examination of American discourse about the Islamic world before the Iranian Revolution can provide a useful comparison for post-1979 developments.

Although there is no comprehensive study of the topic, American depictions of Muslim women as described in scholarly studies reveal a strong Orientalist strand throughout the nineteenth and twentieth centuries, with certain stereotypes fairly consistent over time. Amira Jarmakani identified these as "the cultural mythologies of veils, harems, and belly dancers."[5] These stereotypes held different meanings for Americans over time. In different historical moments, the harem appeared either as a place of exotic sexual fantasy or as a prison. The veil functioned alternately as a sheer covering that added to a harem girl or belly dancer's exotic allure, or as an opaque physical barricade that indicated Islamic women's invisibility. While the meanings of the harem and veil fluctuated between these two polarities, the stereotypes themselves persisted.

Americans first encountered Islamic gender relations in the 1840s and 1850s, when they began to travel as tourists and missionaries to the Middle East. Even more Americans read the numerous travel narratives about Muslim countries published in the United States from midcentury onward. Nineteenth-century American travelers who wrote about Islamic women usually described them as mysterious sexual objects or as slaves whose mistreatment indicated Oriental backwardness. These depictions cast the Muslim world as the inferior opposite of the United States.[6]

The nineteenth-century U.S. public also avidly consumed European tales that depicted Islamic societies as full of harems and exotic sexuality. Unlike Europe, however, the United States did not attempt to colonize Muslim countries. Most Americans who traveled to the Middle East and North Africa during the period sought adventure or were pilgrims to the biblical holy land. They assumed the region would resemble the fantastical places described in *Arabian Nights*, which many Americans read throughout the nineteenth and twentieth centuries.[7] Even the usually cynical Mark Twain referred repeatedly to *Arabian Nights* in *The Innocents Abroad*, his 1869 travelogue. He imagined the Middle East as a "mysterious land where the giants and genii of the *Arabian Nights* once dwelt," replete with "winged horses and hydra-headed dragons" guarding "enchanted castles."[8] Upon arrival, however, U.S. visitors—Twain included—were disappointed. Flying carpets, beautiful princesses, handsome adventurers, and fabulous riches did not abound. They found instead ordinary people with unfamiliar customs.

American men were particularly frustrated that they could not interact with Muslim women. They imagined that veiled Muslim women were exceptional beauties, tantalizingly out of reach, and they longed to gaze upon their bare faces. With his characteristic sarcasm, Twain disputed the fantasy and noted acerbically, "I have caught a glimpse of the faces of several Moorish women . . . and I am full of veneration for the wisdom that leads them to cover up such atrocious ugliness."[9] The travelogue of David Dorr, an enslaved African American who accompanied his master to the Middle East in the 1850s, was more typical of American travel writing. He wrote that not being able to see Muslim women's faces was a "source of low spirits." He described locking eyes with one veiled woman and wrote, "I would have given five pounds to lift her veil."[10] White American men expressed the same wistful longing, often fantasizing about Muslim women's kohl-rimmed eyes and hidden lips.[11] When he visited the Middle East in 1852, poet Nathanial Parker Willis voyeuristically peeped into multiple abodes searching for unveiled women and complained bitterly that Turkish houses had "jealously closed windows." After finally catching a glimpse of a slave girl through an open door, Willis lamented, "To think that only a 'malignant and turbaned Turk' may possess such a Hebe! Beautiful creature!"[12]

The veil frustrated the traveler's gaze, but artists provided access to imaginary Middle Eastern women for the American public. The most popular theme of Orientalist art was the harem woman, or *odalisque*. American artists such as Frederick Arthur Bridgman and Henry Siddons Mowbray produced dozens of paintings of beautiful harem girls in the late nineteenth century.[13] Americans who flocked to the 1893 Chicago World's Fair, where John Singer Sargent's painting *Nude Study of an Egyptian Girl* was on display, also lined up to see imported belly dancers on the fair's Midway dance the "hootchy kootchy."[14] Such titillating performances claimed to provide an "authentic" experience, a glimpse into the harem normally denied to Americans, but they were, of course, a far cry from reality.[15] In an era in which U.S. culture encouraged Victorian gender roles and chaste womanhood, such representations characterized Muslims as both exotic and inferior.

These stereotypes persisted into the twentieth century, even as the status of women in Islamic countries changed dramatically. Egyptians initiated a spirited public debate at the turn of the century about whether women should leave the harem and stop wearing the veil as part of a galvanizing national discussion about Egypt's liberation from Western imperialism.[16] In the 1920s, feminist Huda Shaarawi famously threw off her veil at the crowded Cairo train station. Egyptian feminist and historian Leila Ahmed explained, "If the era of the 1900s to the 1920s was the Age of Unveiling, the 1920s to the 1960s was the era when going bareheaded and unveiled became the norm. A good proportion of the women coming of age during these decades . . . never unveiled because, in fact, they had never veiled."[17] More women pursued formal education and participated in the paid labor force. Women's rights were also expanding in many other Islamic countries.

After World War I, modernizing governments across the Islamic world expanded women's rights. The secularist Kemal Ataturk enshrined gender equality in Turkish law in the 1920s and 1930s by granting women's suffrage, discouraging veiling, and encouraging women's education and employment. Reza Shah, the military officer who overthrew Iran's Qajar dynasty in the 1920s, banned the veil. In Afghanistan during the same period, King Amanullah Khan attempted rapid modernization, which included girls' education and the end of veiling and polygamy. His wife, Queen Soraya, wore Western clothes and was a highly visible participant in her husband's reform programs.

Although religious groups resisted many of these changes—and women did not achieve full equality anywhere—it is nevertheless true that women in Islamic countries won unprecedented freedoms in the twentieth century. Women could choose to appear unveiled in public largely unmolested, especially in cosmopolitan cities like Cairo, Tehran, and Kabul. Many voted, went to college, and had careers. Several countries amended their family laws to grant women more equality in marriage and divorce. A few U.S. newspapers did comment on women's progress in some Islamic countries from the 1920s through 1970s. They applauded modernization in the Third World, and journalists wrote about women's rights as an indicator of progress. The *New York Times* published articles in the 1920s about Egyptian women wearing French fashions and transparent face veils; unveiling and better access to education in Turkey and Iran in the 1930s; and women's suffrage movements in Egypt, Iraq, and Iran in the 1940s and 1950s.[18] However, such news stories were few and unsustained, and these developments did little to corrode American stereotypes.

Meanwhile, the U.S. entertainment industry continued to draw upon long-established motifs of the sensual harem girl as the inaccessible object of desire. American cigarette ads in the 1910s and 1920s enticed customers with beautiful harem women clad in filmy veils and skimpy outfits.[19] The emerging Hollywood film industry also drew upon Orientalist stereotypes to entertain the public. The 1921 silent film *The Sheik*—among the most influential movies in history—told the story of a romanticized desert sheik, played by Rudolph Valentino, who kidnaps and ultimately seduces a European woman. While drawing on the stereotype of the oversexed Arab male, the film also portrayed its few female Muslim characters as slaves and belly dancers.[20] *The Sheik* was a sensation, smashing box office records and inspiring songs and fashion fads.[21] Similar films over the next several decades portrayed Muslim women in the same light.[22]

The 1964 film *The Long Ships* featured an evil sheik's bevy of half-naked beauties, who are delighted when the film's Viking protagonists break into their harem, while Elvis Presley enjoyed the attention of several wide-eyed, buxom harem girls in 1965's *Harum Scarum*.[23] The popular television sitcom *I Dream of Jeannie*, which aired from 1965 to 1970, drew upon well-established Islamic motifs to tell the story of a scantily clad genie's comedic attempts to please her American master.[24] Muslim women also appeared in cartoons published in *Playboy* and *Penthouse* in the 1960s. According to one scholar, these images depicted the harem as "a world in which men are permitted as many women as they can satisfy and veiled women revel in submission to their master."[25] Such portrayals were commonplace in the United States before the Iranian Revolution. Unfree though the Muslim women of U.S. popular culture appeared, there was little indication before 1979 that many Americans felt compelled to help Muslim women claim their human rights.

Orientalist stereotypes about Muslim women persisted after the Iranian Revolution, but U.S. public discourse about Islamic women also increasingly incorporated the language of universal human rights. Orientalism did not disappear, but human rights discourse competed with and often supplanted it as another foundational concept. The story of how this happened, and the "post-Orientalist" terrain, begins not in 1979 but earlier, with the "rights revolution" after World War II, when another organizing concept to understand Muslim women, aside from *The Sheik* and *I Dream of Jeannie*, grew stronger. In postwar America, a host of marginalized groups—African Americans, women, Chicano/as, gays and lesbians, and Native Americans—condemned discrimination and demanded equal rights. The women's liberation movement, also known as Second Wave feminism, was among the most significant and far-reaching of these movements. Feminists exposed the various forms of women's oppression and championed gender equality in all areas of life.

The rights revolution did not eliminate racism, sexism, and other forms of discrimination, and it faced fierce resistance, but it did succeed in sensitizing Americans to inequality and oppression. By 1979, through grassroots activism and federal legislation, U.S. society made real progress toward recognizing and remedying many forms of injustice. It became increasingly unacceptable—and illegal—to deprive people of rights in the United States because of their race or sex.

The domestic rights revolution was part of a concomitant global one. By 1979 many Americans saw oppression and injustice outside the United States in new ways. Globalization and new technologies such as satellite television made the world seem smaller. The American public and policymaking elites began speaking of global "interdependence" and international cooperation to solve common problems.[26] Some embraced the cause to help oppressed people in other countries obtain basic human rights and freedoms. Building upon existing international human rights instruments, such as the UN Charter and the Universal Declaration of Human Rights (UDHR), concerned Americans joined forces with activists from around the world to found NGOs devoted to protecting human rights worldwide. American activists helped found organizations like Human Rights Watch and Amnesty International. They mobilized against apartheid in South Africa, torture in Chile, and genocide in Cambodia.[27] African Americans linked their fight for racial equality to anticolonial movements in Africa and Asia. Even President Jimmy Carter participated, declaring, "Human rights is [*sic*] the soul of our foreign policy."[28] Human rights activists from around the world came together to strengthen international human rights law and shame governments that violated it, and they insisted that human rights were universally applicable.

This transnational human rights movement included activism on behalf of women. American feminists forged strong connections with like-minded women from around the world by the 1970s, and feminist activism affected both national and international human rights instruments. Just as feminists won legislation and judicial decisions in the United States that outlawed sex discrimination in employment and legalized abortion, transnational feminists successfully pushed the United Nations to adopt the Convention on the Elimination of All Forms of Discrimination Against Women (CEDAW) in 1979.[29] The United Nations also declared 1975 the International Women's Year, highlighted by a world conference on women held in Mexico City that summer. Soon afterward, the United Nations designated 1975–85 the Decade for Women. From this point onward, American feminists were involved heavily in various international campaigns for women's rights. Consequently, on the eve of Iran's revolution, many U.S. journalists, feminists, scholars, and the public were primed to see Iranian women in ways that defied simple Orientalist stereotypes.

In January 1979, Shah Mohammad Reza Pahlavi fled Iran. Mass protests that began in 1978 had overthrown one of the United States' most vital allies in the Middle East. Although the Shah's government had appeared stable to outsiders, most Iranians despised their monarch by the 1970s. Popular discontent coalesced around the figure of Ayatollah Sayyed Ruhollah Musavi Khomeini, a religious cleric exiled in the 1960s for criticizing the government. By mid-1981, Khomeini and his fundamentalist followers wrested control of the country from their former allies in the anti-Shah coalition: socialists, communists, secular democrats, moderates, the merchant class (*bazaaris*), and religious traditionalists. With Khomeini's ascendance, Iran became the first Islamic theocracy in modern history.[30] The Ayatollah's government explicitly rejected U.S. culture, values, and modernization theory. The 1979–81 Hostage Crisis demonstrated Iranians' intense hostility toward the United States, which they dubbed the "Great Satan."[31]

Many in Iran blamed the United States for the Shah's repression. They knew the CIA had orchestrated the 1953 coup against Prime Minister Mohammad Mossadegh, which allowed the Shah to transform from a constitutional to an absolute monarch. The United States had been a firm backer of the Shah ever since, providing him with weapons, military advisors, and financial assistance. The monarchy harshly repressed political dissent, and many Iranians, especially the middle class, resented their lack of political freedoms. The SAVAK, the Shah's infamous secret police, notoriously tortured political dissidents on both the left and the right. Government brutality alienated the Iranian people and fostered anti-Americanism, especially after Carter, the champion of human rights, praised the Shah despite his human rights violations.[32]

In the early 1960s, the Shah had launched the "White Revolution," which one historian described as "one of the most ambitious attempts at non-Communist modernization in the Third World."[33] The Shah meant to catapult Iran into the global forefront by providing education, suffrage, and expanded rights for women; enacting land reform; privatizing state-owned industries; improving health care and literacy; adopting new technologies; expanding the size of the educated middle class; and limiting the influence of traditional leaders and religious clerics.[34] While many of the reforms aimed to help the country's poor and middle classes, modernization efforts failed to win popular support. The Shah's attempts to secularize Iranian culture and law also aroused the ire of the mullahs because they undermined religious authority. Reforms that granted more rights to women especially infuriated conservative religious groups.[35]

However, the Shah's programs benefited women, especially those in the middle and upper classes. While many women still chose to veil, many also freely went unveiled, especially in cities like Tehran. They had access to higher education, paid employment, the right to vote and hold office, equal pay, health care, and government institutions dedicated to women's affairs.[36] Before the revolution, several women were elected to the Majlis (Iran's parliament), and two served as cabinet ministers.[37]

Especially notable was the Shah's appointment of Mahnaz Afkhami as the Minister of State for Women's Affairs in 1976. She became just the second cabinet-level official in the world dedicated to women's issues. Intelligent, charismatic, and politically savvy, Afkhami used the novelty of her position to women's advantage. Soon, the heads of twelve other cabinet ministries coordinated with her to ensure that they considered women's rights in their policy decisions. Afkhami had served previously as the secretary-general of the Women's Organization of Iran (WOI). It was largely due to WOI's initiatives and Afkhami's Ministry of Women's Affairs that Iranian women expanded their rights so quickly. The Shah allowed women's rights activists a fair amount of autonomy and co-opted the decades-old Iranian women's movement for state purposes.[38]

Because of this, feminists won reforms in Iran's family law. The 1967 Family Protection Law—and its 1975 amendment—was one of the most progressive family laws in the Islamic world at the time. It largely eliminated polygamy and was a move toward more equitable marriage, divorce, and inheritance.[39] Iran was at the forefront of women's advancement. Many of its reforms were more progressive than those found in the West during the same period. Iranian feminists—including the Shah's wife, Empress Farah, and twin sister, Princess Ashraf—successfully convinced the monarch that women's rights were essential.

Yet the Shah was no feminist, as his public comments occasionally revealed. In a 1973 interview with Oriana Fallaci, he proclaimed, "In a man's life, women count only if they're beautiful and graceful and know how to stay feminine. . . . You may be equal in the eyes of the law, but not, I beg your pardon for saying so, in ability."[40] He raised women's status in part because he wished to appeal to international opinion, and women's issues were on the international agenda at the time.[41] Expanding women's rights signaled progress toward modernization.[42] Promoting women's rights additionally made Iran a more appealing ally to the United States than its Arab rivals, and Iran required U.S. support and weapons sales to transform itself into a formidable regional power.

The White Revolution won the Shah Washington's uncritical support.[43] News sources show that the Shah's reforms for women also played well with the American public. Throughout the 1960s, the New York Times celebrated Iranian programs to educate nurses, the granting of women's suffrage and the election of the first women to the Majlis, Empress Farah's women's rights activism, and Iran's hosting of a session of the UN Commission on the Status of Women.[44] An article published in the Saturday Evening Post in the summer of 1975 indicated that Americans continued to applaud Iranian women's gains well into the 1970s. Titled "Muslim Women: Beyond the Veil," it featured an interview with Farida Ardalan, the wife of an Iranian diplomat in Washington, D.C., and daughter of the Imam of Tehran. It included a photograph of Ardalan, who looked like Farrah Fawcett, with feathered blonde hair and distinctly Western clothing. Highlighting her lack of hijab, the article described Ardalan as "beautiful, her long hair flowing over her shoulders," while the woman told her interviewer that "the Shah is liberating women in Iran just as his father liberated women from the veil."[45] A similar New York Times piece appeared in July 1977 that highlighted the shrinking number of Iranian women who veiled.[46] The thrust of these articles was unambiguous: Iranian women were progressing beyond Islamic backwardness because of the Shah's reforms.

It was precisely such reforms that Khomeini found intolerable. He and other fundamentalists opposed the Shah not because he was undemocratic but because he was a secular modernizer. Khomeini believed that women's subordination was enshrined in the founding texts of Islam: women's equality and proper Islamic observance were incompatible. The Ayatollah wanted to restructure Iranian culture and society so that both adhered more rigidly to his interpretation of Shari'a, or Islamic law. As an integral dimension of his project, Khomeini endeavored to reverse women's gains.

On March 6, 1979, the Ayatollah declared that all women must wear the chador and sought to overturn the Family Protection Law. Fundamentalists ransacked the headquarters of the WOI and threatened prominent feminists.[47] Thousands of Iranian women marched in protest and clashed with pro-Khomeini forces, sometimes violently, for three days until Khomeini rescinded his declarations. Khomeini still shared power with Prime Minister Mehdi Bazargan, a pro-democracy liberal, and had yet to consolidate absolute control. After Khomeini pushed Bazargan out of office in 1980, however, he tried again, firing all female judges and ordering compulsory veiling.[48] Iran's women took to the streets once more, but this time Khomeini and his supporters strong-armed them into compliance.[49] Thus began an era of strict policing of women's dress and behavior by the Iranian state that continues to this day.[50]

Americans, especially journalists and pundits tasked with explaining bewildering events to the public, struggled to make sense of the Iranian Revolution. A survey of U.S. news coverage provides a useful if imperfect window into American reactions to the revolution's impact on women.[51] The news media provide much of the public's knowledge about the outside world, and this was especially the case in the pre-Internet era.[52] Sustained and intense media focus on a particular issue expands the size of the informed public.[53] U.S. news coverage both influenced and reflected American public opinion and discourse about women's rights in revolutionary Iran. The weight of public opinion also influences policymakers' decisions, although to varying degrees. American reporting on women in revolutionary Iran helped set in motion the gradual integration of women's rights into U.S. policy toward Islamic countries.

The revolution and Khomeini's meteoric rise to power surprised U.S. observers, from the general public to the White House. The Iranian Revolution was the United States' first significant encounter with the politicized, militant version of Islam espoused by fundamentalists like Khomeini. Most of the American public had ignored Iran prior to the eruption of mass protests in late 1978, while the Carter administration mistakenly believed the Shah had a firm grip on power.[54] The Shah's ouster left journalists and policymakers scrambling to explain the stunning failure of U.S. policy and the seemingly new brand of radical Islam that had taken root in Iran.

They especially wanted to understand the changing status of Iran's women. During the early stages of the revolution, American journalists struggled to explain why some Iranian women donned the chador to protest the Shah. Previously unveiled women choosing to veil was bewildering. In December 1978, *New York Times* investigative reporter Nicholas Gage interviewed some Iranian women about the potential formation of an Islamic republic. Such a government, Gage contended, "would subjugate them to religious traditions that their parents' generation has been discarding over the last 20 years." He observed that "many college women are donning the chador, a traditional all-enveloping robe, as a gesture of defiance, explaining their actions in words that sound quaint to Western ears."[55]

While Gage portrayed *chadori* as naively misguided, community activist Betsy Amin-Arsala cast such women as a threat to "modern" Iranian women's efforts to resist Khomeini's attempts to force them into "second-class citizenship." In a *New York Times* op-ed, Amin-Arsala characterized women's decision to wear the chador as a "perversion." She argued that young women who donned the chador as a symbol of protest were ignorant of its status as a tool for women's subjugation. By choosing to veil, *chadori* allowed men to blame women for men's bad behavior, since its real purpose was to prevent women from "stimulating men sexually." She concluded, "Refusing the veil is a first step on the long road to liberating women" in Iran.[56] A former Peace Corps volunteer to Afghanistan and wife of a Muslim, Amin-Arsala characterized the veil as a key site of struggle against the Islamic theocracy's oppression of women.

Prominent U.S. feminist Kate Millett, who supported Iran's revolution, was also baffled by Iranian women who wore the chador voluntarily. She traveled to Iran for International Women's Day in early March 1979. When she arrived in Tehran, she encountered *chadori*: "The first sight of them was terrible. Like black birds, like death, like fate, like everything alien. Foreign, dangerous, unfriendly. There were hundreds of them, specters. . . . The men control them. . . . Still wearing the cloth of their majesty, they have become prisoners to it. The bitterness, the driven rage behind these figures, behind these yards of black cloth. They are closed utterly." Only after the first women's protests against compulsory veiling erupted a few days later did Millett imagine Iranian women as like herself. "There are women here—they talk back," she enthused after meeting Iranian women—including *chadori*—who were angry with Khomeini's attempts to restrict their rights.[57]

After Khomeini unveiled his "reforms" for women, the Ayatollah and his supporters became the ones who were truly incomprehensible to the U.S. media. Reports now portrayed Iranian women as victims of male fanaticism. Although some women's earlier choice to veil had been confusing to American observers, it was still a *choice*. Iranian women being *forced* to veil by their government was something else entirely.

By 1981 Khomeini's theocracy had made divorce the sole right of husbands, reinstituted polygamy, reduced the marriage age for girls from eighteen to nine, and banned women from many professions. Khomeini closed the country's universities for two years; when they reopened, they were segregated by sex, as were all public spaces. "Islamic dress" was mandatory. Religious police patrolled the streets on the lookout for improperly veiled women.[58] Across the political spectrum, people in the United States saw Khomeini's laws as unacceptable and sympathized with Iranian women's plight.

Feminists quickly emerged as the foremost American critics of the Islamic Republic's gender policies. By 1979 U.S. feminists had connected with their counterparts from other countries to create a powerful transnational movement for women's rights. Since many American feminists saw the battle against patriarchy as global, they characterized women's struggles in Iran as integral to their own fight for equality.[59] *Ms.* magazine, the "major institution of the second wave of feminism," informed its readers in 1979 that "Iranian feminists need our support—and vice versa."[60]

The burgeoning human rights movement also gave liberal Americans a framework for condemning Iran. Contributors to the *New Republic*, at the time a liberal opinion journal sympathetic to the U.S. women's movement, opposed Iran's theocracy because it violated its citizens' human rights. Calling Khomeini "the worst sort of God-crazed autocrat," the author of a November 1979 article could only hope that Khomeini's attempts to repress women, secular democrats, and ethnic minorities would spark a counterrevolution that would remove the mullahs from power and instill a regime that respected human rights.[61]

As liberals and feminists bemoaned Khomeini's misogyny, American conservatives likewise protested his oppression of women, but for different reasons. While the left and right held conflicting views on women's rights, many intellectuals of the neoconservative "persuasion," as well as more traditional conservatives, found revolutionary Iran's treatment of women reprehensible.[62] Neoconservative thought had coalesced in the 1970s. While neocons disagreed sharply with one another over many issues, one notion they all held dear was a belief in the superiority of U.S.-style freedom and individual rights.[63] Several well-known neocons had ideological roots that extended back to the Old Left; many others had been hawkish Democrats. By the 1970s, they abandoned the Democratic Party in favor of Republicans because they believed the Democrats were too weak to preserve American values and protect U.S. interests.[64]

In most cases, they were committed to social justice, although not the version envisioned by feminists and liberals. It was not unusual to find harsh condemnations of feminism in neoconservative publications such as *Commentary* during the 1970s.[65] Nevertheless, neocons supported women's education and employment, and they counted prominent women such as Reagan's future UN ambassador Jeane Kirkpatrick and Gertrude Himmelfarb among their ranks. What united neocons was their mission to protect liberal democracy at home and promote it abroad. By the mid-1970s, more traditional conservatives accepted them as allies.

Even though neoconservatives' primary foreign policy concern remained communism, they worried about radical Islam.[66] They had warned the rest of America about Islamic extremism in the pages of *Commentary* well before the Iranian Revolution.[67] When the Iranian theocracy imposed restrictions on women, neocons interpreted it as symptomatic of the deeply undemocratic nature of the Islamic Republic, as well as Islam generally. Kirkpatrick wrote in November 1979 that Khomeini was a tyrant "of extremist persuasion" who possessed "intolerance and arrogance that do not bode well for the peaceful sharing of power or the establishment of constitutional governments."[68]

Iran's policing of women's dress and behavior exemplified the suppression of individual liberty that neocons opposed. Their criticisms of Iran, however, may also have served as pointed rebuke to U.S. feminists, who had it pretty good in comparison. As *Commentary* informed its readers in

March 1979, "Indeed, if any situation to which those overused terms 'male chauvinism' and 'women's oppression' can be said to apply . . . it would seem to be in the situation of women in Muslim countries."[69] Given neocons' strong support for the U.S.-Israeli alliance, their critiques of Khomeini's policies on women may also have been intended as an implicit affirmation of Israel's affinity with U.S. values.

Conservatives of a more traditional bent—also no fans of feminism—spoke out against Iran's oppression of women as well. Michael Ledeen criticized Khomeini in a January 1979 *Wall Street Journal* editorial. Ledeen, who later became a special advisor to Ronald Reagan's State Department, found the Ayatollah's treatment of women especially contemptible. Calling Khomeini "a clerical fascist," Ledeen passionately denounced him: "there can be little reason for any democratic citizen of the West to sympathize with Ayatollah Khomeini. For if he has a major voice in the government of Iran, all women and all those not in the good graces of the Muslim divines will be second-class citizens."[70] After the March 1979 women's protests in Iran, the *National Review* predicted that compulsory veiling would generate intensifying discontent and argued that "if, in any culture, one half of the population is excluded from inspiration and action, there will eventually be some form of crisis." One correspondent surmised that the Islamic world had declined precisely because of "the isolation, as a matter of dogma, of women."[71] Such conservative commenters characterized enforced veiling and government-sanctioned gender violence as morally repugnant and deeply inimical to liberty.

Regardless of political ideology, then, there were limits to Americans' tolerance of gender inequality abroad. Americans from across the political spectrum, who disagreed vehemently over many issues, found some common ground and even consensus in their opposition to Iran's treatment of women. For many, condemning revolutionary Iran's oppression of women meant advocating individual freedoms, democracy, human rights, and the "American way of life." This provided some commonality in how Americans viewed Khomeini's policies, whether feminist or anti-feminist, liberal or conservative.

The shift from finding chador-clad women puzzling to oppressed and victimized was not simply an American construction; Khomeini's government did force women into the veil and legally enshrined women's subordination. Transgressors faced severe consequences. In February 1979 the *Washington*

Post observed that many women "find little joy in feeling obliged to don the full-length chador covering their bodies from head to toes to avoid dirty looks or worse on the streets."[72] The *New York Times* had explained what "or worse" meant when it reported, "Women in Western clothes were dragged out of taxis and beaten up" during earlier anti-Shah riots in the city of Tabriz.[73]

Many in the United States blamed Islam for women's situation in Iran and, by association, the rest of the Muslim world. Writers in *Commentary* certainly felt it was the source of women's oppression, as the magazine asserted in March 1979, "No doubt, there are specific elements in Islam as a religion that have contributed to the subjugation of women."[74] Likewise, the centrist *Time* magazine consistently portrayed Islam as medieval. An April 1979 article denounced Shari'a as "a relic of the Dark Ages" and decried the "sexist inequities" of Islamic law in Iran.[75] The magazine observed later that year, "The West and the world of Islam sometimes resemble two different centuries." According to the magazine, "The Iranian crisis has legitimized among Americans a new stereotype of the demented Muslim," who felt threatened by "the full onslaught of secular, materialist modernization" and "young women returning from Paris or Palo Alto in short skirts instead of chadors."[76]

U.S. journalists condemned Khomeini and expressed compassion for Iranian women. The American news media reported approvingly that Iran's women resisted the call for "Islamic dress." Iranian women made similar arguments to those of American journalists: they were fighting for universal rights. As these women resisted attempts to force them into the veil and out of public life, they declared that they fought for freedom, equal rights, and democracy. They spoke Americans' language, figuratively and sometimes literally, which rendered them familiar and sympathetic. By resisting Khomeini, Iranian women also demonstrated that they were not submissive victims, thus contradicting American stereotypes of Muslim women. As Iran's women fought for their rights, American observers applauded.

Major U.S. news outlets especially praised the women's demonstrations that erupted in Tehran, Qom, and other Iranian cities in March 1979.[77] The *Washington Post* reported that fifteen thousand women took to the streets of Tehran, shouting, "Down with Khomeini" and "We won't wear the chador." The demonstrations signaled to the paper "the declining popularity" of the Ayatollah and "women's exasperation with Khomeini's fundamentalist Islam rule."[78] *Newsweek* likewise reported that "thousands of women demonstrated against [Khomeini's] attempt to force them to wear traditional Islamic head covering" and "to protest the suspension of laws enacted by the Shah that severely restricted polygamy and prevented men from unilaterally divorcing their wives."[79] *Time* commented, "Many Iranian women are furious over the Ayatullah's [*sic*] attempt to impose a subservient role on females." The magazine's writers seemed relieved to see women's discontent.[80]

In addition to newspaper coverage, all three major television networks aired footage of thousands of Iranian women—all unveiled, most wearing Western-style clothing and hairstyles—marching peacefully in the streets along with male supporters. ABC reported from Tehran that just "five weeks ago, the women of Iran welcomed Ayatollah Khomeini back from exile." Now, thousands of women took to the streets to protest his policies. One demonstrator, fist in the air, hair uncovered, wore a T-shirt with a Playboy bunny logo—she hardly appeared submissive. Another woman, who spoke English and wore Western clothes, told ABC that Khomeini was a "dictator" and "fanatic."[81] The networks continued to air such stories over the next several days, despite the Iranian government's attempts to suppress reporting on the protests. By this point, more and more Americans were receiving their news about the world from television. TV news coverage of the protests helped shape U.S. public opinion, as Iranian women became legible to Americans through their convergence of worldviews about the desirability of equality and rights.

U.S. feminists certainly saw Iranian women as sisters, and they staged a sympathy protest at Rockefeller Center outside the offices of Iran's provisional government. NBC reported that one thousand American women attended, including Bella Abzug and Gloria Steinem, who wanted "to show their support for the sisters in Iran."[82] According to the *New York Times*, Betty Friedan, Marlo Thomas, and Susan Brownmiller also attended.[83] American demonstrators appeared before NBC's cameras wearing black robes "to show their sympathy with the Iranian women" who were protesting compulsory veiling thousands of miles away.[84] Betty Friedan was more explicit. She told the *New York Times* that the veil went "far beyond the question of modesty in dress, extending into every aspect of human rights."[85] Her decision to draw upon the prevailing language of universal human rights was significant: it implicitly dismissed the notion that what happened in Iran was a cultural issue out of bounds for American concern.

News media reported that Iranian protestors faced violent opposition from dangerous male fanatics. Here, months before the Hostage Crisis, Islamophobia was prominent in U.S. discourse. It combined with Orientalist notions of Muslim men as backward to create the sense that Iranian men were menacing. One scholar has observed, "Considered irredeemably fanatical, irrational, and thus dangerous, Muslim men are also marked as deeply misogynist patriarchs who have not progressed into the age of gender equality, and who indeed cannot."[86] The Hostage Crisis in November reified this notion, but Americans clearly already saw male fundamentalists as fanatics who oppressed women and rejected universal rights. This Islamophobic, Orientalist depiction of Muslim men in U.S. discourse became commonplace thereafter.

This was not simply a U.S. construct, as fundamentalist Iranian men did seek to oppress women, sometimes violently, but such reporting nevertheless rendered invisible the nuanced struggle between fundamentalists and other groups in Iran during this period by creating two totalizing polarities: the familiar female Muslim protagonist, who shared Western or universal values by seeking equal rights, and the alien Muslim male fanatic, who threatened universal values by oppressing women. In describing events in Iran in this way, the media problematically obscured the stories of the many Iranian men who resisted Khomeini's regime (and sometimes died for their dissent) and of religiously conservative Iranian women who found Khomeini's message appealing and collaborated with the government's attempts to impose strict gender roles. This lack of nuance made it easy to dismiss all Iranian men, and Islam itself, as hostile to modern values, contributing to the intense hostility between the United States and Iran that emerged from the revolution.

According to the *Washington Post*, protesting women faced crowds of hostile men as they marched across Tehran: "Harassed by ever nastier, jeering and taunting Moslem men boasting allegiance to Khomeini," the "bareheaded demonstrators were called 'whores.' "[87] NBC reported that the protesters and their male sympathizers "had been roughed up by extremist followers of Ayatollah Khomeini." The station ran footage of angry men pushing and shoving; men with guns intimidated a man who marched with the women.[88] Even more disconcerting were reports that some men threatened to rape unveiled women. According to the *Washington Post*, "Moslem men at a sit-in at the editorial offices [of *Kayham* newspaper in Tehran] became so incensed by the sight of bare-headed women that the men exposed their sex organs and accused the women of really wanting sex, not freedom."[89] Other reports surfaced of men exposing themselves along the protest routes and of men following unveiled women into their workplaces and threatening them with sexual assault.[90] Kate Millett, who witnessed the protests, told the *Washington Post*, "'I've never looked at a situation this tough. This is the first time as a pacifist and a feminist that I've had to face guns. . . . No, I didn't expect so much overt hostility from men. This is quite new.'"[91] Although news footage did include some men supporting the women's marches, the general sense was that Iran's men were violent zealots, while the media portrayed Iranian women as more like Americans than previous stereotypes had allowed.

This was the crucial first step toward integrating women's rights concerns into U.S. foreign policy. During the Iranian Revolution, Americans discovered that many women in Iran did not accept compulsory veiling or legalized subordination. As these women fought to defend their rights, many in the United States rallied to their cause. Iran was not a case of cultural difference or "backwardness"; instead, women had lost rights and were openly and deliberately oppressed by the Islamic Republic. In the context of the transnational feminist movement and the rise of global human rights activism in the 1970s, many Americans felt compelled to oppose such oppression.

Throughout 1979, American journalists, feminists, and political commentators painted a picture for the U.S. public of Iranian women as besieged by male Muslim zealots. These women were not passive or silent victims, however. Through their portrayal in the American media, Iranian women who resisted Khomeini's attempts to force them into the veil and the home emerged as sympathetic figures who fought back against oppression. Muslim women therefore became less alien and stereotypical than they had appeared earlier in the U.S. public sphere. Orientalist imagery persisted, but Islamic women were no longer simply silent slaves or harem girls in American discourse. They were also people who actively fought for their human rights and equality. Significantly, by depicting Muslim women in Iran as "the same"— akin to Americans in their desires—U.S. journalists, feminists, and political pundits made Iranian women intelligible to Western audiences as people who deserved human rights and the same basic freedoms Americans valued.

This was an important moment for the mainstream public's perceptions, but it was not necessarily an important moment for policymakers: the Carter administration did not comment publicly about Iran's women.[92] It was the American public and feminist activists who first identified the issue of Muslim women's human rights as an important area of concern, not policymaking elites. Public discourse about Iranian women in 1979 initiated the development of the common wisdom in the United States that women in Islamic countries were oppressed. Through the 1980s, the notion that Muslim women in general deserved rights that Muslim men denied or tried to strip from them became further entrenched in U.S. discourse through the news media, movies, novels, scholarly publications, memoirs, and other public forums.

Chapter 2

Muslim Women in U.S.
Public Discourse After 1979

An American named Betty Mahmoody traveled to Tehran in 1984 with her
Iranian husband, "Moody," and their four-year-old daughter, Mahtob, to
visit her husband's family for two weeks.[1] Or so she thought. The visit soon
turned into an eighteen-month nightmare when Moody informed Betty that
he had no intention of returning to the United States. The United States and
Iran had severed diplomatic ties in 1980, so the Islamic Republic did not recognize Betty's and Mahtob's American citizenship. To make matters worse,
Iranian law afforded men legal control over their wives and children: Betty
and her daughter required Moody's permission to leave the country. While
he eventually agreed to let Betty go, Moody adamantly refused to allow her
to take Mahtob. Because Betty would not leave her daughter behind, she and
Mahtob became Moody's prisoners. After nearly two years of violent abuse,
Betty and Mahtob finally staged a daring escape on horseback into Turkey
and made their way home.

Their story was sensational and compelling, and in 1987 St. Martin's
Press published Betty's account of their ordeal. *Not Without My Daughter*—
and the 1991 film starring Academy Award winner Sally Field—quickly
became one of the most well-known accounts of women's oppression in the
Muslim world.[2] The book's success catapulted Mahmoody into the national
spotlight. She appeared on *20/20*, *Larry King Live*, the *Phil Donahue Show*,
the *Oprah Winfrey Show*, and *Sally Jesse Raphael*.[3] Through all of these venues, millions of Americans learned of her story.

Mahmoody argued that Muslim men used Islam to justify brutality
against women. Worse still, nations like Iran sanctioned such behavior at the

highest levels. As famous as Mahmoody's story became, however, many Americans already believed that women in Muslim countries were oppressed when her book was published. In the years since the Iranian Revolution, the news media, filmmakers, novelists, women's rights activists, and scholars had contributed to discourse in the United States that identified Muslim men as oppressors of women and Islamic fundamentalism as a growing threat to women's human rights.

In these years, Orientalist and Islamophobic discourses competed with the discourse of universal human rights. The former cast Muslim women as victims and Muslim men as misogynist fanatics, while the latter cast Muslim women as fully complex humans who actively fought for their rights. Feminists from the United States and Islamic countries demonstrated the complex reality of Muslim women's lives. It was in no small part the ability of feminists to bring the weight of public opinion behind their campaigns for Muslim women's human rights that later caused U.S. policymakers to take these issues seriously. The period of the 1980s through the early 1990s incubated public receptivity toward the integration of women's rights into the nation's foreign policy. This idea would gain traction with policymakers later, in the Clinton administration.

Prior to the Iranian Revolution, American policymakers were unconcerned about women's rights in Muslim countries. Equality for women had never been a major goal of U.S. foreign policy. Jimmy Carter's focus on human rights generally as the centerpiece of American policy was unusual, and his record in implementing that agenda was uneven at best.[4] And even Carter, a strong supporter of gender equality, never commented on the restrictions of women's rights in revolutionary Iran, although Iran dominated his agenda throughout his final year in office.[5] Iranian women had captured the attention of U.S. feminists and the public—but not policymakers.

Promoting women's human rights in the Islamic world was not on the Reagan administration's agenda either. Reagan's antipathy toward the feminist movement made him an unlikely candidate to champion women's rights abroad. The year 1980 marked the triumphant resurgence of conservatism in U.S. politics when an unprecedented grassroots mobilization of various conservative groups—from libertarians to neoconservatives to the religious right—coalesced around Reagan.[6] This "New Right" swept him into the White House and gave Republicans a majority in the Senate for the first time since 1952.[7] Aware that grassroots resentment of social and cultural changes wrought by the rights revolution had propelled them to power, Reagan and the Republican Party embraced the New Right's socially conservative agenda. Feminism was a particular target of their ire; women's successes in the United States in the 1970s provoked a powerful backlash as they had in Iran.[8]

Nor did the Reagan administration promote women's equality abroad. In fact, it instituted a "global gag rule," threatening to withhold aid from family planning organizations and other charities worldwide if they so much as mentioned abortion. The United States Agency for International Development (USAID) did issue a 1982 policy paper recommending the integration of women's issues into U.S. development programs because women in development (WID) had become a popular international issue. However, according to a career USAID officer, "these initiatives were not high on priority lists of missions or Washington bureaus."[9] USAID undertook limited education, micro-credit, and family planning initiatives but integrated WID at a glacial pace.[10] Foreign policy infrastructure for women's rights was largely absent in the Reagan and George H. W. Bush administrations.

Reagan's administration also distanced itself from Carter's human rights policies. It focused instead on thwarting the Soviet Union and waging a re-invigorated Cold War.[11] Reagan, like his predecessors, tended to view the Islamic world through the prism of the Cold War. While problems such as the ongoing Arab-Israeli conflict, the Soviet-Afghan War, and the Iran-Iraq War involved many complex factors, the administration followed rather simple, pre-established policy goals: protect Israel, maintain Western access to Middle Eastern oil, and prevent the Soviet Union from gaining influence. This led the United States to become embroiled in the ever more tumultuous affairs of Muslim nations in the 1980s and early 1990s.

Historians have explained how Reagan and his advisors aspired to maintain Western hegemony in the Islamic world by cultivating anti-Soviet alliances with Israel, Egypt, Saudi Arabia, Pakistan, and Turkey. Yet after the Iranian Revolution and the Soviet invasion of Afghanistan, simply arming and aiding key allies was inadequate. Reagan learned this lesson when Israel invaded Lebanon in 1982 in pursuit of the Palestine Liberation Organization (PLO). Reagan deployed the Marines to Lebanon in a disastrous attempt to stabilize the country. Anti-American feeling intensified among Muslim rebels in Lebanon, and after they carried out deadly bombings in 1983 of the U.S. embassy in Beirut and a Marine Corps barracks, the United States withdrew from the conflict. The Lebanese civil war continued, Arab-Israeli hostility escalated, and regional anti-Americanism deepened.[12]

Dispossessed people like the Palestinians and weaker states like Libya turned to terrorist violence to counteract Western and Israeli military superiority. Stateless terrorist networks were difficult to find and neutralize, so Reagan concentrated his efforts on the Libyan dictator Muammar al-Qaddafi. Qaddafi favored the Soviets and publicly supported anti-Western Islamic extremists. Despite Reagan's attempts to cow him in 1981, Qaddafi stepped up covert aid to terrorist groups. After a series of attacks against American and Western targets, Reagan ordered airstrikes against Libya in 1986. Although the raids initially appeared successful, an unchastened Qaddafi retaliated in 1988 when his agents blew up Pan Am Flight 103 over Lockerbie, Scotland, killing 270 people.[13]

More successful—in the short term—was Reagan's covert intervention in Afghanistan. Starting in 1979, Carter had aided anti-Soviet Afghan rebels, known collectively as the mujahideen.[14] Reagan massively increased U.S. aid to roll back Soviet influence by providing funds, expertise, and weapons to the Afghans, using Pakistan as a conduit. Meanwhile, the CIA recruited Muslims from the Middle East to fight a jihad in Afghanistan against the Soviets. The estimated $3 billion in covert aid to the mujahideen contributed invaluably to the 1989 Soviet withdrawal from Afghanistan.[15] In the short term, this was a great victory. However, the administration failed to understand that U.S. assistance in fighting the Soviets would not necessarily lead to pro-American sentiment in Central Asia and the Middle East. Nor did it foresee that recruiting, arming, and training jihadists from across the Islamic world would come back to haunt the United States. Blinded by the Cold War, Reagan's administration simply failed to grasp the depth of the fundamentalist threat.

This was evident in Reagan's treatment of Iran. The Iranians released the last American hostages in January 1981, just as Reagan took office.[16] The end of the Hostage Crisis, Khomeini's consolidation of power, and the start of the Iran-Iraq War in 1980 meant that Iran's theocracy had a firm grip on power, and it would be busy fighting Saddam Hussein's Iraq for much of the decade. Middle East expert Eric Hooglund wrote at the time that administration officials felt that Iran "was contained and could be ignored."[17] Although Iran had become an adversary, Reagan's administration even secretly sold weapons to the Islamic Republic as part of the infamous Iran-Contra scandal. Reagan-era policymakers evidently did not see Iran or Islamic fundamentalism as a serious threat, nor were they particularly concerned about fundamentalists' treatment of women.

The administration's dismissive view differed sharply from U.S. public discourse during the same period. While policymakers did not appear to see fundamentalists' oppression of women as connected to U.S. security or other interests, in the years following Iran's revolution Americans outside of government identified Islamic fundamentalism as a major threat, both to women's human rights and to U.S. interests in the Islamic world. Feminism's growing social and cultural influence at home undergirded the U.S. public's support for women's human rights abroad and their condemnation of Islamic fundamentalists after 1979.

Despite the New Right's rhetoric and fierce political contestation over social issues like abortion, women's equality became an institutionalized assumption in many areas of American life during the Reagan era.[18] Women attended college and professional schools in ever greater numbers, popular culture depicted female sexuality more openly, and the majority of American women worked outside the home.[19] Feminists altered the curricula of schools and colleges, producing what one historian dubbed a "revolution in knowledge," while younger women grew up taking for granted freedoms for which their mothers and grandmothers had fought.[20] There is evidence that public support for gender equality was on the rise during this period, as public opinion polls from the 1980s revealed that a majority of Americans embraced many of the goals of the feminist movement.[21]

Basic women's rights were a given in the United States by the 1980s, so it is unsurprising that there was broad public interest in—and condemnation of—limits on women's rights in Muslim countries. Even anti-feminist conservatives possessed at least a vague belief in women's rights internationally, as demonstrated by their reactions to Khomeini's treatment of women during the revolution. Few Americans agreed with Islamic fundamentalists' attempts to restrict women's education, employment, rights in marriage, freedom of movement, and dress. Although other global developments captured policymakers' attention, Muslim women's rights remained salient to many Americans.

A survey of sources from the U.S. public sphere in the 1980s and early 1990s shows frequent and sustained discussions about Islamic women and reveals conflicting understandings about their situations: some relied on

Orientalist stereotypes, while others used human rights concepts. The two discourses were often in tension, but together they kept Muslim women in the public eye and reinforced the common wisdom that women in the Islamic world lacked rights. Moreover, the human rights framework ensured that many Americans saw Muslim women's oppression not as an immutable feature of Islamic societies, as Orientalist logic implied, but rather as something that rights activism could remedy.

For some Americans, especially Cold War hawks, women's oppression symbolized the larger threat to U.S. interests posed by an Islamic movement that was often explicitly anti-American and that they feared might spread. This was especially worrisome given the reinvigorated Cold War. Radical Muslims were unlikely to become atheist Communists, but anti-Americanism might plausibly invite Soviet influence in the Middle East. Just as troubling, fundamentalists' unapologetic violations of women's rights signaled their deeply undemocratic nature. Their antipathy to pluralism and democracy threatened the spread of American values, which had long been a goal of U.S. foreign policy.

For other Americans—those dedicated to gender equality and human rights—women's situation in and of itself was the issue. Fundamentalists' resistance to the very notion of universal rights threatened to reverse gains made by the human rights and feminist movements through the 1970s. Whether Americans saw Islamic fundamentalists' oppression of women as the main issue or as symbolic of a larger threat to U.S. interests— and it is often difficult to disentangle these viewpoints—Muslim women remained in the U.S. public consciousness. The conventional wisdom that such women were oppressed became firmly entrenched in American understandings of the Islamic world after 1979.

Several developments in the 1980s kept Iranian women in the public eye and caused Americans to maintain their scrutiny of Khomeini's government.[22] The theocracy used harsh measures against all opponents, but women remained special targets, and the U.S. news media continued to condemn this. In May 1980 the *Washington Post* reported approvingly that Iran's women "appear willing to take to the streets again rather than knuckle under to the increasingly despised and mocked clergy," and the paper detailed the creeping clerical interference in women's lives since the revolution.[23] In July, Khomeini reinstituted the restrictions that women protesters had rebuffed in March 1979. Once again, Iranian women took to the streets, and the American media depicted the protesters positively while condemning the government.

This time, however, Iran's women could not resist Khomeini. They were forced to veil, much to the chagrin of U.S. observers. By 1983, the government had criminalized "improper" dress for women, forced women out of certain jobs, segregated universities by sex, banned female university students from majoring in certain subjects, and dismantled the Family Protection Law.[24]

When assessing the state of affairs in Iran five years after the revolution, veteran journalist Terence Smith of the *New York Times* bemoaned the "zealotry" and "fanaticism" of Khomeini's "totalitarian theocracy," which, among other things, forced women "to conform to a strict Islamic code of behavior." Smith described women's "new way of life" for his readers: "Women are not to appear in public except in chador, the shapeless black robe that obscures from head to foot. Those who venture out in Western dress risk arrest by Revolutionary Guards, who function as self-appointed keepers of the public morality. Some of the women arrested are held until they sign statements saying they are prostitutes. . . . The separation of the sexes, a major tenet of Islam, is carried to extremes . . . even the private homes of northern Teheran are not immune from sudden raids by Revolutionary Guards."[25] Even worse was the unabashed violence against women in Iran. Starting in 1980, the government initiated a wave of executions that lasted into the middle of the decade.[26] Revolutionary courts executed people for alleged crimes as varied as dealing drugs, encouraging or engaging in prostitution, "waging war on God," supporting Zionism, committing adultery, demonstrating against the government, and belonging to the Baha'i faith, a minority religion that notably advocates gender equality.

The executions did not spare women. Americans' horror over Iran's execution of women in particular, when the government also killed men in large numbers, interwove Orientalist and human rights concepts. Women's executions in Iran, especially by stoning, reinforced older notions of Oriental despotism and Islamic cruelty.[27] But many Americans also framed the executions as human rights violations. Iranian women who were killed were political prisoners who were denied due process, tortured, and deprived of the most basic human right, the right to life. While activists also used human rights discourse to criticize the death penalty in the United States, Iran's particularly violent and widespread executions of women compelled human rights groups to denounce the Islamic Republic.

In May 1980, Farrokhrou Parsa, the Shah's former minister of education, was executed by firing squad, despite an earlier Khomeini decree that there would be no further executions of Pahlavi-era officials, unless they had committed murder or torture.[28] As the first woman elected to Parliament and first female cabinet minister, Parsa was the notable exception. She represented women's advancement under the Shah that Khomeini and his followers wished to reverse.[29] While in office, she advocated women's education and was a committed feminist. After the revolution, she refused to veil.[30] As a prominent woman, she had to die for her defiance, lest she inspire other women to rebel.

Her execution outraged Americans. Without exception, the U.S. news media denounced Parsa's execution as emblematic of the larger attack on women's human rights in Iran. Like other women who resisted veiling or who actively opposed the theocracy, Parsa faced accusations of engaging in or encouraging prostitution, corrupting public morality, and "waging war on God."[31] Women sentenced to death were often stoned, a method of execution introduced to Iran by the Khomeini regime that Americans found particularly appalling. In July 1980, the *New York Times* reported with disgust that two middle-aged women were buried in holes up to their chests and stoned for "prostitution and ... deceiving young girls." The paper reported that five people threw "stones ranging in size from walnuts to apples ... hurling them at each of the condemned" and included the gruesome detail that it took the prisoners "15 minutes to die."[32]

As American journalists reported on the thousands of executions in Iran over the next few years, they repeatedly highlighted the killing of women. Meanwhile, American human rights activists from organizations like Amnesty International and members of the public who wrote to their local newspapers decried Iran's "murder" and "brutal suppression of women's rights."[33] They signaled the general American horror that the Islamic Republic put women to death as a method of enforcing women's subjugation.

What are we to make of the U.S. outrage? Unsurprisingly, the answer is complex, as the outcry emerged from several different, often competing strands—some Orientalist, some that were selective in their indignation (i.e., overlooking American injustices but focusing intently on those of the Islamic world), and others that were quite novel and groundbreaking. Some groups who decried Iran's executions also opposed the death penalty in the United States, but in other cases this condemnation implied that Americans already upheld universal human rights, while Iran did not. And certainly, the focus on the most sensational forms of violence against Iranian women invited a kind of Orientalist reaction: Americans could cast the Islamic Republic as inherently different from the United States, as the misogynist Other. Rather than seeing the similarities between Iranian and American sexism, or between American Christian fundamentalists and Iranian Islamic fundamentalists, Orientalist and human rights discourses in these examples mutually reinforced each other to cast Iran's fundamentalists as irrational threats to women and universal rights. Sherene Razack has characterized such thinking as the narrative basis of U.S. imperialism, "underpinned by the idea that modern, secular peoples must protect themselves from premodern, religious peoples. . . . We have reason; they do not. We are located in modernity; they are not." Therefore, "it is our moral obligation to correct, discipline, and keep them in line."[34]

Such "narrative scaffolding," as Razack called it, was evident in Americans' outrage over women's executions in Iran. At the same time, however, Iran *did* perpetrate horrific human rights violations against its own people. This was not simply an Orientalist fantasy but, rather, the Islamic Republic's deadly intention to bring its population to heel. One did not need to believe in U.S. superiority to speak out against such clear and blatant human rights violations. For this reason, Americans' concern for Iranian women both was and was not Orientalist. Orientalism perhaps strengthened their reactions, but human rights norms also compelled them to speak out against the regime's murderous subordination of women in an attempt to change Iran's behavior through shaming and pressuring it to stop.

Decrying Iran's abuse of women was part of the process by which Americans eventually came to support more direct U.S. interventions aimed at protecting women's human rights in the Islamic world, and their concerns about Iranian women only deepened throughout the 1980s. Forced veiling, harassment, and executions proved to American observers that rule by Islamic fundamentalists meant the severe restriction of women's rights. Women's plight reinforced fears that Khomeini's success would spread fundamentalism across the Islamic world.[35] While Islamic fundamentalism predated Iran's revolution by half a century, Khomeini's stunning rise to power finally forced Americans to notice the religious revival that had been sweeping across the Muslim world.

Events in the years that followed—religious fanatics' assassination of Egyptian president Anwar el-Sadat, the "Islamization" of Pakistan, and the imposition of Islamic theocracy in Sudan, among other occurrences—gave credence to Americans' fears. Khomeini's ascendancy had already cost the United States a vital ally in the Middle East. Fundamentalism's expansion threatened further setbacks in a strategically important region.[36] To some observers, the erosion of women's rights was a canary in a coal mine, signaling increasing levels of anti-Americanism and anti-democratic sentiment. For others, especially feminists and human rights activists, Islamic fundamentalism's spread and the resulting loss of women's rights in and of itself was the major concern.

The U.S. news media anxiously discussed resurgent fundamentalism's threat to women in countries from Malaysia to Morocco.[37] The *Philadelphia Inquirer* warned in 1980 that Iran intended to export its revolution to Malaysia, "a tinderbox waiting to be set aflame." The result, the paper insisted, would be sex segregation and forced veiling, even for the non-Muslim half of Malaysia's population.[38] That same year, the *Boston Globe* opined that Palestinian sovereignty "would mean terrible treatment for women."[39] In 1983 the *New York Times* informed its readers about "a resurgence of religious fundamentalism" across "the Moslem world from Africa through the Middle East and into Asia." The paper cited as evidence mandatory "modest attire for women and their segregation in public life." Explaining that Iran's theocracy was the model that inspired Islamic fundamentalists everywhere, the *New York Times* worried that in Egypt, "more and more women, especially the young and educated, are donning Islamic clothes," while Kuwait instituted an "effective ban on women working in public."[40]

Discussions about Egypt and Pakistan exemplified American concerns during the period. Egypt was the birthplace of the first modern Islamic fundamentalist group, the Muslim Brotherhood, and was the most populous Arab state. The country had long occupied a central place in the Islamic world. During the 1950s and 1960s, Egypt's Gamal Abdel Nasser inspired the Arab masses with his calls for secular Pan-Arabism. While Nasser's Cold War neutrality had made U.S.-Egypt relations tense, his popularity across the Arab world underscored Egypt's influence. Nasser's successor, Anwar el-Sadat, brought Egypt into the U.S. sphere of influence by signing the Camp David Accords with Israel in September 1978. Following the accords, Egypt became the second-largest recipient of U.S. aid in the Middle East.[41]

American observers therefore worried about fundamentalist opposition to Sadat. Writing in *Foreign Policy* in the summer of 1979, Princeton political science professor Fouad Ajami declared, "The struggle for Egypt's soul is on." The Iranians, he wrote, deemed Sadat a Western lackey and predicted that Islamic revival in Egypt would bring down his government.[42] Americans paid close attention to women's status as a barometer of Egyptian resistance to American influence and an indication of the success or failure of the movement for women's human rights in the Islamic world. Over the next several years, the media reported with alarm the rising numbers of veiled women on the streets of Cairo. *Time* observed in late 1981, "It is a phenomenon that has become startlingly visible over the past year in Cairo. Along the city's crowded sidewalks, on university campuses and in offices, young Egyptian women who once wore the latest in Western fashion are turning toward Islamic dress."[43] This was a portent of what was to come if fundamentalists ousted Sadat.

Such fears were validated when fundamentalists assassinated Sadat in October 1981. U.S. analysts rightly attributed his murder to anger over the Camp David Accords.[44] Astute observers, however, recognized that Sadat's liberal stance on women's rights had also provoked religious hard-liners. One fundamentalist explained to Sana Hasan, daughter of the former Egyptian ambassador to the United States, that Sadat "deserved to be killed" for his support of women's rights. Hasan explained that Egyptian fundamentalists were inspired by Khomeini, and she described for the *New York Times* how the man's demeanor changed when the subject of women arose, especially his intense feelings about Sadat's family law reforms and the role of his wife, Jihan. "'This woman is a disgrace!' the sheik exploded. His eyes were blazing, and the white beard that sprouted limply from his chin seemed animated," Hasan observed. The man continued, woman "is the cornerstone of society. Once she is reformed, all of society will be sound."[45] Based on Khomeini's "reforms," it was easy to imagine how this fundamentalist envisioned women's role in Egypt.

General Mohammad Zia ul-Haq's "Islamization" program in Pakistan, launched in 1979, also disturbed Americans. Pakistan was an important strategic ally. The United States used the country to funnel covert aid to Afghan rebels, and Pakistan trained Afghan mujahideen and foreign jihadis fighting the Soviets.[46] The U.S. government deliberately stirred up Islamic sentiment against the USSR as it waged the Cold War in Central Asia. If Muslim radicals in Pakistan turned against the United States as they had in neighboring Iran, it would be disastrous for U.S. policy at a critical moment. Although the American public did not know about the covert operations, they were aware of the Cold War flare-up in Central Asia. Developments in Pakistan signaled that Americans had reason to worry about fundamentalists in the region.

After seizing power in 1977, Zia turned his attention to "Islamizing" Pakistan. With few exceptions, the American media saw him as an anti-democratic, fundamentalist tyrant. It was common for major news outlets to compare Zia with other notable zealots, from Oliver Cromwell to Jerry Falwell; such reports were anti-fundamentalist rather than anti-Muslim and drew on rights discourse in their critiques. Beyond condemning Zia's general "Islamic Puritanism," journalists especially decried his regressive view of women.[47] The *New York Times* detailed Pakistan's imposition of strict laws and harsh punishments, including stoning for adultery. The paper informed its readers, "The female form must be suitably covered. Female television announcers were prohibited for a time from wearing makeup. . . . There is particular pressure on women to return to the *purdah* of home and kitchen from which many have only recently emerged. There is an eerie feeling at times, even in the big cities, that the country is populated only by males."[48] Israr Ahmad, a Pakistani cleric who supported Zia, explained to the *Wall Street Journal* in 1983 what he and other fundamentalists intended: "he doesn't want women to vote anymore."[49]

For some American observers, such antipathy to women's political rights and participation in public life may have been symbolic of larger concerns about radical Muslims' resistance to U.S. hegemony, or perhaps provided opportunity to advance "hard" U.S. policy imperatives. For others, however, Zia's assault on women's rights *itself* was the problem. Pakistan and countries like it threatened the realization of universal rights when they oppressed women. Paul Gigot of the *Wall Street Journal* wrote from this perspective. In 1983 he condemned the appalling "sexual double standard" in Pakistan that led to the flogging and imprisonment of a blind sixteen-year-old girl who had been raped. Her rapist went free, Gigot explained, because Zia's laws mandated that four adult men witness the act in order to prove rape in court. This was an impossible burden of proof. As a consequence, "the girl, simply because she was pregnant and unmarried, was convicted of adultery under Islamic law. And because she had charged rape but didn't prove it, she was also open to a charge of false accusation."[50] The case of the blind girl was a clear indication of "fanaticism" in Pakistan, one that many other Americans commented upon with horror.[51] Years later, the film *Charlie Wilson's War* (2007) highlighted this rape case, demonstrating the incident's enduring impression on American memory.[52]

The general tenor of American media coverage during this period was that Islamic fundamentalism was on the rise and that it posed a threat both to U.S. interests and to women's human rights. Daniel Pipes, director of the conservative Foreign Policy Research Institute in Philadelphia, warned policymakers and the readers of *Foreign Affairs* in 1986 that "radical fundamentalists are the real danger" and were "even more profound enemies of the United States than Marxists." They controlled Iran, Pakistan, and Sudan, and they challenged the governments of "Morocco, Tunisia, Nigeria, Egypt, Syria, Saudi Arabia, Malaysia, and Indonesia." He concluded, "The application of Islamic law creates human rights problems, so the United States cannot become too closely associated with fundamentalist leaders" who rejected Western "customs relating to the sexes."[53] The inclusion of gender in Pipes's discourse here is striking and indicates that hard power and women's rights concerns were beginning to converge in the arena of policy thought.

While the media drew attention to women's subordination in Islamic countries, especially those places where fundamentalism was on the rise, film and news discussions about women's position in Muslim societies were typically shallow during the 1980s and early 1990s and tended to cast the Islamic world as monolithic. Muslim women more often than not appeared as stereotypical silent victims of Islamic oppression in need of rescue. Jack Shaheen, an authority on American film depiction of Arabs, analyzed the appearance of "mute, enslaved" Muslim women in Hollywood films. He argued that movies like *Not Without My Daughter* "continue to impact viewers without let-up, via TV repeats, big screen revivals, the internet, and movie rentals."[54] American movie portrayals of Muslim women after 1979 both drew upon and reinforced the journalistic conversations about the growing oppression of Muslim women and continued the *Arabian Nights* Orientalist clichés. These portrayals during the 1980s and 1990s were strikingly similar to films made decades earlier. The 1985 film *Harem*, for example, was not appreciably different from the 1921 film *The Sheik*.[55] Iranian women had fought for their rights in front of American news cameras in 1979, but Hollywood was apparently impervious to those images and continued to use familiar Orientalist representations.[56]

In contrast both to mainstream news media, which were often preoccupied with the Cold War, and popular entertainment, which perpetuated familiar Orientalist plots, feminist activists and scholars used human rights discourses to interpret and define Muslim women's history and experiences in a genuinely novel and sympathetic way that challenged not only Orientalist understandings but also Muslim fundamentalists' claims that proper Islamic practice mandated women's subordination. Women from the United States and Islamic countries began publishing scholarship, memoirs, and fiction in the United States during the 1980s and 1990s that examined Muslim women's complex lives.[57] These works both condemned women's oppression in Islamic societies and demonstrated Muslim women's agency. These publications did not reach audiences as large as those for mainstream news media and Hollywood films, but they nevertheless influenced a key segment of the American citizenry that included scholars, undergraduate and graduate students, women's rights activists, policymakers, and the interested public.

Scholarly studies of Muslim women were especially valuable because they provided data and theoretical frameworks to support campaigns for women's equality.[58] During the 1970s, women's rights activists realized that little research existed to support their many campaigns. Feminist theory was in its infancy, leaving researchers to develop their own analytic approaches to collecting and interpreting data. Feminist scholars therefore conducted studies on various topics ranging from women's labor to gender-based violence to women's history. They also produced increasingly sophisticated works of feminist theory that could support activism.

Because of this flurry of scholarship, by the 1980s feminist analysis became "a recognized sphere of academic discourse."[59] The gradual establishment of women's studies programs and feminist publications institutionalized feminism in academe. Feminists made important contributions to disciplines as diverse as philosophy, political science, literary criticism, anthropology, and history, and their heterogeneous perspectives led to lively academic debates.[60] Much of the field's vitality in the 1980s and 1990s came from the increasing diversity of scholars' backgrounds, as previously marginalized groups challenged white, middle-class, heterosexual norms.[61]

This diversification included a flowering of scholarship by and about Muslim women. Such publications demonstrated that Muslim women were, like American women, human beings who had hopes, fears, and aspirations and who struggled for agency and power in their lives despite patriarchal constraints. By deploying universal rights arguments, these authors did not ignore American inequality or cast Islam as unique in its treatment of women. They sought to avoid the self-Other binary that marked Orientalist thought and to place Muslim women's oppression within the context of global patriarchy and other structures of inequality. Nevertheless, this body of scholarship reinforced the conventional wisdom that Islamic societies violated women's rights because scholarly investigation demonstrated that such societies did in fact often subordinate women.

In 1978, historian Nikki Keddie and anthropologist Lois Beck coedited *Women in the Muslim World*, a volume of original articles by scholars from several disciplines. It was the first scholarly book published about Muslim women in the United States. Keddie and Beck consciously positioned the volume within the developing field of women's studies and hoped it would provide a "deepened picture" of the lives of average women living in the Middle East. At the same time, the editors intended for the book to support women's movements in Muslim countries.[62]

The chapters in *Women in the Muslim World* humanized Muslim women and demonstrated that they were "not the horribly oppressed and faceless creatures suggested by some earlier accounts." Indeed, Keddie and Beck argued, "even subject to the constraints of male-dominated society, women are not completely subject to forces outside their control, and they have a variety of strategies enabling them to mitigate the effects of male control." The authors did not minimize Muslim women's struggles, however. Keddie and Beck noted that "today, at least, Muslim women can be shown to be behind the rest of the world by most of the indexes generally used for advance in human rights."[63] According to the authors, Muslim women faced poverty, physical abuse, psychological abuse, polygamy, lack of education, lack of choice in marriage, limited employment opportunities, restricted personal freedoms, and loss of custody over their children in cases of divorce.

In short, Muslim women lacked human rights and "freedom of choice regarding basic life decisions." Keddie and Beck deduced that Muslim women were more oppressed than other women because of Islam.[64] These scholars contended that homegrown women's movements offered the best hope for change in Muslim societies, and their reasoning implied that Islamic law—a complicated and hotly debated matter in women's human rights discourse—had to be replaced for women to overcome oppression.

The interest in Muslim women sparked by the Iranian Revolution and the momentum of women's studies as a scholarly discipline ensured that Keddie and Beck's book was not the last. Throughout the 1980s and 1990s, scholars and activists published a slew of articles and books in the United States about Muslim women. Anthropologists and ethnographers produced much of this early scholarship. They studied Islamic communities in order to understand the "Muslim woman's experience of herself" and to promote cultural understanding.[65] One anthropologist wrote "to convey a sense of women as persons—thinking, feeling, planning, active individuals. . . . The object is to lend a three-dimensionality absent in the caricature of traditional Arab Muslim women."[66] However nuanced, almost all ethnographic studies during this period saw Muslim women as oppressed.[67]

Edited collections, travel narratives, and novels written by American women during the 1980s and 1990s likewise presented audiences with Muslim women's voices and analyses of their situations. These books often argued that Islamic women faced obstacles to equality, as when the main character of the novel *Shabanu*, an independent-minded Pakistani girl, is sold in marriage to a much older man. However, these books also demonstrated that Muslim women actively sought their rights and were agents of social change. Reflecting ongoing debates between Western and Third World women at the time about the feminist movement's agenda, the authors often advised Americans to support the activities of Muslim women without trying to speak for them.[68]

Others produced studies of Muslim women's history, part of the broader scholarly focus on women's history, or "her-story," that came out of Second Wave feminism. Historian Judith Tucker published *Women in Nineteenth-Century Egypt* in 1985 to remedy the invisibility of women in the historiography on the Middle East. Tucker criticized scholarship that cast Islam as monolithic and that suggested "that women lived in a timeless privatized world untouched by historical change." On the contrary, she argued, Egypt's women "helped to shape the sweeping changes" that occurred from 1800 to 1914. Tucker provided a rich picture of the past, full of historical and cultural specificity. Like other scholars who wrote about Muslim women during the period, she argued that women, "because of their sex, were subject to discrimination and constraints," but they were not simply passive victims. Egyptian women's "ability to construct their own institutions or even take their struggle for certain rights to the streets contributed to the making of their history."[69] Other historical scholarship pursued the same goal and revealed that women in Islamic countries had been fighting for their rights for a century or more.[70]

In recovering Muslim women's pasts, Tucker and other historians provided contemporary Muslim women with a legacy of activism that belied fundamentalists' accusations that feminism was a pernicious Western import.[71] Scholarly histories provided women with models of activism drawn from their own cultures and detailed the historically specific and diverse Islamic practices relating to gender across time and space. This body of literature proved that women's status varied according to culture, custom, class, geographic location, and time period. This countered fundamentalists' claims that their views of women's "proper" place were the only authentically Islamic ones. Muslim feminists could point to history and utilize the variety of past practices and Islamic legal systems in their present-day struggle for rights.

Women from Muslim countries began publishing in the United States in large numbers after 1979, as well. A major consequence of the Iranian Revolution and increasing fundamentalist fervor was the immigration of educated, politically impassioned Muslim women to the United States and Western Europe. Whether they left their homes by choice or by necessity, many feminists from the Islamic world became activists-in-exile. Some joined NGOs, while others were drawn to universities, where they worked as students, educators, and intellectuals. These women, and their American feminist allies, attempted to drive the U.S. conversation about Muslim women's human rights through their publications and activism.

Unlike the resigned victims of Islamic tyranny described in *Not Without My Daughter*, Muslim women who wrote for American audiences could and did speak for themselves, and they demanded their rights.[72] They tended to be highly educated and often belonged to the cosmopolitan, secular middle and upper classes in their home countries. Some came to the United States as students and remained, while others, like Iran's Mahnaz Afkhami, were exiles.[73] The perspectives of religiously conservative women, women from the lower classes, or those who supported fundamentalists like Khomeini were absent from the U.S. public sphere during this period. Only those who spoke Americans' language—not simply in the literal sense but also the language of human rights, democracy, and equality—and who had the resources to live or publish in the United States had a voice.[74] Nevertheless, their works contributed a great deal to American understanding through well-researched studies of Muslim women's lives and deeply powerful personal accounts of suffering, loss, and desire for freedom. They provided Americans with insider accounts, and U.S. feminists often drew upon these publications in their own scholarship and activism.

Like the thriving scholarly literature on Islamic women, the growing number of books by women from Islamic countries published in the United States illustrated Americans' growing interest in the wake of the Iranian Revolution.[75] These publications included collaborations between Muslim and American scholars, as well as solo works.[76] Iranian Eliz Sanasarian's pioneering *The Women's Rights Movement in Iran* traced the history of the Iranian women's movement since 1900 and analyzed women's struggles to resist Khomeini. Like American historians at the time, Sanasarian corrected the misconception that Muslim women had never acted to secure their rights. Rather, "in spite of intense social opposition," Sanasarian stressed, they "actively challenged the inferior status of women and suffered much as a result."[77]

Other scholarship aspired to give contemporary Muslim women a voice in Western discussions. In 1988, sociologist Fatima Mernissi published *Doing Daily Battle*, a collection of interviews she conducted with fellow Moroccan women.[78] This provided American and other Western readers with firsthand accounts of these women's lives, from conditions in the harem to the kinds of work they did. Mernissi's later publications did even more to contribute to American understanding. Her memoir of growing up in a Moroccan harem dispelled eroticized, *Arabian Nights*-style fantasies. Instead of providing stories about scantily clad seductresses, Mernissi described the mundane routines, rivalries, and solidarities created by life in a largely female-only environment.[79] Her analyses of Muslim culture and Islamic law, meanwhile, cemented her position as one of the leading Muslim feminists of the age.[80] Mernissi's scathing critique of male authorities' manipulation of Islam and her feminist interpretations of Islamic texts equipped other Muslim feminists to challenge male Islamic scholars.[81] While showing how American stereotypes about Muslim women were wrong, Mernissi's publications reinforced the notion that Muslim women yearned for rights.

Islamic women also published novels, which had a potentially wider audience than academic publications. Nawal el Saadawi, an Egyptian medical doctor, scholar, author, and feminist, began publishing in the United States in the early 1980s. Although her scholarly works such as *The Hidden Face of Eve* powerfully indicated women's inferior status in Islamic culture, her novels gave readers a more intimate account of oppression. Her 1983 novel *Woman at Point Zero* is narrated by an Egyptian prostitute, Firdaus, who chafes under Islamic patriarchy. Firdaus confides to the reader, "Every single man I did get to know filled me with but one desire: to lift my hand and bring it smashing down on his face."[82] Novels written by other women from Islamic countries, from Hanan al-Shayk's *Women of Sand and Myrrh* to Leila Abou Zayd's *Year of the Elephant*, provided U.S. readers with strong female characters and, like Muslim women's scholarship, tended to universalize women's desire for human rights.[83]

Crucially, these Muslim women authors attested that women's human rights were applicable to the non-Western world, contradicting cultural relativists and male fundamentalists alike who argued that women's equality was a foreign concept imposed by Western imperialists.[84] As Mahnaz Afkhami explained, fundamentalists claim that "Islam provides the basic elements of a just society, including the fundamental rights of women. A major contention of this position is that women, in East and West alike, have rights because they belong to certain cultures or religions, not because they are individual human beings."[85]

In contrast, Muslim women who published in the United States argued that women's human rights *are* universal, regardless of religion or culture. These women also challenged the legitimacy of practices that fundamentalists claimed were essential to maintaining "authentic" Islamic culture. Because male religious leaders determined which practices were essential, Muslim feminists declared that customs that harmed women were illegitimate because women had no say in creating them.[86] Their arguments added a rich layer of understanding to U.S. discourse about Islamic women in the years after 1979, providing both the American public and transnational feminist activists with important perspectives as they mobilized on behalf of Muslim women by the 1990s.

It was in the context of these overlapping and often rich discussions about Muslim women in U.S. media and in feminist scholarship that Betty Mahmoody's *Not Without My Daughter* became a best seller. The book became one of the most publicly influential depictions of women's status in Muslim countries, but by the time Mahmoody's book and subsequent film appeared, the American public sphere was already saturated with news coverage, films, and publications that characterized women's oppression as a pervasive problem in the Islamic world. *Not Without My Daughter* was an especially lurid, Islamophobic reflection of American understandings about the place of women in the Islamic world, particularly the notions that East and West were inherently different and that the United States was superior, modern, and rational in its treatment of women.[87] Such binary thinking, which dehumanized Islamic men by casting them as monsters, made it easier for the public to support military interventions against Muslims, whether to bomb Qaddafi, punish Saddam Hussein, or liberate Afghan women.[88] Of all the possible stories and narratives, *Not Without My*

Daughter struck a chord with American audiences because it elicited emotions and drew upon multiple levels of discourse at once. Mahmoody's tale centered on a viscerally disturbing subject. However, as this chapter has shown, the Orientalist and Islamophobic understandings it advanced were not monolithic. They existed in tension with the human rights framework and with feminists' arguments that women everywhere, not just Islamic women, suffered from patriarchal oppression.

Mahmoody did endure horrific abuse at the hands of her husband, and Iran did strip women of their rights. Human rights violations against women in some Islamic countries were not simply Western constructs, although U.S. discourse about Muslim women is sometimes analyzed as such. Orientalist and Islamophobic elements of *Not Without My Daughter* had tremendous emotional appeal to American audiences, which would coexist tensely with universal human rights discourse about oppression in the Islamic world in the years to come. The period of the 1980s through the early 1990s was marked by public consciousness-raising and a consequential deepening of American public attention to women's rights in the Islamic world. The American conversation about Islamic women continued to evolve, with Orientalist, Islamophobic, and human rights discourses overlapping, contradicting, and reinforcing one another at different moments. The result was a complex set of understandings about Muslim women in the United States that undergirded later policy initiatives.

Chapter 3

Sisterhood Is Global:
Transnational Feminism and Islam

Prominent U.S. feminist Robin Morgan published and edited a ground-breaking anthology, *Sisterhood Is Global*, in 1984. At over eight hundred pages, this tome contains national studies and essays on women's status in eighty countries. Each nation's chapter is authored by a woman from that country, and there are fourteen chapters on Muslim-majority nations, exposing both the problems that women shared worldwide and the unique challenges that Islamic women faced in seeking equality.[1] *Sisterhood Is Global* did much to introduce American readers to feminists from the Islamic world, including Mahnaz Afkhami, Fatima Mernissi, Nawal el Saadawi, and Afghanistan's Sima Wali.

The publication of *Sisterhood Is Global* inspired Morgan to found a transnational feminist NGO that same year.[2] The Sisterhood Is Global Institute (SIGI) was a pioneering "international feminist think-tank."[3] Its founding members were women who had contributed to the eponymous book. While SIGI's beginnings were humble and its activities during the 1980s limited, by the 1990s it evolved into the leading transnational NGO that advocated for women's human rights in Muslim societies. Many of its founding members from Islamic countries would become—if they were not already—some of the most well-known Muslim feminists, and several, including Afkhami, Mernissi, and el Saadawi, would later make important contributions to U.S. policymaking.

While many countries had decades-old women's movements with international ties, a truly global feminist movement did not develop until the 1970s.[4] During the UN Decade for Women from 1975 to 1985, women's rights activists from around the globe came together, identified common concerns, brainstormed about strategies, and built transnational networks that internationalized the women's movement. Furthermore, feminist organizations set their sights on international spaces and intergovernmental bodies like the United Nations. While encounters between American women and women from Islamic countries were often fraught, they forged indelible global ties that influenced U.S. discourse and policy decisions about Muslim women's human rights.

The UN Decade proved crucial to the integration of women's human rights concerns into U.S. foreign policy in several ways. While American public discourse about Muslim women expanded after 1979, intensified public interest by itself was not enough to influence policy. In the UN Decade, however, U.S. and transnational feminists developed the organizational might to influence American policymakers and translate ground-level public interest into policy by founding transnational NGOs and networks dedicated to advancing women's rights in the Muslim world, such as Women Living Under Muslim Laws (WLUML) and SIGI. These NGOs and activists gained the necessary international experience through their participation in the UN Decade to equip them to influence U.S. policy effectively in the 1990s. The 1980s through the early 1990s, then, were a crucial period of institution building for activists who wished to promote gender equality in the Islamic world. Additionally, out of the crucible of often fierce debates between women from the United States and Islamic countries concerning the definition of women's human rights, discourses emerged from which policymakers in the near future could draw. They could adopt feminists' language, as policymakers did regularly during the Clinton years, or draw upon competing alternatives from U.S. public discourse, as the George W. Bush administration often did. Feminist engagement during the Decade, then, was directly relevant to later U.S. policy.

A core group of feminists, including Eleanor Roosevelt, had fought successfully for the insertion of language asserting men's and women's equality in the 1945 UN Charter and 1948 Universal Declaration of Human Rights (UDHR).[5] The United Nations also established the Commission on the Status of Women (CSW) to work toward the equal rights mandate set forth in the Charter. Despite these developments, however, the United Nations did little to push for women's equality from its founding through the 1960s.

Instead, it separated women's rights and human rights into different categories and marginalized women's issues.[6]

In 1967, however, the CSW issued the Declaration on the Elimination of
Discrimination Against Women in response to a growing grassroots demand
for women's rights worldwide. Soon afterward, a group of women's organizations proposed to the CSW that the United Nations hold an international
conference on women and declare an International Women's Year, which the
United Nations designated as 1975.[7] The United Nations resolved to hold a
world conference on women in Mexico City that year.[8] Soon thereafter, they
declared the Decade for Women. This necessitated two more conferences:
one in Copenhagen, Denmark, in 1980 and another in Nairobi, Kenya, in
1985. The Decade also included numerous preparatory meetings of UN
agencies, governments, and NGOs to study the status of women globally
and set the world conference agendas.

Although under-studied by historians, the Decade and its three conferences were vital for the evolution of a truly global feminist movement and,
consequently, the creation of transnational NGOs dedicated to Muslim
women's human rights.[9] According to Margaret Snyder, the founding director of the United Nations Development Fund for Women (UNIFEM), the
United Nations became "women's guardian and advocate, the 'unlikely godmother' on whom women have depended to put forth legislation for adoption by all countries, to offer us chances to meet across national and regional
borders, to open doors for us to join discussions of issues that impact our
lives."[10] Women attended the Decade conferences and preparatory events in
the tens of thousands, and the participants became increasingly diverse as
the Decade progressed. Caribbean feminist Peggy Antrobus later asserted,
"It was in this decade, in the context of these global conferences, that the
contours of a global women's movement emerged."[11]

At the 1975 Mexico City conference, governments chose the official delegates. Most were men who toed their states' lines. The official proceedings
in Mexico City excluded all but government delegations, and participating
governments and the United Nations worked out the conference agenda in
advance.[12] To participate in this momentous global conversation about
women, feminist activists and organizations convened at an NGO Forum,
held in parallel to the official conference.[13] Jocelyn Olcott has asserted that
the Mexico City Forum "marked the NGO-ization of activism, particularly

transnational women's activism."[14] Nearly six thousand people from around the world participated in the Mexico City Forum, which scholars agree operated largely as a mass consciousness-raising meeting.[15]

At this Forum, U.S. feminists met their counterparts from Islamic societies and began to link their causes. To mobilize effectively, they had to overcome national, political, and cultural divides, usually along North-South or First World-Third World lines, although there were also East-West tensions stemming from the Cold War, as well as political battles over Palestine and South African apartheid.[16] According to Arvonne Fraser, an American feminist involved in planning the Decade, "The bickering and political rhetoric was, at times, intense."[17] Indeed, the dream of "global sisterhood" ultimately proved illusory in Mexico City. Fault lines developed over questions of identity, culture, political ideology, tactics, and definitions of human rights. Differences between women proved to be as important as what they had in common.[18]

Although these differences were important for many reasons, the most useful for this study—and ones that recurred throughout the Decade—concerned differing human rights conceptions between women from the United States and the Third World. As other scholars have demonstrated, although gender equality was enshrined in the founding documents of international human rights law, neither the United Nations nor the international community treated women's rights as human rights until 1993. Nevertheless, feminists who participated in Decade activities often used human rights concepts to frame their arguments and to push the United Nations and national governments to include women's rights in the human rights agenda. Divergent feminist definitions of human rights from the United States and the Third World, however, became apparent in Mexico City and would resurface in Copenhagen.

Although the UDHR ostensibly treated political, civil, economic, cultural, and social rights equally, a hierarchy of human rights had in fact developed. U.S. feminists tended to privilege individual civil, political, and sexual rights over collective economic, cultural, and social rights. Meanwhile, international human rights law mainly addressed abuses committed by states.[19] The United Nations and many Western countries downplayed or ignored social, economic, and cultural rights, which scholars often refer to as "second generation" human rights.[20] Violations of women's human rights in particular did not receive much international attention before the 1970s in part because individuals, not states, often commit those violations.

Moreover, as Allida Black explained, the international community "focused on legal rather than de facto discrimination and thus neglected discrimination that women encountered from common law, cultural practices, and other extralegal forces."[21] The public/private divide and the premium placed upon civil-political rights prevented the universal application of human rights protections, especially for women.

Feminists recognized this, and those from the United States especially attacked the public/private dichotomy by declaring "the personal is political." And yet—at least during the first half of the Decade—many nevertheless failed to recognize the complex web of power structures that influenced women's situations worldwide. By focusing largely on individual political and civil rights—for example, reproductive freedom, political representation, and legal equality, and by imagining that all women shared a universal experience—many U.S. feminists initially downplayed issues that women from the developing world saw as paramount.

American feminists' perceived lack of sensitivity toward Third World women's perspectives made their initial encounters extremely contentious. Women from the Global South argued that power relationships existed between different groups of women as well as between women and men; U.S. and European women needed to acknowledge that more than just sex discrimination was the problem. By insisting that their particular understandings of rights were universal, the Americans adopted an approach that appeared imperialist to many Third World feminists.[22] As *Ms.* observed about Mexico City, "Unfortunately, it is the Americans who show the most appalling lack of knowledge and understanding about the political and social situation of their sisters in the Third and Socialist worlds . . . some Yankee participants compound the alienation by concentrating on selected issues, 'leading' when they could be following, and turning comatose whenever there is insistence upon redistribution of the world's wealth as a prerequisite to the liberation of women."[23] Women from the Third World prioritized social and economic rights, as well as different forms of structural inequality. Individual political, civil, and sexual rights would have to wait.[24]

Brad Simpson has argued that human rights were "not a trajectory or a gradually expanding set of norms and institutions but an arena of contestation over expertise and representation and therefore power, waged on highly unequal terms."[25] Third World women's attempts to remedy the imbalance between the First World and the Third World led to fierce debates with American and other Western feminists, which profoundly influenced the women who participated in the Decade, as well as the international organizations they founded. Transnational NGOs that focused on women's human rights in the Islamic world would have to reconcile competing rights conceptions when conducting campaigns in the United States in the years that followed.

Mexico City was marked by discord, and so was the conference and Forum in Copenhagen. Originally, Tehran was slated to host the July 1980 conference. The Islamic Revolution forced the United Nations to change the venue, and Khomeini cast a shadow over the proceedings in Copenhagen.[26] Meanwhile, the United Nations' passage of the Convention on the Elimination of All Forms of Discrimination Against Women (CEDAW) in 1979, as well as ongoing efforts to convince UN member states to ratify CEDAW, provided conference participants with a new international instrument to use and a new subject to debate.[27] In the end, the Copenhagen conference and Forum ended up being the most fractious of the three Decade gatherings.[28]

Once again, government delegations clashed over political issues ranging from the Camp David Accords to the ongoing Iran Hostage Crisis.[29] A correspondent covering Copenhagen for *Time* concluded that "global politics had kept the convention from focusing on the plight of women in a man's world."[30] Disagreements were not limited to government delegations. Just as they had in Mexico, NGO Forum participants from the United States and Western Europe clashed with women from the Third World over priorities, strategies, and Western women's cultural insensitivity.[31]

While there had been some discussion of Islam in Mexico City, the topic was more important in Copenhagen because of the Iranian Revolution. Registrants at the Forum included 155 women from ten Middle Eastern nations and dozens more Muslims from Asia and Africa.[32] Several NGOs sponsored workshops specifically dedicated to Muslim women's issues, including the following: Arab women; women in Iraq, Indonesia, Iran, Lebanon, Palestine, and Bangladesh; literacy projects; female genital mutilation; polygamy; family law; health and family planning; and Islam.[33]

The changing status of Iranian women dominated these conversations, particularly because the Iranian delegation was outspoken. *Forum '80*, the Forum's daily newspaper and primary historical record, devoted several articles of scarce column space to the stir the Iranian delegates caused. Iran only permitted its official delegates to leave the country to attend the conference; predictably, they all supported Khomeini.

These women defended the Ayatollah's policies and touted his leadership. They erected a booth dedicated to defending the Islamic revolution and supporting "the return to wearing the chador." According to Fraser, their booth included "a poster of a woman holding a machine gun."[34] Akram Hariri, the head of Iran's delegation, also issued public statements. The majority of her audience's questions focused on the chador and Khomeini's recent restrictions on women. In response, the chador-clad Hariri defended her government and took exception to reports that women were forced to veil, claiming, "Khomeini cannot tell us how to dress. We want to dress like this." When questioned about the absence of women in the new government, Hariri responded, "Because in the past the Shah kept the women down. We don't have such great women yet to go there (into the council) and talk. They (the men) wouldn't mind, they would let us go in; of course I really believe that! We just didn't have great women."[35]

The Iranians' arguments hinted at an alternative framework for understanding women's rights and human rights more generally. Conservative Muslims and others in the Third World have argued that universal human rights concepts represent Western imperialism in disguise.[36] Islamic studies scholar Abdulaziz Sachedina has explained that conservative male religious leaders and scholars "dismissed [universal human rights] as yet another ploy to dominate Muslim societies by undermining their religiously based culture and values system."[37] These conservative Muslims denied that truly universal human rights existed and instead adopted the position of cultural relativism, especially regarding women.

Islamic opponents of universalism claimed that only Islam provides the true rights framework for their societies. They rejected international human rights instruments, such as the UDHR (1948), the International Covenant on Civil and Political Rights (1966), the International Covenant on Economic, Social, and Cultural Rights (1966), and CEDAW (1979). They argued that "authentic" Islam justified women's subordination and gender inequality.[38] The 1990 Cairo Declaration on Human Rights in Islam, adopted a decade after Copenhagen, expressed this view most explicitly when nearly fifty Islamic states asserted that human rights exist only "in accordance with the Islamic Shari'ah."[39] This attitude upheld claims that women do not deserve full human rights because Shari'a—as interpreted by male religious authorities—declares that women are inferior. Copenhagen's Iranian delegation adopted this stance and illustrated it to the vast majority of other conference and NGO Forum participants who condemned Khomeini's policies.

The Iranians defined women's human rights solely within the confines of their religious ideology, and they accepted women's subordinate status within revolutionary Iran.

Feminists working in the Islamic world had to find a way to respond to the challenge of an increasingly influential fundamentalism. Some embraced Islamic feminism, which accepted Shari'a but sought to modify it based on feminist reinterpretations of religious texts—especially the Koran—to argue that Islam guarantees human rights and equal status to all human beings, regardless of gender.[40] While fundamentalists and conservatives argued that Islam and feminism are incompatible, Islamic feminists posited that Islam can be liberating for women but that male religious leaders, especially fundamentalists, misinterpreted religious texts and Islamic law in ways that subordinate women. They argued that interpreting these texts from women's perspectives could bring about justice and equality. In doing so, Islamic feminists rejected the notion—perpetuated by Orientalists but also often asserted by defenders of "tradition" as it applies to women—that Islam is monolithic and cannot, indeed should not, change like other cultures do. Islamic feminists instead questioned cultural norms created by men.[41]

One scholar has characterized Islamic feminists as "political insubordinates" who "refus[ed] the boundaries others try to draw around them" and asserted that "Islam is not necessarily more traditional or authentic than any other identification, nor is it any more violent or patriarchal than any other religion."[42] By doing so, Islamic feminists claimed power within their cultures and religious traditions, pushing back against arguments that feminism was a Western imposition. Meanwhile, other feminists from the Islamic world identified as Muslim but not as "Islamic feminists."[43] They rejected the imposition of Shari'a and pursued a more secular agenda, using Islam to argue for women's equality when it was helpful but not developing their arguments primarily in religious terms.

At Copenhagen, the fundamentalist challenge to universal human rights found powerful expression in the words of the Iranian delegation. Despite their best efforts, however, they failed to convince their skeptics. On July 17, the Iranians led a workshop titled "The Role of Iranian Women in the Revolution," during which they praised the theocracy.[44] Similar to Islamic feminists' claims, they sought to cast Islam and the veil as liberating for women, in contrast to Western imperialism and Western culture. "All we've done is answer questions about the chador—and I said at the beginning that we wouldn't deal with this anymore," remarked a frustrated Leila Bakhtiar, the delegation's English-speaking spokeswoman. To Bakhtiar, the chador was an important symbol of the revolution—"and you don't throw your symbols away."[45]

Their audience rejected the Iranians' arguments, however, and the reporter who covered the workshop characterized the Iranians' statements as "alarming."[46] Just as disconcerting to many Forum attendees was the large portrait of Khomeini that the Iranians hung in the hallway. For many at the Forum, Khomeini's glowering visage was a direct affront to the spirit of the conference.[47]

Although the Iranians' defense of Khomeini put them in the minority and on the most conservative end of the ideological spectrum in Copenhagen, their arguments hinted that some Muslim women wanted to veil and that others might find the issue of veiling less pressing or oppressive than other problems facing Islamic societies. Most women from Muslim countries in Copenhagen were not fundamentalists, but many were frustrated by Western feminists' approaches to discussing women's status in the Islamic world. Many non-Muslim women focused on the hijab; they ignored other serious issues and demonstrated insensitivity to the diversity of Muslim women's views on veiling.

Beyond the veil, Westerners in Copenhagen also condemned female genital mutilation (FGM), a practice many Third World women also opposed. Despite their common opposition to FGM, however, African and Arab women felt that Americans and Europeans "sensationalized" the issue and adopted culturally insensitive, colonialist attitudes when discussing it.[48] As the Association of African Women for Research and Development (AAWORD) argued, Western ethnocentrism regarding such issues not only represented "latent racism" but also ignored "the structures and social relations which perpetuate this situation [violations of women's human rights]." Such factors included "the exploitation of developing countries," they said, but Western feminists downplayed structural causes of inequality in favor of political and sexual rights. Women from developing nations could not focus on sexuality or political representation when they "cannot even satisfy their basic needs," AAWORD asserted.[49] To them, U.S. and European women were putting the cart before the horse.

The conflicts in Copenhagen over issues relating to Islam, such as veiling, FGM, and Khomeini, were certainly acrimonious, and they underscored the broader divisions between Western and Third World women. Many in the Third World had come to see the United States as just the latest incarnation of Western colonialism. They wanted American feminists to recognize the persistent asymmetry of power between their respective countries and to acknowledge that imperialism negatively affected women. When American feminists criticized Islam, their arguments sounded like colonial feminism to many Muslims. Consequently, many Islamic women (and others from the Third World) at Copenhagen questioned whether the term "feminism" even applied to them.[50]

Disagreements, misunderstandings, and differing agendas persisted at the 1985 conference and NGO Forum in Nairobi. By this time, however, the relationship between Western and Third World women—including those from the United States and Islamic countries—was far less acrimonious than it had been during the first half of the Decade.[51] In fact, as Valentine Moghadam has asserted, "The year 1985 was, in many ways, a watershed," while another scholar declared Nairobi "the 'coming of age' of the international women's movement."[52] Historian Judith Zinsser, who participated in the Decade conferences, remarked that "the meeting in 1985 was the most important of all. In Nairobi women demonstrated their ability to cooperate across national, racial, and economic boundaries."[53] Feminist NGOs had acquired the organizational know-how to gain access to the preconference planning sessions, so the official conference agenda incorporated their input. In Nairobi, women's rights activists also managed to overcome many of the North-South divides that had marked the earlier conferences.

There were many reasons for this shift in tone. Feminists had been meeting and exchanging ideas with one another internationally for a decade, so they were more familiar with each other's views. The Nairobi Forum was also better planned. The organizers spent two years in preparation, whereas the earlier forums "had been rather hastily organized."[54] By 1985, the more than 14,000 activists present at the Forum, as well as the 160 national delegations at the official conference, were ready to work together despite their differences.[55]

In addition, worsening global economic conditions—caused in part by Western neoliberal economic policies—made American and Western European women more sympathetic to Third World women's emphasis on bread-and-butter issues. Western feminists were also more willing to acknowledge their relative privilege and the lasting legacy of colonialism. Meanwhile, the rising tide of religious fundamentalism globally brought Muslim and non-Muslim women together to fight reversals in women's rights that fundamentalists from all major religions wished to enforce.[56] Their attacks on women in Islamic countries, from Iran to Algeria to Pakistan, suddenly made legal and sexual equality seem very important. Concerned attendees from both the United States and Islamic countries at Nairobi began to devise common strategies to combat the fundamentalist challenge.

While there were no official statements on religious fundamentalism in Mexico City or Copenhagen, the women in Nairobi—at both the conference and the Forum—issued strong condemnations of fundamentalists and frequently discussed the issue.[57] According to Fraser, "It was agreed that this threat . . . was a worldwide phenomenon which needed to be taken seriously."[58] At the Forum, AAWORD held a session on fundamentalism, which women from around the world attended. The resulting public statement was more explicit than the conference's, calling religious fundamentalism "alarming," "retrogressive," and "dangerous because it questions the rights women have acquired during this decade."[59] Similarly, Nawal el Saadawi wrote an editorial in *Forum '85* condemning "religious obscurantism" and warning that male religious leaders in Egypt were "trying to force women back to a situation which prevailed almost half a century ago." She argued that women had to fight "to ensure that there is no retreat, no going back from what has already been won."[60] While such statements condemned religious fundamentalism generally and did not single out Islam, much of the discussion in Nairobi nevertheless focused on Muslim fundamentalists.

The Forum included dozens of panels and sessions related to Islam, with titles such as "Equality: Women in Islam," "Women, Sex, and Religion," "Egyptian Women in the Eighties," "Women's Rights in Iran," and "Arab Women and Value System."[61] While there was not always agreement between women from Islamic countries and those from the West, or even between Muslim women themselves, the tone of these panels was cooperative and respectful. Remarking on the changing tenor of discussion between Muslim women and non-Muslim (especially Western) women regarding the veil, Palestinian Nadia Hijab wrote that "there is increasing awareness that a veil is not always what it seems."[62]

Similarly, the session "Female Sexuality and Bodily Functions in Different Religious Traditions" concluded with women from many religions—Islam included—agreeing that they needed to work together to reinterpret religious texts in a more feminist light.[63] Just as that session was a site of cooperation and empowerment, *Forum '85* described other sessions dedicated to Muslim women's issues as "lively" and "animated," rather than discordant. When the women did disagree with one another—for instance, over whether or not the veil was a symbol of oppression—they engaged in productive debate rather than heated arguments like they had five years earlier. Even Iran's official delegates were less confrontational and more open to dialogue than they had been in Copenhagen.[64]

The new tone in Nairobi demonstrated the maturation of the global feminist movement.[65] The Decade had provided feminists with spaces to meet, debate, and create a worldwide movement for women's human rights. Just as important, the Decade gave women the opportunity to establish personal ties and transnational networks, which were crucial to waging successful campaigns worldwide. These networks provided women with means to share information, support, and resources around the globe and to mobilize transnational campaigns to pressure states.[66] As Western and non-Western feminist perspectives combined during the Decade, activists used their networks and global communications technology like the fax machine and, later, the Internet to craft a common agenda. This allowed them to develop a transnational community that was an alternative to the prevailing nation-state-based international system. It also allowed them to focus their energies simultaneously on local communities, national governments, and international institutions like the United Nations. As women bridged their divides, they founded transnational organizations to defend and expand their rights. The creation of NGOs in the mid-1980s dedicated specifically to protecting women's human rights in Muslim societies was part of this trend.

The two most influential transnational NGOs that advocated for Muslim women were founded in 1984 and 1986, respectively: SIGI and WLUML. Liberal, secularist, cosmopolitan feminists from the middle and upper classes of Islamic countries dominated both organizations, which enabled them to communicate relatively easily with U.S. feminists and policymakers. None of the main leaders of either organization, for example, wore a hijab, which visually symbolized their liberal, secular agendas. They shared American feminists' commitment to universal human rights, and they knew how to communicate effectively with other organizations and governments. As Mahnaz Afkhami noted in 1995, many Muslim women like herself and her fellow SIGI members were effective advocates for women's human rights because they were "multicultural, familiar with the West, multilingual, and conversant with international organizations and politics."[67] However, while they could speak Americans' conceptual language, their perspectives were not identical to those of U.S. feminists.

In order to be universal, human rights language draws its authority from "the conscience of mankind" and "fundamental freedoms," as the UDHR Preamble explains, rather than from religion or any other culturally bounded framework.[68] According to Sachedina, "Human rights language is modern, firmly rooted in a secular liberalism that safeguards and promotes citizens' rights and that demands privatization of religion from the public sphere to allow the development of a politics independent of religion."[69] Although there were many secular modernizers in the Islamic world, for conservative Muslims and especially for male religious authorities, Islam and secular human rights seemed deeply incompatible. The women of SIGI and WLUML had to confront this reality.

Islam provides a complete way of life, covering all aspects of activity and belief. Removing religion from the public sphere and relegating it to the private is at odds with traditional Islamic theology and jurisprudence.[70] This is especially true with regard to women, whose rights Islam traditionally defines in relation to their roles within the family. SIGI and WLUML knew that acknowledging the religious, historical, and cultural contexts of Islamic societies was necessary to advance women's human rights. Although SIGI and WLUML unequivocally opposed fundamentalism and embraced universal rights, both also accommodated religion in their fight for gender equality. Employing only the secular language of universal rights found in documents like the UDHR and CEDAW would fail to convince many religiously minded Muslims that women are full human beings deserving of equality. Furthermore, using only universal human rights instruments and language would leave feminists open to fundamentalists' charges that they were "inauthentic" lackeys of Western imperialism. SIGI's Afkhami asserted that fundamentalists insisted "on singling out women's relation to society as the supreme test of the authenticity of the Islamic order."[71] By understanding the power of religion in Muslims' everyday lives, then, SIGI and WLUML fought to reclaim power from male religious leaders and fundamentalists who used religion as an excuse to oppress women. These NGOs instead used Islam as a tool to empower them.[72]

The women of SIGI and WLUML were not, however, cultural relativists or Islamic feminists. Although they recognized the importance of religion and culture, they also employed universal, secular instruments of empowerment like CEDAW and international human rights law. They were not bound by Islam; it was simply another tool they could use. As Afkhami explained, "Our difference with Islamic feminists is that we don't try to fit feminism in the Qur'an. We say that women have certain inalienable rights. The epistemology of Islam is contrary to women's rights. But you can use what you need to [to advance women's positions]. I call myself a Muslim and a feminist. I'm not an Islamic feminist—that's a contradiction in terms."[73] This position clearly involved a delicate balance between worldviews that could pull in opposite directions. These women believed deeply in universal human rights, yet they also needed to confront the conditions facing women on the local level to ensure that those rights were realized. They had to work to change religious traditions without appearing to be anti-Islamic, while simultaneously locating women's rights in universal norms and not in one particular tradition. As scholars have recognized, "Human rights are only imaginable with appeal to the global and the universal, but they are only concrete when they are local."[74] Transnational women's organizations operated within this paradox.

Their fundamentalist opponents battled to cast themselves as the sole authorities on women's rights and to keep the rest of the world from interfering by wielding charges of cultural relativism and Western imperialism. To counter these adversaries, SIGI and WLUML had to speak to the global and to the local simultaneously. Afkhami's arguments exemplified the views of the women who dominated these organizations. She wrote, "The struggle is multifaceted, at once political, economic, ethical, psychological, and intellectual. . . . Above all, it is a casting off of a tradition of subjection."[75] Religion and culture were intertwined and valued by Muslim women and therefore had to be included in their fight for equality and human rights.

Muslim women's local struggles were also crucial to the international movement. As Afkhami asserted, "An important part of the ongoing struggle for women's human rights is the effort to find ways and means of bringing together women from different cultures to work toward solutions to common human problems. The global movement for women's human rights, therefore, is not exclusively a women's project; rather, it brings the women's rights perspective, which is fundamentally gender-inclusive, to choices that need to be made for a more productive and humane future for everyone." Cultural and other differences notwithstanding, she stressed, "this historical necessity provides a reason and an opportunity for women from both

South and North to cooperate."[76] In response to the question of "whether Muslim women have rights because they are human beings, or whether they have rights because they are Muslim," SIGI and WLUML emphatically asserted the former.[77]

Algerian feminist Marieme Hélie-Lucas founded WLUML in response to specific, local violations of women's rights in several Muslim countries in 1984. The Algerian government jailed three feminists for nearly a year for attempting to educate other women about the proposed Algerian Family Code, which Hélie-Lucas believed "was intended to reduce women's rights severely."[78] At the same time, a Muslim woman went before India's Supreme Court to challenge her divorce, which her husband accomplished simply by verbally repudiating their marriage. Her case questioned the constitutionality of special family laws that applied only to Muslims in the secular state of India. Meanwhile, a court in Abu Dhabi sentenced a pregnant Sri Lankan to death by stoning for the crime of adultery, and a group of divorced mothers living in France fought custody battles with their ex-husbands in Algeria.[79] The women in all of these cases sought international support, and WLUML formed in response.

As a feminist who opposed the new Algerian family law, Hélie-Lucas felt empowered when she met women from other Islamic countries. As she later explained, despite their contributions to Algeria's war for independence in the 1950s and 1960s, women were being pushed back into the home by the new law: "It was really interesting when I started travelling out of Algeria, mainly to Morocco and Tunisia in the beginning, to see that laws were different in other places when each time we were taught that you can't change anything because this is Islam. So my first contact with women from other Muslim countries showed me that this was a big lie."[80] In July 1984, Hélie-Lucas and eight other Muslim women from Algeria, Bangladesh, Iran, Morocco, Mauritius, Tanzania, Pakistan, and Sudan met at the Tribunal on Reproductive Rights in Amsterdam. As part of the Decade, the Tribunal was the fourth international women's health meeting since 1977; 400 women from sixty-five countries attended.[81] Hélie-Lucas later saw these meetings as crucial to the formation of WLUML. "It is thanks to these international meetings that we have been able to set up our own organisations at the regional and continental levels," she wrote. "It is important to acknowledge the historical role they played in our taking off."[82] The nine Muslim women who met in Amsterdam used the Tribunal to discuss the crises in Algeria, India, and Abu Dhabi. They saw these incidents as evidence of a much broader and more systematic assault on women's rights in the Islamic world, so they formed the Action Committee of Women Living Under Muslim Laws. By 1986, the committee officially became WLUML.[83]

Initially based in France, WLUML was a transnational network that enabled women living in Muslim societies to exchange information, compare different interpretations of Islamic law, learn about their rights, support one another's struggles, share strategies, and organize "collective projects."[84] WLUML was the first transnational feminist network to focus exclusively on Muslim women.[85] Hélie-Lucas, the organization's "guiding light," was a social science professor at the University of Algiers, but she left Algeria for Europe in 1982 because she was being harassed for her activism. As an activist-in-exile, she influenced developments in her home country and countries around the globe through WLUML.

The organization's founders aspired to help Muslim women help themselves. Hélie-Lucas said, "Women who live in Muslim countries and communities are, like women everywhere, actively engaged in promoting positive change—oppressed, no doubt, but not helpless."[86] Her arguments were similar to those expressed simultaneously in scholarly publications about Muslim women. She hoped that WLUML would not only empower Muslim women and challenge Western stereotypes but also break down what she saw as artificial North-South barriers between women. WLUML welcomed support from non-Muslims and forged ties with other international women's groups, including SIGI and organizations in the United States.[87] The inclusion of non-Muslim, Western women within its network was potentially fractious, but Hélie-Lucas avoided this by maintaining women from Muslim societies in leadership positions and treating non-Muslim feminists and NGOs as valued partners. Hélie-Lucas recognized the power that global public opinion—and therefore non-Muslim, Western women—could exert in support of WLUML's attempts to shame Islamic governments that oppressed women.

In 1988, WLUML launched an exchange program for Muslim women, the first of its kind. Women from the program met in Pakistan in 1990 to compare the different ways Koranic verses pertaining to women had been interpreted and to promote feminist interpretations and laws that supported women's equality. WLUML also planned to create a handbook that could assist grassroots activists in challenging Muslim family laws that deprived women of equal rights. Such initiatives reflected the influence of Islamic feminism on WLUML's activities: the secular organization recognized the futility of ignoring religion while campaigning in Muslim societies.[88]

Over time, WLUML proved influential. The network's core in the International Coordinating Office in France shared information with activists, other women's rights organizations, and scholars worldwide. WLUML's *Dossiers* and other publications, distributed in English, French, and Arabic, collected news about women's status in various countries, new scholarship on Muslim women, conferences and events of interest, and calls for support from WLUML's global network. Those who used WLUML to disseminate information included SIGI members such as Nawal el Saadawi and Fatima Mernissi.[89]

WLUML also developed an Alert for Action system, which spread news of urgent situations requiring coordinated action. It mobilized activists around the world to pressure governments of Islamic countries that violated or restricted women's rights. Its alerts and publications were WLUML's main tie to non-Muslim allies and other transnational feminist NGOs like SIGI. The English-language versions of WLUML's alerts and *Dossiers* urged women in the United States to support embattled women in Islamic societies, and they educated non-Muslim feminists about Muslim women's lives. WLUML also disseminated relevant information submitted by American organizations, such as the *Women's International Network News* (*WINN*).[90]

Characterized by Moghadam as "fiercely antifundamentalist," WLUML used its alert system to coordinate mass letter-writing campaigns to protest Muslim family laws that oppressed women, oppose the legalization of fundamentalist political parties, and provide material aid to individual women. The three Algerian feminists arrested in 1984 secured their release later that year due in large part to the international outcry WLUML raised over their incarceration. Similarly, the Sri Lankan woman accused of adultery in Abu Dhabi escaped being stoned and returned home after WLUML intervened.[91] In 1988, members of the network rescued a French-born Algerian woman whose father and brother had kidnapped her from a women's shelter in France. The men smuggled her into Morocco, drugged and beat her, took her identity papers, and planned to marry her off to an Algerian. Because of WLUML members' intervention, including that of supporters in the United States, the woman avoided the marriage, took her case to court in Algeria, and won her freedom.[92]

In subsequent years, WLUML continued to mobilize its supporters globally through its action alerts. It also played a crucial role in disseminating information about new threats to women's rights. By bringing women together across national boundaries, WLUML provided feminist activists in the Islamic world with transnational solidarity and a means of sharing information and strategies. WLUML also gave Muslim feminists a way to garner support and assistance from American and other non-Muslim feminists. This allowed them to exert external pressure on their governments, which was often necessary to the success of their campaigns. By providing a worldwide conduit for information, WLUML later played an important role in the global feminist mobilization against the Taliban in the late 1990s.

Like WLUML, the Sisterhood Is Global Institute emerged mainly in response to the rise of fundamentalism. Although SIGI passed along and built upon information it received from other NGOs like WLUML, it also went beyond WLUML's information-sharing and letter-writing campaigns. SIGI held international conferences, participated in preparations for several UN world conferences, and, most significant, lobbied the U.S. government directly for policies to promote women's human rights in Muslim countries. By the mid-1990s, SIGI had become the premier transnational NGO for the protection and promotion of women's human rights in the Islamic world.

SIGI's beginnings, however, were humble. It was far from obvious in the 1980s that the organization would become any kind of women's rights powerhouse. Robin Morgan published *Sisterhood Is Global* in anticipation of the Nairobi conference.[93] Twenty of SIGI's founding members attended the Nairobi NGO Forum, where they formally launched the organization, but SIGI was barely functional for the next several years.[94] Many of SIGI's original members were not fully committed to the organization, and Morgan herself was often too busy to devote much time to it. More problematic, Morgan and her cofounders decided that SIGI's headquarters and leadership should change every five years so that the organization would "not conform permanently to the culture and environment of any area, and to allow it to focus on women's participation in activities in new regions."[95] SIGI was initially based in New York City. It moved to New Zealand in 1989, to Bethesda, Maryland, in 1993, and to Montreal in 2000. The constant uprooting of SIGI's offices led to administrative instability and limited the organization's effectiveness.[96]

SIGI also struggled for funding as it tried to get off the ground. Writing to Canadian member Greta Hofmann Nemiroff in January 1987, Morgan lamented that "funding dried up in the U.S. to desert proportions vis-à-vis women," and SIGI was floundering.[97] SIGI's early records are full of grant and funding proposal rejections.[98] Because of its early financial limitations, the organization undertook no major projects until the 1990s, when it underwent a renaissance under the leadership of Mahnaz Afkhami, who, like Hélie-Lucas, was an activist-in-exile.

In late 1978, Afkhami had been visiting the United Nations to finalize the creation of the International Center for Training and Research on Women (INSTRAW), which was supposed to be based in Tehran, when her husband called. He passed along a message from Empress Farah warning Afkhami not to come home because fundamentalists had threatened her life. Unable to return to Iran, Afkhami has lived in exile in the United States ever since.[99] A contributor to Morgan's book, she was a member of SIGI throughout the 1980s. She led the NGO starting in 1992, a reflection of U.S. feminists' increased willingness to share leadership with women from the rest of the world. When she became SIGI's executive director, the organization's budget was only $18,000. It had no office space, no permanent staff, and no plans.[100]

Described by Moghadam as "a movement entrepreneur as well as a movement intellectual," Afkhami had the organizational wherewithal to be an effective leader. Her earlier experience as secretary-general of the Women's Organization of Iran and Iran's Minister of State for Women's Affairs proved indispensable.[101] She was capable of working with and outside of governments to advance women's rights. Under Afkhami's leadership, SIGI quickly obtained grants and funding from UNIFEM, the Rockefeller Foundation, the Ford Foundation, and the MacArthur Foundation.[102] While philanthropic giving had expanded by the 1990s, so had the number of NGOs and, consequently, competition for funds. Moreover, with the exception of the Ford Foundation, most new philanthropic funds did not go to organizations that supported women's rights.[103] Afkhami, however, knew how to frame SIGI's applications to appeal to U.S. and international donors and was a major factor in the organization's success in receiving funding for its initiatives.

The influx of money allowed SIGI to maintain an office space with full-time staff and launch a variety of ambitious projects, such as conferences, symposia, workshops, exchange programs, action alerts, research, fund-raising for other organizations, partnerships with the mainstream news media, briefings for governments and other agencies, publications, and the achievement of official consultative status at the United Nations. SIGI could also afford to send delegates to international conferences, including the 1993 UN World Conference on Human Rights in Vienna, the 1994 UN International Conference on Population and Development (ICPD) in Cairo, and the 1995 Fourth World Conference on Women in Beijing. In fact, SIGI member Gertrude Monghella of Tanzania served as the secretary-general of the Beijing conference. By 1999, SIGI's membership included 1,300 women from 70 countries, as well as countless other activists and organizations who received SIGI's alerts through its Sisterhood Is Global Network (SIGN).[104]

Afkhami ensured that SIGI focused its energies primarily on promoting women's rights in the Muslim world. Women from Islamic countries dominated the organization by the early 1990s; focusing on Muslim women made sense. Moreover, no international organization quite like SIGI existed for Islamic women, so the organization's efforts would have a positive effect in that area. Yet Afkhami did not seek to exclude SIGI's non-Muslim membership, which was an important decision. Unlike WLUML, SIGI was founded by an American feminist and had a large non-Muslim membership base. The decision to focus primarily on Muslim women might have alienated Morgan, who had not intended for SIGI to focus on any one particular group, as well as its non-Muslim members who may not have been interested in such a specialized focus. However, the organization's strength, in Afkhami's view, came precisely from its international nature, and she worked to foster harmony and cooperation between its members. At least initially, she was successful.[105]

Afkhami believed that Islamic women needed to work together with others to advance women's human rights both internationally and on the ground. She argued that Muslim women had much to offer the global human rights movement, and "this project requires an equitable representation for the women of the South in setting the criteria, providing the context, and assigning values that will guide the global movement for human rights." Western feminists, meanwhile, also offered much to local movements in Islamic countries. In addition to the benefits that came from U.S. and European feminists' "vitality, good will, and diversity," she wrote, "women from the North can help by mobilizing international support for Muslim women's struggle, particularly through the use of international media and other means of communication to facilitate interaction between Muslim women and the international community as well as among Muslim women themselves."[106] SIGI occupied a space where the local and global movements intersected, providing it the opportunity to serve as a bridge between North and South, between the universal and the particular.

During Afkhami's tenure as leader, SIGI was based in Bethesda, Maryland, providing it with access to U.S. sources of funding and to American policymakers. Its location, resources, and the name recognition of its founder, Robin Morgan, contributed to the organization's renaissance in the 1990s. Because of its success in attracting funding, the organization was able to partner with women's groups in Islamic countries to create formal organizational ties, such as SIGI-Jordan and SIGI-Uzbekistan.[107] SIGI also shared information with and supported the activities of other internationally oriented NGOs, like WLUML, the Center for Women's Global Leadership (CWGL), UNIFEM, Human Rights Watch, and NGOs working toward the eradication of FGM.[108] In fact, SIGI's membership overlapped with that of many of these other organizations, including WLUML.[109]

Through its activities, SIGI raised its profile.[110] By the mid-1990s, the organization set its sights on lobbying the U.S. government for policies to advance women's status in the Muslim world. Such an approach made sense from Afkhami's pragmatic perspective. As the most powerful country, the United States had the ability to improve women's rights internationally. She hoped to convince American policymakers that women's equality was in the national interest and to harness U.S. power for feminist ends.[111] It would take some time, but SIGI and similar groups eventually helped reorient U.S. foreign policy to include women's human rights within its constellation of legitimate policy concerns.

Without the United Nations Decade for Women, it is unlikely that the growing American attention to Muslim women's rights following the Iranian Revolution would have moved beyond the public sphere and into policy. Women's rights NGOs and feminist activists needed to translate the U.S. public's concern for Muslim women into campaigns that lobbied for specific policies to advance women's human rights in Islamic countries. The Decade made these later U.S. policies possible by giving feminists a space to organize transnationally and to craft a language of rights by which to conceptualize their agendas, mobilize the global public, and lobby policymakers.

Through a process of disagreement and debate from Mexico City to Nairobi, feminists from the United States and from Islamic countries who participated in the Decade emerged with a broader definition of women's human rights than they held at the outset. Third World feminists, Muslim women included, increasingly recognized the importance of individual civil, political, and sexual rights, while many U.S. feminists' approaches to international women's issues became more sensitive and nuanced because of their encounters with Third World feminists. American activists increasingly recognized and respected differences between women and embraced a more expansive definition of human rights that included economic, social, and cultural rights.

However, the Western hierarchy of rights did not disappear. Even as many U.S. feminists' human rights conceptions became more inclusive, it was difficult to change the rights definitions held by the American public and policymakers. This difficulty was compounded because not all U.S. feminists benefited from the Decade debates. Many domestically oriented feminist groups that became influential in the 1990s did not participate in the Decade conferences and Forums and therefore continued to espouse narrower conceptions of human rights, as well as colonial feminist rhetoric on issues like veiling. Transnational feminists who sought to harness the power of the United States to uphold women's human rights in the Islamic world in the 1990s and after would therefore continue to be challenged by the general American emphasis on civil and political rights.

Nevertheless, the Decade enabled U.S. and Muslim feminists to found transnational NGOs that focused on the rights of Islamic women, which ultimately proved influential to U.S. policymaking. They developed organizational might over the course of the late 1980s and 1990s that enabled them to influence American foreign policy in various ways. The simultaneous growth of U.S. public concern about Muslim women during the period meant that these organizations could bring the weight of public opinion to bear in support of their campaigns. The first such campaign occurred just a few years after the end of the Decade, when American feminists, servicewomen, and concerned citizens protested the U.S. alliance with Saudi Arabia during the first Gulf War.

Chapter 4

The First Gulf War and Saudi "Gender Apartheid"

U.S. Army major Jane Fisher was stationed in Saudi Arabia during the first Gulf War. While speaking to a *New York Times* correspondent about her experiences, Fisher proclaimed, "I'm thankful I'm not a Saudi woman."[1] Iraq's invasion of neighboring Kuwait in the summer of 1990 had triggered a full-scale mobilization of U.S. military personnel to the Persian Gulf. Large numbers of American troops were stationed in Saudi Arabia as a base of operations for the invasion of Iraq. As American military personnel—including roughly fifteen thousand women—flooded into Saudi Arabia during the Gulf War, U.S. troops and journalists came face-to-face with the conservative Islamic society.[2] The encounter was a culture shock for both.

Prior to the war, the Kingdom of Saudi Arabia was largely closed to Westerners. Americans could only visit the country with the permission of its government, which granted this sparingly. Thus, before 1990, only a handful of Americans—mostly oil workers, businessmen, consultants, and diplomats—had ever set foot on Saudi soil, and the Kingdom closely monitored and limited their activities to shield its citizens from Western influence. When the war started, however, Saudi Arabia opened its doors to over 150,000 U.S. troops and roughly 1,500 journalists.[3] While the Saudi government was a monarchy rather than a theocracy, an ultraconservative version of Sunni Islam that mixed Wahhabism and Salafism was the basis for its laws, social organization, and culture.[4] A strict interpretation of Shari'a characterized the entire legal system, but Saudi laws concerning women were most striking to American troops and journalists who found themselves on the Arabian Peninsula in 1990–91.

All aspects of Saudi life were strictly segregated by gender. Saudi law dictated that women veil themselves entirely—including their faces—while outside their homes or in the presence of unrelated men. Female travelers had to be accompanied by a male relative, and women were forbidden to drive cars or work in mixed-sex environments. Family law permitted polygamy for men and granted men significantly more rights than women in divorce. Meanwhile, male religious police called the *mutawa*, or the Commission to Promote Virtue and Prevent Vice, patrolled public spaces on the lookout for improperly veiled women or those who transgressed the myriad other laws meant to enforce sex segregation. Saudi Arabia was widely considered one of the most restrictive countries in the world for women.

The country also rejected human rights norms, which included the principle of gender equality enshrined in the UN Charter and UDHR. Notably, Saudi Arabia did not abolish slavery until 1962, and it was one of the only countries in the world that did not sign the UDHR in 1948. The Saudis also did not sign any other international human rights conventions save the 1949 Geneva Accords.[5] While many other Muslim countries ratified CEDAW with added reservations during the 1980s, the Saudis refused to ratify the treaty under any circumstances.[6]

Although the United States did not ratify CEDAW either, though for different reasons, American and Saudi attitudes about women were highly incompatible, to say the least.[7] The Saudis struggled to come to terms with unveiled American servicewomen, who worked alongside and often supervised men, carried weapons, and drove vehicles. U.S. military women were shocked by the restrictions placed upon them in Saudi Arabia, the way Saudi men treated them, and the widespread oppression of Saudi women. The media spotlight on American servicewomen's experiences and Saudi society during the war ultimately led some Americans to question the longstanding U.S.-Saudi alliance. Concerned citizens (mostly women) and feminist organizations protested the war because they believed that the United States should not ally itself with Islamic countries like Saudi Arabia that practiced "gender apartheid."

American media coverage of the first Gulf War and Saudi gender inequality therefore sparked a public debate in the United States about what the relationship should be between women's human rights and U.S. foreign policy. Here, the conversation went beyond merely condemning the Islamic oppression of women to include a demand for policy change. A vocal minority argued that U.S. alliances, and especially military action to defend allies, should be based on those allies' commitment to upholding women's equality. Although they failed to alter U.S. policy at the time, wartime protests against Saudi "gender apartheid" were a step toward the integration of women's human rights concerns into U.S. foreign policy. The protests demonstrated how some Americans were beginning to rethink the U.S.-Islamic relationship based upon their understanding of Muslim women's status, and they started to explore new ways to exercise U.S. power in the Islamic world. Instead of pursuing traditional policy goals related to regional stability and oil, the protesters argued that human rights concerns should trump security interests when Islamic allies like Saudi Arabia oppressed women. Never before had women's rights entered public discussions of foreign policy concerns in such a way, especially in wartime. Moreover, the protests advanced a conceptualization and language—particularly the term "gender apartheid"—that future American feminist campaigns utilized.

As the 1990s progressed, the idea that women's rights were relevant to American foreign policy gained influence, and U.S. and Muslim feminist activists accelerated their campaigns for women's human rights in the Islamic world. As the protests about "gender apartheid" during the Gulf War illustrated, the desire to integrate women's rights into U.S. foreign policy came not from policymakers but from grassroots feminist activists and NGOs, the media, and the public. From the perspective of these nongovernmental actors, the legitimate use of U.S. power demanded advancing and defending women's human rights.

Just before the Gulf War began, the international system came unglued with the dramatic end of the Cold War.[8] It fell upon the George H. W. Bush administration to reformulate the United States' international mission. Bush believed the United States had won the Cold War because U.S. policies that emphasized capitalism and democracy were best for the international system.[9] He declared confidently in his inaugural address, "We know what works: Freedom works. We know what's right: Freedom is right. We know how to secure a more just and prosperous life for man on Earth: through free markets, free speech, free elections, and the exercise of free will unhampered by the state."[10] The president was not alone in his optimism. Scholar Francis Fukuyama famously argued that the Cold War's conclusion inaugurated the "end of history," while others theorized that a world dominated by democracies would be a world without war.[11]

It soon became clear, however, that the end of the Cold War did not mean the end of international crises. The Cold War's conclusion might advance world peace or global chaos. To ensure the former, Bush declared that the international community's mission was to build "a new world order, where diverse nations are drawn together in common cause to achieve the universal aspirations of mankind—peace and security, freedom, and the rule of law."[12] He asserted that the greatest threats to this New World Order were, in essence, "rogue states."[13]

Saddam Hussein's Iraq quickly became the poster child for these rogue states. After losing its Iranian ally in 1979, the United States especially relied on Saudi Arabia to maintain Middle Eastern stability; U.S. policymakers were therefore reluctant to push the Saudis on human rights or women's equality. Hussein's regional aggression made the U.S.-Saudi alliance that much more important.

In August 1990, Hussein invaded neighboring Kuwait and seized control of the tiny nation's considerably lucrative oil industry. It was a desperate bid to solve Iraq's economic troubles, the result of the country's costly war with Iran from 1980 to 1988. The international community immediately condemned this brazen violation of Kuwaiti sovereignty, but Hussein began to amass his army near the Saudi border. Bush sent U.S. troops to Saudi Arabia at the monarchy's request to deter an Iraqi invasion that fall. Hussein's aggression—and the fact that occupying Kuwait gave him control of 20 percent of the world's oil supply—could not go unpunished.[14] The United States and a multinational coalition of thirty-four allies, sanctioned by the United Nations, formally declared war on Iraq in January 1991.[15] In the face of overwhelming force, Iraq was defeated within a matter of weeks.

American servicewomen were visible in the Iraq War as they had never been before.[16] When the Cold War ended, the Department of Defense reevaluated its stance on women in the military. Despite the continuing prohibition on women serving in combat roles, the Army and the other military branches opened more jobs to women and began taking the issue of sexual harassment more seriously.[17] The result was a military with a significant number of women within its ranks, performing an unprecedented variety of jobs, when the Gulf War broke out. Ultimately, the United States deployed 41,000 American servicewomen to the Middle East during the war, which historian Beth Bailey characterized as a "major turning point for military women."[18]

It was difficult for military leaders to navigate the largest deployment of female soldiers to date in a sex-integrated military. Even though women were barred from direct ground combat, they still risked coming under fire and being captured by the enemy. In fact, five U.S. servicewomen were killed in action during the Gulf War, and two were taken prisoner.[19] Deploying thousands of female soldiers to a region with very different notions about women's rights made the situation even more challenging. Not only did military leaders have to maintain the morale of soldiers serving in the Gulf, they also had to avoid offending their hosts. To minimize the potential for cultural conflict, the military briefed servicewomen on Saudi customs and ways they should behave in order to minimize conflict with the local populace, yet the briefing was superficial given the rapidity of their deployment.[20] Few servicewomen were truly prepared for life in the Kingdom.

The experience of each servicewoman deployed to Saudi Arabia was unique, and the amount of contact each had with Saudis varied. However, their cumulative perceptions and experiences were crucial to influencing the American public's views of Saudi society during the war. Not only did U.S. servicewomen recount their experiences privately to friends and family, but they also discussed them with journalists, gave oral history interviews, and complained to military leaders. In particular, widespread reporting on U.S. servicewomen in Saudi Arabia wove their perceptions into U.S. public consciousness, sparking public protests about U.S. support for Saudi Arabia during the war.

Upon arriving in the Kingdom, many servicewomen chafed at restrictions that Saudi authorities and the U.S. military imposed upon them. Related largely to their dress and ability to drive, these restrictions aimed to show sensitivity for Saudi culture, but servicewomen found them frustrating and expressed their dissatisfaction. While women in the U.S. military were not required to veil like Saudi women while on the job, the Saudis did request that American women cover their arms and legs completely, and they had to wear the abaya, the black robe worn by Saudi women, while off duty and off base. Although they believed deeply that women should veil, the Saudis made this compromise to accommodate their American allies.

For American servicewomen, however, the dress code was onerous. Montana Army National Guard captain Kareene Ostermiller objected, "Women aren't allowed to wear anything that bares their ankles or their elbows or their neck and in the heat especially for someone like me, I think that's an unreasonable request."[21] They found it particularly unfair that male soldiers did not have to follow the same rules. Eventually, some of the servicewomen rebelled by rolling their sleeves up.[22]

Other restrictions and cultural differences were more troublesome. Customary law prohibited Saudi women from driving. Because the U.S. military did not permit women to occupy combat roles, one of their central tasks was driving supply and transport vehicles. American military planners and Saudi authorities reached another compromise: American servicewomen could drive military trucks, but only while on duty. They were prohibited from driving cars at any time. Servicewomen had to depend on male colleagues or local civilians for transportation, and this often interfered with their military duties. Captain Theresa Cantrell of the Army XVIII Airborne Corps Medical Supply, Optical, and Maintenance (MEDSOM) Battalion complained, "You were second-class citizens. You had no mobility. And in the situation over there, mobility was crucial."[23]

Cantrell's frustration almost got her into trouble with the Saudi police. She and another servicewoman drove illegally from their work site to their base camp late one night, which was the only way they could get back to their camp to sleep. On their way home, a Saudi police officer pulled them over. Cantrell recounted, "The policeman came out and he says 'no, no, you no drive.'" She began to argue with him: "He was very serious. I said, no, no, I can drive. I am in uniform. I go from work. I go to my tent, and he said, no, no, in Saudi you no drive. I said I am an American. I am in the Army. I am a captain. I have been driving for longer than you have been a policeman. And I was becoming somewhat argumentative with him. I was tired. I think it was about 3:00 in the morning, and I did not want to get into this. He said, no, no, and he put his hand on his holster and said, no, you can drive military truck only."[24] She managed to defuse the situation, and that incident was largely the extent of Cantrell's contact with Saudi civilians. Like most American servicewomen—and U.S. military personnel in general—her superiors sharply restricted her interaction with locals in an attempt to reduce the potential for cultural conflict.

What contact U.S. women did have with local men, however, often left them feeling angry, exasperated, or uneasy and reinforced the general American perception that Muslim men were sexist and oppressive. Army sergeant Anne Welch, for example, was left shaken by an encounter she had with Saudi border guards one night while crossing into the Kingdom with her unit. The border guards yelled and pointed at her; she did not understand why. Welch's male colleague responded by threatening the guards with a sword. "Arab men don't have a really good view of American women," she concluded.[25] Army corporal Wendy Taines was more blunt: "They're totally against everything we do from dress to being a woman to everything."[26]

On the rare occasions when American soldiers went into town on liberty, female GIs required a male escort. According to Coast Guard reservist Sandra Mitten, who was stationed on a U.S. ship in the Port of Dammah for the duration of the war, "You always had to have a man with you [when you went into town] because they [Saudis] don't deal with women at all."[27] Many found it "humiliating" to have to ask male colleagues to make purchases for them.[28] Servicewomen on liberty were also ogled by Saudi men. Army captain Kristen Vlahos, who was stationed in Riyadh, recalled, "I had a long sleeve shirt and a skirt down to my ankles with shoes and so my ankles were exposed," and there were "a lot of stares at the ankles."[29]

Oftentimes Saudi men—both civilian and military—simply treated American servicewomen as though they were nonexistent.[30] When they did acknowledge American women, they were not always polite. Vlahos explained that many of the Saudi men she encountered would refuse to get on an elevator if she was on it.[31] A more confrontational incident occurred at a MEDSOM warehouse when a local laborer walked up to a U.S. servicewoman and shoved her because she was in his way.[32]

Captain Ostermiller had more contact with Saudi men because she was a community relations officer with the National Guard's Public Affairs unit. She often went with her colleagues to meet local leaders, and some of those encounters left her feeling threatened. On one occasion, some of the men Ostermiller had met came to her camp to give her a niqab, or face veil, and an abaya. They told her male colleagues, "You can't look on her face anymore. Now she is beautiful." One of Ostermiller's fellow servicewomen who was present bristled at this. "She thought it was absolutely disgusting. She saw it as subjugation. . . . We were under a lot of pressure . . . dealing with a culture that we couldn't acclimatize to," Ostermiller explained.[33]

These women's experiences were crucial to inspiring protests about the U.S.-Saudi alliance back home. Servicewomen also eventually influenced U.S. military policy to see Saudi men as oppressors of women after many complaints and a high-profile lawsuit ended gender-specific restrictions on American soldiers serving in Saudi Arabia.[34] Most important, American servicewomen's complaints about their experiences in the Kingdom found their way into the news media during the war. Journalists who traveled to the Gulf focused intensely on the oppression of Saudi women, the fanaticism of Saudi men, and the "clash of cultures" caused by the presence of female American soldiers. Such stories prompted the protests that emerged shortly after U.S. soldiers arrived in the Gulf in the late summer and early fall 1990.

Kept far from the front lines, journalists searched for newsworthy stories. Having learned its lesson during the Vietnam War, the Department of Defense placed stringent restrictions on the press during the Gulf War. As a result, few reporters witnessed any combat.[35] Of the nearly 1,500 American journalists in Saudi Arabia, the few "pool reporters" permitted to accompany combat units were supervised by military escorts at all times, and they had to clear all reports with military censors. As one scholar explained, "Many ended up covering the desert war from places like the plush-red hotel ballroom or the roof terrace of the Dhahran International Hotel, relaying pieces of second-hand information given to them by cautious briefers and 'pool' reporters authorized to be with combat units."[36] Women journalists found conditions in Saudi Arabia especially limiting. While the Kingdom made exceptions for servicewomen, reporters were subject to all Saudi laws and therefore risked punishment for violating dress codes and traveling with unrelated men.[37]

The combination of military censorship, cultural differences, and reporters' lack of local language skills created a situation in which information about the war was limited. Journalists therefore reported on the information to which they had access. The cultural chasm and "clash of cultures" between American soldiers and Saudi society became one of the most popular themes in U.S. media coverage of the war.[38] Journalists especially focused on the oppression of Saudi women and the difficulties American servicewomen faced in the Kingdom.

Such reporting introduced a broad American audience to Saudi gender norms. Like earlier U.S. discourse about Muslim women, these reports interpreted the veil as a symbol of women's oppression and added to the mix the Saudi ban on women driving. Restrictions on women's freedom of movement and dress—both of which American reporters construed as basic civil rights—symbolized the total lack of women's human rights in Saudi Arabia. This raised serious questions among both journalists and the public about why the United States fought to defend a nation that oppressed women.

Early in the U.S. deployment, in August 1990, *CBS Evening News* anchor Dan Rather reported on American servicewomen in Saudi Arabia. Rather explained, "The biggest problem for American women has been adjusting to the customs of a country where women still are not allowed to drive and many are not allowed to show their faces in public."[39] As Rather spoke, shots of American women in uniform—including an African American officer supervising men who serviced a fighter jet—gave way to scenes of Saudi women on the street shrouded in black. The difference between the women could not have been starker.

A few weeks later, Bob Simon reported for CBS, "Saudis have moved from sand dunes to sparkling new cities without changing their view of the world very much. They've succeeded in resisting change by keeping agents of change, Westerners, out as much as they could—until now." Inviting the United States to defend them from Saddam Hussein, Simon explained, now meant "the most precarious balancing act in the history of their Kingdom: an attempt to maintain a basically feudal society and a quarter million Americans at the same time."[40] The news reports coming out of Saudi Arabia from August 1990 onward did not just report on the differences between Americans and Saudis; they argued that U.S. servicewomen suffered while in Saudi Arabia because of their gender and that Saudi women were horribly oppressed. The result was outrage among some sectors of the American public and a generally negative perception of Saudi and Muslim men in the United States.

The media encouraged this reaction. In September 1990, *ABC World News Tonight* reporter Bill Reddecker described the restrictions on American servicewomen as unfair. He interviewed nineteen-year-old Airman Kimberly Newberger, who headed a unit of mechanics. She told Reddecker, with rolled eyes and a rueful smile, "I have to be careful of what I wear because like I said some Saudi Arabians passing by might become offended by seeing my knees." Reddecker then reported with disapproval that Newberger was confined to base in an attempt to reduce tensions with Saudi men. Explaining that she still sometimes had to interact with Saudi airmen on base, Newberger recounted, "The looks they get on their faces when they see a female out there doing such a demanding job. I've had a few that insisted on doing the work for me, which kind of upset me." When Reddecker asked what she could not do in Saudi Arabia that she could do at home, she responded simply, "Leave."[41]

Other journalists filed similar reports. In January 1991 well-known journalist and future Clinton administration official Strobe Talbott reported for *Time* that an off-duty female U.S. Navy lieutenant was "accosted" by the *mutawa* as she attempted to shop in downtown Riyadh. The lieutenant wore an abaya, but, Talbott recounted, "that wasn't good enough" for the religious police. Describing the *mutawa* as "vigilantes who enforce Muslim religious laws against impiety and immodesty," he described how one of them "prodded her painfully with a long stick and berated her for neglecting to veil her face." A sympathetic merchant explained that she was an American soldier. "Barely missing a beat," Talbott wrote, "the morals cop switched into English and continued his harangue more angrily than ever."[42]

The media coverage pointedly contrasted female GIs and Saudi women and indicated their hope that the mere presence of seemingly liberated American servicewomen would force a change in the Kingdom. *Time* mused about the potential consequences of "the once closed kingdom" of Saudi Arabia "opening its doors to the outside world." Wondering whether the American presence might help Saudi women improve their lot, the magazine explained, "A land that forbids its women to drive, to travel unaccompanied, to wear Western garb or to expose anything more than a scant flash of eyes and cheekbones is now host to thousands of rifle-toting, jeep-driving female G.I.s clad in fatigues."[43] The *Philadelphia Tribune* made a similar comparison when it described a woman soldier in a Saudi supermarket: "Dressed in battle fatigues and sand-caked combat boots, the St. Louis native brushed past heavily veiled Saudi women in floor-length black 'abayas.'" The article described female American "tank mechanics, cargo-plane pilots, doctors, nurses, ammunition haulers and weather forecasters." In contrast, veiled "Saudi women aren't allowed to drive cars." The article characterized the presence of "thousands of American women in uniform" as "an unspoken challenge to custom, tradition and religious teachings that have long made Saudi Arabia one of the most restrictive countries in the world for women."[44]

While the U.S. media most often cast Saudi women—to whom most journalists lacked access—as stereotypically silent, veiled victims, they reported with approval that American women stood up to Saudi men. The *New York Times* ran a piece in February 1991 about Army sergeant Theresa Lynn Treloar, the woman who served closest to the front lines: "While directing a group of American soldiers in putting up a tent, the sergeant said, she confronted a startled Saudi who, apparently unaware that ranking military women had the authority to give orders, urged her to step aside and keep quiet. 'He looked at me and said, "You shouldn't speak. I'll speak for you,"' she recalled with anger. Her response to the Saudi included a stream of obscenities 'and he got the message fast,' she said."[45] The article drove home the point that American women were fighting to defend men who saw them as inferior. Many began to wonder why the United States should ally itself with a Muslim government that deprived women of basic human rights.

American musing about the impact of the U.S. presence was not simply wishful thinking. There was some indication that the American deployment, and the accompanying widespread media attention, did encourage some Saudi women to agitate for more rights. Just weeks after the arrival of U.S. troops, Bob Simon conducted a rare interview for CBS with a Saudi woman, the wife of Saudi newspaper editor Khalid al-Maeena, that indicated simmering resentments among some women. Simon asked the soft-spoken woman, who appeared bareheaded on camera, whether she would like to be able to drive. She responded in English, "I think that I do." She smiled stiffly. "Yes. I resent that more than I resent wearing the veil."[46]

Emboldened by the international spotlight placed upon their country, on November 6, 1990, a group of fifty to seventy Saudi women protested the driving ban. They hailed from some of the country's most prominent families and were highly educated. Many had gotten driver's licenses abroad. The women convened at a supermarket in Riyadh, the nation's capital and the stronghold of religious conservatives. There, they dismissed their chauffeurs and got behind the wheel, driving across the city in an orderly convoy of forty vehicles before being stopped and detained by police. Technically, there was no written law against women driving; the women who took to the wheel that day hoped to push the government to declare the customary ban outdated.

The protest reflected a longstanding debate between Saudis about women driving and larger battles by progressives to reform society. However, the timing of the protest suggests that it was staged to capitalize on the American presence. Although the government suppressed news of the protest in the local press, journalists from the United States and other Western nations circulated information worldwide about the event they dubbed the "drive-in"—a term intended to evoke memories of sit-ins staged by U.S. civil rights activists just a few decades earlier.

The American media celebrated the drive-in, as many journalists saw Saudi Arabia as repressive and retrograde. Youssef Ibrahim of the *New York Times* praised the women's "daring defiance" in launching "the first known open protest by Saudi women." He explained that the protesters had serious grievances: "Under severe Islamic strictures, Saudi women are veiled and robed from head to toe, forbidden from appearing in public with men and from traveling anywhere without permission from husbands or male relatives." Ibrahim concluded that he hoped the protest would lead to "a wider array of rights" for Saudi women.[47]

The U.S. media consistently supported the protesters, and news outlets continued to refer to the incident well into 1991. To the horror of American onlookers, however, rather than initiating reform, the protest provoked a crackdown. Aware that conservative groups held considerable political sway, the women had couched their protest in religious terms. They pointed out that there was no prohibition on women driving in the Koran and that early Islamic women led camels across the desert.[48] They also argued that the customary ban on women driving was actually un-Islamic because it forced women to hire foreign, male chauffeurs to transport them from place to place. As one protester argued, "Islam says that a woman should not be left alone in the company of a man who is not her relative and that is exactly what happens every time I am driven in my car by a Pakistani, Sudanese or other person who is a driver."[49] Wearing veils and driving with female passengers so that they did not violate the law against women traveling alone, the protesters drove in an orderly fashion across Riyadh to prove that women could drive without causing chaos.

Their arguments fell on deaf ears. Religious authorities forced the government to respond harshly to the protest.[50] At first, the police merely detained the women, lectured them, and released them to their families. After all, they had not actually broken any law, but reports soon surfaced about religious groups' "increasingly severe reaction." To placate them and end the debate about women driving, the monarchy formalized the customary ban by issuing a written one. CBS's Bob Simon reported just days after the protest, "The controversy has shaken up the mosques, it has disturbed the campuses, it has 'rocked the casbah.' . . . Yesterday, while American servicewomen drove around American bases, Saudi Arabia's interior ministry announced a formal ban on Saudi women driving, warning that violators will be punished."[51] As a Saudi official told the New York Times, the protest was "an affront to the King" that could not be tolerated.[52]

Religious groups' condemnations of the protestors alarmed American observers, especially when hard-liners threatened the lives of the women and their supporters. During a half-hour Nightline special in December 1990 on the "clash of cultures," an ABC correspondent in Dhahran told Barbara Walters, "It [the drive-in] enormously upset the Kingdom. It enormously upset the Islamic fundamentalists. It was an unprecedented challenge. And when they put it down, they put it down hard." Describing her telephone interview with the husband of one of the protesters, the correspondent explained, "There was incredible fear, even terror, in his voice. He says that the passports of the people involved have been seized.... He has received death threats."[53] The *Wall Street Journal* likewise reported that the women "have been harassed by phone calls branding them infidels and calling on their husbands to divorce them. Even women who didn't take part in the protest but are known to support it have become targets of abuse."[54] Several news outlets reported that many of the women were also dismissed from their jobs.[55]

The *New York Times* related that a member of the royal family claimed that most of the protesters, notwithstanding their coming from prominent families, were "not brought up in an Islamic home." The paper explained, "In this xenophobic and theocratically Islamic country, such a statement borders on categorizing the protesting women as blasphemers and foreigners."[56] This was a serious charge; blasphemy was punishable by death. *Time* reported that religious leaders distributed the women's names, phone numbers, and addresses, while *Ms.* recounted how religious police "demanded that the women be beheaded, that 'their heads roll in the gutters.'"[57] Reports that the protesters feared for their lives underscored the impression that American troops fought to defend Muslim men whose treatment of women was inimical to core U.S. values.

American journalists reporting on the drive-in and its aftermath made this argument explicitly, mirroring feminists' language about the war—and laying some of the groundwork for the antiwar protests by influencing public opinion. In reporting on the swift and harsh reaction against the protesters, Bob Simon interviewed a Saudi woman who defended the drive-in because, she said, "It's not like this is someplace where you can go and talk to your congressman." Simon concluded, "It's not just politics. Saudi Arabia's version of the separate but equal doctrine permeates society. Schools and workplaces here are segregated. Restaurants have separate rooms for women." As the report featured a shot of a Saudi McDonald's, he continued, "And as it once was in the South, it *is* separate. It is not equal."[58] In making such a comparison between Saudi Arabia and Jim Crow, Simon clearly wanted his audience to see Saudi sex segregation as intolerable. His report also highlighted how Americans put a premium on civil and political rights when discussing human rights violations abroad.

Garrick Utley of *NBC Nightly News* went further. When he reported on the drive-in, he informed his viewers that the protestors were stopped by the police, they lost their jobs, and "others report receiving hate calls from people saying they are 'infidels' and their husbands should divorce them." The government, he reported, "sided with the religious authorities—all men—who claim driving 'degrades and harms the sanctity of women.'" Arguing against cultural relativism and using similar logic as feminist organizations who opposed the war, Utley concluded with an impassioned speech: "Well, it is easy to say East is East and West is West and let it go at that. But in Saudi Arabia, the twain—the two—are meeting. If there is war there, American troops— men *and* women—know what they will be fighting against: Iraqi aggression. But what will they be fighting *for*? Oil? For a society where a woman driving a car is seen as a 'stupid act'? American and Saudi officials don't like to talk much about this. It is an awkward problem. In the eyes of many, it is an outrageous one."[59] By asking whether it was worth it for Americans to defend a nation that oppressed its women, Utley boldly questioned the U.S.-Saudi alliance. U.S. feminist organizations and concerned members of the public did the same and argued for a reorientation of U.S. policy in the Gulf.

Journalists' attention to the "clash of cultures" between U.S. troops and the Saudis they defended made the soldiers' experiences, as well as the drive-in, part of U.S. public consciousness about the war. American GIs—male and female—told reporters that Saudis were "basically hostile people who repress women." As a male Marine told the *New York Times*, "America's a democracy. . . . But look at them here. There's no democracy. Women can't drive, and they even have to wear veils."[60] Media coverage helped entrench the negative perception of Saudi men's treatment of women among the American public. When journalists like Utley and Simon publicly compared Saudi gender relations to Jim Crow and asked why American soldiers fought to defend such a nation, they influenced the terms of public debate. Consequently, a substantial "gender gap" developed in the United States on the war, mainly due to Saudi "gender apartheid."

For Americans concerned about women's rights, human rights, and equality, the United States fought a war to defend Saudi Arabia, which oppressed women, and to liberate Kuwait, an Islamic country where women could not vote. This led these Americans, especially women, feminist activists, and journalists, to condemn both the war and the longstanding U.S.

alliance with the Kingdom. While there were other protests based on more traditional antiwar messages, the earliest and most consistently vocal protesters focused on women's oppression as the reason for their opposition to the war.[61] Women's human rights arguments resonated with this segment of the public who emphasized Saudi women's political and civil rights, such as freedom of dress and movement, voting rights, and segregation, issues that were already salient for most Americans. They also drew upon the shameful memory of the United States' own history of racial segregation, as well as South Africa's system of racial apartheid, which by the 1990s the U.S. government and society unequivocally condemned. For those concerned about gender equality and human rights, at least, these were compelling reasons to oppose the war.

One of the first to speak out against the war because of women's oppression was Debra Saunders, a journalist in California. In August 1990, just as American troops deployed to the Gulf, Saunders pointed out the irony that the democratic United States was going to war to defend undemocratic countries. Saunders asserted that "discrimination is wrong, whether it is based on sex or race." What she saw in Saudi Arabia was pure sex discrimination, which she dubbed "gender apartheid." Saunders drew a clear parallel between the situation of women in Saudi Arabia and apartheid in South Africa, which at the time was the target of broad international condemnation. She explained, "I can't help but feel there would be some controversy if American troops were defending a government that practices racial apartheid." Lamenting America's sexual double standard, she worried that "it's a little easier than it ought to be for Washington to stand up for those who hold women down."[62]

U.S. feminists echoed Saunders's arguments about "gender apartheid" and went further by calling for an immediate U.S. withdrawal. The feminist journal *Off Our Backs* cited Saunders in its denunciation of the impending war that October, arguing that "the bitter pill of irony the American conscience must swallow" was that in "Saudi Arabia the US is defending a system of sexual apartheid at least as repugnant to human rights as the racial apartheid we deplore in South Africa." It protested the restrictions placed upon U.S. servicewomen by the military so that they would not offend Saudi sensibilities. "If the press chooses to ignore the nasty moral contradictions of our action in Saudi Arabia, we cannot," the journal declared. "And we too can stir a tempest in the sand."[63]

Feminists did just that. They launched a campaign that November to prevent the United States from going to war to defend Islamic oppressors of women. *Ms.* published an open letter on the Gulf crisis, which criticized U.S. hypocrisy and restrictions on women GIs serving in Saudi Arabia. They urged their readers to send the letter to their friends, political representatives, newspaper editors, and the White House in a mass protest against the U.S.-Saudi alliance.[64] A short time later, *Ms.* editors Gloria Steinem and Robin Morgan teamed up with Kate Millett and Ti-Grace Atkinson to publish a letter of protest in the *New York Times.* They declared, "This is not a war to defend democracy: Women in Kuwait cannot vote; no one in Saudi Arabia can vote, and women cannot even drive cars."[65]

Building upon these protests, the National Organization for Women (NOW) issued a formal statement opposing the Gulf War in late November, citing "gender apartheid" in Saudi Arabia and Kuwait as their reason. "'Saudi Arabia and Kuwait are despotic, clan-run monarchies,' said NOW President Molly Yard. 'Both . . . systematically oppress women. This is gender apartheid in its purest, most brutal form and should deeply offend all Americans.'" NOW additionally decried that American servicewomen faced special restrictions because of their gender. Yard declared, "We would be outraged if the administration sent American troops to defend South Africa from invasion, ordering black soldiers to 'respect the culture' by bowing their heads in the presence of white racists."[66]

NOW's outspoken campaign made national headlines.[67] When *Nightline*'s Barbara Walters reported on NOW's antiwar petition to Congress and the United Nations, she sided with NOW and asked, "Now the fact is we do have a very different definition of human rights and democracy and religious freedom and equal rights for men and women. So leaving aside oil—which is a big leaving aside—why should we defend this regime?"[68] For Walters, an influential figure, to support NOW's campaign suggests how salient women's human rights were for many Americans at the time.

While the feminist protests against the Gulf War primarily advanced the narrower definition of human rights favored by Americans and feminists who had not participated in the UN Decade debates, this historical moment revealed that even domestically oriented feminist groups like NOW had begun to think broadly about oppression. Protests about the U.S.-Saudi relationship focused primarily on civil and political rights for Saudi women, centered on the veil, driving, and the lack of democracy rather than on a more expansive definition of human rights. But those who protested Saudi "gender apartheid" connected patriarchy and gender oppression with other structures of inequality, such as race, when they compared women's status in Saudi Arabia with Jim Crow and South African apartheid. Thus the protesters demonstrated how American feminists and others concerned about Saudi women based moral arguments in favor of women's human rights on examples drawn from multiple cultures and identity categories. As a reflection of nascent feminist intersectionality, antiwar protesters used critiques of racism to strengthen and illuminate their condemnations of Saudi sexism, which was the most striking example of women's inequality worldwide that feminists worked to combat.

Widespread news coverage had helped to spread feminists' antiwar message and the use of the term "gender apartheid" in the United States. Likewise, it indicated that a significant—and vocal—minority of Americans believed that U.S. intervention in the Persian Gulf was wrong because its Muslim allies oppressed women. Journalists reported on a "gender gap" in U.S. polls, which showed a pronounced disparity between men's and women's support for war against Iraq. They explained that 25 percent fewer women supported the war compared to men because of "the fiercely sexist nature of the regimes America is seeking to defend."[69] As a pollster told NBC in December, the gender gap on the war was "the biggest he's ever seen."[70] On the eve of the official start of the war, polls indicated that over 70 percent of women opposed the war, compared to 48 percent of men.[71]

Letters to the editor and color comments by citizens in local newspapers supported the notion that the gender gap was due to women's oppression in the Gulf. "I do not like the idea of fighting for a country where the women have to walk three feet behind their husbands," wrote one woman.[72] Representative Patricia Schroeder (D-Colorado), a staunch advocate for women's rights in Congress, asked publicly, "We do not tolerate 'cultural differences' as an excuse for racial violence. Why do we tolerate it for women?" Citizens writing to their local newspapers expressed similar concerns, asking, "When will gender apartheid . . . be recognized for the crime against humanity that it is?"[73] Even servicewomen protested the war. NBC reported in December 1990 that three women in the California Reserves refused to report for duty to protest the Saudi oppression of women.[74]

In picking up on feminists' rhetoric about "gender apartheid," concerned citizens across America—mainly women—were insisting that women's equality be taken into consideration at the highest levels, particularly when it came to forging alliances with and going to war to defend Islamic countries. The tens of thousands of antiwar protesters were by no means a majority of the American public, but they did gain public recognition. And, as NBC reported, thousands of Republican women—roughly 5 percent of all women polled by NBC—reportedly switched parties because of U.S. policy supporting Islamic oppressors of women in the Persian Gulf.[75]

The first Gulf War deeply shaped how the American public viewed the U.S. relationship with Islamic allies like Saudi Arabia. It helped lay the groundwork for future feminist campaigns for women's rights in the Muslim world by shaping public perceptions and providing a language of human rights and "gender apartheid" that resonated with many Americans. The protests did not alter U.S. policy at the time, but that is unsurprising given the policy imperatives of the Bush administration and the general international consensus that Saddam Hussein's invasion of Kuwait was illegal. Women's human rights were not at the top of Bush's agenda, and doing what the antiwar protesters wanted would have hampered his ability to keep "rogue states" in check.[76] The president also had close personal and financial ties to the Saudi royal family, and he faced myriad unprecedented crises that reinforced the U.S. tendency to prioritize hard power issues and global stability.[77] Moreover, the protesters had failed to articulate alternatives to the war or a clear vision of what the United States could or should do to advance women's human rights meaningfully in the Gulf.

Feminist activists now needed to articulate concrete ways in which U.S. power could be harnessed in the name of women's human rights globally. Nevertheless, the antiwar protests were important in shaping the continually evolving American view of Muslim women that led to U.S. policies that aimed to advance women's human rights in Muslim countries. In particular, the protests pushed back—forcefully—against the U.S. government's hesitancy to criticize Saudi Arabia.[78] Prior to the war, there was little discussion in the United States of women's status in Saudi Arabia beyond scholarly and feminist circles. Mainstream criticism was often met with loud protests by the Saudis and pressure from U.S. officials to back off, as when PBS dared to air the British docudrama *Death of a Princess* in 1980, which told the true story of a Saudi princess executed for committing adultery.[79] Few criticisms of the Saudis appeared in the U.S. media until American troops deployed to the Kingdom during the war.

President Bush was never inclined to acknowledge the wartime protests about "gender apartheid" or to discuss the status of Saudi women.[80] However, feminist protesters and their supporters formulated a compelling argument that women's human rights were central to the U.S. global mission, which soon gained traction with the U.S. public and policymakers. Like Major Jane Fisher, the U.S. encounter with Saudi Arabia during the Gulf War caused many Americans to declare, as Debra Saunders did, "I'm glad I'm not a Saudi woman who must obey religious edicts."[81] The American perceptions that women in Saudi Arabia lacked basic human rights and that Saudi men were oppressors contributed to wider conversations in the United States about the lack of women's rights across the Muslim world. Americans' face-to-face encounter with Islamic patriarchy in Saudi Arabia had forced a debate in the U.S. public sphere about the relationship between women's human rights and U.S. foreign policy. U.S. and transnational feminists drew on the legacy of those protests to shape campaigns against Islamic "gender apartheid" in other countries in the years to come.

A seismic shift occurred in U.S. policy imperatives in the 1990s that the "gender apartheid" protests during the Gulf War helped set in motion, and U.S. priorities began to change in ways that traditional foreign policy assessments are unable to explain. George H. W. Bush lost his bid for reelection in 1992 to Democrat Bill Clinton, a feminist ally who enjoyed a five-percentage-point lead among women voters.[82] Clinton would not ignore arguments in favor of women's human rights like his predecessor had. Within a few years, public concerns about Muslim women and feminist activism would spur Congress and U.S. asylum courts to address the issue of female genital mutilation (FGM), which Americans largely understood to be an Islamic practice. Soon thereafter, the executive branch also took up the cause of Muslim women's human rights.

Chapter 5

Female Genital Mutilation and
U.S. Policy in the 1990s

NBC aired an unusual episode of the long-running drama *Law & Order* in December 1997.[1] Titled "Ritual," the episode at first seemed to follow the show's typical plot formula: a murder occurs, the police investigate and make an arrest, and the district attorneys take it from there. In "Ritual," the murder victim is an Egyptian immigrant, Joseph Moussad, and the police arrest his American nephew-in-law, Eric Martin. The episode takes an unexpected turn, however, when the murderer's motive is revealed. Martin killed Moussad because the man had hired a doctor to come to New York from Cairo to perform a clitoridectomy on Martin's eleven-year-old daughter, Alison. The episode, then, revolves around the real-life issue of female genital mutilation, or FGM. ADA Jamie Ross is so disturbed when she learns of the victim's plans for his niece that she does not wish to prosecute Martin. Even Executive ADA Jack McCoy, a main character who usually sees everything in black and white, is reluctant to take the case to trial. Ross even goes so far as to represent Martin's parents pro bono in family court to prevent Alison's Egyptian mother from retaining custody, lest she cut her daughter while her husband is in prison.[2]

Law & Order boasted that it "ripped" its stories from current headlines, and FGM was indeed a controversial subject in the 1990s, both in the United States and internationally.[3] *Law & Order* was weighing in on the issue and clearly opposed the practice. While grassroots activists had worked internationally for years to end the custom, only in the 1990s did they seek out the power of the U.S. government to combat FGM. Dozens of newspaper and magazine articles, novels, memoirs, and television programs focused American attention on FGM during this period, and *Law & Order* capitalized on this by airing "Ritual."

That the *Law & Order* episode framed FGM largely as a problem related to Islam increased its salience. After all, many Americans had come to see Islam and women's human rights as incompatible during the preceding years. In "Ritual," ADA Ross learns about FGM from an American doctor who witnessed the procedure in Sudan, a predominantly Muslim country.[4] While explaining FGM to her colleagues, Ross stresses, "No religion sanctions it; it's cultural."[5] Many real-life anti-FGM activists and scholars made the same distinction. Nevertheless, "Ritual" reinforces and reflects the link between Islam and FGM. The unsympathetic murder victim, his equally monstrous sister, and his weak-willed niece are all Muslims who believe that cutting Alison is a religious duty.[6] The episode's writers chose to make their FGM-practicing characters Islamic ones.

Anti-FGM activists, scholars, and the media likewise buttressed the American view that female genital mutilation was a Muslim practice, despite their qualifying statements that no religious scripture actually endorsed it. By linking FGM with Islam, activists and the media contributed to the larger discourse in the United States about the lack of women's human rights in the Islamic world, which had inspired protests about the U.S.-Saudi alliance during the first Gulf War. Anti-FGM activism in the 1990s helped keep the Islamic oppression of women in the U.S. public eye.

By the end of the decade, growing public outrage over violations of women's human rights in the Islamic world pushed U.S. leaders to enact policies to promote and protect women's human rights in Muslim countries. In fact, public concerns directly influenced American foreign policy on this issue for the first time when the movement to end FGM motivated Congress in 1996 to criminalize the practice and to tie U.S. foreign aid to efforts to eradicate it abroad. Simultaneously, several groundbreaking U.S. asylum cases set the precedent that a woman's fear of FGM for herself or her children was a legitimate basis for political asylum. The fictional case in *Law & Order* mirrored reality, as FGM went on trial in front of real-life asylum judges.

These legislative, judicial, and foreign aid efforts helped foster an environment in which American foreign policymakers could act more robustly on behalf of women's rights. They also raised important questions about how to define women's human rights, whether and how the United States should approach dealing with human rights in its foreign policy, and which human rights violations abroad were legitimate targets for U.S. action. In seeking to answer these questions and navigate the thorny issue of FGM, Americans began to articulate a vision of the United States' post–Cold War global mission that included championing women's human rights abroad, even when violations of those rights did not directly affect the U.S. national interest. Although this vision was not well-defined, it demonstrated the growing influence of soft power issues such as human rights on American foreign policy by the 1990s.

Condemnation of FGM was not new in the 1990s. What *was* different was the scale of the anti-FGM movement and the engagement of the international mainstream. Islam's connection to FGM particularly resonated with Americans because of the broader context of the well-established U.S. discourse that cast Islam as oppressive for women. International affairs reinforced that understanding. As FGM became a major public issue in the 1990s, the United States was heavily involved in a number of Muslim countries, including Somalia, where FGM was practiced almost universally.[7] The increasing importance of the Islamic world to U.S. interests and growing American public attention to Muslim women's human rights coalesced around the issue of FGM. That Muslims in some countries violated the bodily integrity of women and girls by practicing FGM symbolized Islam's inherent misogyny for many U.S. feminists, journalists, and members of the public.

The Islamic dimension of FGM may not have resonated so powerfully with Americans under different circumstances. FGM is not solely a Muslim custom, nor do all Islamic societies practice it. The Koran does not sanction it. Instead, female genital mutilation is primarily an African practice; it occurs in a broad swath of countries that cuts across the middle of the African continent, from Mauritania and Senegal in the west, to Egypt in the north, to Sudan, Somalia, and Kenya in the east.[8] Scholars have traced the custom to ancient Egypt; it therefore predates Islam by centuries.[9] FGM is not practiced in Saudi Arabia, the birthplace of Islam, or in the rest of the Middle East or the Islamic regions of Asia.

Americans who opposed FGM thus could have framed the issue differently, as a regional issue or perhaps in relation to colonialism, poverty, or development. Transnational activists initially framed it as a public health problem and later a human rights violation not inherently tied to one religious or ethnic group.[10] Americans, however, tended to interpret FGM primarily as the most striking manifestation of the Islamic subjugation of women, and most reacted with visceral horror when first learning of the custom. FGM destroyed the very part of the body that marks it as female. It clearly caused physical harm; the brutal cutting methods deployed in many cases only deepened Americans' revulsion. FGM was sensational, unfamiliar, and lent itself easily to condemnation. The issue was so compelling because FGM deftly connected the two dominant discursive strands about Islam in the United States: Orientalism allowed Americans to characterize FGM as the practice of uncivilized, misogynist Others, while human rights concepts made the women and girls who underwent FGM legible as victims of a custom that violated universal norms. While women also perpetuated FGM, Americans tended to blame men—particularly Muslim men—for the custom.

The centrality of FGM to the culture and religion of those Muslims who practice it may also explain why Americans characterized FGM chiefly as an Islamic practice. Some non-Islamic groups in Africa practice FGM, and there are African Muslim communities who do not. However, the prevalence and severity of FGM, as well as the reasons for it, differ between Muslims and non-Muslims. In countries with non-Muslim majorities where FGM occurs, less than 50 percent of women and girls are cut. In contrast, in FGM-practicing Muslim-majority countries, such as Egypt, Somalia, and Djibouti, the custom is nearly universal.[11]

Moreover, Muslim communities tend to practice the most extensive form of genital cutting. Activists and scholars have identified three forms of FGM. *Clitoridectomy* is the removal of the clitoris. *Excision* involves the removal of the clitoris and all or part of the inner labia. The most severe form of FGM is *infibulation*, in which the clitoris and inner labia are removed entirely. The outer labia are then stitched together to create a "hood of skin," which covers the urethra and most of the vaginal opening. Only a tiny hole about the diameter of a match stick is left for urination and menstruation. Non-Muslim practitioners favor clitoridectomy, excision, or, in some cases, a ritual pricking of the clitoris without removal of tissue. The groups that practice infibulation, on the other hand, tend to be Muslims; infibulation is especially widespread in Somalia, Sudan, southern Egypt, and parts of Ethiopia.[12]

The purpose of FGM for many non-Muslim communities is to initiate girls into womanhood. Girls often undergo FGM in large groups according to their age cohorts around the time they reach puberty. Boys in the community often undergo group circumcision around the same time. Other reasons include hygiene, aesthetic preferences, and claims that it increases fertility, but those are secondary to the cutting ritual's primary purpose of signifying girls' maturity.[13] The problem for anti-FGM activists in these communities is to provide a way for such societies to maintain the cultural significance of girls' transition into womanhood without the physical act of cutting and to provide an alternative form of income for those who make a living performing FGM procedures.

Muslims who practice FGM, on the other hand, do it primarily to protect girls' virginity, and they tend to cut their daughters when they are very young, usually between the ages of five and ten. They use Islam to justify the custom. Such groups characterize female sexuality as a dangerous force that causes social chaos, and their cultures dictate that male honor depends upon the chastity of female family members. Such societies often segregate the sexes, and they see sex outside marriage as a grave sin for women. Most men in these communities insist on marrying virgins, and girls are often married off at a young age. Parents believe that clitoridectomy or excision ensures that girls will remain virgins until marriage because it will remove the source of sexual desire. Parents who infibulate their daughters create an additional physical barrier against intercourse that proves to potential husbands that the girls are virgins. In Muslim countries like Somalia where it is still customary for men to pay a bride-price, proof of virginity yields greater profits for a girl's family.[14] In societies where women must depend primarily on marriage for economic support, parents' refusal to uphold the tradition of FGM often means condemning their daughters to a life of poverty and ostracism.

A complicating factor beyond the cultural and social pressure in these communities is religion. Muslims who cut their daughters believe that FGM is not only socially sanctioned but also a religious duty that all devout Muslims must perform. While the Koran does not mention FGM or female circumcision, many African Muslims do not read Arabic and must rely upon male religious leaders to provide Koranic interpretations. These men preach that FGM is a religious requirement.[15] Religious arguments in favor of FGM and social opprobrium directed against those who do not cut their daughters are mutually reinforcing for FGM-practicing Muslims.[16] The double imperative for families to cut their daughters makes it harder for anti-FGM activists to convince Muslim practitioners to give up the tradition. Thus the custom both is and is not an Islamic one, and Americans have struggled to understand this complicated issue.

While American anti-FGM activists often knew that both Muslims and non-Muslims practice female genital mutilation, they still tended to characterize the custom chiefly as a problem related to Islam. Because FGM was most widespread in Muslim-majority countries and because Muslim practitioners employed its most severe form, characterized it as a religious duty, and clung to the custom most tenaciously, American anti-FGM campaigners found the Islamic practice of FGM most disturbing. Because of the broader context of U.S. public outcry over the violation of women's human rights in Islamic societies since 1979, the notion that FGM was an Islamic practice was powerfully resonant with the American public.

Public outrage over FGM in the United States (and internationally) was considerable by the 1990s, but it had taken many years for the issue to become meaningful to policymakers, journalists, human rights and feminist activists, and the general public. Before the 1980s, few people in the United States had ever heard of "female circumcision," as FGM was known at the time. American conversations about FGM unfolded within the context of the transnational anti-FGM movement, which blossomed in the late 1970s and peaked in the 1990s (although it continues today). Although transnational activists and scholars stressed the need for cultural sensitivity and a nuanced understanding of FGM, their discussions of Islam in relation to the custom linked the two concepts for the American public.

The international movement did not just influence American domestic debates about FGM: it sparked them. Feminists and anti-FGM activists pushed the international community to go beyond its narrow focus on human rights abuses perpetrated by states to include action against human rights violations that occurred in the "private" sphere. Culture, religion, and the family belonged to this sphere, supposedly off-limits for public debates or action. Most practices that harmed women—such as domestic violence, honor killing, bride burning, sex trafficking, rape, child marriage, and FGM—fell into this private category because individuals, rather than governments, committed these acts. Declaring the private sphere off-limits to international intervention effectively ensured the perpetuation of women's subordination worldwide. At the time, this premise was so common that feminists struggled to get the public and government involved in protecting women in the United States from such private sphere abuses.[17] Anti-FGM activists faced the same battle internationally.

Activists followed a three-pronged approach to breaking down the public/ private dichotomy that targeted the local, national, and global simultaneously.

Locally, they launched grassroots community programs to educate FGM-practicing peoples about women's human rights, the harmful effects of FGM, and alternatives to the tradition. Nationally, they pressured governments of countries with FGM-practicing populations not only to support their grassroots campaigns but also to outlaw FGM and actively enforce the ban. Internationally, activists sought to mobilize the United Nations, World Health Organization (WHO), governments of non-FGM-practicing countries, and the public to pressure FGM-practicing nations to eradicate the tradition and to provide financial support for local campaigns. In seeking international support, activists intentionally mobilized the American public.

Early on, despite the efforts of grassroots African activists in the 1960s to secure the assistance of the United Nations and WHO, international organizations refused to discuss the practice. The United Nations and WHO characterized it as a private, cultural issue beyond the purview of international law.[18] It was only in the late 1970s, when the transnational feminist movement challenged the public/private dichotomy and the grassroots human rights movement gained traction, that states and the United Nations began to pay serious attention to the issue.[19]

While African and Arab activists initially struggled to get UN and government assistance, they secured Western feminist support almost immediately. Feminists from North America and Europe saw the eradication of FGM as part of women's common struggle against patriarchy. U.S. feminists in particular were horrified by the custom and raised its visibility in the late 1970s and 1980s. They also initiated therein the problematic and persistent U.S. discourse that linked FGM with Islam.[20]

Fran Hosken was the first American to take up the issue. She mainly targeted the United Nations and WHO, but she also sought to mobilize the international public. Hosken's campaigns heavily influenced how Americans later approached FGM. Austrian-born Hosken, who immigrated with her family to the United States in 1938, was a Harvard-educated journalist and urban planner. She was appalled when she learned about "female circumcision" in 1973 while traveling in Africa and was equally shocked to learn that the international community was largely silent about the issue.[21] She made it her personal mission to eradicate the practice.

Hosken founded *Women's International Network News* (*WINN*) in 1975, a quarterly journal that she published from her basement in Massachusetts.[22] She included a section on FGM in every issue of *WINN* for the next thirty years. Hosken also set out to study FGM after UNICEF and WHO rebuffed her requests that they examine it. She traveled across Africa three times to interview midwives and doctors. Hosken also gathered hundreds of questionnaires from women and institutions in Africa and the Middle East and wrote to the authors of the existing medical publications on FGM.[23] The result of these efforts was the 370-page *Hosken Report*, which she published in 1979.[24]

The first-ever comprehensive study of FGM, *The Hosken Report* documented the geographic scope and history of the practice, described the various types of FGM, enumerated its health effects, explained its purpose, and provided statistics on how many women and girls underwent FGM worldwide. The report also offered suggestions for how to eradicate it. Most subsequent studies relied heavily on Hosken's figures.[25] Because Hosken was the first person to study FGM systematically, she framed how others discussed the tradition thereafter. In fact, Hosken coined the term "female genital mutilation," which became the official term used by the United Nations and much of the NGO community by the late 1980s.[26]

Ultimately, *The Hosken Report* was a manifesto that combined meticulous research with moral outrage. At the most fundamental level, at issue were the reasons why female genital mutilation was performed and how it affected women's status globally. Hosken argued that FGM remained pervasive in so many countries because male religious and political authorities conspired to keep women ignorant about their bodies and subservient to men's sexual desires. Hosken repeatedly singled out Muslim men as culprits. Because she set the parameters of the discussion, her criticisms helped ensure that Islam remained firmly tied to discourse about FGM in the United States.

For Hosken, despite the fact that women often perpetuated FGM, Muslim men deserved special censure. To her, the broader, patriarchal Islamic characterization of women as sexually uncontrollable was at the root of the problem, even if women often performed the ritual. Hosken asserted that Muslim women's "enormous psychological burden" of being responsible for family honor, which FGM supposedly protected, was an expression of patriarchal domination.[27] Muslims were guilty of infibulation, this most horrific violation of women's human rights, according to Hosken, because Islam demanded that women be virgins upon marriage and because Muslim societies were the most oppressive for women generally.

While Hosken attempted to build a broad-based international coalition, her report often alienated potential allies, including other Western feminists. Her critics charged that Hosken was "notoriously short on tact and anti-male."[28] Although she argued that westerners must first and foremost support African and Arab women's efforts to combat FGM, she claimed in her report, "The victims of the practices described here, are for the most part, illiterate and too young to speak for themselves, unaware of the rest of the world and of their own bodies' biological functions. They are quite unable to communicate their needs."[29] Such characterization of FGM's "victims," as well as her attack on Islam, was offensive to activists from FGM-practicing societies and carried racist and colonialist overtones.

When Hosken encountered the respected Egyptian feminist and future SIGI member Dr. Nawal el Saadawi at the NGO Forum in Copenhagen in 1980, the two clashed over Hosken's approach. El Saadawi, a physician, was an internationally influential anti-FGM activist. She protested that Hosken consistently blamed Islam for FGM, whereas el Saadawi argued, "It has to do with patriarchy and monogamy" more than religion, "but she doesn't want to hear any of this."[30] Hosken's approach was therefore problematic for working with women from FGM-practicing countries who should have been ready allies. Her accusatory tone when dealing with male political leaders also undermined her otherwise herculean efforts to push governments and the United Nations to address the issue.

Hosken's contemporaries recognized this and urged her to soften her rhetoric for the good of the cause. In her 1981 review of the second edition of Hosken's report, scholar Margaret Jean Hay praised Hosken's research but called her a "crusader" who weakened the overall impact of her report with her "general tone of outrage and sarcasm," as when Hosken suggested that male castration should replace FGM.[31] Similarly, *Ms.* editors Gloria Steinem and Robin Morgan cautioned Hosken about her "troubling . . . cultural bias," which "could overshadow the enormous value of the work you actually have done" and "confirm the understandable suspicions of Third World women that outside criticism of their countries may have a racist base and agenda."[32]

Despite her undiplomatic approach, Hosken did generate controversy, and attention. This publicity and other feminists' adoption of the issue eventually led to U.S., UN, and other governments' policies by the 1990s that aimed to eradicate FGM. In 1979, after several years of lobbying by Hosken and African women's groups, WHO hosted the first international seminar on FGM in Khartoum, which Hosken attended.[33] She also garnered support in the United States. *Signs*, the leading international women's studies journal at the time, reviewed her report favorably in 1980 and began to feature articles about FGM.[34] Hosken's activism created a space for increasing public discussion of FGM in the United States, despite her problematic approach to the issue.

Hosken's conception of FGM carried powerful overtones of colonial feminism. Although feminist leaders like Morgan and Steinem, as well as others who participated in the Decade's international conversations, cautioned Hosken against her Orientalist, colonial tone, other Americans shared Hosken's stance, making cross-cultural cooperation to end the tradition initially very difficult. Americans' reaction to FGM was often understandably visceral: they were shocked and horrified—and then blamed Islam.

FGM had not been on the agenda in Mexico City, but the Copenhagen Forum held a workshop on it. There, el Saadawi and many other African and Arab women spoke out against FGM, and Western feminists agreed with them, but the issue fell victim to the conference's overriding tensions between Western and non-Western women. North American and European feminists at Copenhagen were shocked and outraged by FGM and were bewildered by African and Arab women's disdain for their horror. Many of them learned about FGM for the first time at the Forum sessions and reacted emotionally. The *New York Times* reported that Western feminists at the sessions "seemed visibly shocked to learn that girls in African and Arab villages are circumcised. . . . Waving a pamphlet entitled, 'Genital and Sexual Mutilation of Females,' a Swedish student asked an American, 'Have you read this? This is barbarism, what they are doing.'"[35] Such statements were precisely what incensed el Saadawi and other women from FGM-practicing countries. She commented, "They call attention to this 'barbaric practice' of 'backward people' instead of looking at it in the context of the whole global and historic oppression of women."[36]

African and Arab women wanted support for their efforts to end FGM, but they did not want Western women to see them as ignorant victims in need of enlightenment or rescue. El Saadawi complained that "the West is exploiting this issue," while AAWORD issued a strong public reprimand of Western feminists for how they discussed FGM.[37] Moreover, terms like "barbaric" implied racism, since Westerners historically cast non-white peoples, especially Africans, as backward, uncivilized savages.

By Nairobi, however, much of the acrimony over FGM dissipated, largely because Western women deferred to the leadership of African and Arab women and, consistent with the evolution of global feminism generally, tried to eschew colonial feminist thinking. The Forum newspaper at the 1985 conference observed that "a big shift has occurred in the fight to stop circumcision," as orderliness and cordiality replaced earlier confusion and tension.[38] The consensus mood in Nairobi shifted the global movement against FGM into high gear. The main efforts to eradicate the custom occurred on the ground in FGM-practicing countries, but transnational NGOs, including WLUML and SIGI, publicized the issue and solicited international moral and financial support for local campaigns. WLUML and SIGI circulated educational information and calls for action to feminists from the United States and non-FGM-practicing Islamic countries. As organizations that focused primarily on the rights of Muslim women, WLUML and SIGI perhaps also helped perpetuate the link between FGM and Islam for Americans.

WLUML's *Dossiers* ran articles on FGM from the mid-1980s onward, informing the women in its global network and resourcing research and eradication efforts.[39] Its third *Dossier*, released in 1988, included a special section devoted to FGM. Its many articles explained that, while the Koran contains no justification for FGM, many Muslims nevertheless saw it as a religious duty, and the tradition was bound up with Islamic sexual mores.[40] Likewise, the article "Female Sexuality and Islam" in WLUML's 1989 *Dossier 5/6* argued that "destructive qualities of female sexuality have been quoted in many Hadith (sayings of the Prophet) as well as in the writings of eminent Muslim scholars. . . . In all the books of Hadith and Fiqh, as well as in the interpretations of the Quran, one can easily find the chapters related to the destructive powers of women's sexuality which strongly support the physical mutilation of women i.e. circumcision. Although Islam does not favour the practice, it provides the ideological justification for it."[41] The NGO's 1997 Plan of Action also proclaimed that FGM's "being propagated as an Islamic requirement" was a prime example of Islamic fundamentalists' desire to subjugate women.[42]

From the perspective of Muslim women working to end FGM, then, Islam was indeed a problem to be confronted. Reportage like this cemented the link between FGM and the Islamic oppression of women for American feminists who received information from transnational organizations. Muslim feminists were not unaware of this. When SIGI sent out an alert about FGM in July 1997, it emphasized, "<u>SIGI wishes to stress that Islam does not condone FGM.</u>"[43] Nevertheless, SIGI passed along action alerts on FGM from other organizations that stressed how people used Islam to justify the custom in countries like Egypt.[44] SIGI's 1995 book *Faith and Freedom: Women's Human Rights in the Muslim World* included a chapter by Pakistani feminist Farida Shaheed, who was also a leader in WLUML. She contended that Islam was a major obstacle to ending FGM.[45] Mahnaz Afkhami herself later characterized FGM as one example among many of how male religious authorities interpreted Islam to justify women's oppression.[46]

It was difficult even for Muslim women to avoid reinforcing the link between Islam and FGM. This was partly because there *were* ties—although far from absolute or universal—between the two in practice, and partly because the link spoke powerfully to the complex hybrid of Orientalism and human rights discourses by which America tended to make sense of international women's issues in the 1980s. Issues that provoked outrage and rose to prominence in the United States tended to resonate with both old, Orientalist thinking and a new, compelling interest in women's rights as human rights. There were plenty of international issues to be seen—but the ones that were seen most vividly tended to mesh with both of these discursive traditions.

Because of well-organized lobbying by women's groups in the 1980s and 1990s, the United Nations and other international agencies paid increasing attention to FGM, as did the U.S. government.[47] Anti-FGM activists initially cast the custom as a health issue. Accordingly, they launched initiatives to educate FGM-practicing communities about the adverse physical and psychological effects of genital cutting on women and girls. The United Nations followed suit.

Much to their chagrin, however, movement leaders realized that many FGM-practicing groups were already aware of the physical risks associated with the custom—including blood loss, infection, difficult childbirth, and death. They simply saw the social costs of not cutting their daughters as outweighing the physical ones. Even worse, families who could afford to responded to the health campaign by taking their daughters to hospitals to be cut or by switching from infibulation to clitoridectomy. The health campaign had failed and, in many cases, further entrenched FGM by prompting its medicalization.

Therefore, in the early 1990s, activists reframed FGM as an issue of women's and girls' human rights—especially the right to bodily integrity—rather than public health. This approach worked better. Many countries—in the West and in Africa—passed legislation to end the practice.[48] As this section explains, U.S. public pressure also spurred congressional action. New NGOs dedicated solely to the eradication of FGM proliferated in the late 1980s and 1990s, feminist organizations included the issue in their campaigns, and scholars and journalists wrote about FGM for American audiences, which combined to build public pressure for action.[49]

The American discourse that ultimately influenced Congress, U.S. asylum courts, and U.S. foreign aid policy sensationalized FGM, which elicited visceral responses from the American public and included a combination of Orientalist and human rights concepts. A sensationalist approach was precisely what transnational feminists had been trying to avoid since their debates in Copenhagen in 1980. The nuance of the international conversation largely disappeared when Americans talked to one another. While the American public, news media, politicians, and feminists genuinely wanted to help women who were at risk of FGM, the ways they discussed the custom also said a lot about how Americans saw themselves.

Those who opposed FGM (and no one argued in favor of FGM in the United States) cast themselves as heroes and the United States as a force for good that upheld human rights and rescued victims of oppression abroad.[50] Their focus on FGM allowed Americans to continue to prioritize certain kinds of human rights by focusing on women's right to bodily integrity, a basic civil right, and largely avoid the ongoing legacy of colonialism and broader economic or social factors that might contribute to FGM and women's inequality generally. Then again, U.S. government action was one of the goals of the transnational anti-FGM movement, and the very unnuanced American domestic discussion of FGM was precisely why the issue grabbed policymakers' attention. Sensationalism and characterization of FGM as a problem of Islam resonated in the 1990s because the broader U.S. public discourse about the general Islamic oppression of women provided a template that Americans could draw upon to interpret FGM.

The U.S. conversation about FGM began in March 1980 when Gloria Steinem and Robin Morgan published a five-page cover story in *Ms.* titled "The International Crime of Genital Mutilation."[51] While Hosken's *Report* had a limited audience, the eight-year-old *Ms.* was popular, with hundreds of thousands of readers each year.[52] Despite Steinem and Morgan's concerns about Hosken's approach, the international attention she drew to the issue prompted them to publish the piece. They carefully stressed that genital cutting rites were not limited to one religion. The tone of the *Ms.* article was more measured than that of Hosken's report, but it still connected FGM with Islam for its readers.[53]

The same issue of *Ms.* also included a piece by Nawal el Saadawi. The article introduced her to American audiences, and it coincided with the publication of *The Hidden Face of Eve*, el Saadawi's first book available in English. The book and her *Ms.* article were powerful indictments of FGM by a woman who experienced the custom firsthand: el Saadawi's own voice reached across cultural divides to American readers. In *The Hidden Face of Eve*, el Saadawi described in terrifying detail her own clitoridectomy at age six, and she testified that "the memory of my clitoridectomy continued to track me down like a nightmare." Her article in *Ms.* reproduced that narrative.[54]

Americans now had a firsthand account of what it was like to undergo genital mutilation. As a woman who experienced FGM, a doctor, and an Egyptian, el Saadawi spoke out against FGM with authority and critiqued Islam in ways that Americans could not. Her story and call for assistance galvanized the U.S. feminist community. Melani McAlister has argued that el Saadawi's story "would, by the mid-1980s, become so widely quoted by American feminists as to make it almost a cliché."[55] Even non-feminists celebrated el Saadawi's outspokenness, however. The mainstream news media, including the *New York Times*, reviewed *The Hidden Face of Eve* positively.[56]

From el Saadawi's book, many Americans could infer that FGM was a Muslim practice, and that inference was understandable. In *The Hidden Face of Eve*, el Saadawi argued that Arab men used Islam to justify their brutal subjugation of women. Because male religious leaders decried sex as shameful and imposed a strict separation of the sexes, she concluded that Arab society had become perverted. Like Hosken, el Saadawi saw Islamic sex segregation as the root of the problem. She reasonably blamed Muslims' obsession with female virginity and family honor for FGM. El Saadawi claimed that "a distorted concept of honour in our Arab society" and "double moral standards" that required girls' virginity but not boys' are "only a reflection of the backwardness that prevails in many aspects of our life."[57]

For el Saadawi, however, patriarchy was the true reason for FGM, not Islam. Using the language of contemporary feminist theory, she argued that FGM would end only when women eliminated patriarchy in Arab society. She attributed the perpetuation of FGM to male religious authorities who intentionally used religion to subordinate women: el Saadawi asserted that "reactionary" Muslims "are making a concerted effort to misinterpret religion and to utilize it as an instrument of fear, oppression, and exploitation." True Islam, in contrast, "aims at truth, equality, justice, love and a healthy wholesome life for all people, whether men or women."[58]

El Saadawi's Western readers were unlikely to appreciate her distinction between true Islam and those who misinterpreted it. Moreover, there were so many competing Islamic interpretations that it was difficult for non-Muslim Americans to determine which version was "true." The Koran does not countenance female genital mutilation, but in practice Muslims use Islam to justify FGM and insist on its perpetuation. In addition, el Saadawi only discussed FGM in relation to Arab, Muslim countries in her book and the *Ms.* article, giving the impression that only Muslims practiced it.

The 1982 *New York Times* review of *The Hidden Face of Eve* underscored this impression and argued that FGM was a uniquely barbaric custom for which Islam was responsible. It condemned FGM's relationship to "the equation still prevalent in the Arab world between a man's honor and a woman's virginity."[59] Here the reviewer echoed el Saadawi's own assertions and opined that "no culture as religion-dominated as Arabic culture can ever accomplish social or political equality for women."[60] El Saadawi's portrayal of Arab society as backward gave credence to this view. While she intended for her readers to see Islam as a potentially progressive force, *The Hidden Face of Eve* also allowed American readers to draw the opposite conclusion.

Seasoned U.S. feminists became increasingly sensitive to African and Arab women's perspectives on FGM over the course of the 1980s—leaning heavily toward an elaboration of women's rights as human rights. Yet new voices joined the U.S. public discussion by the early 1990s that once again emphasized the connection between Islam and FGM. In 1992 Alice Walker published *Possessing the Secret of Joy*, the first novel in the United States to discuss FGM.[61] As the famous author of the Pulitzer Prize–winning *The Color Purple*, Walker had cultural cachet in the United States. *Possessing the Secret of Joy* focuses on Tashi, a minor character from *The Color Purple*, and her struggle to overcome the psychological and physical trauma she experiences after undergoing infibulation as a teen in Africa. In the story, Tashi returns to Africa and murders her mutilator. For Walker, FGM was primarily an African issue that stemmed from a fundamental male desire to control women's bodies. Although she highlighted the regional and cultural nature of FGM, she nevertheless chose to weave Islam into her narrative and implied that Muslim men were to blame for the custom. Tashi's fictional ethnic group practices infibulation, and Walker explicitly identifies them as Muslim. Moreover, "fundamentalists and Muslim fanatics" gather outside of Tashi's prison to attack women who come to support her.[62]

Possessing the Secret of Joy landed Walker on the *Oprah Winfrey Show* and received overwhelmingly positive reviews.[63] Reviewers frequently highlighted the association between FGM and Islam in the novel. One, for example, called the book "more threatening and subversive [to Islam] than Salman Rushdie's *Satanic Verses*."[64] Because every major newspaper in the United States reviewed the novel, discussion of FGM as a dimension of Islam extended further into the American public consciousness.

While Walker used the tools of popular culture to deliver her message, journalists at major media outlets also exposed the public to FGM in the early 1990s. Abe Rosenthal of the *New York Times* consistently wrote about female genital mutilation throughout the decade and condemned it unequivocally as "torture." Rosenthal was the paper's former executive editor and a rare conservative voice at the *New York Times*.[65] Like Americans who discussed FGM before him, he characterized the custom as an Islamic practice that claimed "African Muslim women" as its "principal victims."[66] Rosenthal's repeated references to Islam in his articles drew upon the already existing understanding among his readers that Muslim men were particularly brutal toward women. He used his authority as a respected figure at America's most influential newspaper to increase public and governmental awareness about a practice he found reprehensible.

Rosenthal was not alone. In September 1993, ABC's weekly news program *Day One*, hosted by Forrest Sawyer, aired an episode on FGM called "Scarred for Life," which featured interviews with activists, representatives from international organizations, and people from FGM-practicing countries. Sawyer grilled UN and U.S. officials about why they did not do more to eradicate FGM, and once again, Islam pervaded the discussion. All of the FGM-practicing people featured in the episode were Muslims. The most striking were Hassan and Yasmin, Somalis living in the United States who were deciding whether or not to infibulate their three daughters. "Scarred for Life" won a prestigious Peabody Award.[67]

Other major TV news networks soon aired stories on FGM as well. The most influential was CNN. In September 1994 the network ignited an international firestorm when it broadcast graphic video footage of the clitoridectomy of a young Egyptian girl. Christiane Amanpour aired the footage at the UN International Conference on Population and Development (ICPD), held in Cairo during September 5–13, and CNN televised the video worldwide. The footage showed ten-year-old Nagla Hamza having her clitoris removed without anesthesia or sanitary instruments. *Time* described the video, which depicted "a crowded living room, where relatives smiled and ululated in celebration. As a voice-over explained that no sanitary precautions would be taken, no anesthetic applied, Nagla was tilted onto her back by two men—a plumber and a florist—and her legs prodded into the air in a wide V. While the florist cradled her from behind, the plumber wrapped Nagla's hands around her ankles. Then the plumber quickly leaned in between Nagla's legs and cut off her clitoris with a pair of barber's scissors. The girl barely had time to emit her first gasp of pain before her legs were lowered and her mutilated genitalia were bound with rags."[68] Nagla wore a party dress and had been smiling before the procedure began; afterward, she was clearly in agony. As the men held her down and cut her, she cried, "Father! Father! A sin upon you! A sin upon you all!"[69]

The gripping video did not show Nagla's injuries for obvious reasons, but her heartrending screams were enough to cause "an immediate worldwide public outcry."[70] Partly because of the video, the final platform of the ICPD condemned FGM. Egyptian authorities also arrested Nagla's father, the two men who performed the procedure, and the freelance producer who arranged for CNN to film it. Nagla's father was shocked at his arrest, claiming that "he thought he was participating in a documentary on Islam. . . . As a Muslim, he believes he acted properly."[71] Once again, the face of the victim was a Muslim one.

U.S. audiences were shocked and outraged. The CNN broadcast exposed many to the existence of FGM for the first time. One caller to CNN said that she had not believed written reports on FGM until she saw the video footage from Cairo. The images on-screen proved far more powerful than any written testimony, and CNN reached millions of viewers nightly.[72] The footage even reached American lawmakers, who proved equally susceptible to its power.

The uproar over the CNN footage was the final motivation for the U.S. government to take decisive action against FGM. When American legislators took up the issue, however, it raised thorny questions about the relationship between human rights and the use of U.S. power. Who defined women's human rights, and which human rights abuses were legitimate targets for

U.S. action? What could or should the United States do when private individuals abroad, not states, perpetrated human rights violations? Existing human rights law provided some support for intervention in the affairs of sovereign nations when governments committed human rights abuses, but questions about when and how to intervene remained unanswered. The United States, United Nations, and international community struggled with these issues when responding to genocides in the Balkans and Rwanda during this same period. If there was no clear path for responding to genocide, there was certainly no obvious course regarding human rights abuses that occurred in the private sphere. Indeed, Americans had not figured out how to handle abuses against women at home, as contemporary domestic debates about rape, domestic violence, and the Violence Against Women Act (1994) demonstrated.

Ultimately, U.S. policymakers opted to intervene by using diplomatic, moral, and economic tools, which did not violate the sovereignty of states where FGM occurred. Congress employed moral pressure by banning FGM in the United States in 1996, and they exerted economic pressure by tying U.S. foreign aid to efforts to end FGM in Africa. This approach indicated their belief that certain putatively private human rights abuses against women were legitimate targets for U.S. action, such as violations of the right to bodily integrity. Congress set a precedent for future policymakers to act to promote women's human rights in Islamic countries. Strong public support in favor of using U.S. power to end FGM also implied a future willingness to protect the human rights of Muslim women.

Public opinion was indeed an important factor in the case of FGM. Before the CNN video, the United States had attempted to address the issue, but on a limited scale. USAID quietly began assisting anti-FGM campaigns in Africa in 1993 as part of the Clinton administration's decision to use US-AID as a tool for women's empowerment. The administration did not single out FGM, however; it treated the custom as one among many issues that the United States needed to address to place women's human rights in the mainstream of its foreign policy.[73] Development aid addressed the root causes of FGM more effectively than other tactics, but the administration's discussions of FGM were muted prior to 1994. Representative Patricia Schroeder had also attempted, unsuccessfully, to pass anti-FGM legislation as part of the Women's Health Equity Act in 1993.[74] She reintroduced her anti-FGM bill in early 1994, but despite mounting public outrage over FGM, it took the CNN video to spur other legislators to support Schroeder's endeavors.

Representative Constance Morella (R-Maryland) viewed the film while attending the Cairo conference. When she met later that week with Egyptian president Hosni Mubarak, Morella pressed him on the issue: "I asked him about female genital mutilation, and he said that it does not happen, that it's not legal in Egypt. I said that [the law] must not be enforced . . . that I'd seen the CNN film." A *Washington Post* journalist concluded, "That's probably the best argument for showing shocking and horrifying footage of any atrocity. The world has far too long pretended that female genital mutilation isn't happening."[75] Many who saw the CNN video agreed.

Morella introduced the CNN footage to the House, and a concerned member of the public brought it to the attention of the Senate by telling her longtime friend about it: Senator Harry Reid (D-Nevada). As Reid recounted to the Senate, "I became almost sick to my stomach by listening to her describe what she watched on television."[76] He was so horrified by his friend's account that he watched the footage and immediately commissioned his staff to undertake a thorough study of FGM. He read everything he could find on the practice before introducing a resolution to the Senate Committee on Foreign Relations in late September 1994, which condemned FGM and commended the Egyptian government for arresting the men responsible for Nagla Hamza's mutilation. His resolution passed the Senate without opposition or substantive debate.[77] While the mainstream media was the conduit to policymakers in this case, feminist campaigns had raised the public profile of the issue, which in turn had prompted Amanpour to cover it.

Reid went further than his resolution. Because of the CNN footage, he became the most vocal and untiring supporter of anti-FGM legislation in Congress, aside from Schroeder. Because Reid was a rising star in the Senate, his support gave weight to Schroeder's efforts and allowed both houses of Congress to work together. He and Schroeder cosponsored joint legislation and adopted a dual approach: they proposed to ban FGM in the United States and to tie foreign aid to eradication efforts abroad. Congress ultimately adopted both strategies with little resistance.

In fact, Reid's Senate colleagues rallied to his cause. Reid, Carol Moseley-Braun (D-Illinois), and Paul Wellstone (D-Minnesota) introduced the Federal Prohibition of Female Genital Mutilation Act of 1994. Reid provided his fellow senators with a well-informed description of FGM and an impassioned argument against the custom as a violation of women's and children's human rights. He pointed to recent legislation in the United Kingdom, Sweden, Switzerland, France, and Canada that banned or criminalized FGM, and he called for the Senate to support his proposal to criminalize the practice in the United States. He argued that they must condemn FGM to support the women fighting against the practice in their home countries "until its end is reached."[78] Criminalization was largely a symbolic statement of moral support for anti-FGM campaigns abroad, since the custom was not native to the United States. A ban would affect only immigrants from FGM-practicing countries, a tiny number of people at the time (although an increasing portion of the U.S. population today).[79] Reid introduced the bill to send a message to the international community that Americans took a firm stand.

Reid and his colleagues used the human rights framework espoused by the transnational anti-FGM movement and were careful not to frame FGM as a religious practice or as a cultural issue. They explicitly refused to blame Islam.[80] When supporting the legislation before the Senate, Moseley-Braun stated that "this is not just a matter of difference in cultural points of view. This really goes to a public health concern, a concern for human rights that I think as Americans we all share."[81] She continued, "Female circumcision has been associated with the Moslem [sic] religion, but nowhere in Islamic scripture is it required. Nor is it practiced in Saudi Arabia, the cradle of Islam."[82] Because FGM most often happened to girls under the age of eighteen, the senators framed FGM as an issue of public health, women's right to bodily integrity, and child abuse.

It is possible that, like most Americans, Reid and his colleagues accepted the link between Islam and women's oppression, but they chose to remove religion from the equation for political reasons. There were fierce battles at the time, especially within Congress, over issues like abortion, religion, violence against women, homosexuality, "political correctness," privacy, and multiculturalism. These battles, referred to as the "culture wars," often divided Congress along party lines. It would be easy for FGM to get caught up in the culture wars if it were framed as an issue related to sex or feminism. Further, singling out a religion in proposed legislation could violate the principle of religious freedom. Consequently, many members of Congress might hesitate to support such legislation.[83] Many were also aware of the charges of neoimperialism hurled against the West by defenders of traditional practices whenever Americans criticized customs indigenous to the Global South.

American discussions of human rights were not uncontested, but Reid and his cosponsors could at least appeal to international human rights law and existing U.S. child abuse laws; American abhorrence of child abuse ran across party lines. The fact that several other nations had passed laws banning FGM—including Islamic countries—and the fact that the United Nations had just officially condemned the practice at the ICPD in Cairo (and would do so again at the 1995 Fourth World Conference on Women in Beijing) also gave Reid and his colleagues ammunition. Their approach was politically savvy and successful. The proposed anti-FGM legislation drew bipartisan support—a rare moment of agreement between Democrats and Republicans in an era of congressional gridlock.[84]

Reid wanted to introduce his bill while the CNN video was still a hot topic, at the end of the 1994 congressional term, but Congress adjourned without voting on it. Reid and his allies reintroduced the bill in 1995 to a new Congress. Despite the ongoing acrimony across the aisle, the bill drew strong bipartisan support and five cosponsors, including two Republicans.[85] While Congress worked to pass the legislation, public pressure for government action increased, and reporters began publishing articles about the growing number of immigrant girls and women subjected to FGM in the United States.[86]

Congress passed the legislation in September 1996 as part of the Omnibus Consolidated Appropriations Act of 1997. The act criminalized FGM in the United States and mandated that immigrants from FGM-practicing societies receive information about FGM's negative effects and the federal criminal penalties they faced if they practiced it in the United States. The law also bound the U.S. government to oppose non-humanitarian loans or other funding from international financial institutions to FGM-practicing countries that had not taken steps to end FGM.[87] That the law passed relatively quickly and faced no opposition attested to the salience of women's human rights by the 1990s for American lawmakers.

Public opinion and passage of the anti-FGM law prompted further U.S. action. In June 1995, as it considered passing the ban, the House also passed Schroeder's resolution "urging the President to help end the practice of female [circumcision] worldwide," which pushed Clinton to take up the issue at the executive level. His administration had already taken steps to support the anti-FGM movement through USAID in 1993, and after the furor over the CNN video, USAID also formed a Working Group on FGM to integrate efforts to eradicate the practice into existing reproductive health programs.[88] Meanwhile, First Lady Hillary Rodham Clinton explicitly condemned FGM in Beijing in September 1995 during her groundbreaking plenary speech at the Fourth World Conference on Women.[89]

Although the federal ban and congressional pressure did not alter the type of White House programs directed at FGM, they did cause the administration to refine and reinforce its existing initiatives. The State Department's Office of International Women's Issues (OIWI), which Clinton founded, brought U.S. and African activists to State to discuss concerns that the new U.S. law might cause people in Africa to blame anti-FGM activists for reduced foreign loans. Theresa Loar, who headed OIWI, later asserted that these meetings were highly productive and allowed the administration and African women's organizations to cooperate more effectively against FGM.[90] The President's Interagency Council on Women (PICW) also formed a committee to coordinate efforts across the federal government to implement the 1996 FGM law. Secretary of State Madeleine Albright and the First Lady, among other administration representatives, also continued to reference FGM in public speeches throughout Clinton's time in office.[91]

On September 30, 1996, President Clinton signed the ban on FGM into law, and fifteen states followed suit with anti-FGM legislation of their own.[92] In criminalizing FGM, the United States joined the ranks of dozens of countries that outlawed the custom during the 1990s. This aligned the United States with international opinion. By the year 2000, twenty nations had passed laws specifically outlawing FGM, while seven others declared that their existing civil, criminal, and child protection laws applied to the practice.[93]

The impact of the U.S. legislation depends on one's perspective. The ban did not affect many people. FGM is not an American practice, although recent immigrants from FGM-practicing countries such as Somalia brought the custom with them in the 1990s.[94] The law was also difficult to enforce. Beyond providing information to immigrants about FGM's criminalization, American authorities could do little to prevent people living in the United States from cutting their daughters, especially if they sent them overseas for the procedure. Because of the private nature of the practice, either the victim or someone with intimate knowledge of her mutilation (or her family's plans to cut her) would have to report the situation to the authorities in order for those who violated the law to be apprehended and punished. In tight-knit families that placed a premium on family honor, that did not happen often. In fact, the first prosecution for violating the FGM ban did not occur until 2006.[95] As an attempt to prevent and punish FGM in the United States, the law had limited impact.

However, as a symbolic statement, the law had greater significance. The U.S. government had condemned FGM as an intolerable human rights

violation. This sent a message to FGM practitioners abroad, and tying foreign aid to FGM's eradication made that message more emphatic. Americans
could intervene by refusing aid to governments whose anti-FGM efforts the
United States deemed insufficient and by providing funds through USAID
for grassroots campaigns. Moral and financial support for foreign governments and anti-FGM activists allowed activists from FGM-practicing countries to take the lead and determine exactly how to combat the custom on
the ground.

In enacting this policy, the United States was motivated more by soft
power concerns than by hard power issues that directly involved the national
interest. Unfortunately, Africa historically was less important to U.S. policymakers than other regions, so the potential costs of pressuring FGM-
practicing countries were relatively small. Moreover, most of the world's
governments were on board with the anti-FGM movement, including governments of countries where people practiced the custom. From the perspective of international politics, the U.S. position was hardly controversial or
risky. In fact, it may have been more politically damaging for the United States
not to condemn FGM, given the climate of international opinion at the time.

On the other hand, using foreign aid to push for the eradication of FGM
also had little direct benefit for the United States, at least in hard power
terms. There were no obvious economic, military, or strategic consequences
for Americans whether people in Africa practiced FGM or not. However, if
Americans truly cared about human rights—or at least certain kinds of
human rights—then the moral costs and benefits for the United States were
great. Criminalizing FGM and targeting the practice with foreign aid put the
United States squarely in line with international opinion and human rights
law. It also allowed Americans to see themselves as defenders of human
rights globally and to declare that protecting women's human rights was now
a key component of U.S. global identity.

Governments can also influence foreign affairs with domestic tools such as
political asylum. The categories and conditions by which a country grants
asylum make a statement about which practices it finds reprehensible. In the
1990s, the U.S. judicial system complemented legislative efforts to end
FGM by making the United States a safe haven for women fleeing genital
mutilation.[96] FGM-related asylum cases began to work their way through
American courts just as international scrutiny of the tradition peaked.[97]

Such cases were tricky because of the potential number of women who could seek asylum should the United States declare FGM a legitimate reason for granting it, given the millions of women and girls who were at risk each year. The larger ramifications of such cases also involved declaring gender a persecuted category, theoretically opening the door for other gender-based asylum claims. As American courts put FGM on trial, Islam once again combined with human rights concepts to construct the interpretive lens through which Americans comprehended the practice.

Just before Congress passed its anti-FGM law, a precedent-setting asylum case involving a Muslim girl became a national cause célèbre. American asylum courts had already ruled in favor of a woman's fear of FGM for her children in the case of a Nigerian, Lydia Oluloro, in March 1994. However, the United States had yet to grant any woman asylum based on fear of FGM for herself.[98] The *Kassindja* case changed that. Fauziya Kassindja, a seventeen-year-old Muslim from Togo, fled to the United States and requested asylum in December 1994, shortly after the CNN video aired.[99] Her wealthy parents had gone against tradition by not having her cut as a child. When Kassindja's father died in January 1993, however, her father's relatives exiled her mother and arranged for the girl to marry an older man. Since Kassindja had not undergone FGM, her father's family and the family of her prospective husband insisted that she undergo the procedure prior to her wedding (likely infibulation, based on her description). In response, Kassindja's mother and older sister spirited her to Germany. Once there, she purchased a fake passport, traveled to New Jersey, and applied for asylum at the airport.[100]

Immigration officials sent Kassindja directly to a detention center because she had entered the U.S. illegally, even though she was a minor. After languishing in prison for several months, her cousin secured her legal representation. Layli Miller Bashir, a law student at American University, argued Kassindja's case at her first asylum hearing in Philadelphia in August 1995.[101] The judge denied the girl's petition because he claimed he did not find her account credible.[102] Bashir then sought assistance from the American feminist organization Equality Now. She had met some of the group's members in Beijing at the UN Fourth World Conference on Women that September.[103] Equality Now had worked with Representative Schroeder on her anti-FGM bill, so they were familiar with the custom and readily agreed to publicize Kassindja's situation. They also arranged for Karen Musalo, the head of the International Human Rights Clinic at American University, to take on the girl's case pro bono.[104]

Given the recent attention to the CNN video and the pending federal law, Kassindja's case was ripe for media attention. Equality Now advised Kassindja to write to reporters and to Schroeder, and they organized a public letter-writing campaign that succeeded in getting members of Congress to contact Attorney General Janet Reno about Kassindja's plight.[105] Because of Equality Now's media savvy, Kassindja suddenly found herself thrust into the national spotlight. The *Washington Post, New York Times,* and *Boston Globe* all reported on her case, and members of Congress publicly expressed support for the girl.[106] However, it was Celia Dugger of the *New York Times* who made Kassindja into a news sensation. Equality Now arranged for Dugger to interview Kassindja in the Pennsylvania prison where she was being held, and the resulting article appeared on the front page of the paper on April 15, 1996.

Dugger timed the article perfectly. It came out just before Kassindja appeared before the Board of Immigration Appeals (BIA), the highest tribunal of the INS. Dugger treated Kassindja sympathetically and railed against her unfair treatment in U.S. detention facilities. She pointed out the significance of the girl's case, which would bring gender into asylum law for the first time and create "a new legal framework that would allow genital mutilation to be a reason for granting asylum."[107] Dugger's article did the trick. Within a few days of its publication, Kassindja was released from prison.[108]

In mid-June 1996, the BIA granted Kassindja asylum and ruled that she belonged to a persecuted group: women from her Muslim ethnic group in Togo who refused to undergo FGM.[109] Although the BIA defined this persecuted group narrowly, Kassindja's case had wider implications. In arguing the case, Bashir, Musalo, and the rest of Kassindja's legal team drew upon the existing literature on FGM, presenting first the judge in Philadelphia and then the BIA with Rosenthal's articles and publications by experts who drew explicit connections between FGM and Islam. By granting asylum to Kassindja, the BIA recognized the connection between religion and FGM among Kassindja's ethnic group and ruled that fear of undergoing FGM was a valid basis for an asylum claim.

The BIA's ruling in the Kassindja case established a groundbreaking precedent that all immigration judges in the United States should follow.[110] Soon after, a federal court supported another woman's asylum petition based on this precedent, in the highly publicized case of Adelaide Abankwah.[111] In these cases, the judiciary expanded upon and reinforced congressional efforts to combat FGM by making the United States a safe haven for women fleeing genital mutilation. While these changes in U.S. asylum law helped only a small percentage of at-risk women and girls, namely those who had the means to travel to U.S. soil to request asylum, the cases were still important. The United States had declared that a private human rights abuse against women overseas was a legitimate object for American action. These cases reinforced the message against FGM.

With Kassindja's victory and passage of federal anti-FGM legislation in 1996, the custom remained in the public eye in the United States. New developments maintained Americans' attention to the issue and reified FGM's connection with Islam, such as supermodel Waris Dirie's declaration in a *Marie Claire* interview that she had been infibulated as a child in Somalia.[112] More asylum cases followed and received media attention. By the time *Law & Order* aired "Ritual" in December 1997, the American public had already been exposed to newspaper coverage, magazine articles, television shows, and political and legal arguments that connected Islam with FGM; the episode reflected and reinforced its audience's preexisting understanding. This connection between Islam and the mutilation of women originated with anti-FGM activists, who pushed consistently to publicize the issue and to spur international action to eradicate the practice. Its effect in the U.S. media was to depict Muslims as violators of women's human rights.

The anti-FGM legislation and asylum cases were the first instances in which the American discourse about Muslim women substantively altered U.S. policy. With the exception of the changes in foreign aid policy, these actions affected only a small number of Muslim women in the United States, but Congress and the courts nevertheless sent a signal that Americans were willing to protect women from oppression that originated abroad. This had symbolic significance, and it created context and precedent for subsequent U.S. policy decisions.

Kassindja won asylum and Congress passed its anti-FGM legislation in the summer and fall of 1996, just as the Taliban seized power in Afghanistan. The timing of these events allowed Americans who had been mobilized by FGM to turn their attention to condemning the Taliban's abuse of women, which, like FGM, was sensational and extreme. U.S. public discourse, feminist activism on behalf of Muslim women, and the precedent set by Congress and the judiciary regarding FGM created an environment in which the Clinton administration could condemn the Taliban because of human rights concerns. The rise of the Taliban further cemented the idea that Muslims abused women and that the post–Cold War global mission of the United States included championing Muslim women's human rights.

Chapter 6

The Taliban, Feminist Activism,
and the Clinton Administration

Millions of Afghans have been displaced by warfare since the 1970s. During the Clinton era, refugees fled from the Taliban, who seized Kabul in late 1996. In November 1997, Secretary of State Madeleine Albright visited a refugee camp in Nasir Bagh, Pakistan, which was home to approximately eighty thousand Afghans. Reporters who accompanied Albright described the camp's conditions as "bleak." There, amid the "mud huts and tattered tents," Albright listened intently as a group of Afghan women told her about their experiences with Taliban oppression. "Clearly moved," she promised, "I will do everything I can to help your country." After giving an address in the camp's courtyard, the secretary got down on her knees in the dirt to speak to some schoolgirls, whose small classroom lacked desks and chairs. She told them, "I hope I can come visit you again—but come to an Afghanistan where you can live as full equals."[1] Albright used a significant portion of her brief visit to Pakistan to condemn the Taliban's "despicable" human rights violations against Afghan women and girls, despite her Pakistani hosts' support for the new regime in Kabul.[2]

Albright's intimate moment with the refugees at Nasir Bagh illustrated a broader, revolutionary shift in foreign policy priorities during the Clinton years. Clinton's administration did not abandon traditional American policy goals, but it did try to institutionalize the protection and promotion of women's human rights as a central tenet of U.S. foreign policy. That the nation's top diplomat—and its first female secretary of state—had traveled around the globe to meet with Afghan women and girls underscored the administration's priorities. This policy shift had profound implications for U.S. relations with the Islamic world.

American concern about—and engagement with—Muslim countries intensified during Clinton's eight years in office. Terrorist attacks perpetrated by radical Islamic groups like al Qaeda that targeted Americans both in the United States and abroad frightened the public and concerned policymakers.[3] Civil war in Somalia and genocide in the Balkans prompted U.S. "humanitarian interventions" and global condemnation of Serbians' use of rape as a weapon of war against Bosnian Muslims. The public, journalists, scholars, filmmakers, and others in the United States continued to decry violations of women's human rights in Islamic countries. Beyond the campaign against female genital mutilation, the central issue that mobilized Americans on behalf of Muslim women during this period was the rise of the Taliban in Afghanistan. The Taliban's harshly regressive gender policies were the clearest example of the Islamic oppression of women for those who sought to defend women's human rights.

The growing number, political savvy, and experience of women's NGOs reinvigorated feminist activism in the 1990s in the United States and internationally, demonstrated by the successes of the anti-FGM movement. This increasingly powerful transnational feminist movement, coupled with U.S. policies on FGM, built on the anti–gender apartheid protests during the Gulf War to create an environment in which the defense of women's human rights increasingly became a legitimate expression of American identity on the world stage. Quite simply, human rights, especially women's, were mainstreamed.

The Clinton administration—which included liberal feminists in key government positions—worked to institutionalize women's rights as a major area of concern, both domestically and in foreign policy. Clinton also appointed feminist Madeleine Albright as his second secretary of state just after the Taliban seized power. Feminist NGOs, including SIGI, WLUML, and the Feminist Majority Foundation (FMF), mobilized around the issue of "gender apartheid" in Afghanistan and successfully lobbied the administration to condemn the Taliban. This confluence of factors advanced women's human rights as a major focus of U.S. policy in Afghanistan. By 1998, the United States denied recognition to the Taliban because of their treatment of women. The administration's stance sent a clear message that women's human rights were henceforth a legitimate and important concern for U.S. policy in the Islamic world. This policy may appear overdetermined, but it was actually highly contingent, as U.S. economic and other hard power interests initially pushed some policymakers toward engagement with the Taliban.

The Taliban first emerged as a political force when they seized the southern Afghan city of Kandahar in late 1994. They gained control of Herat the following year and captured international attention in September 1996 when they seized Kabul and overthrew the Afghan government.[4] The Taliban—a group whose name derives from the Arabic word *talib* or "student"—included among their ranks young men from refugee camps in Pakistan, as well as veterans of the Soviet-Afghan War. Most were Pashtuns, the majority ethnic group in Afghanistan and western Pakistan.[5] The Taliban claimed to be "a movement motivated by Islam, desiring to unify and purify Afghanistan."[6] Once in power, they established a theocracy of sorts and sought to implement an ultra-strict, radically fundamentalist version of Islamic law. Like Khomeini a decade and a half earlier, they specifically targeted women in their bid to remake society. The Taliban's rise perplexed many in the West, who had not paid much attention to Afghanistan since the end of the Soviet-Afghan War in 1989.[7] Yet, as one scholar pointed out, "the Taliban did not emerge from nowhere."[8] Their rise was directly related to the Soviet-Afghan War and U.S. policies that aimed to thwart Communist aggression in Central Asia.

The USSR had invaded Afghanistan in December 1979 to prop up the faltering Afghan communist regime, which seized power in 1978 in the midst of political turbulence. A minority group, the Soviet-backed communists embarked upon a course of land redistribution, secularization, and political repression that sparked rebellion among the overwhelmingly Muslim and anti-communist Afghan population.[9] Because communism is atheistic, many Afghans framed their opposition in religious terms. Anti-communist rebels became known as the mujahideen, or "warriors in the way of God."[10] They responded to local leaders' calls for jihad against "the infidel communists."[11] The mujahideen, however, were far from homogeneous. They included at least seven different factions: most were Sunnis, some were Shi'a, and their interpretations of Islam varied widely. The mujahideen were also divided along ethnic, linguistic, and regional lines.[12] The rebels' mutual opposition to the communists bound them together, albeit fragilely, during the war.

From the U.S. perspective, the Soviet invasion of Afghanistan irrefutably proved global communist aggression. What remained of détente by 1979 disappeared completely once the Red Army crossed the Afghan border. To foil Soviet plans for Central Asia, the Carter and Reagan administrations threw their support behind the mujahideen. Despite the troubling rise of fundamentalism in Iran that same year, U.S. policymakers—from Capitol Hill to Langley to the White House—provided a stream of covert military and financial aid to the mujahideen with the assumption that they could wield Islam as a weapon in the Cold War.[13]

Few Americans asked questions about the mujahideen during the war.[14] U.S. newspapers condemned only Soviet war crimes and detailed Afghan suffering.[15] Meanwhile, Helsinki Watch, a U.S.-based human rights NGO (which reconstituted itself as Human Rights Watch in 1988), documented and reported Soviet atrocities but largely ignored rebel brutality.[16] American policymakers, for their part, eagerly touted the Afghans' cause. President Reagan welcomed mujahideen leaders to the White House in 1985 and hailed them as freedom-fighters.[17]

The United States secretly provided an estimated $10 billion in aid to the mujahideen.[18] To the detriment of women, the factions that received the most U.S. aid had the most retrograde views on women's rights. This occurred in part because the United States funneled aid covertly to Afghanistan via Pakistan and relied upon the advice of Pakistani intelligence, the Inter-Services Intelligence (ISI). Supporting the most fundamentalist factions of the mujahideen fit well with Pakistan's agenda, which was after all governed by the fundamentalist general Zia ul-Haq. While Carter initially cut aid to Pakistan after Zia seized power, the Reagan administration reversed course because of the Soviet-Afghan War. Consequently, Pakistan became the third-largest recipient of U.S. foreign aid during the Reagan years.[19]

The rebel leader who received the preponderance of American support was Gulbuddin Hekmatyar, who had led campaigns to throw acid into the faces of unveiled women in the early 1970s.[20] According to one expert, Hekmatyar received "more than half of CIA covert resources, estimated to be worth $2 billion over the ten-year war."[21] The CIA recognized his brutality, but they saw it as an asset when directed against the Soviets. Unfortunately, Hekmatyar unleashed a wave of violence not only upon the communists but also against rival mujahideen factions and civilians. He systematically targeted educated Afghans in the refugee camps in Pakistan, claiming they were "insufficiently Islamic," and Hekmatyar's followers imposed their version of "proper" Islamic veiling and raped and killed women with impunity. Among the women Hekmatyar and his men murdered was Meena Ahmad, founder of the Revolutionary Association of the Women of Afghanistan (RAWA), a secular women's rights organization established in 1977 that resisted both the communists and the fundamentalists.[22] Such persecution ensured that the population of moderate Afghans would later be too small and weak to resist the Taliban.

The USSR withdrew from Afghanistan in defeat in 1989, and the mujahideen finally succeeded in overthrowing the barely surviving communist government in April 1992. The rebels quickly formed a government headed by President Burhanuddin Rabbani, but his administration did not bring peace or stability.[23] Instead, the mujahideen turned on one another almost immediately. The rebel movement fractured along ethnic, linguistic, religious, and ideological lines, and intra-mujahideen disputes were magnified by foreign manipulations.[24] Any chance for national unity evaporated. Instead, faction leaders operated as warlords and waged bloody battles with one another for regional control. As the country descended into civil war, Afghanistan became a "failed state."

The Taliban formed in this context. Their shadowy leader, the one-eyed Mullah Muhammed Omar, mobilized his followers to "restore peace, disarm the population, enforce Sharia law and defend the integrity and Islamic character of Afghanistan." In contrast to the corruption and brutality of the mujahideen, the Taliban cast themselves as "a movement for cleansing society," which appealed to young men who had been born in refugee camps and educated in Pakistani madrassas about "the ideal Islamic society created by the Prophet Mohammed."[25] Ironically, the group's first action was in response to the kidnapping and rape of two teenage girls by a warlord in Kandahar in 1994. The Taliban rescued the girls and hanged the commander from one of his tanks.[26] Mullah Omar later explained, "We were fighting against Muslims who had gone wrong. How could we remain quiet when we could see crimes being committed against women and the poor?"[27] Despite such rhetoric, it quickly became apparent that the Taliban were not Afghans' saviors.

Once they seized control of an area, they imposed draconian codes of "pious" behavior. After capturing Kabul, the Taliban decreed that all men in the city had six weeks to grow a full beard and imprisoned any man whose

beard was insufficient until it grew to the correct length. Homosexuality became a capital offense; prayer five times a day was mandatory. The Taliban
banned television; the Internet; movies; music; singing and dancing; the
keeping of pigeons; kite flying (a favorite hobby in Kabul); making and/or
displaying photographs, portraits, or other images; gambling; long hair for
men; alcohol; and charging interest on loans.[28] They also outlawed many
holidays, including religious ones, because they deemed festivities of any
kind un-Islamic.[29] Armed religious police patrolled the streets and did not
hesitate to beat, imprison, or execute anyone who violated their decrees.[30]

Key to the Taliban's vision was the radical subordination of women.[31] In
every area they controlled, they sought to erase women completely from public life. Thus they prohibited women from working and closed girls' schools.
When women left their homes, they had to be accompanied by male relatives
and wear the burqa, a veil (usually blue or yellow) that covered the entire body,
including the face. A woman wearing a burqa could only see through a mesh
panel that obscured her eyes.[32] The Taliban decreed that women who left their
homes improperly veiled and/or without a male escort "[would] be threatened,
investigated and severely punished."[33] Women were also forbidden from
wearing makeup, Western-style clothing, or high heels. The Taliban closed
beauty parlors, hair salons, and women's bathhouses, which were often the
only places where women had access to hot water. Hospitals were segregated
according to sex, and male doctors were not permitted to treat women.[34]

The Taliban meted out brutal punishments for violating these edicts, including public executions in the Kabul soccer stadium, which RAWA secretly
recorded and publicized internationally.[35] Although Afghan women's status
had slipped since the 1970s as a result of warfare and fundamentalist warlords, the Taliban's treatment of women was radically worse than anything
that had come before.[36] Prior to 1996, "there was no universal standard of
tradition or culture for women's role in society" in Afghanistan, so the Taliban tried to invent one.[37] Given the group's brutality, the international community could not ignore their violations of women's human rights once they
seized Kabul. As they had regarding Iran in 1979, Americans reacted intensely to the loss of women's rights in an Islamic country.

When Taliban abuses came to light in 1996, the transnational feminist movement was in a position to do something about the situation. By the end of
the UN Decade for Women, activists had learned how to lobby governments

and the United Nations effectively, and they used that expertise to launch a well-organized campaign to put women's human rights at the center of the international agenda, aided by the changing international system. When the Cold War ended, the United Nations was revitalized to address concerns common to all nations: human rights, population, development, and environmental degradation. Freed from the confines of the Cold War, it pursued reforms of international law with renewed purpose.

Feminists were particularly successful in getting women's human rights on the itinerary of the 1993 UN World Conference on Human Rights in Vienna, and Americans played a vital role in that campaign.[38] Previously, the United Nations had treated women's rights and human rights as separate categories, so feminists' primary goal was for the Vienna conference to declare that women's rights *are* human rights. The widespread rape of Bosnian women by Serbs as part of their "ethnic cleansing" added urgency to this goal.[39] As other scholars have explained, human rights had an "exploding power" in the 1990s, and violence against women encouraged the "mainstreaming of feminism" internationally.[40]

After a sophisticated campaign, feminists were successful in getting the United Nations to declare that women's rights *are* human rights. The Vienna Declaration and Programme of Action stated unequivocally, "The human rights of women and the girl-child are an inalienable, integral and indivisible part of universal human rights."[41] Significant for activists working in the Muslim world, the Vienna Declaration also called for "the eradication of any conflicts which may arise between the rights of women and the harmful effects of certain traditional or customary practices."[42] This statement negated the Taliban's later claims that their treatment of women was a cultural issue that was not the concern of outsiders.[43]

The expansion of human rights law that they helped bring about allowed feminists to pressure states—including the United States—to take action to protect women from human rights abuses committed in the private sphere. With this shift, transnational feminists influenced international agreements that emerged from the other UN world conferences of the 1990s, particularly the ICPD and the Fourth World Conference on Women.[44] Feminist NGOs that lobbied the U.S. government included WLUML, SIGI, and the Feminist Majority, who became major players in international debates about the rights and status of women in Islamic societies.

Although WLUML was primarily an information network, it helped shape the international response to the Taliban by immediately and consistently publicizing the group's atrocities. WLUML urged other NGOs to lobby governments and the United Nations to act against the new Afghan regime, and it devoted half of its next *Dossier* published after the Taliban seized Kabul to the situation of Afghan women, which included firsthand reports by the Pakistan-based Afghan Women's Network (AWN). AWN, which also received support from SIGI, characterized Kabul as "the world's largest prison for women." It implored those reading the *Dossier* to oppose recognition of the Taliban regime by the United States, the United Nations, and other governments.[45] Every WLUML *Dossier* thereafter contained multiple stories detailing ongoing violations of Afghan women's human rights.[46]

WLUML also publicized other NGOs' campaigns, including those of SIGI and Afghan groups, and urged its members to circulate a petition to the international community—naming the U.S. government specifically—"to hold the Taliban accountable to uphold and respect the human, civil and political rights of Afghan women, girls and men. We call upon these bodies to withhold: recognition of the Taliban; access to the UN seat; and donor assistance."[47] Although WLUML lacked the staff and political access to lobby the U.S. government directly, it provided invaluable information, including firsthand accounts from Afghanistan, for other organizations like SIGI to use when lobbying American policymakers.

The reinvigoration of international feminist activism revitalized SIGI, which played an important role in the eventual U.S. policy of non-recognition. After Mahnaz Afkhami became the NGO's leader in 1992, SIGI chose to focus primarily on Muslim women. Afkhami consulted with fellow members Nawal el Saadawi and Fatima Mernissi, and they decided, "There was hardly anywhere where women were legally as constrained as they were in these societies. So one way of getting a momentum going is starting from a place where on the one hand, there was such oppression of women legally, and on the other you had so many articulate, strong, active, independent women who were willing to work."[48] Work they did. Because of Afkhami's strong leadership, and because the organization included so many committed, prominent feminists from Islamic countries, SIGI soon became the premier transnational NGO working on behalf of Muslim women's human rights.

In addition to attracting donors, launching special projects, and coordinating letter-writing campaigns, SIGI positioned itself to influence U.S. policy.[49] The organization sent a delegation to the Fourth World Conference on Women in Beijing in 1995, where Afkhami met Hillary Clinton. The First Lady then invited Afkhami to the White House a few months later for an event honoring NGOs that provided aid to Bosnia: this included SIGI's work with Bosnian refugees.[50] SIGI was now on the White House's radar. The NGO also raised its public profile by staging dozens of events that brought together scholars and activists and by attending consultative meetings at the United Nations.[51] As part of its initiatives, SIGI published *Faith and Freedom* in 1995, one of the first academic books to connect human rights concepts with the specific conditions for women in the Islamic world. Two years later, SIGI produced another volume, *Muslim Women and the Politics of Participation*.[52] These publications extended SIGI's activism into the academic realm and provided an intellectual framework for its projects.

Most important to SIGI's profile was its grassroots human rights initiative. Its members collaboratively developed the groundbreaking *Claiming Our Rights: A Manual for Women's Human Rights Education in Muslim Societies* in 1996.[53] Funded by the National Endowment for Democracy and the Ford Foundation, the manual was one of the first human rights handbooks written specifically for Muslim women. A "bottom-up and systematic human rights education" project, it laid out the various interpretations of Islamic texts pertaining to women, as well as international law on women's rights.[54] The intent was for small groups of women in Islamic countries as diverse as Iran, Malaysia, and Uzbekistan to meet and discuss how to claim their internationally guaranteed rights within their particular cultural and political contexts. Written by and for women from the Muslim world, *Claiming Our Rights* was a tremendous success. It was published in a dozen languages and spawned human rights education workshops across the Islamic world.[55] SIGI thus established itself as an influential transnational organization just as the Taliban seized power. Largely dominated by feminists from Muslim countries, the NGO put itself in a position to lobby policymakers just as the U.S. government was deciding how to deal with the Taliban.

Feminist organizations were capable of mounting an effective public campaign against the Taliban, but to succeed at the policy level, high-ranking U.S. officials had to listen to organizations like SIGI and take their recommendations seriously. Fortunately for feminists, the Clinton administration was sympathetic. Clinton's election in 1992 (and reelection in 1996) was due largely to the support of women voters, and his administration was the most pro-feminist to date.[56] Key policymakers were predisposed to oppose the Taliban, but non-recognition was not guaranteed when the group first seized

Kabul. Economic and strategic concerns suggested that it would be in the U.S. interest to engage with the Taliban. Feminist NGOs' lobbying on behalf of Afghan women's human rights was therefore necessary for the administration to reject the Taliban.

While Clinton's refusal to recognize the Taliban was not inevitable, his administration's gender politics created the necessary conditions for feminist organizations to succeed in their campaigns. Over the course of his presidency, Clinton proved a staunch advocate of women's rights at home and abroad. He enacted policies that upheld reproductive rights, a key issue for U.S. feminists, and threw his support behind other legislation beneficial to women, such as the Family and Medical Leave Act (1993), the Violence Against Women Act (1994), and the Children's Health Insurance Program (1997).[57] Clinton's concern for women's human rights was attuned to the greater visibility and public opinion in favor of women's rights as human rights internationally. It also meshed with his own and Hillary Rodham Clinton's values. The First Lady was deeply engrossed in policy and instrumental in advancing women's rights during her husband's presidency.[58]

As soon as President Clinton took office, he began to mainstream and institutionalize women's rights in the executive branch.[59] It was a slow process, but the administration immediately signaled its new policy imperatives. Just months after Clinton's inauguration, the U.S. delegation supported the Vienna conference agenda. Secretary of State Warren Christopher later explained, "The June 1993 conference in Vienna provided an excellent opportunity to revitalize American commitment to human rights as an integral part of our foreign policy," which included supporting the conference's special focus on women's rights.[60]

Key U.S. figures used the same language as the global feminist movement to announce American policy. In his address to the opening session of the Vienna conference, Christopher, who had built his career as a defender of civil rights and human rights, highlighted women's human rights as an area of particular concern: "The United States will also act to integrate our concerns over the inhumane treatment of women into the global human rights agenda. . . . Guaranteeing human rights is a moral imperative with respect to both men and women. It is also an investment in making whole nations stronger, fairer, and better."[61] The United States collaborated with women's groups to shape the conference's outcome.

In his September 1993 report to the House Foreign Affairs Committee, Assistant Secretary of State for Human Rights and Humanitarian Affairs

John Shattuck—a longtime human rights advocate—stressed the administration's commitment to making women's rights central to foreign policy. He reiterated, "Women's rights are human rights." After detailing ongoing violations of women's rights in Bosnia, Iran, and Saudi Arabia (unusual for a U.S. official), Shattuck reaffirmed a key point from Vienna: "Some governments excuse the fact that women have a lesser status than men by pointing to culture and tradition. However, culture and tradition cannot excuse gross and systematic violations of human rights. One of our primary goals at the World Conference on Human Rights was to stress that human rights are universal. As Secretary Christopher said in his speech to the conference, 'We cannot let cultural relativism become the last refuge of repression.' . . . Governments that promote or turn a blind eye to gender-based violence are denying basic human rights." Shattuck concluded his testimony by enumerating various U.S. policies to implement the principles of Vienna, such as new USAID programs to "increase women's access to education, health care, and income" and institutionalize women in development (WID) principles in U.S. foreign aid. This included programs to help end FGM in Africa, which predated the 1996 congressional legislation on FGM by almost three years.[62]

Shattuck also announced that the administration sought U.S. ratification of CEDAW, support for the establishment of a UN High Commissioner for Human Rights, the prosecution of rape "as a war crime and a tool of ethnic cleansing" in the former Yugoslavia, the inclusion of women's human rights data in U.S. human rights reports, a focus on women's rights in U.S. democracy promotion initiatives, and the creation of a full-time position in the State Department for women's issues.[63] These demonstrated a serious attempt at gender mainstreaming within Clinton's foreign policy apparatus and a deliberate alignment of the administration's gender framework with transnational feminists' agenda.

Significantly, in its later policies to uphold women's human rights in Islamic countries, the administration consistently deployed the women's human rights framework rather than the discursive logic of colonial feminism, Islamophobia, or Orientalism. This aligned Clinton's administration with the transnational feminist movement, the United Nations, and international human rights law. Though not without problems, Clinton's approach to women's human rights in the Islamic world tried to eschew neoimperialism. When subsequent administrations took up the issue, they did not always employ the same logic.

Before the Taliban's rise, Clinton had institutionalized women's human rights in the executive branch: he "maintained special channels relating to women's policy issues" through the White House Office for Women's Initiatives and the President's Interagency Council on Women (PICW).[64] Clinton created the PICW to ensure that his administration followed through on its commitments to women's human rights after the Beijing conference. The PICW facilitated cooperation and coordination between agencies across the executive branch and brought high-level representatives from each agency together. The First Lady was the PICW's deeply involved honorary chair. Donna Shalala, the secretary of health and human services and co-chair of the U.S. delegation to Beijing, was its first chair from 1995 to 1996; Secretary of State Madeleine Albright chaired the PICW from 1997 until Clinton left office. Theresa Loar, a career foreign service officer, was tapped to serve as the council's director and as the representative from the State Department.[65]

The PICW not only accelerated gender mainstreaming, but it also laid the groundwork for U.S. non-recognition of the Taliban in important ways. Notably, the council brought its members together with NGOs and women's human rights activists. According to Loar, "Bringing NGOs into the process of government" was a key goal of the PICW, something that U.S. foreign policy institutions had done only rarely in the past.[66] To that end, the PICW held regular public briefings for NGOs and interested members of the public, as well as a nationwide satellite briefing in 1996 in which 60,000–80,000 people participated.[67] By giving NGOs more access to government, the PICW helped set in motion the process by which feminist NGOs directly influenced U.S. policy toward Afghanistan.

Loar herself also became a key player in foreign policy circles. In addition to serving as the PICW director, she served as the Senior Coordinator for International Women's Issues (SCIWI) through the State Department's Global Affairs Office starting in late 1996. Her experience as a career foreign service officer, combined with her position on the PICW, ensured that she could push effectively for women's human rights to be at the center of U.S. policy on Afghanistan.[68] Her contacts from the PICW, especially the First Lady's Office and the NGO community, proved invaluable to her work on the Taliban after she began her position as SCIWI.

The creation of the SCIWI position was part of a broader reorganization of the State Department that also influenced the outcome of U.S. policy deliberations on Afghanistan. In February 1993, the administration announced the creation of a new office that reflected the changing nature of the international system: the Office of Global Affairs, which became operational in May 1994.[69] Undersecretary of State Timothy Wirth, whom one historian characterized as a "feminist ally," headed the new office.[70] The reorganization reflected the administration's increasing focus on issues that did not fit neatly into State's existing regional divisions. Wirth oversaw the Bureaus of Democracy, Human Rights, and Labor; Narcotics, Terrorism, and Crime; Population, Refugees, and Migration; and Oceans, Environment, and Science.[71] Wirth initiated the opening of State to NGO access, consultation, and cooperation.[72] While it had not been part of the culture at State to work with NGOs before the Clinton era, the initiatives of Wirth and the PICW made consultation and cooperation with NGOs more commonplace.

These changes in the State Department included the creation of the Office of International Women's Issues (OIWI) in 1994 under the auspices of the Office of Global Affairs.[73] The Senior Coordinator for International Women's Issues was a senior-level diplomatic position meant to initiate the process of gender mainstreaming by coordinating the many bureaus of State. According to Loar, this was "the first position really focused across the whole State Department and embassies around the world on promoting women's human rights as a foreign policy objective."[74] The first SCIWI was Gracia Hillman, who had been executive director of the League of Women Voters. During Hillman's tenure, OIWI focused on preparing State for the upcoming Beijing conference. Hillman left government shortly after Beijing, and her post remained unfilled for most of 1996.[75]

When Loar replaced Hillman in October 1996, the OIWI began to have a real impact. Unlike Hillman, Loar had an intimate knowledge of the State Department, extensive foreign policy experience, and connections with NGOs and high-ranking members of other government agencies. She remained committed to working with NGOs as she took up her new position. In her later years as SCIWI, Loar worked closely with the First Lady's office to launch the Vital Voices Initiative, which promoted democracy and women's full participation in multiple countries, and to develop an anti–human trafficking program.[76] Her first task, however, was responding to the rise of the Taliban, which seized Kabul just days before Loar began her new position.

In addition to the administration's institutional changes, the First Lady played a crucial role in supporting, developing, and articulating Clinton's global gender policies. A key example of the First Lady's public activism was her trip to the Beijing conference, which she attended over the objections of congressional Republicans to deliver Beijing's most memorable keynote address.[77] There Hillary declared, "Human rights are women's rights and women's rights are human rights."[78] She later wrote, "I hoped my presence would signal the U.S. commitment to the needs and rights of women in international policy."[79] In her speech, Hillary condemned the worldwide abuse of women and affirmed U.S. support for women's human rights. As she concluded her address, the audience leapt to its feet for a lengthy standing ovation.[80] The First Lady's declaration was international front-page news; the *New York Times* declared that the speech "may have been her finest moment in public life."[81] Bill Clinton later characterized the Beijing address as "one of the most important speeches delivered by anyone in our administration during our entire eight years."[82] Hillary's speech was not merely rhetoric; it was a reaffirmation of the policy shift underway since 1993.

The First Lady was also an important advisor to the president regarding political appointments.[83] Relevant to this story, Clinton appointed the first female secretary of state when he replaced Warren Christopher with Madeleine Albright at the start of his second term. Albright had served as Clinton's UN ambassador during his first term, and she was a strong advocate for women's rights. Hillary Clinton "enthusiastically" backed Albright's nomination, and her appointment underscored the importance of women's rights in foreign policy.[84] When President Clinton declared in December 1996, "We are putting our efforts to protect and advance women's rights where they belong—in the mainstream of American foreign policy," he was asserting his administration's ongoing commitment.[85]

Thus, when the Taliban took power in the fall of 1996, they faced a U.S. administration with very different foreign policy priorities than those of its predecessors. Clinton's focus on women and myriad efforts to institutionalize women's human rights in U.S. foreign policy created a situation in which it was unlikely that high-ranking American policymakers would embrace an Islamic regime that oppressed women. But U.S. non-recognition of the Taliban was not preordained.

Traditional policy concerns suggested that the United States should work with the Taliban; consequently, Warren Christopher's State Department was cautiously friendly toward the Taliban at first. Confidential government documents indicate that U.S. officials, including Assistant Secretary of State for South Asia Robin Raphel, met with Taliban representatives starting in early

1995.[86] Within a few days of the fall of Kabul, State Department representatives declared they sought dialogue with the new regime and indicated interest in reopening the U.S. embassy in Kabul, despite expressing reservations about the Taliban's "heavy-handed style of conservative Islam."[87]

Although much of the State Department record remains classified, the available evidence suggests that its embrace of the Taliban did not come from Secretary Christopher or the White House. Rather, the South Asia Bureau took the lead in developing State's initial response to the Taliban takeover. Christopher, who was planning his retirement, did not speak publicly about the Taliban and was deeply engaged elsewhere when Kabul fell.[88] While the secretary had a long history of supporting human rights, the people who staffed the Afghan desk and South Asia Bureau do not appear to have shared Christopher's priorities or the administration's commitment to women's human rights. Clinton's mainstreaming efforts were, after all, only three years old; they had not yet permeated all State Department bureaus. While Raphel appears to have been largely indifferent to women's rights concerns, Loar described some members of the Afghan desk, such as Lee Coldren, as actively hostile to the idea of prioritizing women's human rights over other, more traditional policy considerations: Coldren "considered this annoying focus on women to be distracting."[89]

There were several reasons why some members of Christopher's State Department were willing to deal with the Taliban. Most of them had to do with the fact that the culture at State and its historical structures predisposed it to pursue a traditional policy agenda, which privileged hard power issues like geostrategy and economics over ones that less clearly affected the national interest, such as human rights. One primary motivation for engaging the Taliban was regional stability. After over fifteen years of bloodshed and political crisis in Afghanistan, to which U.S. policy had contributed, some at Foggy Bottom welcomed a force that promised peace and order. Since they controlled the majority of Afghanistan, the Taliban appeared to be the most likely candidates to bring stability to Central Asia.[90]

Some at State also hoped that the new regime would curb Afghan opium production.[91] The international drug trade was a major concern, and U.S. reports indicated that the Taliban opposed opium cultivation on religious grounds. Some officials hoped that the Taliban would prove useful partners in the global war on drugs.[92] The State Department wrote to the U.S. embassy in Islamabad in late September 1996, "We have welcomed your reassurances that the Taliban condemn narcotics as un-Islamic. . . . We hope that the

Taliban will make one of its first tasks the public condemnation in clear terms of narcotics growing and trafficking." State expressed its additional (albeit misguided) desire that the Taliban might help the United States fight terrorism, asking them to assist with locating "ex-Saudi financier and radical Islamist Osama bin Laden," who, the United States believed, was in Afghanistan.[93]

Furthermore, in 1996 the United States still relied on Pakistani advice about Central Asia. Pakistan's government supported the Taliban and may even have helped orchestrate their rise to power. It was one of only three nations to recognize the Taliban as a legitimate government; Islamabad extended recognition almost immediately after the fall of Kabul.[94] It is likely, therefore, that some State Department officials were influenced by Pakistan's counsel.[95]

Perhaps most important, there was strong economic motivation to establish a working relationship with Afghanistan. The U.S. oil company Unocal had developed a plan with a Saudi company to build oil and gas pipelines across Central Asia, which would connect the oil and gas reserves of Turkmenistan, Uzbekistan, and Kazakhstan to global markets via Pakistan. The project would enrich all those connected with it. Analysts at the time believed that there were vast, untapped oil and natural gas reserves estimated to be worth $4 trillion waiting to be exploited in Central Asia, making the region the "next Middle East."[96] Beyond its obvious economic appeal, the project had the added benefit of bypassing Iran, the common rival of Saudi Arabia, Pakistan, and the United States for influence in the region.

For the project to succeed, however, the pipelines had to cross Afghanistan. The Rabbani government had been unable to provide the necessary security for pipeline construction, and before they even ousted Rabbani, the Taliban promised protection for the project.[97] Unocal representatives therefore advocated a U.S. policy of engagement and, once the Taliban seized Kabul, spoke "glowingly about the immediate prospects of doing business with them."[98] Unocal clearly hoped that U.S. foreign policy would help its bottom line.

The company spent $2 million in 1996–97 to lobby Capitol Hill, the White House, and State to support the pipeline deal. Unocal also hired consultants, including ex-U.S. officials like Robert Oakley, the former U.S. ambassador to Pakistan, and Zalmay Khalilzad, who worked the State Department Afghan desk in the 1980s. Khalilzad, who later became a key advisor to George W. Bush, worked particularly hard to convince the American public to see the Taliban positively.[99] In an October 1996 *Washington Post* op-ed, Khalilzad claimed, "The Taliban does not practice the anti-U.S. style of fundamentalism practiced by Iran," so Americans had nothing to fear from them. Moreover, he asserted that the United States had a "moral obligation" to bring peace to Afghanistan; the United States should engage the Taliban diplomatically and support the Unocal pipeline. He wrote, "We should use as a positive incentive the benefits that will accrue to Afghanistan from the construction of oil and gas pipelines across its territory" as a way to bring peace and stability.[100] He neglected to mention that the Taliban brutalized women and girls.

Administration officials appreciated the potential strategic and economic benefits of the pipeline. As early as 1995, the United States expressed support for it when Clinton convinced the president of Turkmenistan to sign a contract with Unocal. Robin Raphel announced official U.S. backing for the project in early 1996 and held a lengthy meeting with President Niyazov of Turkmenistan to help the pipeline deal move forward. The situation in Afghanistan dominated their discussion.[101] Meanwhile, the U.S. embassy in Islamabad, which was the conduit for early U.S. contacts with the Taliban, reportedly hosted functions on behalf of Unocal, and U.S. intelligence analysts briefed oil company representatives "extensively."[102]

Despite incontrovertible evidence that the Taliban committed human rights abuses, South Asia Bureau representatives initially sought to depict the group positively. After her first meeting with the Taliban in April 1996, Raphel claimed, "They have wonderful senses of humor," despite the fact that she had to sit with her back to them because they refused to look upon her unveiled face.[103] The day after the Taliban seized Kabul, bureau spokesperson Glyn Davies went so far as to tell the press, "We've seen some of the reports that they've moved to impose Islamic law in the areas that they control, but at this stage we're not reading anything into that. I mean, there's on the face of it nothing objectionable."[104] The combined policy imperatives for stability, curbs on opium production, and oil revenues led some in the South Asia Bureau to take an initially benign view of the Taliban. Moreover, their public statements gave the impression that the administration might welcome the new regime in Kabul.

The State Department's stance puzzled many journalists. Almost as soon as the Taliban marched into Kabul, American reporters began to file stories detailing the human rights abuses women suffered at their hands.[105] Such reports reinforced already existing American perceptions of the status of women in Islamic countries, kindled by the "gender apartheid" accounts from the Gulf War. They also spurred the public—which had recently mobilized to condemn FGM—to speak out against the abuse of Afghan women.

Kathy Gannon of the Associated Press told her readers in early October about the Taliban's regressive views. Drawing upon the Orientalist theme of uncivilized Muslim men, she described a Taliban leader, who had "one eye, a wooden leg and a patchy grizzled beard beneath his black turban" with an "artificial foot shod in a ragged shoe, his good foot totally bare" who became "enraged" when he caught some of his men meeting with Gannon and three other American reporters. His "voice shaking with fury," he "roared at his local commanders: 'Why are you talking to these infidels?'" The mullah was especially upset about Gannon's presence, so he slapped one of his men in the face for speaking to her.[106]

After framing her story with this encounter, Gannon went on to describe how the Taliban immediately moved "to establish their version of Islamic law." This included closing girls' schools, banning women from working, and forcing women "to envelop themselves in yards of material from head to foot." The result was that women "have virtually disappeared from the streets." Those who did venture out, she explained, faced violent abuse, even when properly veiled. "Taliban fighters were seen whipping two women with a car radio antenna in Kabul. It is not clear why the women were attacked, as both were dressed according to the rules. No one attempted to intervene," she reported.[107]

Countless similar stories appeared in the U.S. media that cast doubt on the wisdom of State's apparent overtures to the new regime.[108] One *Washington Times* reporter commented that "the Clinton State Department's reaction to the recent tumult in Afghanistan is surprising" given the administration's earlier stance on women's human rights. The Taliban were "a bloodthirsty and obscurantist pseudo-Islamic militia" that forced women to "wear an all-enveloping laundry-bag-like garment in public," he wrote. "The Iranians—the Iranians!—attack the new rulers' 'medieval' mentality," so he wondered why State would "cozy up" to the Taliban.[109] Another journalist was equally incredulous and could not fathom why "the United States says it's ready and willing to work with the hard-line Taliban movement.... How can this be?"[110]

Such questions ignored the historic U.S. alliance with Saudi Arabia, but they did point out the inconsistency in the administration's emphasis on women's rights but apparent embrace of the Taliban. In addition to the media's numerous condemnations of the Taliban from September 1996 onward, feminist organizations launched campaigns to mobilize the public. NOW (which had spearheaded the Gulf War protests) and the Feminist Majority denounced the Taliban and Unocal's pipeline plans, while SIGI and WLUML issued Action Alerts to mobilize their constituencies.[111] According to Valentine Moghadam, "WLUML and SIGI were especially effective in transmitting information, news, and action alerts, and in working with UN agencies to keep up the pressure on the Taliban."[112]

Confronted with mounting public outcry, in October the administration moved to distance itself from the Taliban. *New York Times* reporter Elaine Sciolino charged that Clinton did not want his administration—or reelection campaign—associated with an Islamic regime that oppressed women. Sciolino described how State Department spokespeople scrambled to retract Davies's remarks from earlier that month. Senior officials now claimed there was a "total misperception that we were recognizing and embracing the Taliban." To correct course, State expressed its "concern about the Taliban's human rights record."[113]

Based on the available evidence, more than simple electoral politics were at play here. Reelection considerations aside, the South Asia Bureau's approach directly contradicted the administration's core values, and there was a power struggle occurring behind the scenes in the State Department. The most influential members of the South Asia Bureau and Afghan desk advocated a policy of engagement with the Taliban and opposed putting human rights at the center of U.S. policy. Meanwhile, Loar believed that women's human rights must be the focus of U.S. policy in Afghanistan. Because Loar's position was so new, it was unclear whether the Afghan hands or SCIWI carried more institutional weight. As a highly competent policy entrepreneur, Loar used the novelty of her position to define her own status and to turn the OIWI into a truly influential office. The administration's prior human rights policies added weight to her initiatives, and she worked to wrest control of Afghan policy away from the South Asia Bureau. Given State's earlier, positive statements about the Taliban and the dire situation Afghan women faced, Loar had to act fast to change course.[114]

Because of the coincidence of the timing of her appointment and the Taliban's rise, Afghanistan dominated Loar's agenda for the next several years. She later explained, "When the Taliban came, it was almost like a direct challenge to that whole concept [women's human rights]." It was "a very black and white issue."[115] Loar tirelessly waged the uphill battle of changing the bureaucracy to put women's human rights on the agenda of every State Department bureau.

Loar was aware that the South Asia Bureau rejected her views. Had she held a different position, the Bureau might have been able to block her agenda: typically, the South Asia Bureau signed off on policy recommendations for Afghanistan. Loar, however, embraced the ambiguity of her position to invent a new bureaucratic hierarchy. Instead of asking the Bureau to approve her initiatives, Loar simply circumvented it and went straight to Nick Burns, spokesman of the Department of State and acting assistant secretary for public affairs. He was a close advisor to Christopher and quickly became a staunch ally of OIWI.[116]

Burns began issuing condemnations of the Taliban to backpedal from Raphel's and Davies's earlier remarks. Loar later explained that she "needed that counterweight to the very aggressive, hostile . . . bordering-on-bullying tactics coming from the South Asia Bureau." When she went to the Bureau to share the advice she gave to Burns, "there was yelling, and there was slamming of doors, and there were disparaging remarks" from the Afghan desk. As a goodwill gesture, Loar kept the Bureau informed and hoped that they would "come around," but she was unable to win over the Afghan hands.[117]

Her efforts began to pay off elsewhere, as Loar and OIWI cultivated more powerful allies. Burns consistently highlighted the issue of women's rights in Afghanistan from late 1996 until he became the U.S. ambassador to Greece in 1997.[118] Undersecretary Wirth, Loar's superior, did not personally focus on Afghanistan, but he gave Loar free rein to pursue her agenda. Wirth also brought Loar with him to weekly meetings of the assistant secretaries from across State so that she could brief them about Afghan women's issues. Through such meetings, Loar cultivated a close working relationship with Allan Jury, director of policy and resource planning at the Bureau of Population, Refugees, and Migration. Loar cleared diplomatic cables for him and attended donor meetings to ensure that aid reached Afghan women through Jury's office.[119] Most important, the secretary of state himself supported Loar's initiatives.[120]

While Christopher remained publicly silent about Afghanistan, he allowed Burns to express concern about Afghan women. Christopher also weighed in on the issue outside the public eye. Supporting a regime like the Taliban surely violated his core beliefs about human rights. On December 10, 1996, just before he retired, Christopher directed Raphel to respond to a

November letter from the Taliban's acting foreign minister, Mullah Ghaus. Although the Taliban's original letter is unavailable, Ghaus appears to have written seeking U.S. support for the Taliban to fill Afghanistan's seat at the United Nations. Raphel's reply repeated many of the concerns expressed in earlier State Department reports about opium, regional stability, and terrorism. However, her cable also emphasized women's rights, a theme absent in her earlier interactions with the Taliban. She wrote, "The Taliban's gender policies have cost it the necessary support of the international community. The discriminatory treatment of women, especially the prohibitions forbidding women to work and girls from attending school, violates international human rights covenants and general principles of customary international law binding on Afghanistan." Raphel continued, "The policy of the United States towards the Afghan groups has not changed since Kabul fell to Taliban control. We continue to maintain contacts with all the various groups. We urge all parties to continue pursuing political talks under UN auspices aimed at achieving a broad-based, fully representative national government. . . . Whatever government is formed in Afghanistan must respect the rights of all its citizens."[121] Given that Raphel favored engagement and consistently downplayed human rights as late as that November, the letter undoubtedly reflected Christopher's stance, not hers.[122] It was clear that State's mood had changed by late 1996, largely due to the efforts of OIWI.

In addition to orchestrating this shift, Loar cooperated with a variety of people from other organizations to craft a policy that condemned the Taliban's repeated violations of women's human rights: NGOs; Afghan exiles; the heads of UN agencies, such as UNICEF, UNIFEM, and the World Food Program; officials from other agencies across the State Department; and the First Lady—who, according to Loar, was intimately involved with "all of the women's human rights agenda." Loar coordinated with NGOs in particular, which were not only sources of information and counsel but also influencers of public opinion. She was particularly anxious that the NGO community learn of Burns's statements so that the administration did not appear hypocritical or insincere in its gender policies.[123] Loar cultivated the Capitol Hill constituency as well. Loar testified before Congress several times about Afghan women and the integration of women's human rights into U.S. foreign policy generally. According to Loar, condemning the Taliban's abuse of women was a topic of daily concern within the administration from October 1996 onward, so much so that she assigned staff to work on Afghanistan full-time. She explained, "Every day, it was very clear, if you're going to have women's human rights be integrated into foreign policy, be part of considerations, then you can't ignore the Afghan women's issue."[124]

Clinton's creation of OIWI and Loar's appointment had a clear impact on the development of U.S. policy toward Afghanistan. The White House went further, however, in making women's human rights an important policy consideration. Perhaps the most important step the president took to change the culture of State, and one that underscored the salience of women's issues, was his appointment of Madeleine Albright to replace Warren Christopher, who retired after Clinton won reelection. Clinton appointed Albright in December, and she took office in late January 1997. The situation in Afghanistan was not the only reason why Clinton appointed Albright, but global attention to women's human rights and public criticism of State's initial stance on the Taliban surely played a role in that decision.

The new secretary immediately instituted a sea change in State's approach to the Taliban. Although Foggy Bottom had begun to turn away from its initial statements, its public criticism of the Taliban was muted and intermittent between October and January. The South Asia Bureau also remained at odds with OIWI. Albright settled the remaining power struggle between the two, and as soon as she took office, she articulated an Afghan policy grounded in women's human rights.

The secretary "was adamant in her disdain" for the Taliban because of their mistreatment of women.[125] She made personnel changes in State that brought the Afghan desk and South Asia Bureau into alignment with her views. Every person on the Afghan desk under Christopher either retired or was reassigned by the summer of 1997, including Robin Raphel. Her replacement, Karl "Rick" Inderfurth, became a key ally to OIWI. Coldren retired and was replaced by Don Camp, who embraced the women's human rights agenda. New Afghan hands Sheldon Rapoport and Tom Hushek also became allies of OIWI.[126] The result of these personnel shifts was a 180-degree change. One scholar noted, "The new team brought with it a new outlook and a new vocabulary. What had once been vague references to international 'misgivings' about the Taliban's human rights violations became unapologetic condemnations."[127]

A month after taking office, Albright hosted a celebration of International Women's Day, where she declared, "Advancing the status of women is not only a moral imperative; it is being actively integrated into the foreign policy of the United States. It is our mission." She explicitly linked America's global identity with the promotion of women's rights—rights she saw as universal and non-negotiable. She argued, "Unfortunately, today, around the world, appalling abuses are being committed against women. There are those who suggest that many of these abuses are cultural and there's nothing we can do about them. I say they're criminal and it's the responsibility of each and every one of us to stop them."[128] The First Lady also spoke at the event. She, too, condemned the Taliban in unambiguous terms and later explained, "I believed that the United States should not recognize their government because of its oppression of women; nor should American business enter into contracts for pipeline construction or any other commercial enterprise."[129] When the First Lady condemned the Taliban, noted a journalist, "the writing was on the wall."[130]

The administration continued to criticize the Taliban throughout 1997. According to Loar, "There was never a wavering with Secretary Albright, [and Hillary] Clinton."[131] In May 1997, the PICW issued a report on America's commitment to implementing the 1995 Beijing Platform for Action. Chaired by the First Lady and secretary of state, the council reported, "State Department officials, in public statements regarding restrictions against and treatment of women in Taliban-controlled areas of Afghanistan, have linked women's human rights to a fundamental expression of foreign policy."[132] That included adopting universal human rights discourse and the principle that women's rights *are* human rights, which the transnational feminist movement had worked so successfully to enshrine in international law. Although such an approach was not unproblematic, it demonstrated a conscious attempt by the Clinton administration to avoid the yet more problematic colonialist, Islamophobic, and Orientalist approaches to women's equality by not making Islam the lens through which they saw Afghan women's situation.

That November Albright traveled to Nasir Bagh and met with Afghan girls, as described at the beginning of this chapter. Hers was the first trip by a secretary of state to South Asia in fourteen years. That Albright used a significant portion of her limited time to meet Afghan women made her priorities clear.[133] Despite the U.S. alliance with Pakistan, which maintained its pro-Taliban stance, Albright did not hesitate to warn Pakistani officials, "Your country is in danger of being isolated because of its support for the Taliban."[134] She declared, "We are opposed to the Taliban because of . . . their despicable treatment of women and children."[135] Commenting on the trip, *Washington Post* reporter Thomas Lippman wrote, "The sight of Albright on her hands and knees, greeting children in the mud-walled school of an

Afghan refugee village . . . showed how much attitudes in Washington have changed."[136]

As of 1997, the administration had yet to decide whether to adopt a formal policy of non-recognition or to pursue a more ambiguous wait-and-see approach. American policymakers needed a push, and in large part it came from NGOs like the Feminist Majority and SIGI. Western feminists were largely silent about Afghan women before 1996, but they immediately responded to Afghan and Pakistani feminists' appeals for support after the Taliban seized Kabul. They mobilized their constituents, aided by the "computer revolution" that allowed them to share information and coordinate activities much more quickly than before. Feminists worked to deny the Taliban diplomatic recognition by the United States and the international community.

The feminist campaign was effective in the United States because much of the American public already shared their negative view of Islamic fundamentalists. Because of feminism's successes over the previous three decades, the public largely accepted certain rights for women as the norm. A foundation of awareness, described in earlier chapters and built on Muslim and Western feminist voices, further primed Americans to hear the message.[137] Whatever disagreements about feminism or problems faced American women, the majority of Americans nevertheless believed that women deserved rights to education and employment, freedom of movement, choice in marriage, freedom of dress, and freedom from violence—rights denied to Afghan women by the Taliban.

The Feminist Majority launched the most vocal and publicly visible campaign against the Taliban in the United States. Founded in the late 1980s as a domestically oriented organization concerned mainly with reproductive rights, the FMF became interested in international affairs during the 1990s.[138] Because it was a group with little transnational experience, the FMF's rhetoric on international matters often contained vestiges of colonial feminism and Orientalism, as well as a rescue narrative. In contrast, experienced transnational NGOs like SIGI approached Afghan women's situation with more nuance. These groups self-consciously avoided colonial feminist approaches and situated the oppression of Afghan women in the context of universal human rights and global patriarchy.

Despite its problematic approach, the FMF proved effective domestically. It first raised alarms about the Taliban in the fall of 1996. The NGO officially launched its Campaign to End Gender Apartheid in Afghanistan in 1997, which garnered publicity. According to FMF leader Eleanor Smeal, "We decided the target would be to deny recognition of the Taliban government." Because of State's initial statements, the FMF worried that U.S. recognition was imminent, and "we saw this as a threat to our own democracy."[139] The campaign title consciously echoed the protests against the Gulf War and likened condemnation of the Taliban to the successful campaign to dismantle the South African apartheid regime.

The FMF publicized violations of Afghan women's rights and urged members of the public to contact their political representatives to demand that the United States withhold recognition from the Taliban and pressure them to stop oppressing women. The FMF also raised money to provide humanitarian and educational assistance to Afghan women.[140] Celebrity involvement enhanced the FMF's profile and brought the weight of public opinion behind its efforts. Mavis Leno, wife of *Tonight Show* host Jay Leno, chaired the campaign and was its primary spokesperson. She appeared on multiple TV shows ranging from *Larry King Live* to *Entertainment Tonight* and gave interviews to *Newsweek*, *Time*, *Vanity Fair*, *Us*, *People*, the *Washington Post*, and the *Los Angeles Times*. Each time, she highlighted the Taliban's violations of women's rights by pointing to the burqa.[141]

Without prior experience with Muslim women's issues, Leno fell back on common American stereotypes, which echoed the initial approaches of U.S. feminists in the 1970s and 1980s that Muslim feminists had fought so hard to counteract. Her focus on the veil carried Orientalist overtones and was problematic, yet her message resonated with U.S. audiences precisely because it fit with the preexisting American narrative that Muslim men oppressed women. Moreover, nuanced discussions of complex issues often fail to gain traction with the public, while sensationalized and oversimplified rhetoric can often be galvanizing. When Leno wrote an article in the popular syndicated newspaper column "Dear Abby," the FMF's telephone system crashed because of the volume of calls it received from the public about it.[142] Three hundred women's groups, trade unions, and human rights organizations also signed onto the FMF campaign.[143]

The Lenos donated $100,000 to the cause, and in early 1999 they hosted a headline-grabbing benefit event that attracted "100 A-list names," including musician Lionel Richie, comedian Lily Tomlin, and actors Sidney Poitier, Marlo Thomas, Halle Berry, Tyne Daly, Geena Davis, Kathy Bates, and "all the Judds."[144] The FMF also invited Albright, who did not attend.[145] In all, one thousand people attended the star-studded event, and powerhouse journalists Christiane Amanpour and Diane Sawyer, who traveled to Afghanistan, sent videos to the gala "about the virtual house arrest of the female population" so that "the dimmest bulb in Hollywood could hardly misunderstand what the Taliban is about."[146]

On the one hand, the Lenos and Smeal spoke in terms evocative of colonial rescue narratives that situated Americans as the liberators of the passive Afghan female captive.[147] On the other hand, notwithstanding this problematic element of their discourse, the FMF undoubtedly coordinated a sophisticated campaign that made use of mass media, the Internet, and the weight of celebrity support to get their message across to a wide American audience. They were highly successful in mobilizing public opinion against the Taliban.[148]

The Feminist Majority also targeted Unocal. Even after policymakers and the public turned against the Taliban, Unocal continued to press for the pipeline deal. It hired scholars to build goodwill toward the group in the United States. Unocal promised $1.8 million over two years to the University of Nebraska's Center for Afghanistan Studies, run by Dr. Thomas E. Gouttierre, then hired Gouttierre to establish training programs in Afghanistan to build a pipeline workforce. In return, Gouttierre told the press that the Taliban "are not out there oppressing people."[149] Such efforts were no match for the FMF. In 1998 the NGO embarrassed the company by petitioning California's state legislature to revoke Unocal's charter.[150] Mavis Leno even convinced one of Unocal's shareholders to give her his seat at a corporate meeting, where she took the company to task for promoting oppressors of women.[151] It finally became politically impossible for Unocal to continue with the pipeline. The U.S. government no longer backed the deal, and public outcry eventually forced the company to abandon the project.[152]

This was a remarkable accomplishment. Despite the FMF's troubling deployment of colonial feminist and Orientalist rhetoric, their blockage of the pipeline was inherently anti-imperial. The group had prevented Unocal from setting the political agenda in Afghanistan so that it could profit from extracting the resources of Central Asia. In this instance, the FMF foiled the profit motive that has long driven many American foreign policy decisions in the name of Afghan women's rights, which had no material benefit for the United States. Such a policy victory for human rights was rare in U.S.

history. Their actions also ensured that the Taliban were denied the ability to profit from the pipeline, which sent a clear message that violating women's human rights carried serious consequences.

SIGI also played a crucial role in influencing U.S. policy. A few months before the Taliban seized Kabul, SIGI met with Madeleine Albright, who at that time was U.S. ambassador to the United Nations. The meeting was Fatima Mernissi's idea, and Afkhami supported it. The women hoped to engage with policymakers to bring U.S. might behind their efforts in Islamic countries.[153] Albright seemed an appropriate entrée to the inner circle. She was already aware of SIGI's reputation and sympathetic to its agenda; she agreed to meet several SIGI members at her office in Washington, D.C., in early May 1996.[154] According to Afkhami, SIGI impressed upon Albright the "fact that the United States' security interests, United States' well-being depends upon moderate, tolerant democratic societies. And the people who are at the forefront of these movements and are the mobilizing elements are the women." If the United States wanted to bring about a peaceful, democratic world, "the women are the ones who are going to do it. And they need to be paid attention to. They need to be talked to, and they need to also have their needs reflected. And the policymakers in the United States need to have those issues in mind."[155] Theresa Loar, who also attended, recalled it as "a really interesting, vibrant discussion."[156] According to SIGI's report on the meeting, Albright "expressed interest in continuation of the dialogue in future meetings."[157]

For the next several years, the State Department, OIWI, and First Lady's Office sought SIGI's input regarding Afghanistan.[158] Sima Wali, an Afghan feminist and one of SIGI's founding members, also testified before Congress.[159] SIGI consistently urged U.S. policymakers to withhold recognition from the Taliban.[160] In all likelihood SIGI's urgings reinforced the administration's predisposition, but this reinforcement was pivotal. More than any other NGO in the United States, SIGI maintained contacts with prominent Afghan feminists and organizations, including Wali, RAWA, and AWN.[161] It also received and passed along information from WLUML. This allowed SIGI's members to understand and communicate Afghan women's viewpoints to policymakers, giving it authority that American groups, including the FMF, lacked.[162] Afkhami in particular was also a major asset, according to Loar.[163]

Ultimately, U.S. non-recognition was the result of lobbying by NGOs and the efforts of feminists and their allies within the administration. The

Taliban formally applied for U.S. recognition in 1997, likely at the urging of Unocal. Although neither the president nor the secretary of state met with them, Taliban representatives did meet with Rick Inderfurth and Theresa Loar. At one meeting, Loar and Inderfurth questioned the Taliban closely and sent a clear signal that the United States would not do business with a regime that violated the human rights of women and girls. They did not accept the Taliban's explanation that they were merely "protecting" their women. Unocal representatives also met with Loar around the same time to urge her to support recognition, but to no avail.[164]

At another meeting in early December 1997, three "senior members of the Taliban delegation visiting the U.S. under the auspices of Unocal" met with Inderfurth and several other U.S. officials. Acting on orders from Mullah Omar, the Taliban representatives urged the United States to reopen its embassy in Kabul, pushed for resurrection of the Unocal pipeline, and insisted they desired "friendly relations with the U.S. and all countries of the world based on mutual respect and non-interference." When the main spokesman attempted to preempt criticism by explaining that three thousand girls attended school in Kabul and that the Afghan people wanted women to veil, Inderfurth did not accept this ruse. According to a State Department report, when the spokesman "argued that there were differences between the sexes," Inderfurth "corrected him and noted that a society needed the contributions of all of its members to go forward. Further, he said our attitude toward the Taliban would be influenced by its behavior related to medical care, education, and opportunities made available to women. This was not the U.S. view alone but was held by the entire international community." The Taliban retorted that "much of the international community's information on the circumstances of Afghan women was wrong." Inderfurth, however, was adamant. He reiterated the U.S. commitment to women's human rights and announced that the United States would not recognize their government.[165] The Taliban representatives failed to secure U.S. support, and by spending approximately half the meeting discussing Afghan women, Inderfurth reaffirmed the administration's refusal to acknowledge a regime that violated women's human rights.

Following this meeting, Inderfurth testified before the Senate Foreign Relations Committee that State followed a policy of "strict neutrality" between the various factions vying for control of Afghanistan.[166] This indicated publicly that the United States would not recognize the Taliban. Soon thereafter, the administration released several statements clearly articulating a policy of non-recognition. It stated, "The United States does not plan to extend diplomatic recognition to the Taliban," and insisted, "We do not plan to recognize any government unless it is broad-based, representative of all Afghans and respects international norms of behavior in human rights, including the human rights of women and girls."[167]

This declaration brought U.S. policy into alignment with that of the rest of the world, which—aside from Pakistan, Saudi Arabia, and the United Arab Emirates—consistently refused to acknowledge the Taliban as legitimate. The administration also closed the Afghan embassy in Washington to prevent the Taliban from sending an ambassador.[168] In March 1998, at the request of Senator Diane Feinstein (D-California), Loar testified before the Senate, "Promoting the observance of human rights, particularly the rights of women and girls, is one of our highest foreign policy priorities in Afghanistan." She stated, "We are facing in Taliban controlled Afghanistan, one of the worst examples of the treatment of women in history," so the United States would not recognize their regime.[169] Once those on Capitol Hill heard about the Taliban's violations of women's rights, there was full congressional support for non-recognition.[170] Despite the acrimonious relationship between Democrats and Republicans at the time, there was strong bipartisan support for Clinton's policy.[171]

Thereafter, the administration repeatedly affirmed non-recognition. On International Women's Day in 1998, the president himself vowed "that there would be no recognition until treatment of women improved."[172] That August, al Qaeda simultaneously bombed the U.S. embassies in Dar es Salaam, Tanzania and Nairobi, Kenya, killing hundreds of people and wounding many more. Al Qaeda's elusive leader, Osama bin Laden, based his operations in Afghanistan, and Clinton had pursued him unsuccessfully for some time.[173] Because of the embassy bombings, the administration's attention in Afghanistan largely shifted to terrorism after 1998, yet it never wavered in its emphasis on women's rights and continued to insist that the Taliban improve their women's human rights record.[174] In fact, the United States toughened its stance through increased economic sanctions after the embassy attacks.[175] As he pursued bin Laden, Clinton met with Smeal and Leno in 1999 and repeated his assurance that the United States would never recognize the Taliban unless they changed their policies toward women.[176]

To underscore its ongoing commitment to women, the administration paired its rejection of the Taliban with aid programs intended to empower Afghan women. Non-recognition was a powerful symbolic statement, but the

United States needed to do more if it wanted to help women on the ground. Clinton was already using USAID as a tool for women's empowerment; he now turned that tool against the Taliban. By the time Clinton left office, the United States was the largest single provider of humanitarian aid to Afghans. As was consistent with Clinton's foreign aid programs, U.S. funds were channeled through UN agencies and NGOs.[177] The administration worked closely with these agencies to ensure that aid reached its intended recipients and did not benefit the Taliban.[178]

In March 1998, shortly after the administration formally announced non-recognition, Albright and Hillary Clinton announced that the United States would provide $2.5 million to grassroots organizations in Pakistan and Afghanistan to help Afghan women.[179] By the end of fiscal year '98, the administration had spent $8.3 million on aid to the Afghan people, $3.3 million of which it specifically earmarked for programs that targeted women and girls. The United States gave an additional $14.8 million to the UN Refugee Agency (UNHCR) and the Red Cross, much of which went to Afghanistan.[180] According to Inderfurth, the administration spent close to $200 million total in humanitarian assistance to Afghanistan.[181] A significant portion of that benefited Afghan women. Although Afghans continued to suffer as long as the Taliban held power, this aid program was a start toward helping them recover from decades of war and oppression. By using foreign aid to empower Afghan women, the Clinton administration ensured that its condemnations of the Taliban were not merely rhetoric but rather represented the clearest example of Clinton's attempts to position women's human rights in the mainstream of U.S. foreign policy.

Non-recognition of the Taliban was the crucial moment when women's human rights concerns were integrated seriously into U.S. foreign policy toward the Islamic world. Such a policy came about because several key factors converged just as the Taliban seized power: the maturation of transnational feminism; the growing profile and effectiveness of NGOs like WLUML, SIGI, and the FMF; sustained and growing American public attention to Muslim women; the election of a president with feminist sympathies who sought to incorporate women's human rights into the mainstream of U.S. foreign policy; and the appointment of Madeleine Albright as secretary of state. These factors created an environment in which the public and high-ranking policymakers could be mobilized on behalf of women. By declaring that the United States refused to recognize the Taliban specifically because of their abuse of women, the Clinton administration sent a strong signal that women's human rights were now central to the U.S. international mission—even overriding hard power policy concerns and interests regarding regional stability and an oil pipeline. Such a policy move was unprecedented, and its importance cannot be understated.

Feminists working within and outside the U.S. government had won the day over an oil company and traditional hard power interests. If analyzed using traditional interpretations of U.S. foreign policy, this decision would be totally inexplicable. Historians who employ traditional approaches have long argued that hard power concerns primarily drive policy decisions. In this analysis, women's human rights are either irrelevant or at most serve as window dressing to justify decisions that are motivated primarily by other concerns. Clinton's policy toward the Taliban contradicts this interpretation. The United States had clear economic and strategic motives to engage with the Taliban. Afghan women's suffering, on the other hand, had no direct impact on the U.S. national interest, and non-recognition carried with it material consequences. Clinton's policy was driven almost purely by moral and soft power concerns in this instance—or as close to such a policy as is possible in the complex world of foreign affairs. U.S. policy imperatives were therefore shifting in important and unpredictable ways by the 1990s, and historians must pay closer attention to this development.

Clinton's decision also had significant consequences. Rejecting the Taliban meant that the Unocal pipeline project had to be scrapped, which meant that the United States would not profit from Central Asian oil (at least temporarily); it also left a potential opening for Iran to exert more influence in the region.[182] Unocal, which had invested heavily in the project, was left out in the cold. Given the resources of the oil lobby and its influence in Washington, such a situation could have caused oil lobbyists to retaliate against Clinton or Democrats more generally. Yet abandonment of the pipeline also ensured that the Taliban would not profit from it either. In addition, the Clinton administration joined most other governments in successfully isolating the Taliban regime, putting the United States in line with the rest of the world and demonstrating the power of global opinion. Clinton's administration was sincere in its focus on Afghan women, but even if it had little interest in women's issues, it would have been difficult to ignore the Taliban's abuse of women because international attention to human rights at the time demanded action.

U.S. non-recognition and the scrapping of the pipeline also represented a major victory for transnational feminism. Feminist organizations like SIGI and the FMF successfully mobilized public opinion and lobbied the U.S. government to put concerns for women's human rights at the center of American policy in Afghanistan. By bringing feminists' concerns into the mainstream, the Clinton administration made the protection of women's human rights an integral part of U.S. national identity and rejected the imperialist and hard power status quo. This set a precedent for the way future administrations could approach the Muslim world and created an ongoing role for women's human rights activists in policymaking circles. Muslim women remained in the public eye as the United States became even more entangled in the affairs of Islamic nations in the years that followed. Especially after 9/11, concerns about women's rights continued to be a central point of tension in U.S.-Islamic relations.

Yet this is not simply a story of policy success or feminist triumph. There was also a significant downside to the administration's decision. Non-recognition, in the end, did not end women's suffering in Afghanistan. The Taliban were not moved by international pressure. While they did attempt to negotiate with the United States, especially following U.S. airstrikes in 1998, they were unwilling to change their policies on women in order to earn diplomatic recognition or secure a better relationship with the United States.[183] While non-recognition was a major step forward for women's human rights globally, women in Afghanistan remained at the mercy of the Taliban.

Non-recognition, therefore, was not a magic bullet. The administration did use economic tools to empower Afghan women, and Loar and other members of the administration worked closely with UNICEF, UNIFEM, and other organizations to ensure that Afghan women received aid. However, these programs did not remove the most serious obstacle to human rights in Afghanistan. As long as the Taliban remained in control, women's situation continued to deteriorate. U.S. policymakers, feminist and human rights activists, the United Nations, and the international community continued to face one of the central conundrums of human rights advocacy: How can the international community end human rights abuses committed by governments against their own people?

The policy of non-recognition and Clinton's positioning of women's human rights at the center of U.S. policy on Afghanistan left a complicated legacy for subsequent policymakers. On the one hand, it was a major accomplishment for feminist activists that the U.S. government declared that the protection and expansion of women's human rights was an important policy goal. What is more, the Clinton administration did not simply pay lip service to women's rights in the abstract. The highest-ranking members of the administration prioritized Afghan women's human rights, and they supported that policy with significant foreign aid expenditures. This made it more likely that future policymakers would also take women's human rights seriously.

On the other hand, non-recognition—as momentous as it was—did not solve the problem in Afghanistan because the Taliban refused to relinquish their insistence on women's subordination when faced with international pressure. Which rights to promote and how exactly to make a positive difference in Muslim women's lives without making such women more vulnerable or resorting to imperialist approaches that breed anti-Americanism remained an open question. Expanding and protecting women's human rights takes time and political capital, and Clinton was already halfway through his beleaguered second term by the time non-recognition became policy. Moreover, if economic and development aid was the answer to Afghan women's troubles (and that is unclear), there were limits to what Clinton could accomplish. Serious use of foreign aid advances a vision of social and economic human rights—and raises serious questions about imperialism and global inequality—that never resonated with most Americans.

When later presidential administrations grappled with the same questions about whether and how to push for women's human rights in Islamic countries, they used some of the same tools as Clinton, including development aid. Their use of such tools, however, would be accompanied by military intervention and a return to Orientalist, Islamophobic, and colonialist frameworks. Following the 9/11 attacks, the George W. Bush administration built upon Clinton's policies by naming women's rights as a central concern in the War on Terror. Such policies would make the relationship between women's rights and U.S. policy in the Islamic world infinitely more complex in the years that followed.

Chapter 7

Muslim Women's Human Rights and U.S. Foreign Policy Since 9/11

In the years after Clinton left office, American attention to women's human rights in Islamic countries only grew. Given public concerns and continued feminist campaigns, policymakers in the administrations of George W. Bush and Barack Obama often followed Clinton's lead. While many in Islamic countries and in the United States deemed America's attention to Muslim women neoimperialist, a review of Bush's and Obama's women's rights policies suggests a more complex understanding. This was more than just a politically expedient or opportunistic policy position. Although such elements were undeniably evident in Bush's approach, U.S. women's rights policies toward Islamic countries since 9/11 also attest to how successfully feminism and women's human rights discourse had penetrated the foreign policy sphere in the preceding decades.

After the United States invaded Afghanistan in late 2001, the George W. Bush administration proclaimed that the United States was fighting the Taliban because they supported terrorism and because they oppressed women. When the president signed the Afghan Women and Children Relief Act that December, he asserted, "The central goal of the terrorists is the brutal oppression of women." Under the Taliban, Bush explained, "Afghan women were banned from speaking or laughing loudly. They were banned from riding bicycles or attending school. They were denied basic health care and were killed on suspicion of adultery." He continued, "We strongly reject the Taliban way. We strongly reject their brutality toward women and children."[1]

Bush was an unlikely champion of women's rights. As a socially conservative Republican, he promoted the traditional family, opposed reproductive rights, and advocated cutting federal funds for social welfare programs, which disproportionately affected women and children.[2] Leading U.S. feminist organizations, including NOW, Planned Parenthood, and NARAL Pro-Choice America, opposed his policies and saw him as an adversary. Counterintuitively, then, following the 9/11 attacks, his administration launched a vigorous and sustained campaign for women's human rights in the Islamic world. Liberating women, according to the president and high-ranking members of the administration, was a professed U.S. war goal in Afghanistan. After the United States also invaded Iraq in 2003, Bush justified toppling Saddam Hussein's government in part by calling for expanded rights for Iraqi women. While Bush's positions on women's rights domestically and in the Islamic world appear to have been contradictory, it is also possible that he felt that American women had achieved a measure of equality and that the brutal, deliberate oppression of women in Afghanistan was not akin to women's issues in the United States.

Despite Bush's conservative stance on the family and reproductive rights, it appeared as though he did embrace civil and political rights for women and sought to promote them globally as part of a campaign to promote U.S.-style democracy and freedom.[3] By supporting women's education, employment, and political representation in Afghanistan and Iraq, Bush was very much in line with the reality of U.S. society and norms. Although he appointed fewer women to federal positions than Clinton did, he did appoint several to high-profile federal and cabinet-level positions. Three women served in Bush's first-term cabinet, while his second-term cabinet featured four.[4] As some scholars observed, Bush "surrounded himself with professional and accomplished women."[5]

Ultimately, the Bush administration envisioned a far more limited set of rights for women than U.S. or Muslim feminists did; nevertheless, it further integrated women's human rights into U.S. foreign policy. The administration's motives were less straightforward than Clinton's. Bush also abandoned Clinton's adoption of transnational feminists' human rights discourse and often fell back upon imperialist, Islamophobic, and Orientalist frameworks. Given Bush's silence about Muslim women prior to 9/11 and the administration's opposition to policies that would have ensured greater gender equality in the United States, one could argue that these policymakers opportunistically exploited the broad public support for Islamic women's human rights to bolster support for war in Afghanistan and Iraq. And they took up Muslim women's rights zealously so that women's human rights arguments overlaid the policy debates about terrorism and U.S. military intervention. The reality, however, was more complex than simple opportunism.

Although the Bush administration's relationship with American feminist organizations was initially hostile, following the 9/11 attacks, it "courted" the leaders of the Feminist Majority, as well as Martha Burk, head of the National Council of Women's Organizations.[6] The administration invited feminists, including Smeal and Leno, to brief White House counselor Karen Hughes, National Security Advisor Condoleezza Rice, Secretary of State Colin Powell, Deputy Secretary of Defense Paul Wolfowitz, and Deputy Secretary of State Richard Armitage on Afghan women. According to Smeal, "They were *anxious* to meet with us," and "they apologized" for not meeting with FMF earlier.[7] Like Clinton, Bush drew upon feminist organizations' expertise while formulating policy, but the cast of characters had changed. U.S. groups who had little direct experience with the Islamic world, like the FMF, now had the White House's ear, while SIGI found itself on the policy margins. The result was the deployment of colonial feminist rhetoric by both the White House and the FMF, which unfortunately tied women's equality to U.S. imperialism.

In 1999 the Feminist Majority had set its sights on pushing the United States to designate the Taliban as a terrorist organization, but the FMF enjoyed little direct access to the Clinton administration. Following 9/11, however, they suddenly had significant influence in Washington. In addition to briefing Bush administration officials, Leno and Smeal testified before Congress to encourage U.S. military intervention in Afghanistan. The FMF staunchly supported the bombing and invasion that began in October 2001.[8] This situation was somewhat ironic: American feminists had opposed a war in 1990 because of Islamic violations of women's human rights; the FMF now advocated war for the same reason. As other feminists tried to distance themselves from the NGO's bellicosity, the FMF stepped up its campaign to rally the public to support U.S. efforts to liberate Afghan women.[9]

SIGI, meanwhile, was in disarray. Mahnaz Afkhami's term as the NGO's leader had ended in 1999. Canadian Greta Hofmann Nemiroff succeeded her as president, and the organization's offices moved to Montreal. The move disrupted SIGI's operations, while the leadership transition ultimately ripped the organization apart. Although SIGI had carved out an influential role, Nemiroff and Robin Morgan felt that the organization had become too narrowly focused on Muslim women, so they pushed to shift SIGI's priorities to the depletion of fisheries and micro-credit projects for single mothers. Morgan was also concerned that working with policymakers would drive the organization to the right politically.[10] SIGI thus relinquished its seat at the policy table just as Bush took office, ensuring that it had little influence on how the United States approached women's rights in Afghanistan, Iraq, and other Islamic countries during the Bush years.

This decision was catastrophic for the organization. The changes undid much of what Afkhami and the other Muslim members had spent nearly a decade building, and Nemiroff and Morgan quickly alienated them. Morgan bizarrely characterized SIGI's reputation as an organization dedicated to Muslim women's rights as an "image problem," and the two openly disparaged Afkhami to SIGI's members.[11] Morgan, it appears, was unhappy that Afkhami's star had eclipsed her own. Personal grievances became entangled with disapproval of SIGI's specialized focus, as Morgan and Nemiroff's attempts to reorient the NGO turned into an anti-Afkhami campaign.[12] As a result, SIGI's members split into two factions by August 2000.[13]

Two decades after the contentious Mexico City and Copenhagen conferences, Western and Muslim feminists once again found themselves at odds over which issues to prioritize, and the conflict within SIGI prefigured the sharp post-9/11 divisions between feminists over the issue of Islam. The situation only resolved when Afkhami left SIGI to found her own organization, the Women's Learning Partnership for Rights, Development, and Peace (WLP). Many members left with her.[14] SIGI continued to hold workshops on Muslim women, but by 9/11 the organization was a shadow of its former self. SIGI was moribund by 2004.[15]

SIGI was no longer capable of influencing U.S. policy after Afkhami's departure, but some of its members did participate in the discussions in Washington. Although they supported programs to aid Afghan women, they were decidedly less enthusiastic about military intervention than the FMF was. Sima Wali, by then the head of the NGO Refugee Women in Development, traveled to Bonn, Germany, in December 2001, where the United States and the international community drew up a UN-brokered plan for Afghanistan's new government. There, she advocated for the new political system to include women and promote women's equality.[16] A week later, Wali and a delegation of other Afghan women, including representatives from RAWA, traveled to

Washington, D.C., and New York to urge the U.S. government to make women's human rights a priority in Afghanistan. Eleanor Smeal and Gloria Steinem joined them as they met with the Senate Foreign Relations Committee, the State Department, members of the House of Representatives, and UN officials. "We need sustained, international support and a commitment to make sure that women's rights, which have been taken away from us, are restored," Wali insisted.[17] The earlier conduits built between SIGI, Afghan feminists, and the American government enabled women like Wali to have a voice, albeit one that fought for influence, in policymaking circles.

Policymakers needed to consider Afghan women's perspectives, although they did not speak with one voice. RAWA—the oldest and most influential Afghan feminist organization—argued vehemently against military intervention, as did several other groups. Meanwhile, other Afghans wanted to overthrow the Taliban, and the FMF enthusiastically backed military action. In the end, because it already intended to go to war, the administration privileged the views of those who shared its desire to use the full might of the United States to remake Afghanistan, and it largely attempted to impose its American understanding of women's equality on Afghanistan rather than following the lead of experienced Afghan groups like RAWA.[18]

Although 9/11 was the primary motivation for the war, leading U.S. officials argued that it was about more than just terrorism. The war was also about promoting freedom, democracy, and capitalist prosperity, they argued, and women's rights were central to those goals. Starting in October 2001 and continuing for the next several years, the president, First Lady, and high-ranking members of the administration continually drew attention to the Taliban's violations of women's human rights and pushed for greater equality for Afghan women.

Because of the decades-long history of American discourse about Muslim women's rights and the events of the previous decade, the public supported Bush's policies. The U.S. public's fascination with—and condemnation of—the status of women in the Islamic world reached an all-time high after 9/11. Thus the administration's decisions coincided with increasingly intense public attention to Islamic women. Muslim women both participated and were depicted in U.S. public conversations after 9/11 in varied and complex ways, but the outpouring of attention underscored the centrality of gender in U.S.-Islamic encounters and maintained public pressure for policymakers.

While counterintuitive in light of Bush's generally conservative stance on gender issues, the administration's posture regarding Islamic women was very much politically on key.

As in earlier periods, the news media galvanized public debate. In September 2001, CNN aired *Beneath the Veil*, a documentary directed by the London-based Afghan Saira Shah and filmed with RAWA's help. It graphically depicted the Taliban's brutal treatment of women and girls. The documentary's first airing that August had received little attention, but because of 9/11, its second airing attracted 5.5 million viewers, "making it the network's most-watched documentary ever."[19] Suddenly Afghan women were everywhere in American media. TV programs contrasted images of burqa-clad women living in horrid conditions in Taliban-controlled areas before the war with images of women tossing aside their burqas after the arrival of U.S. soldiers. Magazines described Afghan women's lives, while experts and Muslim women appeared on TV to debate women's place in Islam.[20]

While these depictions often cast Afghan women as victims and drew on stereotypes of Islamic backwardness, American public discourse about Muslim women after 9/11 was in fact highly complex. As they had increasingly since 1979, Muslim women spoke for themselves by giving interviews and telling their own stories. They wrote op-eds and newspaper articles. They testified before Congress and appeared on TV. RAWA member Taheema Faryal made the rounds on *Larry King Live, Good Morning America*, the *News Hour with Jim Lehrer*, and *CBS Evening News.*[21] Afghan women claimed space for themselves in the U.S. public sphere and told Americans that Afghan women should take the lead in determining their own futures.[22]

The media frenzy aroused public sympathy for women in Afghanistan and provided a strong base of public support for the administration's policies. Policymakers apparently realized this and used it to their advantage. The First Lady was the first to capitalize on the issue by launching a public campaign to draw attention to the plight of women under Taliban rule, which rallied public support for war. In November 2001, Laura Bush delivered her husband's weekly radio address—an unprecedented move by a First Lady—in which she "kick[ed] off a world-wide effort to focus on the brutality against women and children" in Afghanistan. Calling the Taliban's policies "deliberate human cruelty," she linked the War on Terror with women's equality.[23] Liberating women would presumably counteract radicalism and set Islamic societies on the path to enlightenment and freedom.

The president echoed this argument when he signed the Afghan Women and Children Relief Act into law, and the narrative of rescue espoused by the administration appeared to play well politically. The bill was cosponsored by over a dozen women senators, and Bush's declarations at the signing ceremony received a standing ovation from women's rights activists—most of whom were Democrats.[24] In his 2002 State of the Union address, the president once again stressed the importance of women's rights: "The last time we met in this chamber, the mothers and daughters of Afghanistan were captives in their own homes, forbidden from working or going to school. Today women are free, and are part of Afghanistan's new government . . . America will always stand firm for the non-negotiable demands of human dignity."[25]

High-ranking administration officials reinforced this message. The State Department pointedly stressed the centrality of women's human rights to U.S. policy after consulting an array of women's rights activists and experts on Afghanistan, including Theresa Loar and Afghan feminist Belquis Ahmadi.[26] Two days after the First Lady's radio address, Secretary Powell declared at a conference on Afghan women, "The rights of the women of Afghanistan will not be negotiable." Using language reminiscent of Madeleine Albright, Powell asserted, "The new government of Afghanistan must be broad-based and representational, and that means it must include women. It must respect the rights of Afghan women to choose how they will participate in their society."[27] As Powell asserted in March 2002, "The worldwide advancement of women's issues is not only in keeping with the deeply held values of the American people; it is strongly in our national interest as well. . . . Women's issues affect not only women; they have profound implications for all humankind."[28] This indicated a recognition that women's equality was bound up with other issues—including hard power concerns. State recognized that it had broad support for such policies, and Undersecretary of State for Global Affairs Paula Dobriansky stressed that "it strengthens our message that these are universal rights that we believe should be restored to Afghan women."[29]

While on the surface such statements appeared to align with the framework of universal human rights, they also reflected longstanding notions of American exceptionalism. Bush articulated this most clearly in 2002 when he declared, "The United States will use this opportunity to extend the benefits of freedom across the globe. We will actively work to bring the hope of democracy, development, free markets, and free trade to every corner of the world."[30] Central to his logic was the assumption that U.S.-style freedom, democracy, and capitalism are universally appealing. There was a long history of U.S. leaders using such beliefs to justify U.S. actions.[31] Here, human rights as the Bush administration defined them functioned as the twenty-first-century version of earlier calls to establish "liberty" worldwide.

The Bush administration followed its words with substantive action. State released its "Report on the Taliban's War Against Women" in November 2001, which detailed the Taliban's "appalling" and "egregious" treatment of women and advocated women's inclusion in building a post-Taliban government.[32] State then created the U.S.-Afghan Women's Council in January 2002, which was headed by Dobriansky and cochaired by Afghanistan's Minister of Women's Affairs Sima Samar and Foreign Minister Dr. Abdullah Abdullah.[33] The council coordinated efforts to ensure gender balance in the new Afghan government, and it brought together resources and expertise for the education and training of Afghan women and girls.

The administration expended significant resources to implement its policies. The United States provided $178 million in humanitarian assistance during the first month of the war, and it earmarked an additional $320 million for maternal and child health programs and women's education.[34] OIWI reported in 2004 that the United States had spent $4 billion and secured pledges of over $8 billion more from international donors to reconstruct Afghanistan. The priority was to fund USAID's Afghan Women's Empowerment Program. In its first three years alone, the program implemented over two hundred separate initiatives, which included initiatives addressing violence against women, sex trafficking, political and social participation, health programs, education, refugee resettlement, and economics.[35] Over the next several years, the president, First Lady, and high-ranking members of the administration continued to emphasize to the public and to the new Afghan government that women's human rights and women's full participation in politics, education, and the economy were U.S. priorities.[36]

As many people have pointed out, despite the Bush administration's enthusiastic embrace of Afghan women's rights, its approach was incredibly problematic. Its rhetoric allowed many in the Islamic world to argue that women's rights represented a form of U.S. imperialism and an attack on Islam that had to be resisted. Even worse, the administration's programs fell far short of their goals. Poorly conceived and poorly implemented, these policies—and the war that accompanied them—made it difficult for Afghan women to improve their situation. Critics of the administration advanced their arguments on many fronts.[37] Many characterized Bush's focus on women's rights as a cynical ploy to lure female voters away from the Democratic Party or as a ruse to broaden public support for war.[38]

The most serious problems with the Bush administration's policies related to their flawed conceptualization and implementation. The concept of universal human rights is imperfect, but a conscientious adoption of this framework would have allowed the administration to take part in a global, multilateral conversation that included Islamic viewpoints and potentially cultivate buy-in from a broad array of Afghans. Clinton's approach had been constructed carefully to avoid employing imperialist and unilateralist policies as much as possible to give grassroots women's rights campaigns the greatest chances of success. Clinton also recognized that the United States itself was not a paragon of gender equality and coupled his international programs with domestic policies that upheld women's rights at home. The Bush administration, in contrast, adopted exceptionalist and imperialist frameworks that cast the United States as the most enlightened and democratic nation, duty-bound to spread its supposedly universal values and freedom to less advanced nations. Its women's rights policies ultimately represented colonial feminism, a significant step backward for U.S.-Islamic understanding.

This was troubling to many activists and scholars. One commenter contended that Bush "embraced the gendered logic of neocolonialism, which Gayatri Spivak (1985) has documented time and again: heroic white men set out to 'rescue' brown women from 'barbaric' brown men."[39] Many others agreed.[40] This disguised the U.S. drive for empire in Central Asia and the Middle East, both of which were oil-rich regions, and feminists risked becoming imperialists if they supported the administration's policies. One scholar asserted, "The geo-politics of US imperialism, packaging itself as a movement to create democracy and 'freedom' through militarism and force, uses the rhetoric of the Feminist Majority's Campaign to serve its own interests," which are "the right to control, the right to invade and the right to occupy."[41] Likewise, historian Emily Rosenberg observed that, despite using the language of human rights, "the visual focus on the burka, in short, may reinforce an orientalist perspective that renders some people as exotic and wholly foreign while mobilizing the domestic emotions of humanitarian sympathy to buttress American exceptionalism. Discourses of gender disorder and the necessity of 'civilized' nations' setting things aright . . . can become especially emotive rallying cries in times of war."[42] Many worried that feminism had become Bush's pawn.[43] This put American feminists who supported Afghan women but opposed war in an uncomfortable position.

For Afghan women, the situation was even more serious. They faced the dislocating effects of war and potential reprisals from fundamentalists if they used the opportunity provided by the U.S. presence to claim their rights; they also valued their cultural identities and did not wish to seem un-Islamic. Their decisions about education, political participation, and other improvements in their status could be life-and-death, as those who sought greater autonomy and rights after the U.S. invasion became Taliban targets. Massouda Jalal, who eventually became a cabinet minister, received death threats when she ran against Hamid Karzai for the Afghan presidency in 2004.[44] The Taliban also attacked teachers, aid workers, feminists, health care workers, and schools, declaring, "There is no difference between the armed people who are fighting against us and civilians who are co-operating with foreigners."[45] While the U.S. presence made women's programs possible by dislodging the Taliban, it also made Afghan women vulnerable as fundamentalists claimed to defend Afghanistan and "authentic" Islam from the American invaders.

Beyond the problematic rhetoric, Bush's policies also had mixed results at best. The United States after 9/11 continued to reward abusers of women by welcoming former mujahideen warlords—who now called themselves the "Northern Alliance"—as allies in the war against the Taliban. These were the same groups who had mandated veiling and raped and killed women with impunity during the 1990s. President Hamid Karzai, whom the United States handpicked, had ties to such groups; he served as the deputy foreign minister in the mujahideen government and had been one of the Taliban's earliest supporters.[46]

Consequently, despite the fact that the new Afghan constitution declared the equality of men and women, the government still based its legal system on Shari'a. The constitution asserted, "No law shall contravene the tenets and provisions of the holy religion of Islam," and included no provisions expressly protecting women's rights; given the persistence of conservative interpretations of Shari'a in Afghanistan, this upheld patriarchy.[47] RAWA and other Afghan feminists vehemently opposed this development—they preferred secular democracy and laws that aligned with CEDAW. Karzai, meanwhile, proved quick to sacrifice women's rights to maintain the support of conservatives.[48]

Moreover, while Afghan women did improve their position in some ways after the U.S. invasion, they continued to suffer in other areas. After the arrival of U.S. forces, Afghan women became increasingly visible in all sectors, and the country made some progress toward its development goals, such as increasing numbers of children—especially girls—in school.[49] Several women also entered the political arena.[50] However, Afghan women faced continued lack of security, poverty, unemployment, dislocation, patriarchal laws and attitudes, fear, and violence.[51] The American focus on women also created tension with Afghan men, who felt ignored and excluded, and thousands of Afghan women and children died in U.S. bombing campaigns.[52]

Tragically, as the United States turned its attention to Iraq in 2003, U.S. funding and commitment to Afghan women waned, allowing the Taliban to stage a comeback. Twice as many Afghans died in 2006 compared to 2005, while 80,000 were displaced by continued fighting. The year 2007 was the bloodiest one for Afghan civilians since 2001, and many areas became "no go" zones for aid workers.[53] By that point, women's literacy rates remained abysmal, and Afghanistan's Gender Development Index was the second lowest in the world.[54] After years of U.S. presence, the administration could point to no clear evidence that its policies had actually helped Afghan women. Of the $2 billion it spent between 2001 and 2013, the United States could only verify that $64 million had gone to women's programs, and it could not confirm that the money had reached its intended recipients or achieved its objectives.[55]

And yet, starting with U.S. public criticism of Islamic fundamentalists after 1979 and continuing with feminist campaigns and the Clinton administration's policies in the 1990s, one could see the Bush administration's focus on Afghan and Iraqi women not only as the appropriation of feminist rhetoric in the service of U.S. empire but also as a sign of feminists' success in reframing the terms of U.S. foreign policy debate. As Michaele Ferguson wrote, "If we dismiss the [Bush administration] rhetoric as mere words, then we fail to appreciate the work feminists have done to make the connection between women and security sound reasonable and mainstream."[56] To suggest that Bush's policies represented nothing more than an updated version of colonial feminism, as many critics have, ignores the many years that non-Muslim and Muslim feminists worked to get U.S. policymakers to take women's human rights seriously.

The defense of women's rights certainly provided a convenient way for U.S. policymakers to mobilize public support for military intervention after 9/11, both in Afghanistan and later in Iraq. However, the Bush administration began to advocate women's human rights in the Islamic world more generally, even in places where the United States did not have boots on the ground. This indicated the continuing salience of Muslim women's rights for U.S. policymakers and the American public, beyond providing justification for military action.

In May 2004, a year after the United States ousted Saddam Hussein, Bush condemned Islamic terrorists everywhere for seeking to create "a harsh society in which women are voiceless and brutalized."[57] A year later, Secretary of State Condoleezza Rice spoke out in favor of women's rights during a trip to Egypt. "Half a democracy is not a democracy," she told the men in attendance. Rice pointedly remarked that she hoped women would gain political rights in Kuwait and Saudi Arabia and exploited a press conference with Saudi foreign minister Saud al-Faisal in Riyadh to publicize her point.[58] It was daring, given U.S. officials' historical reticence to criticize the Saudis on human rights issues. Karen Hughes, at that point the under secretary of state for public diplomacy and public affairs, also visited Saudi Arabia a few months later and boldly condemned its ban on women driving.[59] When Laura Bush visited the Middle East in 2005, she, too, underscored America's commitment to upholding women's rights in the Muslim world.[60] This risked tension with allies but provoked a response.[61] Partly because of international pressure, King Abdullah instituted incremental reforms that, while modest relative to those of other countries, indicated that Saudi Arabia was open to very slowly granting women more freedom.[62]

Through the last years of the Bush administration, even absent military intervention, U.S. policymakers continued to embed Muslim women's human rights in foreign policy. The American military promoted U.S. servicewomen's grassroots efforts to forge connections with Afghan and Iraqi women.[63] U.S. and NATO projects, as well as the efforts of the United Nations and myriad NGOs, built schools and other infrastructure to promote girls' and women's education, economic independence, and political rights in Afghanistan and Iraq. The administration continued to consult feminists and created government positions to keep attention focused on women's human rights. While Dobriansky spearheaded State's women's human rights projects under Colin Powell, when National Security Advisor Condoleezza Rice took over as secretary of state in Bush's second term, she further institutionalized

women's rights. Rice brought with her Dr. Shirin Tahir-Kheli, a political
scientist and longtime foreign policy specialist, as her senior advisor for
women's empowerment (SAWE).

Indian-born Tahir-Kheli had served in various positions in the National Security Council and State Department since the 1980s.[64] Under
George H. W. Bush, Tahir-Kheli was the only, and first, Muslim to hold
ambassadorial-level security clearance. Although she spent most of her
career focused on nuclear non-proliferation and India-Pakistan relations,
she came to her new post with experience in human rights diplomacy: she
was the head of the U.S. Delegation to the UN Commission on Human
Rights from 2001 through 2003.[65]

Tahir-Kehli's appointment, Islamic identity, and ambassadorial-level
rank demonstrated deepening U.S. commitment to women's human rights.
Her work as SAWE focused on using soft power tools to empower women—
economic aid, educational exchanges, health programs, and network building. Tahir-Kheli helped U.S. ambassadors to develop a roster of influential
women in their countries. She also created a "women leaders working group,"
chaired by Rice, which convened female heads of state, foreign ministers,
attorney generals, and others to promote women's empowerment. Sixty-eight
women participated in the working group by the time Rice and Tahir-Kheli
left office in early 2009; almost half were leaders from Islamic countries,
including Pakistan, the UAE, Morocco, Oman, and Kuwait.[66]

Much of Tahir-Kheli's work focused on Muslim countries. Her office
faciliated a partnership between Harvard and a women's college in Saudi
Arabia in which students from both universities built houses in Jordan for
Habitat for Humanity. Rice and Tahir-Kheli also coordinated a public-
private partnership to construct a children's hospital in Basra at the request
of Iraqi mothers. Regarding her time as SAWE, Tahir-Kheli later explained,
"We built on stuff that the Clinton administration did, and we hoped that
they [Obama administration] would build on stuff we did. . . . Women were
very front and center of all programming . . . it was kind of an overwhelming amount of commitment . . . everybody felt that it [promoting women's
rights] was a good thing to do."[67]

As he prepared to leave office, President Bush urged Americans to remain committed to women's human rights in the Islamic world. At a meeting in June 2008 on economic cooperation with Middle Eastern leaders,
Bush lauded Kuwait's recent decision to grant women the right to vote and
cautioned, "It is costly and unwise to keep half the population from fully

contributing to the life of a nation."[68] As an outgoing second-term president, Bush found that he had less power and popularity, so he had little to gain politically from what he said. However, Bush's statement indicated his abiding desire for the United States to promote democracy and freedom—not just in Afghanistan and Iraq but also in the entire Middle East—by expanding political and civil rights for women.

Even after leaving office, George and Laura Bush continued to advocate Muslim women's human rights. The former First Lady now heads the Women's Initiative of the George W. Bush Institute, which works to promote women's rights and focuses on the Muslim world.[69] Bush kept a low profile during the first few years after he left office, but the only substantive public remarks he did make pertained to Muslim women. In April 2011, he opposed the Obama administration's plan to withdraw U.S. troops from Afghanistan. In an interview on Fox News, Bush explained, "My concern of course is that the United States gets weary of being in Afghanistan, it is not worth it, let's leave. . . . And Laura and I believe that if that were to happen, women would suffer again. We don't believe that's in the interests of the United States or the world to create a safe haven for terrorists and stand by and watch women's rights be abused."[70] For Bush, Muslim women's rights had become an enduring foreign policy issue.

Bush's policies and ongoing wars in Iraq and Afghanistan left the incoming Barack Obama administration with an unclear and difficult path in 2009. The rhetoric of Bush and his supporters regarding women's issues often offended Muslims, including women's rights activists, which made the necessary cross-cultural cooperation elusive. Despite the Bush administration's attempts to differentiate between terrorists/fundamentalists and the peaceful majority of Muslims, it still drew upon and perpetuated stereotypes of oppressive, barbaric Islamic men and victimized Muslim women. The Feminist Majority did likewise, often seeking to speak *for* Afghan women rather than *with* them. Such an approach gave radical groups like the Taliban and al Qaeda, as well as Muslim men who were simply religiously conservative and anti-imperialist, reason to resist women's calls for equality. Bush-era policies regarding terror suspects that violated the Geneva Accords had made the United States vulnerable to charges of hypocrisy on human rights issues as well.[71]

The Obama administration had to tread carefully. All of the public attention to Muslim women in the years after 9/11, combined with the momentum of policy precedents set by the Clinton and Bush administrations, made it difficult for Obama to ignore Muslim women's rights. Public opinion still strongly favored helping Muslim women. Some observers have claimed that Afghan women's disappearance from the headlines after mid-2002 indicated waning public interest. Although media attention did turn away from Afghanistan, Muslim women in general were still central to conversations in the U.S. public sphere.

Books by and about Muslim women flew off the shelves. Memoirs like Azar Nafisi's *Reading Lolita in Tehran* (2003), Marjane Satrapi's *Persepolis* (2003), and Ayaan Hirsi Ali's *Infidel* (2007) topped the best-seller lists.[72] By reading novels and memoirs, American audiences could put themselves in Muslim women's shoes and see the world through their eyes. Films featuring Muslim women were also popular, while scholarship about women and Islam continued to expand.[73] Feminists worked to foster cultural sensitivity and dialogue across religious and cultural boundaries. Journalists, too, kept Muslim women in the public eye by publishing a flood of articles and reports about Islamic women following 9/11, with reportage that was increasingly attuned to the perspectives of Islamic peoples.

American Muslims—a growing segment of the U.S. population—faced Islamophobic backlash from certain groups, but they also embraced the controversy engendered by 9/11 to educate their fellow Americans about Islam. They produced their own publications, such as *Azizah*, a magazine founded in 2002 for Muslim women, and *Islamic Horizons*, a bimonthly magazine founded by the Islamic Society of North America (ISNA) in 2003.[74] American Muslims also gave interviews, wrote articles for mainstream publications, and authored books about their religion and their lives. Muslim American women explained that veiling, or not, was their choice. They demonstrated that the Islamic world was varied, complex, and dynamic and that Muslims were far more diverse than most Americans assumed.[75]

Hence, Obama's foreign policy decisions regarding Islamic countries unfolded in an environment of great public and media interest in Muslim women's human rights and of dynamic, rich, often contentious public debates about whether and how to promote gender equality in Islamic societies. Feminists especially had high expectations that Obama would handle the issue better than his predecessor had. Like Clinton, Barack Obama enjoyed women's political support. Domestically, Obama was the opposite of Bush in his positions on reproductive rights and gender issues. He promoted women's equality domestically and appointed women to his administration. Hillary

Clinton, his rival for the Democratic presidential nomination in 2008, became his secretary of state. A slew of personnel from the Clinton administration returned to government as well, and Secretary Clinton brought with her to State her ongoing and lifelong commitment to women's human rights.

With the United States' increasing entanglement in Islamic countries' affairs—from the wars in Iraq and Afghanistan to the wave of revolutionary upheaval known as the Arab Spring that swept across North Africa and the Middle East starting in late 2010—it would have been natural for Muslim women's human rights to play a central role in Obama's policies. Yet tension developed within the administration over the issue. On the one hand, Bush-era policies had proven problematic, and the American public had grown weary of war. On the other, the U.S. public still supported human rights for Muslim women, and the United States had made promises to Afghan and Iraqi women in particular.

President Obama signaled early on that he would change the direction of U.S. policy to improve American-Islamic relations. He was more cautious and pragmatic than Bush, and Obama was well aware that the 9/11 attacks and the ensuing wars had engendered hatred and mistrust between Americans and Muslim peoples. In June 2009, Obama gave a groundbreaking speech in Cairo. He envisioned a "new beginning" between the United States and Muslim countries "based upon mutual interest and mutual respect" and "common principles of justice and progress; tolerance and the dignity of all human beings." Obama also avoided colonialist rhetoric as he addressed the issue of women's rights: "Issues of women's equality are by no means simply an issue for Islam . . . I do not believe that women must make the same choices as men in order to be equal, and I respect those women who choose to live their lives in traditional roles. But it should be their choice. That is why the United States will partner with any Muslim-majority country to support expanded literacy for girls, and to help young women pursue employment through micro-financing that helps people live their dreams."[76] Obama here affirmed previous U.S. policies promoting women's human rights, yet qualified his support. The president limited his focus to specific economic and educational rights for women in this speech and did not mention political rights, violence against women, or cultural and social rights for which feminists in Muslim countries and elsewhere had been fighting. He was far more muted than Bush or Clinton, which indicated that Obama might not promote women's rights in the Islamic world as consistently or forcefully as his predecessors had.

His secretary of state, on the other hand, was determined to keep women's rights at the center of American policy. In April 2009, two months before Obama's Cairo speech, Hillary Clinton announced the creation of the Office of Global Women's Issues (OGWI) under the auspices of the State Department. The OGWI replaced OIWI and had greater status within State's bureaucracy, making permanent the attempts to build foreign policy institutions dedicated to women's rights during her husband's presidency. As part of this effort, Clinton appointed Melanne Verveer, her former chief of staff, as the first U.S. ambassador-at-large for global women's issues.[77] A few months later, Clinton declared that women's rights were "now a cornerstone of American foreign policy."[78] Journalists soon dubbed this "The Hillary Doctrine."[79]

In the years that followed, Clinton and Verveer insistently drew attention to the oppression of women worldwide. Although they did not single them out, Muslim women still featured prominently in their initiatives. Several programs aimed specifically to promote gender equality in Islamic countries and advanced an expansive definition of human rights for women. Among many others, these programs included ones on democracy, development, FGM, political and economic rights, women's leadership, and violence against women.[80] Clinton's State Department also maintained contacts with transnational feminists and NGOs working on women's rights in the Muslim world. When Clinton became secretary of state, Mahnaz Afkhami's new organization, the WLP, was up and running in Maryland. Afkhami had ongoing contacts with Clinton and other members of the Obama administration, which reflected the ties she built with Democratic policymakers during the 1990s.[81] The message coming out of State during Obama's first term was that women's human rights were central to America's global mission.

This message was sometimes at odds with those coming from the White House. Although Obama never declared that he was putting women's rights aside, he clearly downplayed them. He was cautious because of the policy blowback from the Bush years, and he was pragmatic about the limits of U.S. power. Obama stepped back from rhetoric about nation-building, democracy promotion, and women's oppression. In fact, he was cautious about pushing a human rights–based policy in general, as demonstrated by his reluctance to intervene in the Syrian civil war, his muted response to government violence in Egypt, and his general silence on human rights when dealing with China. Moreover, the president worked continually to counteract the virulent Islamophobia that appeared in U.S. political and public discourse following 9/11. Singling out the Islamic oppression of women may have undermined this attempt.

Beyond improving the image of the United States among Muslim peoples, Obama's main policy goals in the Islamic world were to find Osama bin Laden and to extricate the United States from two unpopular wars as quickly as possible. His increasingly tepid support for Afghan women's equality troubled feminists and others. The institutionalization of women's human rights in foreign policymaking ultimately constrained Obama's options: he faced criticism if the U.S. war in Afghanistan ground on, but he also risked public outcry if he withdrew and reneged on the U.S. commitment to Afghan women.

In early April 2009, shortly after Obama took office, the Afghan parliament passed a family law governing the country's Shi'a minority. It included, among other provisions, legalizing marital rape, lowering the age of marriage for girls, and requiring husbands' permission for married women to leave the home. Karzai signed the bill into law, so hundreds of Afghan women took to the streets in protest, where they faced angry fundamentalist men who threw stones and threatened them.[82]

Secretary Clinton's reaction was immediate and unequivocal: the new law was unacceptable. At a press conference on April 3, she stated, "My message is very clear. Women's rights are a central part of American foreign policy in the Obama administration. They are not an add-on or an afterthought."[83] Obama's response, however, was less forcefully clear. When questioned about the law while at a NATO summit, the president called the law "abhorrent" but added the qualification, "But I want everybody to understand that our focus is to defeat al Qaeda."[84] Obama's comments prompted criticism from feminists, while the strong international outcry from other NATO governments and private diplomacy by Clinton forced Karzai to revise the law.[85]

Even more problematic for U.S. and Afghan feminists was Obama's announcement that the United States would withdraw from Afghanistan in 2014, regardless of conditions on the ground. In setting a firm timetable for withdrawal, the president appeared to accept sacrificing Afghan women, and the hard-fought progress they made since 2001, to end an unpopular war. Starting in 2010, the administration even indicated a willingness to negotiate with the Taliban and, potentially, to allow them a share in Afghanistan's future governance, which would legitimize their views. The Taliban's stance on women had not changed. Including them in the government would certainly mean renewed restrictions on women.

According to the *Washington Post*, a top U.S. official indicated that some members of the administration were willing to accept that: "Gender issues are going to have to take a back seat to other priorities. . . . There's no way we can be successful if we maintain every special interest and pet project. All those pet rocks in our rucksack were taking us down."[86] Women's human rights are not a "pet rock," however, and the return of the Taliban to power could literally be a matter of life-and-death for many Afghan women who have tried to get an education or pursue employment or other freedoms since 2001. Indeed, women were already targets of Taliban retribution during the protracted U.S. occupation.[87]

While Obama sought to step back from women's rights promotion to focus on other, more traditional policy priorities, there was a significant public reaction against this. Many feminists had opposed the war in 2001, but they nevertheless believed that the United States must follow through on its promises. Otherwise, America's longest war would have been for naught, and Afghan women would suffer the consequences of this policy failure. Women's human rights had become so connected to U.S. foreign policy, both institutionally and in the minds of the public, that it was an issue American policymakers had to consider, or at least appear to consider, when formulating policy toward the Islamic world. (This is still the case today.) Feminist activism and public opinion did not permit Obama to downplay or ignore the issue.

Immediately after the president indicated in the summer of 2010 that the United States might be willing to negotiate with the Taliban, *Time* magazine responded with a cover story on Afghan women. Its cover featured a photo of an eighteen-year-old Afghan girl named Aisha, whose ears and nose the Taliban had cut off the year before. The girl's face was strikingly disfigured, and she looked directly at the reader, accusingly. Superimposed over the photo was the headline "What Happens If We Leave Afghanistan."[88] The extensive cover story followed the lives of Aisha and several other Afghan women who struggled for rights in a country still very much threatened by Taliban extremism. They suffered for the sake of American political expediency.

The issue of *Time* drew worldwide attention.[89] A few days later, Christiane Amanpour hosted the first episode of her weekly television news talk show, *This Week with Christiane Amanpour*. While interviewing her first guest, House Speaker Nancy Pelosi (D-California), Amanpour confronted her with the *Time* cover. "Is America going to abandon the women of

Afghanistan again?" Amanpour demanded.[90] A clearly uncomfortable Pelosi struggled to respond. That the world-renowned war correspondent and foreign affairs expert would bring up the issue of Afghan women with her first guest on her first episode demonstrated the issue's enduring salience.

Amanpour gave weight to the growing chorus of voices that called for the Obama administration not to abandon Afghan women and maintain its commitment to putting women's human rights at the center of American foreign policy. Internet and print articles with titles like "Obama Backpedals on Empty Promises to Afghan Women," "Betrayed," and "Don't Abandon Us, Obama" became commonplace, while Afghan feminist organizations, such as RAWA, AWN, and Women for Afghan Women, along with American journalists, maintained a public spotlight on women's human rights despite the president's attempts to move the issue to the back burner.[91] All made the argument articulated by *Washington Post* journalist Michael Gerson that "Afghanistan, without the participation of women, will remain a failed and dangerous state. . . . The dignity of women is not the only reason America fights in Afghanistan—but it is a good one."[92] The widespread criticism of Obama's attempts to sidestep the issue of Afghan women indicated not only abiding public concern for Muslim women but also the fact that women's human rights had become an important variable that U.S. leaders must address when formulating foreign policy.

The policy discourse since 9/11 revealed two different yet interrelated foreign policy impulses at work simultaneously. The first was a genuine concern for human rights, especially women's human rights. The Bush administration always maintained that its policies were "grounded in the non-negotiable demands of human dignity and reflect universal human values," and Hillary Clinton's State Department returned to universal human rights discourse.[93] This put the United States squarely in line with many other governments, the United Nations, and the climate of international opinion, including in Islamic societies; indeed, the influence of global opinion on these issues cannot be overstated. Human rights and women's rights were and are on the international agenda. That the United States focused primarily on women's human rights in the Islamic world is also unsurprising. The United States became increasingly entangled in the affairs of Muslim countries, and the Islamic world experienced much instability in the early twenty-first century. Other nations grappled with similar concerns about human rights and Muslim women during the same period, as demonstrated by the headscarf debates in France.[94]

Second, Americans' understanding of human rights issues is inextricably entangled with the nature of U.S. power and identity. Americans have long believed in their own exceptionalism and have seen themselves as a model for the world. In declaring their commitment to human rights and in implementing policies that aimed to advance women's rights in countries like Iraq and Afghanistan, U.S. officials and groups like the FMF advanced a vision of what they thought the United States was, or at least what they wanted it to be: a beacon of liberty, democracy, and individual freedom and the protector of the vulnerable and oppressed. In this conception, the Muslim world and its fundamentalists in particular were the mirror opposite of the United States.

Simultaneous commitments to universal human rights and to notions of American exceptionalism might appear to be contradictory, but older discourses and frameworks for understanding the world can exist alongside and become entangled with newer ones.[95] While aspects of colonial feminism persisted in early twenty-first-century U.S. discourse, they existed alongside another discourse of universal human rights. By the 1990s, international law treated women's rights and human rights as one and the same. After several decades, the language and logic of the transnational human rights movement had influenced the thinking of U.S. policymakers.

Similarly, decades of feminist activism in the United States and internationally changed American society and ways of thinking about gender. Emily Rosenberg explained, for example, the uneasily coexisting "imaginaries" of a "discourse of gender and rescue" and a "largely twentieth-century tradition of transnational networks, which emphasizes . . . human welfare and women's empowerment."[96] Post-9/11 policies on women in Afghanistan and Iraq stemmed from these interrelated and sometimes conflicting impulses to spread American ideals abroad and to uphold universal human rights.

U.S. policies, then, have not simply represented colonial feminism or the expedient and politically opportunistic co-optation of feminist rhetoric. In the context of post-1979 American discourse, feminist campaigns, and Clinton-era policy precedents, the Bush administration's focus on women's human rights in Afghanistan and Iraq makes sense. Only by understanding the complex and nuanced history of Americans' engagement with the issue of gender equality in the Islamic world, along with the variety of historical actors who made women's human rights into a foreign policy issue, can historians gain a better understanding of U.S. policymakers' approaches to promoting Muslim women's equality.

The serious and profound challenges to women's human rights in Islamic countries, described in these chapters, continue. Even worse, new radical Islamic groups have arisen whose tactics go beyond even the Taliban's brutality. Boko Haram in Nigeria has kidnapped and raped hundreds of girls, while the so-called Islamic State (ISIS) has unleashed a wave of terror in Syria and parts of Iraq that has included, among other atrocities, enslaving women. The challenges to women's human rights go on.[97]

I wish I could contemplate the prospects for women's human rights under a Hillary Clinton presidency, but alas, I cannot. She likely would have implemented the most far-reaching gender equality policies, both foreign and domestic, in U.S. history. Instead, as a gleeful misogynist, the current president is hardly likely to take women's human rights seriously, either at home or abroad. If he discusses Muslim women's rights at all, it will be to use them to support naked imperialism abroad and Islamophobic and xenophobic policies at home. The future for U.S. women's human rights policy indeed looks bleak in the wake of the 2016 election. But feminist and human rights activists, as well as the American public, must not allow policymakers to relegate women's rights to the margins once again, regardless of who occupies the White House. If the United States seeks a peaceful, more democratic world—as it claims—that world cannot come about without women's access to education, political rights, economic independence, physical safety, and basic human dignity. Traditional American policy goals—like stability and prosperity—depend on women, and *all* people, enjoying the full measure of equality. Soft power and hard power issues are inextricable. As Ambassador Melanne Verveer put it, "Women are a foreign policy issue. Seriously, guys."[98]

Notes

For a complete bibliography of sources used in this book, please go to http://www
.kellyjshannon.com.

Introduction

1. "Liberating the Women of Afghanistan," *New York Times*, November 24, 2001,
A26.

2. George W. Bush, "Address to the Joint Session of the 107th Congress," September 20, 2001, *Selected Speeches of George W. Bush, 2001–2008*, White House Archives,
http://georgewbush-whitehouse.archives.gov/infocus/bushrecord/documents
/Selected_Speeches_George_W_Bush.pdf (accessed October 13, 2015).

3. Laura Bush, "Radio Address by Mrs. Bush," November 17, 2001, American
Presidency Project, ed. Gerhard Peters and John T. Woolley, http://www.presidency
.ucsb.edu/ws/index.php?pid=24992 (accessed October 1, 2009).

4. According to polls conducted by CNN, Gallup, *USA Today*, CBS, ABC, the
Washington Post, and *New York Times* from October 2001 through September 2002,
83–94 percent of Americans supported the war in Afghanistan. Karlyn Bowman,
America and the War on Terrorism, American Enterprise Institute for Public Policy
Research, July 24, 2008, 58–60, http://www.aei.org/publicopinion3 (accessed May 12,
2010).

5. The burqa is a form of Islamic veil traditionally worn by Pashtuns in Afghanistan and Western Pakistan, which the Taliban forced all women to wear once they
seized control of Afghanistan in the mid-1990s. The burqa is a large piece of cloth—
often blue, yellow, or brown—that covers a woman's entire body from head to foot. The
headpiece includes a screen over the eyes, forcing the woman to see and breathe out of
small holes in the screen. No part of the woman's body should be visible to others. It is
the most extreme form of veiling in the Islamic world. Although the burqa is specific

to Central Asia, since 2001 many in the West began using the term "burqa" (also spelled "burka") to refer to any veil that covers a woman's head, body, and face.

6. A Google News Archive search yielded 21,200 articles written about Afghan women in the United States from September through December 2001. Examples include "Tahmeena Faryal: Democratic Government Is Best Hope for Afghan Women," *Time*, December 4, 2001, http://archives.cnn.com/2001/COMMUNITY/12/04/faryal .cnna/index.html (accessed November 24, 2009); Richard Lacayo, "About Face for Afghan Women," *Time*, November 25, 2001, http://www.time.com/time/nation/article /0,8599,185651,00.html (accessed November 24, 2009); Janelle Brown, "Any Day Now," *Salon*, December 3, 2001, http://dir.salon.com/story/mwt/feature/2001/12/03 /afghan_women/index.html (accessed November 24, 2009); Debbie Howlett, "Afghan Women Fight Oppression," *USA Today*, October 16, 2001, http://www.usatoday.com /news/sept11/2001/10/17/afghan-women.htm (accessed November 24, 2009); LaShawn Jefferson, "Out Go the Taliban, But Will Afghan Women Be Excluded Again?" *New York Times*, November 16, 2001, http://www.nytimes.com/2001/11/16/opinion/16iht -edjeff_ed3_.html (accessed November 24, 2009); Scott Peterson, "For Many Afghan Women, Bare Faces and Lives Resumed," *Christian Science Monitor*, November 16, 2001, http://www.csmonitor.com/2001/1116/p1s3-wosc.html (accessed November 24, 2009); "Veiled Women with Voices," *Wired*, October 31, 2001, http://www.wired.com /techbiz/media/news/2001/10/48040 (accessed November 24, 2009).

7. "As the World Pays New Attention to Women in Afghanistan, Muslim Women Debate Feminism and Fundamentalism," *Democracy Now*, December 13, 2001, text and mp3, http://www.democracynow.org/2001/12/13/as_the_world_pays_new_attention (accessed May 12, 2010).

8. Gayatri Spivak, "Can the Subaltern Speak?" in *Colonial Discourse and Post-Colonial Theory: A Reader*, ed. Patrick Williams and Laura Chrisman (New York: Columbia University Press, 1994), 93. For a sampling of critical analyses, see Miriam Cooke, "Saving Brown Women," *Signs* 28, no. 1 (Autumn 2002): 468–70; Susan Faludi, *The Terror Dream: Fear and Fantasy in Post 9/11 America* (London: Atlantic Books, 2008), 52–57; Liz Halloran, "The Lifting of the Burkas," *Hartford Courant*, November 25, 2001, http://articles.courant.com/2001-11-25/news/0111250038_1_ women-s-rights-national-women-s-law-center-burkas (accessed January 21, 2013); Michaele L. Ferguson and Lori Jo Marso, eds., *W Stands for Women: How the George W. Bush Presidency Shaped a New Politics of Gender* (Durham, NC: Duke University Press, 2007); Charles Hirschkind and Saba Mahmood, "Feminism, the Taliban, and the Policies of Counter-Insurgency," *Anthropological Quarterly* 75, no. 2 (Spring 2002): 339–54; Emily Rosenberg, "Rescuing Women and Children," *Journal of American History* 89, no. 2 (2002): 456–65.

9. David Stout, "The First Lady; Mrs. Bush Cites Women's Plight Under Taliban," *New York Times*, November 18, 2001, B4.

10. Barbara J. Keys, *Reclaiming American Virtue: The Human Rights Revolution of the 1970s* (Cambridge, MA: Harvard University Press, 2014), 5.

11. Gail Bederman, *Manliness & Civilization: A Cultural History of Gender and Race in the United States, 1880–1917* (Chicago: University of Chicago Press, 1995), 24.

12. While historians point to many periods as the origin of the human rights movement, the three main ones are the Enlightenment, the 1940s, and the 1970s. See Elizabeth Borgwardt, *A New Deal for the World: America's Vision for Human Rights* (Cambridge, MA: Harvard University Press, 2005); G. Daniel Cohen, "The Holocaust and the 'Human Rights Revolution': A Reassessment," in *The Human Rights Revolution: An International History*, ed. Akira Iriye, Petra Goedde, and William I. Hitchcock (New York: Oxford University Press, 2012), 53–71; Mary Ann Glendon, *A World Made New: Eleanor Roosevelt and the Universal Declaration of Human Rights* (New York: Random House, 2002); Lynn Hunt, *Inventing Human Rights: A History* (New York: W. W. Norton, 2007); Micheline Ishay, *The History of Human Rights: From Ancient Times to the Globalization Era* (Berkeley: University of California Press, 2004); Jonathan Israel, *Democratic Enlightenment: Philosophy, Revolution, and Human Rights, 1750–1790* (Oxford: Oxford University Press, 2011); Barbara Keys, "Anti-Torture Politics: Amnesty International, the Greek Junta, and the Origins of the Human Rights 'Boom' in the United States," in *The Human Rights Revolution*, ed. Iriye, Goedde, and Hitchcock, 201–21; Samuel Moyn, *The Last Utopia: Human Rights in History* (Cambridge, MA: Harvard University Press, 2010); Devin O. Pendas, "Toward a New Politics? On the Recent Historiography of Human Rights," *Contemporary European History* 21, no. 1 (2012): 95–111.

13. Samuel Moyn, "Substance, Scale, and Salience: The Recent Historiography of Human Rights," *Annual Review of Law and Social Science* 8 (2012): 125.

14. See Borgwardt, *New Deal for the World*; Mark Philip Bradley, "The United States and the Global Human Rights Politics in the 1940s," in *Civil Religion, Human Rights and International Relations*, ed. Helle Porsdam (London: Edward Elgar, 2012), 118–35; Keys, *Reclaiming American Virtue*; Samantha Power, *"A Problem from Hell": America and the Age of Genocide* (New York: Harper, 2002); Bradley R. Simpson, *Economists with Guns: Authoritarian Development and U.S.-Indonesian Relations, 1960–1968* (Stanford: Stanford University Press, 2008); Sarah B. Snyder, *Human Rights Activism and the End of the Cold War: A Transnational History of the Helsinki Network* (New York: Cambridge University Press, 2011); David F. Schmitz and Vanessa Walker, "Jimmy Carter and the Foreign Policy of Human Rights: The Development of a Post–Cold War Foreign Policy," *Diplomatic History* 28, no. 1 (January 2004): 113–43.

15. Snyder, *Human Rights Activism*; Carl Bon Tempo, "From the Center-Right: Freedom House and Human Rights in the 1970s and 1980s," in *The Human Rights Revolution*, ed. Iriye, Goedde, and Hitchcock, 223–44.

16. Allida Black, "Are Women 'Human'? The UN and the Struggle to Recognize Women's Rights as Human Rights," in *The Human Rights Revolution*, ed. Iriye, Goedde, and Hitchcock, 133–58.

17. See Mahnaz Afkhami, ed., *Faith and Freedom: Women's Human Rights in the Muslim World* (Syracuse, NY: Syracuse University Press, 1995); Charlotte Bunch and

Niamh Reilly, *Demanding Accountability: The Global Campaign and Vienna Tribunal for Women's Human Rights* (New Brunswick, NJ: Center for Women's Global Leadership, 1994).

18. Kenneth Cmiel, "The Emergence of Human Rights Politics in the United States," *Journal of American History* 86, no. 3 (December 1999): 1239.

19. Keys, *Reclaiming American Virtue*, 3, 7.

20. Cmiel, "Human Rights Politics," 1242.

21. See Frank Costigliola, *France and the United States: The Cold Alliance Since World War II* (New York: Twayne, 1992); Frank Costigliola, *Roosevelt's Lost Alliances: How Personal Politics Helped Start the Cold War* (Princeton, NJ: Princeton University Press, 2012); Kristin Hoganson, *Fighting for American Manhood: How Gender Politics Provoked the Spanish-American and Philippine-American Wars* (New Haven: Yale University Press, 1998); Amy Kaplan, *The Anarchy of Empire in the Making of U.S. Culture* (Cambridge, MA: Harvard University Press, 2002); Christina Klein, *Cold War Orientalism: Asia in the Middlebrow Imagination, 1945–1961* (Berkeley: University of California Press, 2003); Michelle Mart, "Tough Guys and American Cold War Policy: Images of Israel, 1948–1960," *Diplomatic History* 20, no. 3 (Summer 1996): 357–79; Mary A. Renda, *Taking Haiti: Military Occupation and the Culture of U.S. Imperialism, 1915–1940* (Chapel Hill: University of North Carolina Press, 2001); Andrew J. Rotter, *Comrades at Odds: The United States and India, 1947–1964* (Ithaca, NY: Cornell University Press, 2000); Naoko Shibusawa, *America's Geisha Ally: Reimagining the Japanese Enemy* (Cambridge, MA: Harvard University Press, 2006); Judy Tzu-Chun Wu, *Radicals on the Road: Internationalism, Orientalism, and Feminism During the Vietnam War* (Ithaca, NY: Cornell University Press, 2013).

22. Robert Buzzanco, "Where's the Beef? Culture Without Power in the Study of U.S. Foreign Relations," *Diplomatic History* 24, no. 4 (Fall 2000): 623.

23. See Ervand Abrahamian, *The Coup: 1953, the CIA, and the Roots of Modern U.S.-Iranian Relations* (New York: New Press, 2013); H. W. Brands, *Into the Labyrinth: The United States and the Middle East, 1945–1993* (New York: McGraw-Hill, 1994); Matthew Connelly, *A Diplomatic Revolution: Algeria's Fight for Independence and the Origins of the Post–Cold War Era* (New York: Oxford University Press, 2002); Lloyd C. Gardner, *Three Kings: The Rise of an American Empire in the Middle East After World War II* (New York: New Press, 2009); Peter L. Hahn, *Caught in the Middle East: U.S. Policy Toward the Arab-Israeli Conflict, 1945–1961* (Chapel Hill: University of North Carolina Press, 2004); Mahmood Mamdani, *Good Muslim, Bad Muslim: America, the Cold War, and the Roots of Terror* (New York: Pantheon, 2004); Salim Yaqub, *Containing Arab Nationalism: The Eisenhower Doctrine and the Middle East* (Chapel Hill: University of North Carolina Press, 2004).

24. See Matthew F. Jacobs, *Imagining the Middle East: The Building of an American Foreign Policy, 1918–1967* (Chapel Hill: University of North Carolina Press, 2014); Douglas Little, *American Orientalism: The United States and the Middle East Since 1945* (Chapel Hill: University of North Carolina Press, 2002); Melani McAlister, *Epic*

Encounters: Culture, Media, and U.S. Interest in the Middle East, 1945–2000 (Berkeley: University of California Press, 2001); Michael B. Oren, *Power, Faith, and Fantasy: America in the Middle East, 1776 to the Present* (New York: W. W. Norton, 2007); Rosenberg, "Rescuing Women and Children."

25. See Hoganson, *Fighting for American Manhood*; Mart, "Tough Guys"; Robert Dean, *Imperial Brotherhood: Gender and the Making of Cold War Foreign Policy* (Amherst: University of Massachusetts Press, 2001).

26. The small body of literature that does include women in the history of U.S. foreign relations is usually authored by female historians. See Harriet Hyman Alonso, *Peace as a Woman's Issue: A History of the U.S. Movement for World Peace and Women's Rights* (Syracuse, NY: Syracuse University Press, 1993); Kristin Hoganson, *Consumers' Imperium: The Global Production of American Domesticity, 1865–1920* (Chapel Hill: University of North Carolina Press, 2007); Helen Laville, *Cold War Women: The International Activities of American Women's Organizations* (Manchester: Manchester University Press, 2002); Shibusawa, *America's Geisha Ally*; Wu, *Radicals on the Road*; Mari Yoshihara, *Embracing the East: White Women and American Orientalism* (New York: Oxford University Press, 2003). The exception is Rhodri Jeffreys-Jones, *Changing Differences: Women and the Shaping of American Foreign Policy, 1917–1994* (New Brunswick, NJ: Rutgers University Press, 1995).

27. Many studies of Western perceptions of Muslim women center on Europe rather than the United States. Emily Rosenberg's "Rescuing Women and Children" provides an excellent analysis of Bush administration rhetoric about Afghan women, but as an article published only a year after the U.S. invasion of Afghanistan, her study necessarily is not comprehensive. For studies of Western characterizations of Muslim women more generally, see Malek Alloula, *The Colonial Harem* (Minneapolis: University of Minnesota Press, 1986); Holly Edwards, ed., *Noble Dreams, Wicked Pleasures: Orientalism in America, 1870–1930* (Princeton, NJ: Princeton University Press, 2000); Mohja Kahf, *Western Representations of the Muslim Woman: From Termagant to Odalisque* (Austin: University of Texas Press, 1999); Patricia M. E. Lorcin, *Imperial Identities: Stereotyping, Prejudice, and Race in Colonial Algeria* (London: I. B. Tauris, 1995); Fatima Mernissi, *Scheherazade Goes West: Different Cultures, Different Harems* (New York: Washington Square, 2001); Joan Wallach Scott, *The Politics of the Veil* (Princeton, NJ: Princeton University Press, 2007); Faegheh Shirazi, *The Veil Unveiled: The Hijab in Modern Culture* (Gainesville: University Press of Florida, 2001).

28. Edward Said, *Orientalism* (New York: Vintage Books, 1978), 2.

29. See Alloula, *Colonial Harem*; Mernissi, *Scheherazade*; Shirazi, *Veil Unveiled*; Jack Shaheen, *Reel Bad Arabs: How Hollywood Vilifies a People* (Northampton, MA: Olive Branch Press, 2001, 2009).

30. A useful overview of historians' critiques and uses of *Orientalism* can be found in Andrew Rotter, "Saidism Without Said: *Orientalism* and U.S. Diplomatic History," *American Historical Review* 105, no. 4 (October 2000): 1205–17.

31. McAlister, *Epic Encounters*, 40.

32. Ibid., 12.

33. George Morgan and Scott Poynting, "Introduction: The Transnational Folk Devil," in *Global Islamophobia: Muslims and Moral Panic in the West*, ed. George Morgan and Scott Poynting (Surrey, UK: Ashgate, 2012), 2; Deepa Kumar, *Islamophobia and the Politics of Empire* (Chicago: Haymarket Books, 2012), 3; Stephen Sheehi, *Islamophobia: The Ideological Campaign Against Muslims* (Atlanta: Clarity Press, 2011), 31. Much of the scholarly literature also contends that Islamophobia is a racist ideology. However, most of these studies do not provide concrete evidence to support this claim. Moreover, Islam is not a race but rather a religion that has members from every racial and ethnic group. This study therefore does not employ a racial analysis. I am not ignoring an issue that might come naturally to the minds of some readers, but there is not sufficient evidence in my primary sources to warrant stronger emphasis on race than I have provided. Likewise, I do not include Christianity as a lens of analysis because, even more than race, it does not appear in my sources.

34. Bederman, *Manliness & Civilization*, 24.

35. Sherene H. Razack, *Casting Out: The Eviction of Muslims from Western Law and Politics* (Toronto: University of Toronto Press, 2008), 16.

36. Lata Mani, "Contentious Traditions: The Debate on *Sati* in Colonial India," in *Recasting Women: Essays in Indian Colonial History*, ed. Kumkum Sangari (New Brunswick, NJ: Rutgers University Press, 1990), 88–126; Clare Midgley, "British Women, Women's Rights and Empire, 1790–1850," in *Women's Rights and Human Rights: International Historical Perspectives*, ed. Patricia Grimshaw, Katie Holmes, and Marilyn Lake (Houndmills: Palgrave, 2001), 3–15.

37. Leila Ahmed, *Women and Gender in Islam: Historical Roots of a Modern Debate* (New Haven: Yale University Press, 1993), 152–53.

38. Hester Eisenstein, *Feminism Seduced: How Global Elites Use Women's Labor and Ideas to Exploit the World* (Boulder, CO: Paradigm, 2009), 179; Ahmed, *Women and Gender in Islam*, 151.

39. Todd Shepard, *The Invention of Decolonization: The Algerian War and the Remaking of France* (Ithaca, NY: Cornell University Press, 2006), 186–89; Hal Lehrman, "Battle of the Veil in Algeria," *New York Times Sunday Magazine*, July 13, 1957, SM14.

40. Richard H. Immerman, *Empire for Liberty: A History of American Imperialism from Benjamin Franklin to Paul Wolfowitz* (Princeton, NJ: Princeton University Press, 2010), 5–6.

41. See Haideh Moghissi, *Feminism and Islamic Fundamentalism: The Limits of Postmodern Analysis* (London: Zed, 1999), vii–viii, 4–6, 49–63, 73–76; Mahnaz Afkhami, "Cultural Relativism and Women's Human Rights," in *Women and International Human Rights Law: Volume 2*, ed. Kelly D. Askin and Dorean M. Koenig (Ardsley, NY: Transnational Publishers, 1999), 479–86.

42. See William Appleman Williams, *The Tragedy of American Diplomacy* (New York: W. W. Norton, 1959, 1962, 1972); Noam Chomsky, *Towards a New Cold War:*

U.S. Foreign Policy from Vietnam to Reagan (New York: New Press, 1982, 2003); Greg Grandin, *Empire's Workshop: Latin America, the United States, and the Rise of the New Imperialism* (New York: Henry Holt, 2006).

43. See John Lewis Gaddis, *We Now Know: Rethinking Cold War History* (Oxford: Oxford University Press, 1997); Paul Kengor, *The Crusader: Ronald Reagan and the Fall of Communism* (New York: Regan Books, 2006).

44. Muslims also use a shorthand term, "Dar al-Islam," to refer to Muslim-majority areas, so the "Islamic world" is not simply a Western construct.

45. Pew Research Religion and Public Life Project, "Major Religious Traditions in the U.S.," Religious Landscape Survey, April 2007, http://religions.pewforum.org /reports (accessed June 9, 2014).

46. "The Future of the Global Muslim Population," Interactive Map, Pew Forum on Religion and Public Life, http://features.pewforum.org/muslim-population -graphic (accessed March 15, 2013).

47. Scholars debate the use of the term "fundamentalist" in reference to Muslims. Since fundamentalism originated as a self-description for a particular kind of U.S. Protestantism in the early twentieth century, some argue that the term is inappropriate when applied to Muslims. They propose as alternatives "Muslim radicalism," "Islamism," "Muslim revivalism," "Muslim traditionalism," and "religious nationalism." While sensitive to the problematic nature of the term "Islamic fundamentalism," I find the alternative descriptors even more unsatisfying. Because "fundamentalist" was the most commonly used term during the period under examination, and because I am persuaded by Haideh Moghissi's arguments in favor of the term, I use "fundamentalist" in this book to refer to politically motivated, radically conservative Muslims like Ayatollah Khomeini and the Taliban. See David Harrington Watt, "What's in a Name?: The Meaning of 'Muslim Fundamentalist,' " *Origins* 1, no. 10 (July 2008), http://ehistory.osu.edu/osu/origins/article.cfm?articleid=15 (accessed March 27, 2008); Moghissi, *Feminism and Islamic Fundamentalism*, 64–73.

Chapter 1

1. The chador is a traditional Iranian veil. It is a long black piece of fabric that covers a woman's entire body, leaving only the hands and face visible. *Chadori* refers to women who wear the chador.

2. "Khomeini and the Veiled Lady," *Time*, October 22, 1979, http://www.time.com /time/magazine/article/0,9171,947512,00.html (accessed May 9, 2008). The *New York Times Sunday Magazine* published the full transcript of Fallaci's interview with Khomeini. See Oriana Fallaci, "An Interview with Khomeini," *New York Times*, October 7, 1979, SM8. After 9/11, Fallaci published highly controversial criticisms of Islam. See Oriana Fallaci, *The Rage and the Pride* (New York: Rizzoli, 2002).

3. Michael E. Latham, *The Right Kind of Revolution: Modernization, Development, and U.S. Foreign Policy from the Cold War to the Present* (Ithaca, NY: Cornell University Press, 2011), 143–52; David Ekbladh, *The Great American Mission: Modernization*

and the Construction of an American World Order (Princeton, NJ: Princeton University Press, 2011), 231.

4. McAlister, *Epic Encounters*, xvii.

5. Amira Jarmakani, *Imagining Arab Womanhood: The Cultural Mythology of Veils, Harems, and Belly Dancers in the U.S.* (Houndmills: Palgrave Macmillan, 2008), 6, 9.

6. Oren, *Power, Faith, and Fantasy*, 149–76. The number of Americans who traveled to the Islamic world prior to the 1840s–1850s was very small. For views of American missionaries, see Annie Van Sommer and Samuel M. Zwemer, *Our Moslem Sisters: A Cry of Need from Lands of Darkness Interpreted by Those Who Heard It* (New York: Fleming H. Revell Co., 1907), 5–6; Nima Naghibi, *Rethinking Global Sisterhood: Western Feminism and Iran* (Minneapolis: University of Minnesota Press, 2007), 1–34.

7. Oren, *Power, Faith, and Fantasy*, 13–14, 44–45, 150, 152, 160–61, 172; Naghibi, *Rethinking Global Sisterhood*, xv. See also Mernissi, *Scheherazade*. *Arabian Nights* is the shortened title Americans often use in place of the original, *A Thousand and One Arabian Nights*.

8. Mark Twain, *The Innocents Abroad, or, The New Pilgrims' Progress* (Hartford, CT: American Publishing Company, 1869), 373, Electronic Text Center, University of Virginia Library, http://etext.lib.virginia.edu/toc/modeng/public/TwaInno.html (accessed February 15, 2010).

9. Twain, *Innocents Abroad*, 85.

10. David F. Dorr, *A Colored Man Round the World*, ed. Malini Johar Schueller (Cleveland: Printed for the author, 1858; Ann Arbor: University of Michigan Press, 1999), 122–23, PDF, the Internet Archive, https://archive.org/details/acoloredmanroun00dorrgoog (accessed May 14, 2010).

11. Oren, *Power, Faith, and Fantasy*, 156–57.

12. Nathaniel Parker Willis, *Summer Cruise in the Mediterranean on Board an American Frigate* (London: T. Bosworth, 1853), 260, 200, PDF, the Internet Archive, https://archive.org/details/summercruiseinm01willgoog (accessed December 3, 2014).

13. Lynne Thornton, *Women as Portrayed in Orientalist Painting* (Paris: ACR Edition Internationale, 1994), 20. See Frederick Arthur Bridgman, *Soir*, oil on canvas, 1888, Orientalist Gallery, http://theorientalistgallery.blogspot.com/2009/03/summer-evening.html (accessed February 15, 2010); Henry Siddons Mowbray, *Harem Scene*, oil on canvas, 1884–1900, Metropolitan Museum of Art, Works of Art: American Paintings and Sculpture, http://www.metmuseum.org/works_of_art/collection_database/american_paintings_and_sculpture/harem_scene_henry_siddons_mowbray/objectview.aspx?collID=2&OID=20011989 (accessed May 14, 2010). Other Bridgman paintings depicting Muslim women include *L'Indolence*; *The Orange Seller*; *Almeh Flirting with an Armenian Policeman, Cairo*; *The Siesta*; *In the Seraglio*; *Orientalist Interior*; *On the Terrace*; *The Harem*; *Queen of the Brigands*; *Moorish Girl, Algiers Countryside*; *In the Garden at Mustapha*; *The Card Players*; *An Eastern*

Veranda; A Veiled Beauty of Constantinople; After the Bath; Aicha, a Woman of Morocco; and dozens more. See Frederick Arthur Bridgman: The Complete Works, http://www.frederickarthurbridgman.org (accessed March 20, 2012). See also Edwin Lord Weeks: The Complete Works, http://www.edwinlordweeks.org (accessed June 13, 2012); Edwards, *Noble Dreams*.

14. Jarmakani, *Imagining Arab Womanhood*, 55, 63–66; John Singer Sargent, *Study from Life* (a.k.a. *Nude Study of an Egyptian Girl*), oil on canvas, 1891, Art Institute of Chicago, http://www.artic.edu/aic/collections/artwork/121629?search_no=5&index=27 (accessed December 11, 2013).

15. For firsthand accounts of harem life, see Leila Ahmed, *A Border Passage: From Cairo to America—A Woman's Journey*, reprint ed. (New York: Penguin, 2012); Fatima Mernissi, *Dreams of Trespass: Tales of a Harem Girlhood* (Cambridge, MA: Perseus Books, 1994); Huda Shaarawi, *Harem Years: The Memoirs of an Egyptian Feminist (1879–1924)*, trans., ed., and introduced by Margot Badran (New York: Feminist Press, 1986).

16. Ahmed, *Women and Gender in Islam*, 144–88. See also Qasim Amin, *The Liberation of Women and The New Woman: Two Documents in the History of Egyptian Feminism*, trans. Samiha Sidhom Peterson (originally published 1899, 1900; Cairo: American University in Cairo Press, 2000).

17. Leila Ahmed, *A Quiet Revolution: The Veil's Resurgence, from the Middle East to America* (New Haven: Yale University Press, 2011), 46.

18. "The Harem Compartment," *New York Times*, March 21, 1920, XX9; "Egypt's Women Waking Up," *New York Times*, November 21, 1920, 123; "Tourist Tide Turns to Egypt Again," *New York Times*, May 15, 1921, 34; Ameen Rihani, "Moslem Women Are Advancing at Different Paces," *New York Times*, August 17, 1930, 103; Felix Howland, "Iran Women Lift Veils," *New York Times*, November 17, 1935, X11; "Women Again Demanding Egyptian and Iraqi Votes," *New York Times*, January 16, 1944, 11; "Vote for Women Proposed in Egyptian Parliament," *New York Times*, February 28, 1951; "Iran's Women Seek Vote," *New York Times*, January 17, 1952, 2; "Egyptian Feminist to Fast for Rights," *New York Times,* March 13, 1954, 5; "Egyptian Leader of Women's Rights Tells of Literacy and Suffrage Gains in Land," *New York Times*, November 2, 1954, 30; Jay Walz, "Women of Iran Seek the Ballot," *New York Times*, September 25, 1960, 10.

19. Jarmakani, *Imagining Arab Womanhood*, 103–37.

20. *The Sheik*, directed by George Melford (1921; Image Entertainment, 2002), DVD.

21. Emily W. Leider, *Dark Lover: The Life and Death of Rudolph Valentino* (New York: Farrar, Straus and Giroux, 2003), 154.

22. For similar films, see *The Thief of Bagdad*, directed by Raoul Walsh (1924; Kino Video, 2004), DVD; *The Son of the Sheik*, directed by George Fitzmaurice (1926; Image Entertainment, 2002), DVD; *The Garden of Allah*, direct by Richard Boleslawski (1936; Metro-Goldwyn-Mayer, 2004), DVD; *Ali Baba Goes to Town*, directed by David Butler (1937; 20th Century Fox, 2013), DVD; *Road to Morocco*, directed by David Butler

(1942; Paramount, 2002), DVD; and *Kismet*, directed by Vincente Minnelli (1955; Warner Home Video, 2005), DVD. Earlier film versions of *Kismet* appeared in 1920, 1930, and 1944.

23. *The Long Ships*, directed by Jack Cardiff (1964; Sony, 2003), DVD; *Harum Scarum*, directed by Gene Nelson (1965; Turner Entertainment, 2007), DVD. Sidney Poitier played the evil sheik in *The Long Ships*.

24. *I Dream of Jeannie*, created by Sidney Sheldon, starring Barbara Eden and Larry Hagman, NBC, 1965–70.

25. Shirazi, *Veil Unveiled*, 43.

26. Daniel Sargent, *A Superpower Transformed: The Remaking of American Foreign Relations in the 1970s* (New York: Oxford University Press, 2015), 35–36, 165–66.

27. United Nations Development Programme, *Human Development Report 2000* (New York: Oxford University Press, 2000), 47. See also Iriye, Goedde, and Hitchcock, eds., *The Human Rights Revolution*.

28. Jimmy Carter, "Universal Declaration of Human Rights Remarks at a White House Meeting Commemorating the 30th Anniversary of the Declaration's Signing," December 6, 1978, American Presidency Project, ed. Gerhard Peters and John T. Woolley, http://www.presidency.ucsb.edu/ws/index.php?pid=30264&st=human+rights &st1=soul (accessed May 18, 2010). Carter declared a commitment to human rights consistently, beginning with his inaugural address. Jimmy Carter, "Inaugural Address," January 20, 1977, American Presidency Project, ed. Gerhard Peters and John T. Woolley, http://www.presidency.ucsb.edu/ws/index.php?pid=6575 (accessed May 18, 2010).

29. United Nations, "Convention on the Elimination of All Forms of Discrimination Against Women," 1979, http://www.un.org/womenwatch/daw/cedaw/text /econvention.htm (accessed August 12, 2009).

30. Sudan became an Islamic theocracy in 1983, and the Taliban in Afghanistan instituted a theocracy of sorts in 1996. Moghissi, *Feminism and Islamic Fundamentalism*, 67–68.

31. William O. Beeman, *The "Great Satan" vs. the "Mad Mullahs": How the United States and Iran Demonize Each Other* (Westport, CT: Praeger, 2005); Abbas Amanat, "Khomeini's Great Satan: Demonizing the American Other in Iran's Islamic Revolution," in *U.S.-Middle East Historical Encounters: A Critical Survey*, ed. Abbas Amanat and Magnus T. Bernhardsson (Gainesville: University Press of Florida, 2007), 142–61.

32. Yaqub, *Containing Arab Nationalism*, 13–14, 29–30; David Farber, *Taken Hostage: The Iranian Hostage Crisis and America's First Encounter with Radical Islam* (Princeton, NJ: Princeton University Press, 2005), 13, 51–60; Latham, *Right Kind of Revolution*, 143–47; Odd Arne Westad, *The Global Cold War: Third World Interventions and the Making of Our Times* (Cambridge: Cambridge University Press, 2007), 289–90; Jimmy Carter and Shah Mohammad Reza Pahlavi, "Tehran, Iran Toasts of the President and the Shah at a State Dinner," December 31, 1977, American Presidency Project, ed. Gerhard Peters and John T. Woolley, http://www.presidency.ucsb.edu/ws/

?pid=7080 (accessed December 4, 2015). See also Abrahamian, *The Coup*; James A. Bill, *The Eagle and the Lion: The Tragedy of American-Iranian Relations* (New Haven, CT: Yale University Press, 1989); David Crist, *The Twilight War: The Secret History of America's Thirty-Year Conflict with Iran* (New York: Penguin, 2012); Stephen Kinzer, *All the Shah's Men: An American Coup and the Roots of Middle East Terror*, 2nd ed. (Hoboken, NJ: Wiley, 2008).

33. Westad, *Global Cold War*, 289.

34. A. K. Ramakrishnan, *US Perceptions of Iran: Approaches and Policies* (New Delhi: New Century Publications, 2008), 32–33; Latham, *Right Kind of Revolution*, 148.

35. Sandra Mackey, *The Iranians: Persia, Islam, and the Soul of a Nation* (New York: Penguin, 1996), 221–38; Westad, *Global Cold War*, 291–93.

36. Eliz Sanasarian, *The Women's Rights Movement in Iran: Mutiny, Appeasement, and Repression from 1900 to Khomeini* (New York: Praeger, 1982), 79–105.

37. Mahnaz Afkhami, "At the Crossroads of Tradition and Modernity: Personal Reflections," *SAIS Review* (Summer/Fall 2000): 87–88. The two women cabinet ministers were Minister of Education Farrokhrou Parsa and Mahnaz Afkhami.

38. Mahnaz Afkhami, oral history interview with author, December 10, 2009, Bethesda, MD; Jane Afary, "Mahnaz Afkhami: A Memoir," *Journal of Middle East Women's Studies* 1, no. 1 (Winter 2005): 150–53. For a comprehensive history of the Iranian feminist movement up to the Revolution, see Sanasarian, *Women's Rights Movement in Iran*.

39. Irene Schneider, "Iran," in *Encyclopedia of Women & Islamic Cultures: Family, Law, and Politics*, vol. 2, ed. Suad Joseph (Leiden: Brill, 2005), 392; Noushin Ahmadi, "Reform and Regression in Iran: Advocating for Change of Family Laws Before and After the Revolution," http://learningpartnership.org/en/advocacy/campaign/familylaw/iranreformprerevolution (accessed May 28, 2009); Afary, "Mahnaz Afkhami," 151.

40. Oriana Fallaci, "The Shah of Iran," *New Republic* (December 1, 1973): 18.

41. Afkhami, "Crossroads," 88.

42. Deniz Kandiyoti, "Reflections on the Politics of Gender in Muslim Societies: From Nairobi to Beijing," in *Faith and Freedom*, ed. Afkhami, 22.

43. Latham, *Right Kind of Revolution*, 148–52.

44. Jay Walz, "Iranian Girl, 24, Teaches Nursing," *New York Times*, May 5, 1963, 22; "Iranians to Elect Parliament Sept. 17," *New York Times*, August 6, 1963, 4; "Iranian Women to Vote Tuesday," *New York Times*, September 15, 1963, 8; "Iran Parliament Is Back in Session," *New York Times*, October 7, 1963, 7; "Farah to Open U.N. Talks in Iran," *New York Times*, February 28, 1965, 2.

45. Joy Billington, "Muslim Women: Beyond the Veil," *Saturday Evening Post* (May/June 1975): 79.

46. Marvine Howe, "Iranian Women Return to Veil in a Resurgence of Spirituality," *New York Times*, July 30, 1977, 15.

47. Afkhami, "Crossroads," 89.

48. Refusing to support Bazargan's call for the release of the American hostages taken at the U.S. embassy on November 4, 1979, Khomeini supported the hostage takers and directly undermined the prime minister's authority. Bazargan was forced to resign in protest.

49. Masoud Kazemzadeh, *Islamic Fundamentalism, Feminism, and Gender Inequality in Iran Under Khomeini* (Lanham, MD: University Press of America, 2002), 9–10; Moghissi, *Feminism and Islamic Fundamentalism*, 100–101.

50. Since the 1990s, Iranian women have collectively pushed back against the veiling laws. Many Iranian women now wear just a headscarf and manteau, a long jacket, instead of the chador, and they allow a daring amount of hair to peek out from under their hijabs. The Iranian government periodically cracks down on "improper" veiling.

51. Edmund Ghareeb, introduction to *Split Vision: The Portrayal of Arabs in the American Media*, ed. Edmund Ghareeb (Washington, DC: American-Arab Affairs Council, 1983), xvii; Melvin Small, "Public Opinion," in *Explaining the History of American Foreign Relations*, 1st ed., ed. Michael J. Hogan and Thomas G. Paterson (Cambridge: Cambridge University Press, 1991), 172.

52. Karin Gwinn Wilkins, "Middle Eastern Women in Western Eyes: A Study of U.S. Press Photographs of Middle Eastern Women," in *The U.S. Media and the Middle East: Image and Perception*, ed. Yahya R. Kamalipour (Westport, CT: Greenwood, 1995), 50.

53. Thomas Roach, "Competing News Narratives, Consensus, and World Power," in *The U.S. Media and the Middle East*, ed. Kamalipour, 33, 28.

54. Farber, *Taken Hostage*, 4–5, 76. Historians have argued that U.S. policymakers missed clear signs of impending unrest in Iran during the 1960s–1970s. See Matthew Shannon, "'Contacts with the Opposition': American Foreign Relations, the Iranian Student Movement, and the Global Sixties," *The Sixties* 4, no. 1 (June 2011): 1–29.

55. Nicholas Gage, "Young People of Iran, Rejecting Modernism, Revive Islamic Values," *New York Times,* December 17, 1978, 1, 12.

56. Betsy Amin-Arsala, "In Iran, to Veil or Not to Veil?" *New York Times*, April 21, 1979, 23.

57. Kate Millett, *Going to Iran* (New York: Coward, McCann and Geoghegan, 1982), 49–50, 73.

58. Afkhami, "Crossroads," 89.

59. Naghibi, *Rethinking Global Sisterhood*, 74–107.

60. Amy Farrell, "Attentive to Difference: *Ms.* Magazine, Coalition Building, and Sisterhood," in *Feminist Coalitions: Historical Perspectives on Second-Wave Feminism in the United States*, ed. Stephanie Gilmore (Urbana: University of Illinois Press, 2008), 48–49; Mim Kelber, "Iran: Five Days in March," *Ms.*, June 1979, 90. In the late 1970s, *Ms.* sold approximately 300,000 issues each month and had over one million estimated

readers, making it the most widely read feminist publication in the United States. Farrell, "Attentive to Difference," 60.

61. Steven Erlanger, "Iran's Shaky Theocracy," *New Republic* (November 10, 1979): 13.

62. Irving Kristol, often described as the "godfather" of neoconservatism, stated, "I think the term 'impulse' or 'persuasion' would be more accurate" than the term "movement" when describing neoconservatism. Irving Kristol, *Neoconservatism: The Autobiography of an Idea* (New York: Free Press, 1995), ix.

63. Sargent, *Superpower Transformed*, 206.

64. David Farber, *The Rise and Fall of Modern American Conservatism: A Short History* (Princeton, NJ: Princeton University Press, 2010), 201.

65. See Michael Levin, "The Feminist Mystique," *Commentary* (December 1980): 25–30; David Gutmann, "Men, Women, and the Parental Imperative," *Commentary* (December 1973): 59–64; Michael Novak, "A Radical Feminist," *Commentary* (February 1976): 90; Jane Larkin Crain, "Feminist Fiction," *Commentary* (December 1974): 58–62. See also Susan Faludi, *Backlash: The Undeclared War Against American Women* (New York: Doubleday, 1991), 281.

66. John Ehrman, *The Rise of Neoconservatism: Intellectuals and Foreign Affairs, 1945–1994* (New Haven, CT: Yale University Press, 1995), 33–62; Jeane Kirkpatrick, "Neoconservatism as a Response to the Counterculture," in *The Neocon Reader*, ed. Irwin Stelzer (New York: Grove, 2004), 236–40. See also Norman Podhoretz, *Breaking Ranks: A Political Memoir* (New York: HarperCollins, 1980).

67. Jacob Heilbrunn, *They Knew They Were Right: The Rise of the Neocons* (New York: Doubleday, 2008), 244; Bernard Lewis, "The Return of Islam," *Commentary* (January 1976): 39–49.

68. Jeane Kirkpatrick, "Dictatorships & Double Standards," *Commentary* (November 1979): 34–35.

69. Brigitte Berger, "Observations: What Women Want," *Commentary* (March 1979): 63.

70. Michael Ledeen, "Khomeini's Theocratic Vision," *Wall Street Journal*, January 5, 1979, 10.

71. Erik von Kuehnelt-Leddhin, "Ayatollah-ism," *National Review* (June 22, 1979): 810.

72. Jonathan C. Randal, "Views Differ on Islam Role in Republic; Role of Islam Murky as Khomeini Aides Ponder Republic," *Washington Post*, February 4, 1979, A1.

73. Paul Hofmann, "Behind Iranian Riots, a Web of Discontent," *New York Times*, March 5, 1978, 7.

74. Berger, "Observations," 63.

75. "A Faith of Law and Submission," *Time*, April 16, 1979, http://www.time.com /time/magazine/article/0,9171,912497,00.html (accessed May 9, 2008).

76. "Islam Against the West?" *Time*, December 17, 1979, http://www.time.com /magazine/article/0,9171,92012,00.html (accessed on May 5, 2008).

77. While the women's protests did not displace news reports on other issues in Iran during this period, they did comprise a significant portion of the American news coverage. Of the 757 articles published in the *New York Times* about Iran from March 8 through March 20, 1979, 143 or over eighteen percent of the articles focused on the women's protests, and many of the articles made front-page news. See Pro-Quest Historical Newspapers: *New York Times* (1851–2011) database.

78. Jonathan C. Randal, "Women Protest in Iran, Shout 'Down with Khomeini,'" *Washington Post*, March 9, 1979, A1.

79. Fay Willey with Elaine Sciolino, "Iran: Who's in Charge?" *Newsweek*, March 19, 1979, 47.

80. "You Are Weak, Mister," *Time*, March 19, 1979, http://www.time.com/time /magazine/article/0,9171,047014,00.html (accessed May 9, 2008).

81. *ABC World News Tonight*, March 8, 1979, Television News Archive, Vanderbilt University Libraries, DVD (hereafter Television News Archive). See also *CBS Evening News*, March 8, 1979, Television News Archive.

82. *NBC Nightly News*, March 15, 1979, Television News Archive.

83. Judith Cummings, "Demonstrators in City Back Iranian Women's Rights," *New York Times*, March 16, 1979, A7.

84. *NBC Nightly News*, March 15, 1979.

85. Cummings, "Demonstrators in City," A7. Friedan had gone to Iran in 1970 and met with key feminists there. Naghibi, *Rethinking Global Sisterhood*, 82–83.

86. Razack, *Casting Out*, 16.

87. Jonathan C. Randal, "Militant Women Demonstrators Attack Khomeini Aide Who Heads Iran Radio," *Washington Post*, March 12, 1979, A10.

88. *NBC Nightly News*, March 12, 1979, Television News Archive.

89. Randal, "Militant Women."

90. Kelber, "Five Days," 96.

91. Jonathan C. Randal, "Sexual Politics in Iran; Kate Millet Finds That Tehran's Feminists Are Not United," *Washington Post,* March 12, 1979, B1.

92. A search through the *Public Papers of the Presidents* and of the available FRUS documents yields no mention of the changing status of women's rights in Iran by the Carter administration in 1979–80.

Chapter 2

1. Betty's husband's full name was Sayyed Bozorg Mahmoody, but he went by the nickname "Moody." Betty Mahmoody with William Hoffer, *Not Without My Daughter* (New York: St. Martin's Press, 1987), 2.

2. As of 2010, St. Martin's Press had sold over twelve million copies of the book. Email from Emily White, Macmillan academic marketing assistant, to author, March 29, 2010. The film was not a critical or box-office hit in 1991, but through its countless airings on television and through VHS/DVD sales, it became incredibly well-known. It is impossible to track how many times *Not Without My Daughter*

aired on network and cable television, but it has appeared on TV regularly since the 1990s. *Not Without My Daughter*, directed by Brian Gilbert (1991; Metro-Goldwyn-Mayer, 2001), DVD. The enduring popularity of both the book and film can be gauged in part by Internet searches. According to Google Keyword Tool, as of 2012 there were on average 27,100 Internet searches per month worldwide (8,100 in the United States) for "Not Without My Daughter." The average monthly number of searches for "Betty Mahmoody" was 12,100 worldwide (2,900 in the United States).

3. American Entertainment International Speakers Bureau, "Betty Mahmoody," http://www.aeispeakers.com/Mahmoody-Betty.htm (accessed March 24, 2010). Mahmoody became an expert on international kidnapping for the State of Michigan and the State Department.

4. See Schmitz and Walker, "Carter and Human Rights"; Kenton Clymer, "Jimmy Carter, Human Rights, and Cambodia," *Diplomatic History* 27, no. 2 (April 2003): 245–78.

5. In addition to FRUS and the *Public Papers* containing no references to Iranian women, Carter's memoir discussed the Iranian Revolution in detail but did not mention women's rights. Jimmy Carter, *Keeping Faith: Memoirs of a President* (Fayetteville: University of Arkansas Press, 1995), 114, 260–61, 342, 421, 441–79, 493–98, 506–34, 553, 566–69, 572–75, 579–80.

6. See William C. Berman, *America's Right Turn: From Nixon to Bush* (Baltimore: Johns Hopkins University Press, 1994); Robert M. Collins, *Transforming America: Politics and Culture During the Reagan Years* (New York: Columbia University Press, 2007); Farber, *Modern American Conservatism*; Michael Schaller, *Right Turn: American Life in the Reagan-Bush Era, 1980–1992* (New York: Oxford University Press, 2007); Jules Tygiel, *Ronald Reagan and the Triumph of American Conservatism* (New York: Pearson Longman, 2004); Sean Wilentz, *The Age of Reagan: A History, 1974–2008* (New York: Harper Collins, 2008).

7. Schaller, *Right Turn*, 47.

8. Wilentz, *Age of Reagan*, 6; Farber, *Modern American Conservatism*, 119–58; Ruth Rosen, *The World Split Open: How the Modern Women's Movement Changed America* (New York: Penguin, 2000, 2006), 270, 275, 331–32. For the most well-known analysis of anti-feminism, see Faludi, *Backlash*.

9. Samuel Hale Butterfield, *U.S. Development Aid—An Historic First: Achievements and Failures in the Twentieth Century* (Westport, CT: Praeger, 2004), 269–70. See also USAID, *Gender Equality and Female Empowerment Policy* (Washington, DC: USAID, March 2012), 4, http://www.usaid.gov/policy/gender-female-empowerment (accessed January 27, 2014).

10. Butterfield, *U.S. Development Aid*, 270–72.

11. David Carleton and Michael Stohl, "The Foreign Policy of Human Rights: Rhetoric and Reality from Jimmy Carter to Ronald Reagan," *Human Rights Quarterly* 7, no. 2 (May 1985): 208–11.

12. Peter Hahn, *Crisis and Crossfire: The United States and the Middle East Since 1945* (Washington, DC: Potomac Books, 2005), 69, 78–80; Mamdani, *Good Muslim, Bad Muslim*, 119–77.

13. Hahn, *Crisis and Crossfire*, 81–82.

14. According to Zbigniew Brzezinski, Carter's national security advisor, U.S. aid to the mujahideen began in July 1979, several months before the Soviet invasion. Bill Blum, "The CIA's Intervention in Afghanistan," *Le Nouvel Observateur* (Paris), January 15–21, 1998, http://www.globalresearch.ca/articles/BRZ110A.html (accessed December 14, 2015).

15. Hahn, *Crisis and Crossfire*, 78.

16. Farber, *Taken Hostage*, 181; Mark Bowden, *Guests of the Ayatollah: The First Battle in America's War with Militant Islam* (New York: Atlantic Monthly, 2006), 279–89.

17. Eric Hooglund, "Reagan's Iran: Factions Behind US Policy in the Gulf," *Middle East Report* 151 (March/April 1988): 29.

18. See Rosen, *World Split Open*, 264–335; Faludi, *Backlash*, ix–45; Gail Collins, *When Everything Changed: The Amazing Journey of American Women from 1960 to the Present* (New York: Little, Brown, 2009), 304, 308–12, 320; Sara Evans, "Feminism in the 1980s: Surviving the Backlash," in *Living in the Eighties*, ed. Gil Troy and Vincent Cannato (New York: Oxford University Press, 2009), 85–97.

19. Schaller, *Right Turn*, 161; Collins, *When Everything Changed*, 293, 332.

20. Rosen, *World Split Open*, 266, 274.

21. A 1986 Gallup poll revealed that 56 percent of all women identified as feminists, while 67 percent said they believed a continued strong women's movement was necessary. Equally striking, there was a remarkable "diffusion" of support for gender equality across many different groups. A 1989 poll indicated that 51 percent of all American men, 64 percent of white women, 72 percent of Latino women, and 85 percent of African American women supported the feminist movement. Rosen, *World Split Open*, 271, 314, 337–38; Faludi, *Backlash*, xix; Collins, *When Everything Changed*, 293, 308.

22. See, for example, "Four in Iran Executed by Stoning," *New York Times*, July 4, 1980, A1, A5; *NBC Nightly News*, July 6, 1980, Television News Archive.

23. Jonathan C. Randal, "Iranian Women Foresee More Battles with Moslem Clergy," *Washington Post*, May 22, 1980, A19.

24. Charles J. Hanley, "Iran's Revolutionaries Are Said to Be Showing a Gradual Shift to Right," *Philadelphia Inquirer*, June 25, 1983, A12.

25. Terence Smith, "Iran: Five Years of Fanaticism," *New York Times*, February 12, 1984, SM22, SM30.

26. By 2009 Iran had executed more of its citizens per capita than any other government and more people total than any country save China. Iran Human Rights, "Annual Report on the Death Penalty in Iran 2009," http://iranhr.net/spip.php?article1616 (accessed October 28, 2011); Amnesty International, "Death Penalty Statistics 2010,"

http://www.amnestyusa.org/our-work/issues/death-penalty/international-death
-penalty/death-penalty-statistics-2010 (accessed October 28, 2011); International
Federation for Human Rights, "Iran/Death Penalty: A State Terror Policy," 1–64 (date
unknown, most likely 2010), PDF, www.fidh.org/IMG/pdf/Rapport_Iran_final.pdf
(accessed August 10, 2012).

27. Said, *Orientalism*, 4, 32, 102, 153, 172, 203, 205.

28. John Kifner, "Iran Executes Female Ex-Minister, Confirms Arrest of a U.S.
Woman," *New York Times*, May 9, 1980, A3; Jonathan C. Randal, "Iran Refuses to
Compare Takeovers of Embassies," *Washington Post*, May 7, 1980, A21; Jonathan C.
Randal, "Bani-Sadr's Plan to Name Premier Encounters Resistance," *Washington
Post*, May 9, 1980, A20; Associated Press, "US Confirms 8 Bodies/Iran Courts Hit,"
Boston Globe, May 10, 1980.

29. Mahnaz Afkhami, "Iran: A Future in the Past—The 'Prerevolutionary' Women's
Movement," in *Sisterhood Is Global: The International Women's Movement Anthology*,
ed. Robin Morgan (New York: Anchor Books, 1984), 330.

30. Farrokhrou Parsa, quoted in "A Woman for All Seasons: In Memory of Farrokhrou Parsa" by Ardavan Bahrami, *Iranian.com*, May 9, 2005, http://www.iranian
.com/ArdavanBahrami/2005/May/Parsa/index.html (accessed on November 30,
2009). Parsa served in government from 1968 to 1974.

31. Kifner, "Iran Executes Female Ex-Minister," A3.

32. "Four in Iran Executed by Stoning," A1. See also Associated Press, "Iranian
Regime Revives Execution-by-Stoning," *Boston Globe*, July 3, 1980.

33. Charlotte Williams, "Barbarity of Khomeini Regime in Documents and Pho-
tos," *New York Amsterdam News*, January 8, 1983, 46. See also Associated Press, "Iran
Executes Children, Amnesty Asserts," *Boston Globe*, September 28, 1983; John Kimmey,
letter to the editor, *Wall Street Journal*, January 3, 1983, 23; "Around the World: Iran
Reports Execution of 12 for Various Offenses," *New York Times*, August 24, 1980, 5;
"Firing Squad Executes 7 in Iran," *New York Times*, May 6, 1981, D23; "Aide to Kho-
meini Praises Firing Squad Executions," *New York Times*, June 27, 1981, 3; "33 High
Iranian Officials Die in Bombing at Party Meeting; Chief Judge Is Among Victims,"
New York Times, June 29, 1981, A1; "Iran Shoots 9 Foes and Ousts Reuters," *New York
Times*, July 8, 1981, A3; "Execution of 149 Reported by Iran," *New York Times*, Septem-
ber 21, 1981, A4; "Iran Reports 45 More Executions as Drive Against Leftists Goes
On," *New York Times*, September 22, 1981, A4; "Iran Reports Execution of 7," *New
York Times*, January 17, 1982, 34; "Iran Executions Are Reported," *New York Times*,
August 25, 1982, A7; Lynn Rosellini, "Students from Iran March with a Message," *New
York Times*, August 30, 1982, A12; "Amnesty International Says Iran Continues to Ex-
ecute Prisoners," *Wall Street Journal*, September 28, 1983, 33; Caryle Murphy, "Execu-
tions, Arrests in Iran," *Washington Post*, July 6, 1983.

34. Razack, *Casting Out*, 9–10.

35. See Youssef M. Ibrahim, "War Seems to Bolster Khomeini's Appeal to the
People Across the Arab World," *New York Times*, October 26, 1980, 20; Jim Hoagland,

"CIA Will Survey Moslems Worldwide," *Washington Post*, January 20, 1979, A1; Edward Cody, "Fervor Against West in Islamic World Picks U.S. as Chief Target," *Washington Post*, December 3, 1979, A24; William Clairborne, "Moslem Militance Stirs Up Israel's Arabs," *Washington Post*, January 30, 1980, A16; Flora Lewis, "Basis of the New Moslem Fervor Seen as Rejection of Alien Values," *New York Times*, December 28, 1979, A1; Ray Vicker, "Moslem Justice: Islam's Revival Spreads Use of the Sharia Law, a Flexible Legal Setup," *Wall Street Journal*, May 11, 1979, 1; Maurice Guindi, "Islam Beset by Conflicts, Amidst Its Resurgence," *Baltimore Afro-American*, December 8, 1979, 17.

36. Daniel Pipes, "Fundamentalist Muslims Between America and Russia," *Foreign Affairs* 64, no. 5 (Summer 1986): 939–59.

37. See Alan Cowell, "Clamor for Change Is Sounding Across the Sudan," *New York Times*, February 17, 1982, A2; "Anti-U.S. Sentiment Sweeping Through Nations of Islam," *Atlanta Daily World*, November 25, 1979, 3; "The Explosion in the Moslem World: A Roundtable on Islam," *New York Times*, December 11, 1979, A16; "33 Accused in Turkey of Seeking Islamic State," *New York Times*, April 1, 1983, A7; Thomas W. Lippman, "Islam and Its Discontents," *Washington Post*, December 11, 1983, BW4; Raymond Carroll with Ron Moreau, "The Rule of Islam," *Newsweek*, February 26, 1979, 38.

38. Lewis M. Simons, "Iran Firing Islamic Zeal in Malaysia," *Philadelphia Inquirer*, August 7, 1980, A21.

39. Christina Robb, "Women of Israel Locked Firmly in the Role of Subservient Sex Object: A Woman in the Mideast Can't Even Go Out in Public Without Ceaseless Harassment. And It's Not Getting Better," *Boston Globe Magazine*, April 6, 1980.

40. Judith Miller, "Moslem World Is Unsettled by Surge in Fundamentalism," *New York Times*, December 18, 1983, 1, 20.

41. Oren, *Power, Faith, and Fantasy*, 513–28, 539–41; McAlister, *Epic Encounters*, 84–124; Mamdani, *Good Muslim, Bad Muslim*, 126. See also Yaqub, *Containing Arab Nationalism*.

42. Fouad Ajami, "The Struggle for Egypt's Soul," *Foreign Policy* 35 (Summer 1979): 3.

43. "Back to Fundamentals," *Time*, September 21, 1981, http://www.time.com/time/magazine/article/0,9171,953075,00.html (accessed December 2, 2009).

44. John Kifner, "After Sadat," *New York Times*, October 11, 1981, E2.

45. Sana Hasan, "Egypt's Angry Islamic Militants," *New York Times*, November 20, 1983, SM143–44.

46. Mamdani, *Good Muslim, Bad Muslim*, 149–53.

47. William K. Stevens, "In Pakistan, Islam Leaves Little Room for Freedom," *New York Times*, August 28, 1983, E3; Robert Trumbull, "Pakistan Adopting Islamic Laws with Their Severe Punishments," *New York Times*, February 11, 1979, 1; "Backward March in Pakistan," *New York Times*, October 19, 1979, A34.

48. Stevens, "Little Room for Freedom," E3. Purdah refers to the custom of segregating the sexes in India and Pakistan by keeping women in the home.

49. Paul A. Gigot, "Moslems in Turmoil: Islam Fundamentalism Stirs Up Much Discord in Pakistan, Elsewhere," *Wall Street Journal*, December 1, 1983, 1.

50. Ibid., 20.

51. Carol Anne Douglas, "Women of Pakistan: Two Steps Forward . . . One Step Back," *Off Our Backs* 18, no. 3 (March 31, 1988): 26; Mohammad Rafique, "Woman Who Eloped Gets Lash, Jail, Man Goes Free," *Globe and Mail*, January 38, 1984 (accessed via LexisNexis Academic on April 1, 2010). The sixteen-year-old girl, Safia Bibi, was punished under Pakistan's Zina Ordinance, instituted by Zia. The law treats rape and adultery/fornication as similar crimes. In order to prove that a rape has occurred, four male Muslim witnesses of good moral character must testify that they witnessed the act of penetration. Such a requirement made it very difficult for Pakistani women to prove they had been raped, and the fact that many were punished as adulterers ensured that most Pakistani rape victims were reluctant to come forward. Rubya Mehdi, *Dossier 18: The Offense of Rape in the Islamic Law of Pakistan*, Women Living Under Muslim Laws, October 1997, WLUML Records, provided to the author by Aisha Shaheed, WLUML International Coordination Office, London (hereafter WLUML Records).

52. *Charlie Wilson's War*, directed by Mike Nichols (2007; Universal Studios, 2008), DVD.

53. Pipes, "Fundamentalist Muslims Between America and Russia," 958, 945, 959, 940.

54. Shaheen, *Reel Bad Arabs*, 29, 3, 11.

55. *Harem*, directed by Arthur Joffe (1985; Sara Films/Universal Studios, 1987), VHS.

56. For examples of films, see *Aladdin*, directed by John Musker and Ron Clements (1992; Walt Disney Home Entertainment, 2004), DVD; *Allan Quatermain and the Lost City of Gold*, directed by Gary Nelson (1987; Metro-Goldwyn-Mayer, 2004), DVD; *Baby Boom*, directed by Charles Shyer (1987; Metro-Goldwyn-Mayer, 2001), DVD; *Indiana Jones and the Raiders of the Lost Ark*, directed by Steven Spielberg (1981; Paramount, 2008), DVD; *Intimate Power*, directed by Jack Smight (1989; Lionsgate, 2003), DVD; *The Jewel of the Nile*, directed by Lewis Teague (1985; 20th Century Fox, 2006), DVD; *Never Say Never Again*, directed by Irvin Kershner (1983; Metro-Goldwyn-Mayer, 2000), DVD; *Rambo III*, directed by Peter MacDonald (1988; Lionsgate, 2004), DVD. See also Lina Khatib, *Filming the Modern Middle East: Politics in the Cinemas of Hollywood and the Arab World* (London: I. B. Tauris, 2006).

57. The number of books published about Muslim women—both scholarly and fictional—increased substantially after 1979 and continued to increase exponentially each decade thereafter. This was significant because there were practically no studies or novels focused on Muslim women published in the United States before the Iranian Revolution.

58. Imelda Whelehan, *Modern Feminist Thought: From the Second Wave to "Post-Feminism"* (New York: NYU Press, 1995), 126, 34–87.

59. Ibid., 131.

60. Ibid., 143.

61. Some important feminist authors from the 1980s and early 1990s who challenged the dominant feminist norms of the 1970s included bell hooks, Chandra Mohanty, Alice Walker, Cherrie Moraga, Gloria Anzaldua, Vivian V. Gordon, Angela Davis, and Audre Lorde.

62. Nikki Keddie and Lois Beck, introduction to *Women in the Muslim World*, ed. Nikki Keddie and Lois Beck (Cambridge, MA: Harvard University Press, 1978), 2. According to Keddie, "This was the first such volume published." Nikki Keddie, "My Life and Ideas: A Brief Overview," http://nikkikeddie.com (accessed May 28, 2009).

63. Keddie and Beck, introduction, 27, 19, 16.

64. Ibid., 18, 27.

65. Unni Wikan, *Behind the Veil in Arabia: Women in Oman* (Baltimore: Johns Hopkins University Press, 1982), 5. See also Susan Schaefer Davis, *Patience and Power: Women's Lives in a Moroccan Village* (Cambridge, MA: Schenkman, 1983), 2–6.

66. Susan Dorsky, *Women of 'Amran: A Middle Eastern Ethnographic Study* (Salt Lake City: University of Utah Press, 1986), 9.

67. Wikan, *Behind the Veil*, 5; Dorsky, *Women of 'Amran*, 9; Erika Friedl, *Women of Deh Koh: Lives in an Iranian Village* (Washington, DC: Smithsonian Institution Press, 1989), 4; Barbara J. Callaway, *Muslim Hausa Women in Nigeria: Tradition and Change* (Syracuse, NY: Syracuse University Press, 1987), xv.

68. For edited collections, see Elizabeth Warnock Fernea and Basima Quattan Bezirgan, eds., *Middle Eastern Muslim Women Speak* (Austin: University of Texas Press, 1977); Elizabeth Warnock Fernea, ed., *Women and the Family in the Middle East: New Voices of Change* (Austin: University of Texas Press, 1984); Jane I. Smith, ed., *Women in Contemporary Muslim Societies* (Lewisburg, PA: Bucknell University Press, 1980). Examples of novels include Hilary Mantel, *Eight Months on Ghazzah Street* (New York: Henry Holt, 1988); Barbara-Chase Riboud, *Valide* (New York: William Morrow, 1986); Suzanne Fisher Staples, *Shabanu: Daughter of the Wind* (New York: Alfred A. Knopf, 1989). Memoirs available in the United States by Westerners who spent time in Muslim countries include Millett, *Going to Iran*; Eileen MacDonald, *Brides for Sale? Human Trade in North Yemen* (Edinburgh: Mainstream Publishing, 1988); Sandra Mackey, *The Saudis: Inside the Desert Kingdom* (Boston: Houghton Mifflin, 1987). Even male scholars began to take interest in Muslim women, although not to the extent that women scholars published on the subject. See Peter Knauss, *The Persistence of Patriarchy: Class, Gender, and Ideology in Twentieth Century Algeria* (New York: Praeger, 1987); John L. Esposito, *Women in Muslim Family Law* (Syracuse, NY: Syracuse University Press, 1982).

69. Judith E. Tucker, *Women in Nineteenth-Century Egypt* (Cambridge: Cambridge University Press, 1985), 3, 5.

70. Shaarawi, *Harem Years*, 7.

71. Abdulaziz Sachedina, *Islam & the Challenge of Human Rights* (New York: Oxford University Press, 2009), 117–19.

72. Mahmoody, *Not Without My Daughter*, 35, 38, 103.

73. Mahnaz Afkhami, *Women in Exile* (Charlottesville: University of Virginia Press, 1994), 1–16, 78–99, 124–39, 191–208.

74. This was especially true in the 1980s. Islamic feminists, who interpret women's rights through a religious lens, did not have much of a voice in the United States at that time. Secular feminists from Muslim countries did, however, begin to adopt Islamic feminists' tactics in the 1990s, and some Islamic feminists were able to publish and speak in the United States in later periods. Secular feminists from Muslim countries still dominate the conversation in the United States today.

75. It is impossible to find figures on the number of books published by Muslim women in the United States since the 1970s, but a search of library catalogs, Amazon, and other sites reveals few, if any, such books published before 1979 and a marked increase each decade thereafter, with a significant spike after 9/11.

76. See Fernea and Bezirgan, *Muslim Women Speak*; Fernea, *Women and Family*; Keddie and Beck, *Women in Muslim World*; Azizah al-Hibri, *Women and Islam*, published as a special issue of *Women's Studies International Forum*, vol. 5, no. 2 (New York: Pergamon Press, 1982); Robin Morgan, ed., *Sisterhood Is Global: The International Women's Rights Movement Anthology* (New York: Anchor Books, 1984); Nawal el Saadawi, *The Hidden Face of Eve: Women in the Arab World*, trans. and ed. Sherif Hetata (London: Zed, 1980, 2007); Sanasarian, *Women's Rights Movement in Iran*; Fatima Mernissi, *Doing Daily Battle: Interviews with Moroccan Women*, trans. Mary Jo Lakeland (London: Women's Press, 1988); Azar Tabari and Nahid Yeganeh, *In the Shadow of Islam: The Women's Movement in Iran* (London: Zed, 1982); Naila Minai, *Women in Islam: Tradition and Transition in the Middle East* (New York: Seaview Books, 1981); Malik Ram Baveja, *Woman in Islam* (New York: Advent Books, 1981); Farah Azari, ed., *Women of Iran: The Conflict with Fundamentalist Islam* (London: Ithaca Press, 1983); Jamila Brij Bhushan, *Muslim Women: In Purdah and Out of It* (New York: Advent Books, 1980); Samira Rafidi Meghdessian, *The Status of the Arab Woman: A Select Bibliography* (Westport, CT: Greenwood, 1980); Baba of Karo, *Baba of Karo, a Woman of the Muslim Hausa* (New Haven, CT: Yale University Press, 1981); Guity Nashat, ed., *Women and Revolution in Iran* (Boulder, CO: Westview, 1983); Fatna Aït Sabbah, *Woman in the Muslim Unconscious* (New York: Pergamon Press, 1984); Soha Abdel Kader, *Egyptian Women in a Changing Society, 1899–1987* (Boulder, CO: Lynne Rienner, 1987); Bouthaina Shaaban, *Both Right and Left Handed: Arab Women Talk About Their Lives* (London: Women's Press, 1988); Minou Reeves, *Female Warriors of Allah: Women and the Islamic Revolution* (New York: Dutton, 1989); Soraya

Altorki, *Women in Saudi Arabia: Ideology and Behavior Among the Elite* (New York: Columbia University Press, 1986); Laila Abou-Saif, *A Bridge Through Time: A Memoir* (New York: Summit Books, 1985); Lila Abu-Lughod, *Veiled Sentiments: Honor and Poetry in Bedouin Society* (Berkeley: University of California Press, 1986); Freda Hussain, ed., *Muslim Women* (New York: St. Martin's, 1984); Jehan Sadat, *A Woman of Egypt* (New York: Simon and Schuster, 1987).

77. Sanasarian, *Women's Rights Movement in Iran*, 1. Dozens of scholarly articles have cited Sanasarian's book, according to the database Arts & Humanities Citation Index, run by ISI Web of Knowledge (search conducted on April 3, 2010). Most books published about Iranian women since the publication of Sanasarian's book in 1982 also draw upon her work.

78. Mernissi, *Doing Daily Battle*.

79. Mernissi, *Dreams of Trespass*.

80. Fatima Mernissi, *The Veil and the Male Elite: A Feminist Interpretation of Women's Rights In Islam*, trans. Mary Jo Lakeland (New York: Basic Books, 1992); Fatima Mernissi, *Beyond the Veil: Male-Female Dynamics in Modern Muslim Society*, rev. ed. (Bloomington: Indiana University Press, 1987).

81. There was a body of literature by men that asserted that the Koran and hadith, as well as other sources of Islamic jurisprudence, justified women's subordination. See Mernissi, *The Veil and the Male Elite*.

82. Nawal el Saadawi, *Woman at Point Zero* (London: Zed, 1983), 10.

83. Novels published by Muslim women available in the United States in the 1980s include Leila Abou Zayd, *Year of the Elephant* (Austin: University of Texas Press, 1989); Alifa Rifaat, *Distant View of a Minaret and Other Stories* (Oxford: Heinemann, 1983); Assia Djebar, *A Sister to Scheherazade*, trans. Dorothy S. Blair (London: Quartet, 1989); Nawal el Saadawi, *God Dies by the Nile* (London: Zed, 1985); Hanan al-Shayk, *The Story of Zahra* (London: Quartet, 1986); Hanan al-Shayk, *Women of Sand and Myrrh* (New York: Anchor, 1989).

84. For descriptions of cultural relativist and fundamentalist denial of the universality of human rights, especially pertaining to women, see Courtney W. Howland, "Women and Religious Fundamentalism," in *Women and International Human Rights Law: Volume 1*, ed. Kelly D. Askin and Dorean M. Koenig (Ardsley, NY: Transnational Publishers, 1999), 533–621; Christina M. Cerna and Jennifer C. Wallace, "Women and Culture," in *Women and International Human Rights Law: Volume 1*, ed. Askin and Koenig, 623–50.

85. Afkhami, "Cultural Relativism," 481.

86. Cerna and Wallace, "Women and Culture," 630, 648–49.

87. See Mahmoody, *Not Without My Daughter*, 35, 38, 103, 419.

88. Razack, *Casting Out*, 8–11.

Chapter 3

1. Those countries were Afghanistan, Algeria, Egypt, Indonesia, Iran, Kuwait, Lebanon, Libya, Morocco, Pakistan, Palestine, Saudi Arabia, Senegal, and Sudan. It also contained a chapter on Nigeria, which had a significant Muslim minority.

2. Morgan, introduction to *Sisterhood Is Global*, 3; Robin Morgan, "Sisterhood Is Global," 1996, http://www.feminist.com/resources/artspeech/inter/sisterhood.htm (accessed October 4, 2012).

3. SIGI, "About the Sisterhood Is Global Institute," Sisterhood Is Global Institute website, http://www.sigi.org/about.html (accessed January 13, 2010). See also Administrative Files Series, 1975–2004, Membership Files Subseries. Sisterhood Is Global Institute Records, Boxes M1–M7, Rare Book, Manuscript, and Special Collections Library, Duke University (hereafter SIGI Records).

4. Valentine Moghadam, *Globalizing Women: Transnational Feminist Networks* (Baltimore: Johns Hopkins University Press, 2005), 1. Women's rights activists did forge international ties during the late nineteenth and early twentieth centuries around issues like the abolition of slavery, women's suffrage, peace, and labor. Women's international organizing waned after the 1930s, however. Transnational feminism experienced a resurgence in the 1970s, and the organizations formed in the late twentieth century differed in organizational structure, political tactics, strategies and goals, funding, ideology, and membership from their predecessors.

5. Marilyn Lake, "From Self-Determination via Protection to Equality via Non-Discrimination: Defining Women's Rights at the League of Nations and the United Nations," in *Women's Rights and Human Rights*, ed. Grimshaw, Holmes, and Lake, 254–71; Glendon, *World Made New*, 31, 65–78; Black, "Are Women 'Human'?" 133–41; United Nations, Charter of the United Nations, preamble and Article I, 1945, http://un.org/en/documents/charter/index.shtml (accessed August 12, 2009); United Nations, Universal Declaration of Human Rights, Article 2, 1948, http://www.un.org/en/documents/udhr (accessed August 19, 2009).

6. Arvonne S. Fraser, *The U.N. Decade for Women: Documents and Dialogue* (Boulder, CO: Westview, 1987), 2; Margaret E. Galey, "Women Find a Place," in *Women, Politics, and the United Nations*, ed. Anne Winslow (Westport, CT: Greenwood, 1995), 13–14; Black, "Are Women 'Human'?" 139–42; Claire de Hedervary, "Good Grief, There Are Women Here!" in *Sisterhood Is Global*, ed. Morgan, 692–94.

7. Galey, "Women Find a Place," 21–23; Fraser, *U.N. Decade*, 2, 17, 18; Peggy Antrobus, *The Global Women's Movement: Origins, Issues and Strategies* (London: Zed, 2004), 34; Jocelyn Olcott, "Globalizing Sisterhood: International Women's Year and the Politics of Representation," in *The Shock of the Global: The 1970s in Perspective*, ed. Niall Ferguson, Charles S. Maier, Erez Manela, and Daniel J. Sargent (Cambridge, MA: Belknap Press of Harvard University Press, 2010), 283.

8. Fraser, *U.N. Decade*, 18; Antrobus, *Global Women's Movement*, 34; United Nations, *Meeting in Mexico: The Story of the World Conference of the International Women's Year* (New York: United Nations, 1975), 18–19.

9. Most of the existing literature on the Decade has been produced by feminists who participated in the Decade conferences and NGO Forums or the United Nations. The Mexico City conference has the most extant historiography of the three conferences—driven largely by the work of historian Jocelyn Olcott—but even that body of literature is small.

10. Margaret Snyder, "Unlikely Godmother: The UN and the Global Women's Movement," in *Global Feminism: Transnational Women's Activism, Organizing, and Human Rights*, ed. Myra Marx Ferree and Aili Mari Tripp (New York: NYU Press, 2006), 24.

11. Antrobus, *Global Women's Movement*, 32.

12. Virginia R. Allan, Margaret E. Galey, and Mildred E. Persinger, "World Conference of International Women's Year," in *Women, Politics, and the United Nations*, ed. Winslow, 40.

13. The first NGO Forum was held in Stockholm in 1972 at the UN environmental conference, and the second convened in Bucharest in 1974 during the UN population conference. Fraser, *U.N. Decade*, 55–56.

14. Olcott, "Globalizing Sisterhood," 287.

15. Fraser, *U.N. Decade*, 59–60; Allan, Galey, and Persinger, "World Conference," 60; Olcott, "Globalizing Sisterhood," 292; Judith P. Zinsser, "The United Nations Decade for Women: A Quiet Revolution," *History Teacher* 24, no. 1 (November 1990): 23.

16. The divisions between women did not always fall along neat geographical lines. They were also divided by class and race, and wealthier women from the developing world often found themselves in agreement with Western women and in conflict with women from the lower classes within their own countries. Women of color from the United States felt they had more in common with women from the Third World, but their feelings of racial solidarity were not always reciprocated. The webs of agreement and conflict were highly complex. When I speak of North-South divisions, I necessarily generalize.

17. Fraser, *U.N. Decade*, 61.

18. Olcott, "Globalizing Sisterhood," 283.

19. Ibid., 282–92; Moghadam, *Globalizing Women*, 5–6, 85; Allan, Galey, and Persinger, "World Conference," 35–36; Mary Jo McConahay, "Trials at the Tribune," *Ms.* (November 1975): 101–4; Hanna Papanek, "The Work of Women: Postscript from Mexico City," *Signs* 1, no. 1 (Autumn 1975): 215–26; Brad Simpson, "'The First Right': The Carter Administration, Indonesia, and the Transnational Human Rights Politics of the 1970s," in *The Human Rights Revolution*, ed. Iriye, Goedde, and Hitchcock, 180, 187; Black, "Are Women 'Human'?" 141–42.

20. Berta Esperanza Hernandez-Truyol, "Human Rights Through a Gendered Lens: Emergence, Evolution, Revolution," in *Women and International Human Rights Law, Volume 1*, ed. Askin and Koenig, 25–26.

21. Black, "Are Women 'Human'?" 142.

22. See Domitila Barrios de la Chungara, "The Woman's Problem" (Bolivia, 1980), in *The Essential Feminist Reader*, ed. Estelle B. Freedman (New York: Modern Library, 2007), 346–50; Association of African Women for Research and Development (AAWORD), "A Statement on Genital Mutilation" (Senegal, 1980), in *The Essential Feminist Reader*, ed. Freedman, 351–54.

23. McConahay, "Trials at the Tribune," 103–4.

24. For an analysis of Third World women's priorities in Mexico City, see Jocelyn Olcott, "Cold War Conflicts and Cheap Cabaret: Sexual Politics at the 1975 United Nations International Women's Year Conference," *Gender & History* 22, no. 3 (November 2010): 733–54.

25. Simpson, "'The First Right,'" 195.

26. Afary, "Mahnaz Afkhami," 154.

27. CEDAW did not become legally enforceable until 1981, but it was passed in 1979 prior to the conference.

28. Jane S. Jaquette, "Losing the Battle/Winning the War: International Politics, Women's Issues, and the 1980 Mid-Decade Conference," in *Women, Politics, and the United Nations*, ed. Winslow, 45; Charlotte Bunch, "What Not to Expect from the UN Women's Conference in Copenhagen," *Ms.* (July 1980): 80, 83; John Nielsen with Frederick Kempe, "Cacophony in Copenhagen," *Newsweek*, August 4, 1980, 35.

29. Moghadam, *Globalizing Women*, 85; *Evening News*, CBS, July 15, 1980, Television News Archive; Tony Hall, "Hostages: It's Up to Carter Iranians Tell Bella," *Forum '80*, July 17, 1980, 1, International Women's Tribune Centre Collection, 89S-29, Box 13, Sophia Smith Collection, Smith College (hereafter IWTC Collection). The IWTC records at Smith are unprocessed, and the collection is divided into several batches according to accession date. I have included the batch number (89S-29) to indicate which batch of IWTC records I am citing.

30. John Leo, "Cacophony in Copenhagen," *Time*, August 4, 1980, 52, Betty Friedan Papers, 1960–1993, Box 20, Schlesinger Library, Radcliffe Institute, Harvard University (hereafter Friedan Papers).

31. Jaquette, "Losing the Battle/Winning the War," 48–49; Leo, "Cacophony," 52.

32. International Women's Tribune Centre, "Mid-Decade Directory: Participants at the NGO Mid-Decade Forum and World Conference of the UN Decade for Women, Copenhagen, Denmark, July 14–28, 1980," April 1981, Sisterhood Is Global Institute Records, Box CONF8, David M. Rubenstein Rare Book and Manuscript Library, Duke University, Durham, NC (hereafter SIGI Records).

33. Planning Committee Mid-Decade Forum Copenhagen '80, "Organisations Sponsoring Workshops," 1980, IWTC Collection, 89S-29, Box 5; Planning Committee Mid-Decade Forum Copenhagen '80, "List of Workshops Held at the Forum," 1980, IWTC Collection, 89S-29, Box 5; "Islam Advocates Equal Rights," *Forum '80*, July 24, 1980, 2, IWTC Collection, 89S-29, Box 13. The NGOs that sponsored workshops on issues related to Muslim women included AAWORD, the Association of Arab Women Scientists, the Association of Bangladesh, the General Union of Palestinian

Women, the Indonesian Association of Women's Organizations, the International Committee for the Abolition of Genital Mutilation, the Revolutionary Women's Organization of Iran, the League of Lebanese Women's Rights, and *Women's International Network News* (*WINN*). For discussion of female genital mutilation, see Chapter 5.

34. Fraser, *U.N. Decade*, 152.

35. Tony Hall, "The Sayings of Akram Hariri," *Forum '80*, July 16, 1980, 2, IWTC Collection, 89S-29, Box 13.

36. Bert B. Lockwood, introduction to *Women's Rights: A "Human Rights Quarterly" Reader*, ed. Bert B. Lockwood (Baltimore: Johns Hopkins University Press, 2006), ix.

37. Sachedina, *Islam and the Challenge of Human Rights*, 5.

38. Ibid., 117–18; Mahnaz Afkhami, preface to *Faith and Freedom*, ix. See also UN, UDHR; UN, CEDAW; United Nations, International Covenant on Civil and Political Rights, December 16, 1966, http://www.ohchr.org/en/professionalinterest/pages/ccpr.aspx (accessed April 16, 2014); United Nations, International Covenant on Economic, Social, and Cultural Rights, December 16, 1966, http://www.ohchr.org/EN/ProfessionalInterest/Pages/CESCR.aspx (accessed April 16, 2014).

39. Organization of the Islamic Conference, Cairo Declaration on Human Rights in Islam [CDHRI], August 5, 1990, U.N. GAOR, World Conf. on Hum. Rts., 4th Sess., Agenda Item 5, U.N. Doc. A/CONF.157/PC/62/Add.18 (1993) [English translation], University of Minnesota Human Rights Library, http://www1.umn.edu/humanrts/instree/cairodeclaration.html (accessed April 30, 2014). The CDHRI currently has fifty-seven signatories. John Humphrey Centre for Peace and Human Rights, "Cairo Declaration on Human Rights in Islam (CDHRI)," Understanding Human Rights, http://www.jhcentre.org/understanding-human-rights/human-rights-around-world/cairo-declaration-human-rights-islam-cdhri (accessed April 30, 2014).

40. For studies of Islamic feminism, see Ahmed, *A Quiet Revolution*; Elizabeth Warnock Fernea, *In Search of Islamic Feminism: One Woman's Global Journey* (New York: Doubleday, 1998); Valentine Moghadam, "Islamic Feminism and Its Discontents: Toward a Resolution of the Debate," *Signs* 27, no. 4 (Summer 2002): 1135–71.

41. Martha Nussbaum, "Women and Cultural Universals," in *Feminist Theory: A Philosophical Anthology*, ed. Ann E. Cudd and Robin O. Andreasen (Malden, MA: Wiley-Blackwell, 2005), 315.

42. Miriam Cooke, *Women Claim Islam: Creating Islamic Feminism Through Literature* (New York: Routledge, 2001), 60.

43. For an explanation of the debates within the Iranian community (both in Iran and among expatriates) regarding Islamic feminism, see Moghadam, "Islamic Feminism."

44. Planning Committee Mid-Decade Forum Copenhagen '80, "List of Workshops Held at the Forum," 1980, IWTC Collection, 89S-29, Box 5.

45. Hall, "Hostages," 1.

46. Ibid., 2.

47. Letters from M. P. Cullimore and Ms. Baraz, "Heads at NGO," *Forum '80*, July 21, 1980, 5, IWTC Collection, 89S-29, Box 13; Letter from the Women's Organization of the Islamic Revolution of Iran, "Imam Khomeini," *Forum '80*, July 23, 1980, 5, IWTC Collection, 89S-29, Box 13; Cartoon, *Forum '80*, July 18, 1980, 7, IWTC Collection, 89S-29, Box 13.

48. FGM has a complicated relationship to Islam. Chapter 5 analyzes this issue in depth. As an example of Third World women's sensitivity to the ways in which Western women discussed FGM, see Maggie Jones, "African Women Must Speak Out on Circumcision," *Forum '80*, July 21, 1980, 2, IWTC Collection, 89S-27, Box 13.

49. AAWORD, "Statement on Genital Mutilation," 352–54.

50. Eisenstein, *Feminism Seduced*, 77.

51. Carolyn M. Stephenson, "Women's International Nongovernmental Organizations at the United Nations," in *Women, Politics, and the United Nations*, ed. Winslow, 147.

52. Moghadam, *Globalizing Women*, 1; Jaquette, "Losing the Battle/Winning the War," 57.

53. Zinsser, "The United Nations Decade for Women," 23.

54. Fraser, *U.N. Decade*, 200.

55. Zinsser, "The United Nations Decade for Women," 21; Susan Tifft, "Conferences: The Triumphant Spirit of Nairobi," *Time*, August 5, 1985, http://www.time.com/time/magazine/article/0,9171,1048453, 00.html (accessed December 9, 2009); Charlotte G. Patton, "Women and Power: The Nairobi Conference," in *Women, Politics, and the United Nations*, ed. Winslow, 65.

56. Elaine Sciolino, "Islam: Feminists vs. Fundamentalists," *New York Times*, July 25, 1985, C1, C12, IWTC Collection, 97S-9, Box 3; Moghadam, *Globalizing Women*, 6–7.

57. United Nations, "Report of the World Conference to Review and Appraise the Achievements of the United Nations Decade for Women: Equality, Development, and Peace," Nairobi, July 15–26, 1985 (New York: United Nations, 1986), introduction, paragraph A, http://www.un.org/womenwatch/confer/nfls/Nairobi1985report.txt (accessed October 15, 2012).

58. Fraser, *U.N. Decade*, 205.

59. AAWORD, "Nairobi Manifesto," *Issue: A Journal of Opinion* 17, no. 2 (1989): 46.

60. Nawal el Saadawi, "End of the Decade," *Forum '85*, July 12, 1985, 6, Women's Rights Collection, Box 19, Sophia Smith Collection, Smith College (hereafter Women's Rights Collection).

61. Forum '85 Workshop Programme, Friedan Papers, Box 22.

62. Nadia Hijab, "Veils: In Eyes of Beholder," *Forum '85*, July 10, 1985, 4, Women's Rights Collection, Box 19.

63. "Religion and Sexuality," *Forum '85*, July 16, 1985, 7, microfiche, Women's Rights Collection, Box 19.

64. Nadia Atif, "Workshops: Circumcision," *Forum '85*, July 15, 1985, 6, microfiche, Women's Rights Collection, Box 19; Nadia Hijab, "Young Arab Women Roundtable," *Forum '85*, July 18, 1985, 8, microfiche, Women's Rights Collection, Box 19; "Woman from Iran," *Forum '85*, July 19, 1985, 6, Women's Rights Collection, Box 19; Rima Sabban, "Social Scientists Debate Women," *Forum '85*, July 19, 1985, 10, microfiche, Women's Rights Collection, Box 19; Mervat Hatem, "Arab Women Value System," *Forum '85*, July 22, 1985, 3, microfiche, Women's Rights Collection, Box 19; Letter from Leila Abd el-Wahhab, Egypt, "Arab View," *Forum '85*, July 23, 1985, 5, microfiche, Women's Rights Collection, Box 19; Nadia Hijab, "Islamic Family Law Changing," *Forum '85*, July 24, 1985, 7, microfiche, Women's Rights Collection, Box 19; Nadia Hijab, "Attempting to Tackle a Sensitive Issue," *Forum '85*, July 25, 1985, 2, microfiche, Women's Rights Collection, Box 19; Hizbullah Women's Organization, Islamic Republic of Iran, "Iranian Women Appeal for Peace," *Forum '85*, July 17, 1985, 5, microfiche, Women's Rights Collection, Box 19; Letter from Haideh Daragah, Iran, "Veiling," *Forum '85*, July 18, 1985, 5, microfiche, Women's Rights Collection, Box 19.

65. Moghadam, *Globalizing Women*, 8, 6.

66. "Report—Planning Committee: NGO Activities at the World Conference of the UN Decade for Women," IWTC Collection, 89S-27, Box 18; Georgia Dullea, "At Women's Conference, Delegates Notice Informal Network of Contacts Emerging," *New York Times*, July 25, 1980, A12.

67. Mahnaz Afkhami, introduction to *Faith and Freedom*, 5.

68. UN, UDHR, Preamble. See also David Little, foreword to Sachedina, *Islam and the Challenge of Human Rights*, vii–viii.

69. Sachedina, *Islam and the Challenge of Human Rights*, 6.

70. Ibid., 7.

71. Afkhami, introduction to *Faith and Freedom*, 1.

72. SIGI member Fatima Mernissi, for example, worked to reinterpret Islamic texts and "craft a feminist theology." Moghadam, "Islamic Feminism and Its Discontents," 1150. See also Mernissi, *The Veil and the Male Elite*.

73. Mahnaz Afkhami, interview with Valentine Moghadam, Washington, DC, November 21, 1999, quoted in Moghadam, "Islamic Feminism and Its Discontents," 1152.

74. Steve J. Stern and Scott Straus, "Introduction: Embracing Paradox: Human Rights in the Global Age," in *The Human Rights Paradox: Universality and Its Discontents*, ed. Steve J. Stern and Scott Straus (Madison: University of Wisconsin Press, 2014), 4.

75. Afkhami, introduction to *Faith and Freedom*, 2.

76. Ibid., 5.

77. Ibid., 1.

78. Marie Aimée Hélie-Lucas, "Women Living Under Muslim Laws," in *Ours by Right: Women's Rights as Human Rights*, ed. Joanna Kerr (London: Zed, 1993), 56.

79. WLUML, *Dossier 1*, February 1986, 2, Women Living Under Muslim Laws Records, copies provided to author by Aisha Shaheed, WLUML, International Coor-

dination Office, London (hereafter WLUML Records). Though India was and is a secular state, it instituted specific laws for minority groups that did not apply to the society as a whole, largely as a result of the demands of those groups. Muslims, a minority in the predominantly Hindu society, were one such group. They lobbied for and received special laws that applied to family issues like marriage and divorce, which had the effect of depriving Muslim women of rights guaranteed by the Indian constitution.

80. Marieme Hélie-Lucas, "The WLUML Interview: Marieme Hélie-Lucas," October 30, 2009, audio recording, WLUML website, http://www.wluml.org/node /5615 (accessed October 3, 2012).

81. Jutta Joachim, *Agenda Setting, the UN, and NGOs: Gender Violence and Reproductive Rights* (Washington, DC: Georgetown University Press, 2007), 134-41.

82. Marie-Aimée Lucas, "Women Living Under Muslim Laws: How It Started," *Women's World* 21-22 (December 1989), ISIS-WICCE: 6, WLUML Records.

83. WLUML, *Dossier 1*, 2; Farida Shaheed, "Linking Dreams: The Network of Women Living Under Muslim Laws," in *From Basic Needs to Basic Rights: Women's Claim to Human Rights*, ed. Margaret Schuler (Washington, DC: Women, Law & Development, 1995), 307-8. WLUML chose its name specifically to acknowledge that not all women living in societies under Islamic law are Muslim.

84. Hélie-Lucas, "Women Living Under Muslim Laws," 56-57. WLUML's headquarters moved from France to London in 2001.

85. Moghadam, *Globalizing Women*, 144.

86. Hélie-Lucas, "Women Living Under Muslim Laws," 52.

87. WLUML and SIGI shared information and supported one another's initiatives. Mahnaz Afkhami, quoted in Moghadam, *Globalizing Women*, 167. See also, WLUML, 1992-2000 folders, SIGI Records, Box ORG12.

88. Hélie-Lucas, "Women Living Under Muslim Laws," 57-58. SIGI later produced such a handbook. I do not know whether they got the idea for the handbook from WLUML.

89. Fatima Mernissi, "The Fundamentalist Obsession with Women," in WLUML, *Dossier 4*, August/September 1988, 40, WLUML Records; Nawal el Saadawi, "The Impact of Fanatic Religious Thought: A Story of a Young Egyptian Moslem Woman," in WLUML, *Dossiers 5-6*, December 1988-May 1989, 38-40, WLUML Records; Nawal el Saadawi, "Fundamentalism: A Universal Phenomenon," in WLUML, *Dossiers 9-10*, June 1991, 78-80, WLUML Records. WLUML's *Dossiers* also announced books by SIGI members; see WLUML *Dossier 3*, June/July 1988, 75, WLUML Records; WLUML, *Dossier 17*, June 1997, 157, WLUML Records; WLUML, *Dossier 21*, September 1998, 163, WLUML Records.

90. WLUML, *Dossier 1*; WLUML, *Dossier 2*, April 1986, WLUML Records; WLUML, *Dossier 3*; WLUML, *Dossier 4*; WLUML, *Dossiers 5-6*; WLUML, *Dossiers 7-8*, June 1989-March 1990, WLUML Records.

91. Shaheed, "Linking Dreams," 307.

92. Hélie-Lucas, "Women Living Under Muslim Laws," 61.

93. Moghadam, *Globalizing Women*, 143.

94. "Empowering Women Through the Law," *Forum '85*, July 15, 1985, 5, micro-fiche, Women's Rights Collection, Box 19; "Sisterhood Is Global," *Forum '85*, July 22, 1985, 6, microfiche, Women's Rights Collection, Box 19.

95. Moghadam, *Globalizing Women*, 146.

96. Afkhami interview with author.

97. Robin Morgan to Greta Hofmann Nemiroff, January 1, 1987, SIGI Records, Box GHN1.

98. Funding Rejections for SIGI Meeting, 1984, Robin Morgan Papers, Box S12, David M. Rubenstein Rare Book & Manuscript Library, Duke University (hereafter Morgan Papers); Grant Rejections, 1981–1988, Morgan Papers, Box S12.

99. Afkhami interview with author; Afary, "Mahnaz Afkhami," 155.

100. Moghadam, *Globalizing Women*, 147.

101. Ibid., 143; Mahnaz Afkhami, Curriculum Vitae, "Profiles: Mahnaz Afkhami," Women's Learning Partnership for Rights, Development, and Peace, http://www.learningpartnership.org/viewProfiles.php?profileID=389 (accessed December 8, 2009).

102. Moghadam, *Globalizing Women*, 166; Funding folder, SIGI Records, Box GHN2; Financial Papers Subseries, 1984–2004, SIGI Records, Boxes FP1–FP19; Funding Files Subseries, 1984–2002, SIGI Records, Boxes FF1–FF16.

103. Joan E. Spero, *The Global Role of U.S. Foundations* (New York: Foundation Center, 2010), 7–16; Lydia Alpizar Duran, "20 Years of Shamefully Scarce Funding for Feminists and Women's Rights Movements," May 14, 2015, AWID, http://www.awid.org/news-and-analysis/20-years-shamefully-scarce-funding-feminists-and-womens-rights-movements (accessed December 27, 2015).

104. Moghadam, *Globalizing Women*, 145.

105. After Afkhami stepped down as SIGI's leader, divisions arose between SIGI's Muslim and non-Muslim members, especially between Morgan and Afkhami. See Chapter 7 for further explanation.

106. Afkhami, introduction to *Faith and Freedom*, 6.

107. Afkhami interview with author; Moghadam, *Globalizing Women*, 166; Mahnaz Afkhami, "Promoting Women's Rights in the Muslim World," *Journal of Democracy* 8, no. 1 (1997): 161.

108. Afkhami interview with author; Mahnaz Afkhami, quoted in Moghadam, *Globalizing Women*, 167; WLUML, 1992–2000 folders, SIGI Records, Box ORG12; Feminist Majority 1994–1998, 2000 folder, SIGI Records, Box ORG5; Female Genital Mutilation folder, SIGI Records, Box SUBJ3. See also Council on Foreign Relations, 1996–1997 folder, SIGI Records, Box ORG4; CWGL [Center for Women's Global Leadership], 1993–1999 folder, SIGI Records, Box ORG4; Equality Now folders, SIGI Records, Boxes ORG4 and ORG5; Human Rights Watch, 1996–1998 folder, SIGI Records, Box ORG6; International Women's Tribune Centre folders, SIGI Records,

Box ORG7; Middle East Institute folder, SIGI Records, Box ORG7; U.S. State Department folder, SIGI Records, Box ORG11; Women's Foreign Policy Council, 1985–1988 and undated folder, SIGI Records, Box ORG12.

109. Moghadam, *Globalizing Women*, 167.

110. Ibid., 9–10.

111. Afkhami interview with author.

Chapter 4

1. James LeMoyne, "Army Women and the Saudis: The Encounter Shocks Both," *New York Times*, September 25, 1990, A1.

2. Beth Bailey, *America's Army: Making the All-Volunteer Force* (Cambridge, MA: Belknap Press of Harvard University Press, 2009), 218.

3. Alberto Bin, Richard Hill, and Archer Jones, *Desert Storm: A Forgotten War* (Westport, CT: Praeger, 1998), 67; Alastair Finlan, *The Gulf War 1991* (Oxford: Osprey, 2003), 76.

4. While many Muslims object to the term "Wahhabism," there is no better term available for the distinct form of Islam practiced in Saudi Arabia. The Ottomans dubbed Muhammad ibn al-Wahhab's eighteenth-century variant of the Sunni Hanbali legal school "Wahhabism" to discredit it, implying that its adherents venerated al-Wahhab rather than God. Although the Ottomans meant the term to be derogatory, it has stuck. Wahhabi ulama dominated Saudi Arabia at its inception in the early twentieth century and still do. The version of Islam practiced by many Saudis today is a mixture of Wahhabism and Salafism, a modern fundamentalist movement that developed in the late nineteenth and early twentieth centuries and is best exemplified by the Muslim Brotherhood. In the 1950s, Saudi Arabia opened its doors to the Brotherhood, who were persecuted in Nasser's Egypt. Since many members of the Brotherhood became teachers in Saudi Arabia, they spread Salafism to the Saudi rank and file. For further discussion, see Mohammed Ayoob and Hasan Kosebalaban, eds., *Religion and Politics in Saudi Arabia: Wahhabism and the State* (Boulder, CO: Lynne Rienner, 2008).

5. Human Rights Watch, "Saudi Arabia," *World Report 1992*, http://www.hrw.org /reports/1992/WR92/MEW2-02.htm#P415_151501 (accessed May 22, 2014).

6. Saudi Arabia did finally ratify CEDAW in 2000 but with reservations, including, "in case of contradiction between any term of the Convention and the norms of Islamic Law, the Kingdom is not under the obligation to observe the contradictory terms of the Convention." United Nations Committee on the Elimination of Discrimination Against Women, "Consideration of Reports Submitted by States Parties Under Article 18 of the Convention on the Elimination of All Forms of Discrimination Against Women, Combined Initial and Second Periodic Reports of States Parties, Saudi Arabia," United Nations, CEDAW/C/SAU/2, March 29, 2007, 8, UN Women, CEDAW, Country Reports, http://www.un.org/womenwatch/daw/cedaw/reports.htm#s (accessed May 23, 2014).

7. Congress to this date has not ratified CEDAW, despite efforts by the Clinton and Obama administrations to convince them to ratify it. The United States generally has refrained from ratifying most international conventions, so not ratifying CEDAW fits with this larger trend. It also fits with ongoing gender inequality in the United States. Some specific objections to CEDAW that have prevented ratification include conservatives' opposition to the convention's language upholding women's reproductive rights. The U.S. failure to ratify CEDAW leaves it open to charges of hypocrisy when it criticizes other states' treatment of women. However, the Saudis' refusal to ratify the convention was not among the criticisms American protesters leveled at the Kingdom in 1990–91, and U.S. protesters were not responsible for the fact that the United States did not ratify CEDAW. Many feminists have pressed the United States to ratify the convention since its adoption by the United Nations in 1979.

8. "Malta Summit Ends Cold War," BBC News, December 3, 1989, http://news .bbc.co.uk/onthisday/hi/dates/stories/december/3/newsid_4119000/4119950.stm (accessed February 1, 2010).

9. Jeffrey A. Engel, "A Better World . . . But Don't Get Carried Away: The Foreign Policy of George H. W. Bush Twenty Years On," *Diplomatic History* 34, no. 1 (January 2010): 29.

10. George H. W. Bush, "Inaugural Address," January 20, 1989, http://www .nationalcenter.org/BushInaugural.html (accessed February 9, 2010).

11. Francis Fukuyama, *The End of History and the Last Man* (New York: Free Press, 1992); Michael E. Brown, Sean M. Lynn-Jones, and Steven E. Miller, eds., *Debating the Democratic Peace* (Cambridge, MA: MIT Press, 1996).

12. George H. W. Bush, "Address Before a Joint Session of the Congress on the State of the Union," January 29, 1991, American Presidency Project, ed. Gerhard Peters and John T. Woolley, http://www.presidency.ucsb.edu/ws/?pid=19253 (accessed February 9, 2010).

13. George H. W. Bush, "Remarks at the Aspen Institute Symposium in Aspen, Colorado," August 2, 1990, American Presidency Project, ed. Gerhard Peters and John T. Woolley, http://www.presidency.ucsb.edu/ws/?pid=18731 (accessed May 23, 2014); Bush, "State of the Union." For a discussion of the concept of "rogue states" in postwar U.S. foreign policy, see Alexandra Holomar, "Rebels Without a Conscience: The Evolution of the Rogue States Narrative in US Security Policy," *European Journal of International Relations* 17, no. 4 (November 2011): 705–27.

14. Finlan, *Gulf War 1991*, 25–27, 29; Lawrence Freedman and Efraim Karsh, *The Gulf Conflict 1990–1991: Diplomacy and War in the New World Order* (Princeton, NJ: Princeton University Press, 1993), 37–41, 73–74, 80–84.

15. Holomar, "Rebels Without a Conscience," 713.

16. Bailey, *America's Army*, 132–33, 163, 171, 217–18.

17. Sexual harassment of and sexual assault upon military women by military men remains a considerable problem in the U.S. armed forces today, and the American military has a long way to go in improving its handling of these matters.

18. Judith Hicks Stiehm, "Just the Facts, Ma'am," in *It's Our Military, Too! Women and the U.S. Military*, ed. Judith Hicks Stiehm (Philadelphia: Temple University Press, 1996), 69; Bailey, *America's Army*, 218.

19. Bailey, *America's Army*, 218; Stiehm, "Just the Facts, Ma'am," 69; CNN, "War in the Gulf," February 11, 1991, Television News Archive, DVD. For an account of an American woman POW, see Rhonda Cornum, as told to Peter Copeland, *She Went to War: The Rhonda Cornum Story* (Novato, CA: Presidio, 1992).

20. Department of Defense, "Conduct of the Gulf War: Final Report to Congress" (Washington, DC: Department of Defense, April 1992), 490; Kareene Ostermiller, transcript of oral history interview with John Terreo, August 3, 1992, 5, 20th Century Montana Military Veteran's Oral History Project, OH 1463, Montana Historical Society; Captain Theresa O. Cantrell, Accountable Property Officer, 32d Medical Supply, Optical and Maintenance Battalion, transcript of oral history interview by Major Robert B. Honec III (116th Military History Detachment), June 1991, 5–6, Operations Desert Shield and Desert Storm Oral History Interviews, DSIT AE 107, Department of the Army, XVIII Airborne Corps and U.S. Army Center of Military History, http://www.history.army.mil/documents/SWA/DSIT/DSIT107.htm (accessed January 30, 2010); Deidre Jean Wright, Major, Air Force Veteran, Veterans History Project, Library of Congress, http://lcweb2.loc.gov/diglib/vhp/story/loc.natlib.afc2001001.12502/transcript ID?=sr0001 (accessed January 30, 2010); Molly Moore, *A Woman at War: Storming Kuwait with the U.S. Marines* (New York: Scribner's, 1993), 33.

21. Kareene Ostermiller, transcript of oral history interview with John Terreo, December 9, 1990, 6, 20th Century Montana Military Veteran's Oral History Project, OH 1222, Montana Historical Society.

22. Cantrell interview transcript, 8, 9; Major Jenette Wade, G-2 Operations Section, XVIII Airborne Corps, transcript of group oral history interview of Major Jenette Wade and Captain Kristen B. Vlahos by Major Robert B. Honec III (116th Military History Detachment), June 6, 1991, 8, Operations Desert Shield and Desert Storm Oral History Interviews, DSIT AE 106, Department of the Army, XVIII Airborne Corps and U.S. Army Center of Military History, http://www.history.army.mil/documents/SWA/DSIT/DSIT106.htm (accessed January 30, 2010); Wendy Marie Wamsley Taines, Corporal, Army Veteran, oral history interview with Mary Ann Donahue, January 26, 2005, Veterans History Project, Library of Congress, http://lcweb2.loc.gov/diglib/vhp/story/loc.natlib.afc2001001.24791/transcript?ID=sr0001 (accessed January 30, 2010); Moore, *Woman at War*, 33.

23. Cantrell interview transcript, 9–10. See also Wade and Vlahos interview transcript, 7; Ostermiller interview 1 transcript, 62.

24. Cantrell interview transcript, 12.

25. Anne Welch, Sergeant, Army Veteran, Veterans History Project, Library of Congress, http://lcweb2.loc.gov/diglib/vhp/story/loc.natlib.afc2001001.17760/transcript?ID=sr0001 (accessed January 30, 2010).

26. Taines interview transcript.

27. PSC Sandra L. Mitten, USCGR, transcript of oral history interview with Michael J. Salkowski, September 18, 2007, 8, U.S. Coast Guard Oral History Program, Operation Desert Shield/Desert Storm, http://www.uscg.mil/history/weboralhistory /SandyMittenOralHistory.asp (accessed January 30, 2010).

28. Moore, *Woman at War*, 33.

29. Wade and Vlahos interview transcript, 14.

30. Ibid., 4.

31. Ibid., 6–7.

32. Cantrell interview transcript, 7.

33. Ostermiller interview 1 transcript, 30–31, 65–66.

34. The lawsuit was initiated in 1995; the policies formally ended in 2002. See Daniel Pipes, *Nothing Abides: Perspectives on the Middle East and Islam* (New Brunswick, NJ: Transaction Publishers, 2015), 152–54; Elaine Sciolino, "Servicewomen Win, Doffing Their Veils in Saudi Arabia," *New York Times*, January 25, 2002, http:// www.nytimes.com/2002/01/25/international/25SAUD.html (accessed January 6, 2016).

35. Gary C. Woodward, "The Rules of the Game: The Military and the Press in the Persian Gulf War," in *The Media and the Persian Gulf War*, ed. Robert E. Denton Jr. (Westport, CT: Praeger, 1993), 1.

36. Woodward, "Rules of the Game," 2. See also R. W. Apple, "Correspondents Protest Pool System," *New York Times*, February 12, 1991, A14; Malcolm W. Browne, "The Military vs. the Press," *New York Times Magazine*, March 3, 1991, 27–30, 44–45; Walter Cronkite, "What Is There to Hide?" *Newsweek*, February 25, 1991, 43; Jason DeParle, "17 News Executives Criticize U.S. for 'Censorship' of Gulf Coverage," *New York Times*, July 3, 1991, A4; R. Michael Schiffer and Michael F. Rinzler, "No News Is No News; Pentagon Restrictions Distort Coverage on the Gulf," *New York Times*, January 23, 1991, A19; "15 Top Journalists See Cheney and Object to Gulf War Curbs," *New York Times*, May 2, 1991, A16; Richard Zoglin, "Press Coverage: Volleys on the Information Front," *Time*, February 4, 1991, http://www.time.com/time/magazine/ article/0,9171,972261,00.html (accessed February 26, 2010); United States Senate, Hearing Before the Committee on Governmental Affairs, February 20, 1991 (Washington, D.C.: U.S. GPO, 1991).

37. Woodward, "Rules of the Game," 19–20.

38. While quantitative studies of the major themes of Gulf War news coverage are not available, a Lexis-Nexis Academic keyword search that I conducted in February 2016 of one thousand U.S. newspaper articles published about the Gulf War between August 1990 and February 1991 revealed that approximately 20 percent of the articles discussed U.S. servicewomen or Saudi women.

39. *CBS Evening News*, August 23, 1990, Television News Archive, DVD.

40. *CBS Evening News*, September 5, 1990, Television News Archive, DVD.

41. *ABC World News Tonight*, September 7, 1990, Television News Archive, DVD.

42. Strobe Talbott, "America Abroad," *Time*, January 21, 1991, http://www.time.com/time/printout/0,8816,972155,00.html (accessed February 26, 2010).

43. "The Gulf: Lifting the Veil," *Time*, September 24, 1990, http://www.time.com/time/printout/0,8816,971218,00.html (accessed February 24, 2010).

44. Steve Raymer, "GI Women in Saudi Arabia Make Presence Felt," *Philadelphia Tribune*, January 11, 1991, 5A.

45. Philip Shenon, "At Combat's Doorstep, She Confronts Peril and Male Doubt," *New York Times*, February 24, 1991, 16.

46. *CBS Evening News*, September 5, 1990.

47. Youssef M. Ibrahim, "Saudi Women Take Driver's Seat in a Rare Protest for the Right to Travel," *New York Times*, November 7, 1990, A18.

48. William Dowell, "Saudi Arabia Life in the Slow Lane," *Time*, November 26, 1990, http://www.time.com/time/printout/0,8816,971791,00.html (accessed February 27, 2010).

49. Ibrahim, "Saudi Women Take Driver's Seat," A18.

50. Thomas W. Lippman, *Inside the Mirage: America's Fragile Partnership with Saudi Arabia* (Boulder, CO: Westview, 2004), 308–9.

51. *CBS Evening News*, November 14, 1990, Television News Archive, DVD.

52. James LeMoyne, "Ban on Driving by Women Reaffirmed by Saudis," *New York Times*, November 15, 1990, A19.

53. *Nightline*, ABC, December 18, 1990, Television News Archive, DVD.

54. Geraldine Brooks, "Americans Bring Ideas That Disrupt Saudi Life," *Wall Street Journal*, November 15, 1990, A14.

55. *Nightline*, ABC, December 18, 1990, Television News Archive, DVD; Brooks, "Americans Bring Ideas," A14; LeMoyne, "Ban on Driving," A19; "Saudi Women Disciplined," *New York Times*, November 13, 1990, A14; James LeMoyne, "Saudi Interior Minister Prohibits All Protests for Change by Women," *New York Times*, November 18, 1990, 16; "Action Alert: Saudi Arabia: Driving Home Women's Rights," *Ms.* (January/February 1991): 8.

56. LeMoyne, "Interior Minister," 16.

57. Dowell, "Saudi Arabia Life in the Slow Lane"; "Saudi Arabia: Update on Women at the Wheel," *Ms.* (November/December 1991): 17.

58. *CBS Evening News*, November 14, 1990, Television News Archive, DVD.

59. *NBC Nightly News*, November 17, 1990, Television News Archive, DVD.

60. James LeMoyne, "U.S. Troops and Saudis: A Silent Clash of Cultures," *New York Times*, November 21, 1990, A10.

61. For a discussion of other, more traditional antiwar protests, see Peter Applebome, "War in the Gulf: Antiwar Rallies; Day of Protest Is the Biggest Yet," *New York Times*, January 27, 1991, http://www.nytimes.com/1991/01/27/us/war-in-the-gulf-antiwar-rallies-day-of-protests-is-the-biggest-yet.html (accessed January 11, 2016).

62. Debra J. Saunders, "U.S. House Can Hardly Throw Stones at Riyadh," *Daily News* (Los Angeles), August 9, 1990, N21; Debra J. Saunders, "A Double Standard on

Equality," *San Jose Mercury News*, August 13, 1990, 7B. The *San Jose Mercury News* article is a verbatim reprint of the L.A. *Daily News* piece. Saunders appears to identify as a political conservative today, but I do not know what her politics were in 1990.

63. Marie DeSantis, "The Middle East Crisis: Democracy, Kings, and Sexual Apartheid in Saudi Arabia," *Off Our Backs* 20, no. 9 (October 31, 1990): 8.

64. "A Ms. Open Letter on the Persian Gulf Crisis," *Ms.* (November 1990): 21.

65. Kate Millett, Robin Morgan, Gloria Steinem, and Ti-Grace Atkinson, "A Feminist Issue Still," *New York Times*, January 20, 1991, E18.

66. Knight-Ridder, "NOW Urges Gulf Withdrawal," *Washington Post*, November 28, 1990, A30.

67. "NOW Issues Call for US Withdrawal," *Boston Globe*, November 28, 1990, 15; Thrity Umrigar, "NOW Condemns Saudi Sexism; Group Against U.S. Defending a Nation Oppressive to Women," *Akron Beacon Journal*, November 29, 1990, A8; Carl M. Cannon, "NOW Calls for Pullout over 'Gender Apartheid,'" *Philadelphia Inquirer*, November 28, 1990, A4; Associated Press, "Pull Out—NOW," *Philadelphia Daily News*, November 28, 1990, 50; Carl M. Cannon, "U.S. Women Question Fighting for Sexist Regime," *Lexington Herald-Leader*, November 29, 1990, A1; Janet Williams, "American Rights Bow to Saudi Customs," *Pittsburgh Post-Gazette*, December 9, 1990, B1.

68. *Nightline*, ABC, December 18, 1990, Television News Archive, DVD.

69. Carl M. Cannon, "Islamic Sexism Widens Gender Gap in Support for U.S. Action in Gulf," *The State* (Columbia, SC), November 29, 1990, 2A.

70. *NBC Nightly News*, December 8, 1990, Television News Archive, DVD.

71. Michael X. Delli Carpini and Ester R. Fuchs, "The Year of the Woman? Candidates, Voters, and the 1992 Elections," *Political Science Quarterly* 108, no. 1 (1993): 33. The gender gap closed somewhat as the war wore on, but it remained throughout. See Clyde Wilcox, Lara Hewitt, and Dee Allsop, "The Gender Gap in Attitudes on the Gulf War: A Cross-National Perspective," *Journal of Peace Research* 33, no. 1 (February 1996): 67–82.

72. Cannon, "Islamic Sexism Widens Gender Gap," 2A.

73. Deborah C. England, "Letters to the Editor," *San Francisco Chronicle*, November 17, 1990, A14. For similar letters, see Jacqueline T. Banks, "Letters from the People," *Sacramento Bee*, December 7, 1990, B11; Dawn E. Bell, "Letters from the People," *Sacramento Bee*, December 7, 1990, B11; Barbara Krabec, "Letters from the People," *Sacramento Bee*, December 30, 1990, F5; Gloria Freund, "NOW Speaks Up for All Women," *Newsday* (Melville, NY), January 2, 1991, 88.

74. *NBC Nightly News*, December 8, 1990, Television News Archive, DVD.

75. Ibid.

76. Bush continued to enforce the Reagan-era global gag rule and pursued an anti-abortion agenda at home. "President George H. W. Bush on Women's Issues," Women in Focus: Key Debates, *WeWomen.com*, http://www.wewomen.com/key-debates /george-h-w-bush-womens-issues-n158886.html (accessed May 21, 2014). When the

Bush administration stuck by his appointment of Clarence Thomas to the Supreme Court in 1991, even after Anita Hill testified during Thomas's confirmation hearings that he had sexually harassed her, it provided further evidence for many who believed that Bush was not committed to women's equality.

77. David Hancock, "The Tangled Web of U.S.-Saudi Ties," *CBS News.com,* April 20, 2004, http://www.cbsnews.com/news/the-tangled-web-of-us-saudi-ties (accessed May 27, 2014).

78. Saudi Arabia only officially outlawed slavery in 1962 reportedly at the urging of President John F. Kennedy, yet American leaders established a close relationship with the Kingdom in the 1930s and offered little public comment on Saudi slavery, either during the time period or since. Recent reports on human trafficking and slave labor name Saudi Arabia as a country where these human rights violations continue to occur, but American policymakers remain publicly silent about such issues.

79. "Introduction," *Death of a Princess, Frontline,* PBS, April 12, 2005, http://www .pbs.org/wgbh/pages/frontline/shows/princess/etc/synopsis.html (accessed July 17, 2012); Transcript of *Death of a Princess,* a film by Anthony Thomas, *Frontline,* PBS, http://www.pbs.org/wgbh/pages/frontline/shows/princess/etc/script.html (accessed July 17, 2012); *Death of a Princess,* dir. by Anthony Thomas, Youtube video, 1:56:33, posted by "the people want to destroy idols," July 25, 2011, https://www.youtube.com /watch?v=kDUsKJTkOaE (accessed July 17, 2012).

80. A search of the George H. W. Bush Presidential Library and Museum website, the *Public Papers of the Presidents,* and news coverage from August 1990 through March 1991 reveals no mention of Saudi women, women's rights in the Gulf, or the protests against "gender apartheid." See http://bushlibrary.tamu.edu/research/public _papers.php (accessed May 19, 2014). The closest Bush came to acknowledging the antiwar protests was an open letter he sent to college newspapers in January 1991. See George H. W. Bush, "Open Letter to College Students on the Persian Gulf Crisis," January 9, 1991, American Presidency Project, ed. Gerhard Peters and John T. Woolley, http://www.presidency.ucsb.edu/ws/index.php?pid=19205&st=open+letter&st1 =college+students (accessed May 19, 2014).

81. Debra J. Saunders, "Just Being an American Is Cause for Thanksgiving," *Daily News* (Los Angeles), November 22, 1990, N23.

82. Carpini and Fuchs, "Year of the Woman," 36.

Chapter 5

1. *Law & Order* debuted in 1990 and, according to NBC, was "the second-longest-running drama series in the history of television." See http://www.nbc.com/Law_and _Order/about (accessed May 21, 2010). Its twentieth and final season ended in May 2010, but its several spin-offs continue.

2. "Ritual," *Law & Order,* Season 8, Episode 10, first broadcast December 17, 1997, NBC, directed by Brian Mertes and written by Kathy McCormick (New York: Wolf Films in association with Universal Media Studios, 1997). DVD of episode provided

to the author in February 2009 by Professor Kenneth Pybus, Abilene Christian University.

3. The various rituals that involve cutting the female genitalia are also referred to as "female genital cutting" (FGC), "female circumcision," "female genital modification," and "female genital surgeries" (FGS). "Female circumcision" was the earliest term and most closely approximated local terms for the practice, while FGM came into common use by the late 1970s. FGC, FGS, and "female genital modification" are more recent names coined in response to debates about finding terminology that is accurate but not pejorative or offensive to practitioners, although others continue to use FGM. This chapter does not engage with these debates. I am aware of them but have chosen to use "female genital mutilation" because it was the most commonly used term during the period under examination, and I feel it is an accurate term to describe these practices.

4. During this period, Sudan encompassed the present-day Republic of the Sudan and Republic of South Sudan, which were created in 2011.

5. "Ritual," *Law & Order.*

6. Ibid.

7. For accounts of the U.S. intervention in Somalia, see Chester A. Crocker, "The Lessons of Somalia: Not Everything Went Wrong," *Foreign Affairs* 74, no. 3 (May/June 1995): 2–8; Mark Bowden, *Black Hawk Down: A Story of Modern War* (New York: Atlantic Monthly, 1999); Ken Rutherford, *Humanitarianism Under Fire: The US and UN Intervention in Somalia* (Sterling, VA: Kumarian Press, 2008); Jonathan Stevenson, *Losing Mogadishu: Testing U.S. Policy in Somalia* (Annapolis: Naval Institute Press, 1995); Walter S. Clarke, *Somalia and the Future of Humanitarian Intervention* (Princeton, NJ: Princeton University Press, 1995); Michael Barnett, *The Empire of Humanity: A History of Humanitarianism* (Ithaca, NY: Cornell University Press, 2011), 171–94.

8. Nahid Toubia, *Female Genital Mutilation: A Call for Global Action* (New York: RAINBO, 1995), 22–25. As of the mid-1990s, there were reports that it also occurred in Oman and Yemen, and immigrants from countries that practiced FGM brought the custom with them to the West.

9. Elizabeth Heger Boyle, *Female Genital Cutting: Cultural Conflict in the Global Community* (Baltimore: Johns Hopkins University Press, 2002), 27–28; Hanny Lightfoot-Klein, *A Woman's Odyssey into Africa: Tracks Across a Life* (Binghamton, NY: Haworth Press, 1992), 47–48.

10. See Kelly Shannon, "The Right to Bodily Integrity: Women's Rights as Human Rights and the International Movement to End Female Genital Mutilation, 1970s–1990s," in *The Human Rights Revolution*, ed. Iriye, Goedde, and Hitchcock, 285–310.

11. "Prevalence of Female Genital Mutilation (FGM) in Africa," Map and Data Table, *Afrol News*, http://www.afrol.com/Categories/Women/FGM/netscapeindex.htm (accessed May 21, 2010). This source is based upon data collected by Amnesty International and the U.S. government. See also Stanlie M. James and Claire C.

Robertson, "Introduction: Reimaging Transnational Sisterhood," in *Genital Cutting and Transnational Sisterhood: Disputing U.S. Polemics*, ed. Stanlie M. James and Claire C. Robertson (Champaign: University of Illinois Press, 2002), 9–10.

12. Toubia, *Female Genital Mutilation*, 10, 25; "Prevalence of FGM" data table.

13. Boyle, *Female Genital Cutting*, 30–31; James and Robertson, "Introduction," 11–12.

14. El Saadawi, *Hidden Face of Eve*, 22, 43, 47; Boyle, *Female Genital Cutting*, 29–30; Lightfoot-Klein, *A Woman's Odyssey into Africa*, 49–50; Ayaan Hirsi Ali, *Infidel* (New York: Free Press, 2007), 31.

15. Boyle, *Female Genital Cutting*, 32.

16. See Ali, *Infidel*; Waris Dirie and Cathleen Miller, *Desert Flower: The Extraordinary Journey of a Desert Nomad* (New York: William Morrow, 1998); Fadumo Korn, *Born in the Big Rains: A Memoir of Somalia and Survival*, trans. and afterword by Tobe Levin (New York: Feminist Press, 2006).

17. See Estelle B. Freedman, *No Turning Back: The History of Feminism and the Future of Women* (New York: Ballantine, 2002), 276–302. American feminists did not succeed in getting Congress to pass the Violence Against Women Act (VAWA) until 1994. The debates about FGM occurred during this period of heightened feminist campaigns for public action against abuses of women's rights in the private sphere.

18. Boyle, *Female Genital Cutting*, 41.

19. For more on this, see Shannon, "Right to Bodily Integrity," 285–310.

20. Boyle, *Female Genital Cutting*, 45.

21. Joseph P. Kahn, "Fran P. Hosken, 86; Activist for Women's Issues Globally," *Boston Globe*, February 12, 2006, http://www.boston.com/news/globe/obituaries/articles/2006/02/12/fran_p_hosken_86_activist_for_womens_issues_globally (accessed November 6, 2008); Fran P. Hosken, "A Personal View," in *The Hosken Report: Genital and Sexual Mutilation of Females* (Lexington, MA: Women's International Network News, 1979), 1. Hosken numbered each chapter separately in her report, so citations hereafter will contain the chapter title and page number.

22. "She Studies Societies That Brutalize Women," *New York Times*, February 28, 1978, 39.

23. Hosken, "A Personal View," 1–20.

24. Hosken, *Report*. Hosken revised the report several times. See Fran P. Hosken, *Female Sexual Mutilations: The Facts and Proposals for Action* (Lexington, MA: Women's International Network News, 1980); Fran P. Hosken, *The Hosken Report: Genital and Sexual Mutilation of Females*, 3rd rev. ed. (Lexington, MA: Women's International Network News, 1982); Fran P. Hosken, *The Hosken Report: Genital and Sexual Mutilation of Females*, 4th rev. ed. (Lexington, MA: Women's International Network News, 1993). Hosken issued a preliminary report in 1976; however, its extremely limited availability meant that her research only received notice when she published *The Hosken Report* in 1979. Fran P. Hosken, *Genital Mutilation of Women in Africa* (Pasadena, CA: Munger Africana Library, 1976).

25. For example, Dr. Nahid Toubia, a notable anti-FGM activist from Sudan, stated that she relied upon Hosken's figures when no national studies were available. Toubia, *Female Genital Mutilation*, 22.

26. Hosken, "Medical Facts and Summary," in *Report*, 1; Hosken, "A Personal View," in *Report*, 2. Hosken coined FGM because she believed the term "female circumcision" was not an accurate descriptor of the rituals she studied because it implied a specious correlation between female "circumcision" and male circumcision. Terms like FGC, FGS, and so forth have only come into vogue in the twenty-first century.

27. Hosken, foreword to *Report*, 4.

28. Tobe Levin and Augustine H. Asaah, preface to *Empathy and Rage: Female Genital Mutilation in African Literature*, ed. Tobe Levin and Augustine H. Asaah (Oxfordshire: Ayebia Clarke Publishing, 2009), xv.

29. Hosken, "Geographic Overview," in *Report*, 6.

30. Nawal el Saadawi, quoted in Tiffany Patterson and Angela Gillam, "Out of Egypt: A Talk with Nawal El Saadawi," *Freedomways* 23, no. 3 (1983): 190–91. AAWORD was also outraged by Hosken's workshop in Copenhagen. Levin and Asaah, preface to *Empathy and Rage*, ed. Levin and Asaah, xv.

31. Margaret Jean Hay, review of *The Hosken Report* in *International Journal of African Historical Studies* 14, no. 3 (1981): 523–26. See also Hosken, "A Personal View," 13–14.

32. Gloria Steinem and Robin Morgan to Fran Hosken, March 26, 1980, Letters to Ms., 1972–1980, 7, Schlesinger Library, Radcliffe Institute, Harvard University. A dispute between Hosken and *Ms.* arose because, when Hosken heard the magazine was considering running a piece on FGM, she proposed that she be the author. She was insulted when Morgan and Steinem decided to write the article themselves, and she objected when they included the article by el Saadawi rather than focus on Hosken's work. Fran Hosken to Gloria Steinem, May 28, 1979, Gloria Steinem Papers, Box 151, Sophia Smith Collection, Smith College.

33. World Health Organization, "Seminar on Traditional Practices Affecting the Health of Women and Children," February 10–15, 1979, A/CONF.94/BP/9, microfiche, Women's Rights Collection, Conferences Series, Box 19.

34. Elizabeth Fee, review of *The Hosken Report* in *Signs* 5, no. 4 (Summer 1980): 807–9.

35. Georgia Dullea, "Female Circumcision a Topic at U.N. Parley," *New York Times*, July 18, 1980, B4.

36. Jones, "African Women Must Speak Out," 2.

37. Ibid.; AAWORD, "Statement on Genital Mutilation," 351–54. African and Arab women at the sessions on FGM were particularly insulted when photographs of excised female genitalia were shown during the workshop on FGM. See Pierrette Herzberger-Fofana, "Excision and African Literature: An Activist Annotated Bibliographical Excursion," in *Empathy and Rage*, ed. Levin and Asaah, 145.

38. Atif, "Workshops: Circumcision," 6. See also Hijab, "Attempting to Tackle a Sensitive Issue," 2.

39. WLUML, "Female Circumcision," *Dossier 7/8*, June 1989 and March 1990, 89, WLUML Records; Barbara Crossette, "Egypt: Court Backs Egypt's Ban on Genital Cutting of Girls," WLUML, *Dossier 20*, July 1998, 146–47, WLUML Records; WLUML, Books and Papers: "Against the Mutilation of Women," *Dossier 20*, July 1998, 155, WLUML Records; WLUML, Audiovisuals: "In the Name of God: Changing Attitudes Towards Mutilation," *Dossier 20*, July 1998, 166–67, WLUML Records; Azza M. Karram, "Contemporary Islamisms and Feminisms in Egypt," WLUML, *Dossier 19*, February 1998, 45, WLUML Records; WLUML, Resource Index: "Awaken/L'Eveil," *Dossier 19*, February 1998, 148, WLUML Records; WLUML, Declarations and Sentiments: "Muslim Thinkers' Plea to Rulers," *Dossier 19*, February 1998, 154, WLUML Records; Hooma Hoodfar, "Muslim Women on the Threshold of the Twenty-First Century," WLUML, *Dossier 21*, February 1999, 113, WLUML Records.

40. "Sexual Mutilations: Case Studies Presented at the Workshop: African Women Speak on Female Circumcision, Khartoum, October 21–25, 1984," WLUML, *Dossier 3*, June/July 1988, 49–64, WLUML Records. See also "Women's Group for the Abolition of Sexual Mutilation (CAMS-F)," WLUML, *Dossier 3*, June/July 1988, 64, WLUML Records; "Foundation for Women's Health, Research and Development (FORWARD)," WLUML, *Dossier 3*, June/July 1988, 65–66, WLUML Records.

41. Farhat Rahman, "Female Sexuality and Islam," WLUML, *Dossier 5/6*, December 1988–May 1989, 30, WLUML Records.

42. WLUML, "Plan of Action—Dhaka 1997," 8, WLUML Records.

43. Sisterhood Is Global Alert, "Government Backlash to Campaign Against Female Genital Mutilation," July 11, 1997, SIGI Records, Box PF8. Underlining in the original.

44. SIGI actively participated in the anti-FGM movement, and it acted as a "financial conduit" for Sudanese activist Dr. Nahid Toubia's international campaign. Dr. Nahid Toubia, "Presentation to USAID on Female Genital Mutilation," July 27, 1993, SIGI Records, Box SUBJ3; Dr. Nahid Toubia to Mahnaz Afkhami, May 20, 1992, SIGI Records, Box SUBJ3.

45. Farida Shaheed, "Networking for Change: The Role of Women's Groups in Initiating Dialogue on Women's Issues," in *Faith and Freedom*, ed. Afkhami, 86. FGM is not practiced in Pakistan.

46. SIGI Alerts, Equality Now, Women's Action 8.1, "Egypt: Government Efforts to Medicalize Female Genital Mutilation (FGM)," March 1995, SIGI Records, Box PF9; Afkhami interview with author.

47. Shannon, "Right to Bodily Integrity," 299–301.

48. Ibid., 292–98, 300–301.

49. For examples of publications that targeted American audiences, see Olayinka Koso-Thomas, *The Circumcision of Women: A Strategy for Eradication* (London: Zed, 1987); Hanny Lightfoot-Klein, *Prisoners of Ritual: An Odyssey into Female Genital*

Circumcision in Africa (New York: Haworth Press, 1989); Raqiya Haji Dualeh Abdalla, *Sisters in Affliction: Circumcision and Infibulation of Women in Africa* (New York: Zed, 1982); Blaine Harden, "Africans Keep Rite of Girls' Circumcision," *Washington Post,* July 13, 1985, A12, A13; Margaret Strobel, "African Women," *Signs* 8, no. 1 (Autumn 1982): 109–31; "Africa: A Ritual of Danger," *Time,* November 8, 1990, http://www.time.com/printout/0,8816,971611,00.html (accessed February 27, 2010).

50. Feminists pushed for Congress to pass VAWA precisely because violence against women in the United States was such a problem. Women faced rape, domestic violence, murder, and other abuse because of their gender, and as the 1991 Anita Hill testimony against Clarence Thomas brought home to U.S. women at the time, they also faced regular sexual harassment and discrimination.

51. Robin Morgan and Gloria Steinem, "The International Crime of Genital Mutilation," *Ms.* (March 1980): 65–67, 98, 100.

52. At its peak in the 1970s, *Ms.* sold 550,000 copies per year. Patricia Bradley, *Mass Media and the Shaping of American Feminism, 1963–1975* (Jackson: University Press of Mississippi, 2003), 182.

53. Morgan and Steinem, "International Crime," 66–67. The hadith are the sayings of Muhammad. They are not considered the word of God the way the Koran is, but they are one of the main texts for the interpretation of Islamic law. Many scholars and experts on Islamic law, as well as Muslims who do not practice FGM, have argued that the particular hadith that pertain to FGM are not authentic and cannot be attributed to Muhammad. FGM therefore cannot be justified by using any Islamic holy text, according to this interpretation.

54. Nawal el Saadawi, "The Question No One Would Answer," *Ms.* (March 1980): 68–69.

55. Melani McAlister, "Suffering Sisters? American Feminists and the Problem of Female Genital Surgeries," in *Americanism: New Perspectives on the History of an Ideal,* ed. Michael Kazin and Joseph A. McCartin (Chapel Hill: University of North Carolina Press, 2006), 251. McAlister cited Amal Amireh, who wrote that el Saadawi is one of the most translated Arab writers and that her books are found on syllabi across the United States for various graduate and undergraduate courses, from literature to politics to women's studies. See Amal Amireh, "Framing Nawal El Saadawi: Arab Feminism in a Transnational World," *Signs* 26, no. 1 (Autumn 2000): 215–49.

56. Vivian Gornick, "About the Mutilated Half," *New York Times,* March 14, 1982, BR33.

57. El Saadawi, *Hidden Face of Eve,* 36–37, 48, 41–42.

58. Ibid., 313, 63–54.

59. Gornick, "About the Mutilated Half," BR33.

60. Ibid.

61. Alice Walker, *Possessing the Secret of Joy* (New York: Washington Square Press, 1992). The second novel to discuss FGM appeared the same year and featured

an infibulated major character; however, this character was a Jewish girl from Ethiopia, not a Muslim. See Gloria Naylor, *Bailey's Café* (New York: Vintage Books, 1992).

62. Walker, *Possessing the Secret of Joy*, 139–40.

63. See Janette Turner Hospital, "What They Did to Tashi," *New York Times*, June 28, 1992, http://www.nytimes.com/books/98/10/04/specials/walker-secret.html (accessed November 15, 2008); Dierdre Donahue, "Walker's Disturbing 'Secret': Novelist Explores Trauma of the Mutilation of Women," *USA Today*, June 18, 1992, 1D; Patricia A. Smith, "'Secret of Joy': Walker's Tender, Terrifying Tour de Force," *Boston Globe*, July 6, 1992, 38; Mel Watkins, "Book of the Times: A Woman in Search of Her Past and Herself," *New York Times*, July 24, 1992, C20; Lisa Schwartzbaum, "Book Review: *Possessing the Secret of Joy* (1992)," *Entertainment Weekly*, July 24, 1992, http://www.ew.com/ew/article/0,,311217,00.html (accessed August 24, 2009); Jacqueline Trescott, "The Stories That Cry to Be Read: Caught in the Truths of 3 Unconventional Best Sellers," *Washington Post*, July 2, 1992, C1.

64. Carol Treloar, "Casting the First Stone: Provocative Challenge to Islam," *Advertiser/Sunday Mail*, July 11, 1992 (accessed via LexisNexis Academic November 15, 2008).

65. Heilbrunn, *They Knew They Were Right*, 204; Robert D. McFadden, "A. M. Rosenthal, Editor of the *Times*, Dies at 84," *New York Times*, May 11, 2006, http://www.nytimes.com/2006/05/11/nyregion/11rosenthal.html (accessed June 2, 2009).

66. A. M. Rosenthal, "Female Genital Torture; How Many Millions More?" *New York Times*, December 29, 1992, A15; A. M. Rosenthal, "The Torture Continues," *New York Times*, July 27, 1993, A13. See also A. M. Rosenthal, "Female Genital Torture," *New York Times*, November 12, 1993, A33; A. M. Rosenthal, "Female Genital Mutilation," *New York Times*, December 24, 1993, A27; A. M. Rosenthal, "A Victory in Cairo," *New York Times*, September 6, 1994, A19; A. M. Rosenthal, "The Possible Dream," *New York Times*, June 13, 1995, A25; A. M. Rosenthal, "Fighting Female Mutilation," *New York Times*, April 12, 1996, A31.

67. "Scarred for Life," *Day One*, ABC News, September 20, 1993, transcript, 22 pages (purchased from the Transcription Company at http://www.transcripts.tv on October 23, 2008).

68. Jill Smolowe, "A Rite of Passage—or Mutilation?" *Time*, September 26, 1994, 65 and http://www.time.com/time/magazine/article/0,9171,981483,00.html (accessed September 13, 2008).

69. *World Today*, CNN, September 7, 1994, Television News Archive, DVD.

70. Nada Khader, "Hope for Our Sisters: Ending Female Genital Mutilation," Proutworld, 2001, http://www.proutworld.org/features/hopesis.htm (accessed October 22, 2008).

71. Smolowe, "Rite of Passage," 65.

72. Judy Mann, "When Journalists Witness Atrocities," *Washington Post*, September 23, 1994, E3.

73. John Shattuck, "Violations of Women's Human Rights," Assistant Secretary for Human Rights and Humanitarian Affairs, Statement Before the Subcommittee on International Security, International Organizations, and Human Rights of the House Foreign Affairs Committee, Washington, D.C., September 29, 1993, in State Department, *Dispatch* 4, no. 41 (October 11, 1993), http://dosfan.lib.iuc.edu/ERC/briefing /dispatch/1993/html/Dispatchv4no41.html (accessed via Electronic Research Collections April 21, 2015).

74. Anika Rahman and Nahid Toubia, eds., *Female Genital Mutilation: A Guide to Laws and Policies Worldwide* (London: Zed, 2000), 240; Toubia, "Presentation to USAID."

75. Mann, "When Journalists Witness Atrocities," E3.

76. Harry Reid, "Senate Resolution 263—To Express the Sense of the Senate Condemning the Cruel and Tortuous Practice of Female Genital Mutilation," 103rd Cong., 2nd Sess., *Congressional Record—Senate*, vol. 140, no. 133 (September 21, 1994), 140, Cong. Rec. S. 13100: page 2 of 5 (accessed via LexisNexis Congressional on October 2, 2008).

77. Reid introduced the resolution on September 21, 1994, and the Senate adopted the resolution on September 27, 1994. "Chamber Action," 103rd Cong., 2nd Sess., *Congressional Record—Senate, Daily Digest,* vol. 140, no. 137 (September 27, 1994), 140, Cong. Rec. D. 1136: page 3 of 18 (accessed via LexisNexis Congressional on October 2, 2008).

78. Harry Reid, "Statements on Introduced Bills and Joint Resolutions," 103rd Cong., 2nd Sess., *Congressional Record—Senate*, vol. 140, no. 143 (October 5, 1994), 140, Cong. Rec. S. 14243: page 2 of 9 (accessed via LexisNexis Congressional on October 2, 2008).

79. Monica Anderson, "African Immigrant Population in U.S. Steadily Climbs," Pew Research Center, November 2, 2015, http://www.pewresearch.org/fact-tank /2015/11/02/african-immigrant-population-in-u-s-steadily-climbs (accessed February 25, 2016).

80. "Senator Harry Reid, Speaking on September 21, 1994, to Express the Sense of the Senate Condemning the Cruel and Tortuous Practice of Female Genital Mutilation," S. Res. 263, 103rd Cong., 2nd Sess., *Congressional Record*, 140, pt. 133: 140 Cong. Rec. S. 13100: page 5 of 5 (accessed via LexisNexis Congressional on October 2, 2008).

81. Carol Moseley-Braun, "Statements on Introduced Bills and Joint Resolutions," 103rd Cong., 2nd Sess., *Congressional Record—Senate*, vol. 140, no. 143 (October 5, 1994), 140, Cong. Rec. S. 14244: page 6 of 9 (accessed via LexisNexis Congressional on October 2, 2008).

82. Moseley-Braun, "Statements," 140 Cong. Rec. S. 14245: page 7 of 9.

83. For a contemporary discussion of the "culture wars," see James Davison Hunter, *Culture Wars: The Struggle to Define America* (New York: Basic Books, 1991); Mary E. Williams, ed., *Culture Wars: Opposing Viewpoints* (San Diego: Greenhaven, 1999).

84. Democrats and Republicans in Congress during the 1990s not only locked horns in the "culture wars" but also clashed over the federal budget; the government shut down over budget disputes between the parties in 1995–96. Republicans also impeached President Bill Clinton in 1998, and the final Senate vote (which resulted in Clinton's acquittal) fell along strict party lines.

85. S. 1030: "Federal Prohibition of Female Genital Mutilation Act of 1995," Bill Tracking Report, 104th Cong., 1st Sess., U.S. Senate, 1995 Bill Tracking S. 1030; 104 Bill Tracking S. 1020: page 3 of 4 (accessed via LexisNexis Congressional on November 30, 2008).

86. See Barbara Crossette, "Female Genital Mutilation by Immigrants Is Becoming Cause for Concern in US," New York Times, December 10, 1995, http://query .nytimes.com/gst/fullpage.html?sec=health&res=9904E7DE1639F933A25751C1A963 958260 (accessed November 28, 2008); Linda Burstyn, "Female Circumcision Comes to America," Atlantic, October 1995, http://www.theatlantic.com/unbound/flashbks /fgm/fgm.htm (accessed November 28, 2008); Wren MacCager, "Rite Is Wrong," Los Angeles View, December 1, 1995, http://130.94.183.89/magazine/july96/fgm.html (accessed via Flashpoint! Electronic Magazine on February 16, 2009).

87. "Omnibus Consolidated Appropriations Act of 1997," HR 3610, September 30, 1996, Pub. L. 104-208, 110 Stat. 3009, 104th Congress, sec. 579, 645. The law identified "international financial institutions" as the International Bank for Reconstruction and Development, the Inter-American Development Bank, the Asian Development Bank, the Asian Development Fund, the African Development Bank, the African Development Fund, the International Monetary Fund, the North American Development Bank, and the European Bank for Reconstruction and Development (Section 352(b)).

88. Rahman and Toubia, Female Genital Mutilation, 240; Toubia, "Presentation to USAID."

89. "House Passes Schroeder Resolution on Female Genital Mutilation," Congressional Press Releases, June 7, 1995; Hillary Rodham Clinton, Remarks by First Lady Hillary Rodham Clinton to the United Nations Fourth World Conference on Women (Washington, D.C.: Executive Office of the President, 1995), 6.

90. Theresa Loar, interview by Charles Stuart Kennedy, initial interview date August 8, 2001, Foreign Affairs Oral History Collection, Association for Diplomatic Studies and Training, Arlington, VA, 176–79, http://www.adst.org (accessed December 18, 2014).

91. Karen Garner, Gender & Foreign Policy in the Clinton Administration (Boulder, CO: FirstForum Press, 2013), 231–32.

92. Rahman and Toubia, Female Genital Mutilation, 237; Isabelle R. Gunning, "Women and Traditional Practices: Female Genital Surgery," in Women and International Human Rights Law: Volume 1, ed. Askin and Koenig, 671.

93. Rahman and Toubia, Female Genital Mutilation, 101–41.

94. There are reports, however, of some American women undergoing clitoridectomy during the late Victorian era and early twentieth century as a "cure" for "hysteria" or masturbation.

95. "Man Arrested for Mutilating Daughter," *Washington Post*, November 2, 2006, A2.

96. "In re: Fauziya Kasinga, Applicant," Interim Decision #3278, File A73 476 695—Elizabeth, Decided June 13, 1996, U.S. Department of Justice, Executive Office for Immigration Review, Board of Immigration Appeals: 1–22; Corinne A. Kratz, "Seeking Asylum, Debating Values, and Setting Precedents in the 1990s: The Cases of Kassindja and Abankwah in the United States," in *Transcultural Bodies: Female Genital Cutting in Global Context*, ed. Ylva Hernlund and Bettina Shell-Duncan (New Brunswick, NJ: Rutgers University Press, 2007), 167–201; Charles Piot, "Representing Africa in the Kasinga Asylum Case," in *Transcultural Bodies*, ed. Hernlund and Shell-Duncan, 157–66; Equality Now, "Women's Action 9.3," June 1996, http://www.equalitynow.org/english/actions/action_0903_en.html (accessed June 18, 2008); Timothy Egan, "An Ancient Ritual and a Mother's Asylum Plea," *New York Times*, March 4, 1994, A25; Celia W. Dugger, "Woman's Plea for Asylum Puts Tribal Ritual on Trial," *New York Times*, April 15, 1996, A1, B4; Pamela Constable, "INS Says Mutilation Claim May Be Basis for Asylum," *Washington Post*, April 24, 1996, A03; Patricia D. Rudloff, "In Re Oluloro: Risk of Female Genital Mutilation as 'Extreme Hardship' in Immigration Proceedings," *St. Mary's Law Journal* 26 (1995): 877.

97. United States Court of Appeals for the Ninth Circuit, "Matter of Lydia Omowunmi Oluloro," March 23, 1994, Portland, Oregon, http://www.unhcr.org/refworld/docid/3ae6b65a18.html (accessed August 21, 2009); Kratz, "Seeking Asylum," 173; Egan, "An Ancient Ritual," A25. In March 1994, Lydia Oluloro, a Yoruba woman from Nigeria, successfully petitioned to have her deportation suspended after arguing that her U.S.-born daughters would be subjected to FGM against her will if she were sent back to Nigeria.

98. See Rudloff, "In Re Oluloro."

99. Kassindja's name was misspelled in court documents and press coverage as "Kasinga," but I use the correct spelling when not using direct quotations.

100. Kratz, "Seeking Asylum," 174–75; Piot, "Representing Africa," 158–59. See also Equality Now, "Women's Action 9.3"; Dugger, "Woman's Plea," A1, B4.

101. Bashir is now named Layli Miller-Muro and is the founder and director of Tahirih Justice Center, a nonprofit dedicated to protecting immigrant women and girls from gender-based violence. See http://www.tahirih.org (accessed August 21, 2009).

102. Constable, "INS Says Mutilation Claim May Be Basis for Asylum," A03; BIA, "In re: Fauziya Kasinga, Applicant," Interim Decision #3278, 1.

103. Fauziya Kassindja, *Do They Hear You When You Cry*, with Layli Miller Bashir (New York: Delta, 1999), 381–82. Equality Now was founded in 1992 and was based in New York.

104. Kratz, "Seeking Asylum," 175; Kassindja, *Do They Hear You When You Cry*, 384.

105. Kratz, "Seeking Asylum," 175; Kassindja, *Do They Hear You When You Cry*, 428.

106. Rosenthal, "Fighting Female Mutilation," A31; Linda Burstyn, "Asylum in America: Does Fear of Female Mutilation Qualify?" *Washington Post*, March 17, 1996, C5; Judy Mann, "When Judges Fail," *Washington Post*, January 19, 1996, E3; Ellen Goodman, "Mutilated by Her Culture," *Boston Globe*, April 7, 1996, 69; Associated Press, "INS Frees Woman, 19, Who Fled Genital Mutilation in Togo," *Boston Globe*, April 25, 1996, 2; Kratz, "Seeking Asylum," 181.

107. Dugger, "Woman's Plea," B4.

108. *Nightline*, ABC, May 2, 1996, Television News Archive, DVD; Kassindja, *Do They Hear You When You Cry*.

109. BIA, "In re: Fauziya Kasinga, Applicant," Interim Decision #3278, 1–22.

110. Kratz, "Seeking Asylum," 173.

111. For a description of the Abankwah case, see Kratz, "Seeking Asylum," 178–80, 189–94. The case (1997–99) received much publicity, but after Abankwah won asylum, evidence came to light that she had stolen another woman's identity and lied about being from an ethnic group that practiced FGM.

112. Laura Ziv, "The Tragedy of Female Circumcision: One Woman's Story," *Marie Claire* (March 1996): 65–70; Dirie, *Desert Flower*, 213–20.

Chapter 6

1. David S. Cloud, "Albright Lambastes [*sic*] Taliban over Treatment of Women," *Chicago Tribune*, November 19, 1997, 1, 4 (accessed via Proquest April 15, 2015); Steven Erlanger, "In Afghan Refugee Camp, Albright Hammers Taliban," *New York Times*, November 19, 1997, http//:www.nytimes.com/1997/11/19/world/in-afghan-refugee-camp-albright-hammers-taliban.html (accessed April 15, 2015); Madeleine Albright, *Madam Secretary: A Memoir* (New York: Hyperion, 2003), 462–63.

2. George Gedda, "Secretary of State Madeleine Albright Tells Afghan Refugrees U.S. Will Not Recognize Taliban Government Due to Its 'Despicable' Treatment of Women and Children," Associated Press, November 18, 1997, http://www.apnewsarchive.com/1997/Secretary-of-State-Madeleine-Albright-Tells-Afghan-Refugees-U-S-Will-Not-Recognize-Taliban-Government-Due-To-Its-Despicable-Treatment-of-Women-and-ChildrenBy-GEORGE-GEDDA/id-e8e80f6adf81cf72d39b3c88737343d6 (accessed April 15, 2015).

3. These included the February 26, 1993, bombing of the World Trade Center; the June 25, 1996, bombing of the U.S. military housing complex in Dhahran, Saudi Arabia; the August 7, 1998, bombings of the U.S. embassies in Nairobi, Kenya and Dar es Salaam, Tanzania; and the October 12, 2000, bombing of the U.S.S. *Cole*.

4. William Maley, "Introduction: Interpreting the Taliban," in *Fundamentalism Reborn? Afghanistan and the Taliban*, ed. William Maley (New York: NYU Press, 1998), 1–2; Larry P. Goodson, *Afghanistan's Endless War: State Failure, Regional Politics, and the Rise of the Taliban* (Seattle: University of Washington Press, 2001), 108.

5. The Pashtuns constituted 40 percent of the Afghan population of 20 million. Ahmed Rashid, *Taliban: Militant Islam, Oil and Fundamentalism in Central Asia* (New Haven, CT: Yale University Press, 2000), 2. Other ethnic groups in Afghanistan included Persian and Turkic groups, Hazaras, and Tajiks. Rashid, *Taliban*, 7–8.

6. Goodson, *Afghanistan's Endless War*, 108.

7. Sonali Kohlhatkar and James Ingalls, *Bleeding Afghanistan: Washington, Warlords, and the Propaganda of Silence* (New York: Seven Stories Press, 2006), xv; Richard Mackenzie, "The United States and the Taliban," in *Fundamentalism Reborn?* ed. Maley, 95; Rashid, *Taliban*, vii.

8. Maley, "Interpreting the Taliban," 14.

9. Steve Coll, *Ghost Wars: The Secret History of the CIA, Afghanistan, and Bin Laden, from the Soviet Invasion to September 10, 2001* (New York: Penguin, 2004), 39. See also Shahnaz Khan, "Between Here and There: Feminist Solidarity and Afghan Women," *Genders* 33 (March 2001), http://www.colorado.edu/gendersarchive1998 -2013/2001/03/01/between-here-and-there-feminist-solidarity-and-afghan-women (accessed March 4, 2017); Maley, "Interpreting the Taliban," 6–7; Rashid, *Taliban*, 12–13; Amin Saikal and William Maley, *Regime Change in Afghanistan: Foreign Intervention and the Politics of Legitimacy* (Boulder, CO: Westview, 1991), 9–32.

10. Maley, "Interpreting the Taliban," 9; Mamdani, *Good Muslim, Bad Muslim*, 153. Secular groups resisted the Soviets as well, but they were not included in the mujahideen and for the most part did not receive foreign aid. Such groups included the Revolutionary Association of the Women of Afghanistan (RAWA). The only faction of the mujahideen that was not fundamentalist (though it was religious) was the National Islamic Front of Afghanistan, led by Syed Ahmad Gailani. Kolhatkar and Ingalls, *Bleeding Afghanistan*, 8. For an in-depth examination of the various factions, see Barnett R. Rubin, *The Fragmentation of Afghanistan: State Formation and Collapse in the International System* (New Haven, CT: Yale University Press, 1995).

11. Rashid, *Taliban*, 13.

12. Maley, "Interpreting the Taliban," 9.

13. Mamdani, *Good Muslim, Bad Muslim*, 123–49; Coll, *Ghost Wars*, 46, 51, 58, 65.

14. Only a few journalists raised questions about the mujahideen's motives and views on women. They included the *New York Times*' Donatella Lorch and Henry Kamm. See Donatella Lorch, "An Afghan Exile, Her School and Hopes for Future," *New York Times*, June 12, 1988, 14; Henry Kamm, "Isolated Afghan Refugee Camp Life Turns Women into 'Birds in a Cage,'" *New York Times*, March 27, 1988, 16; Henry Kamm, "Afghan Rebel Opposes Talks; Vows Battle for Islamic State," *New York Times*, March 19, 1988, 1; Henry Kamm, "Afghan Rebels' Discord Widens as Pullout Nears," *New York Times*, March 9, 1988, A10; Henry Kamm, "Afghan Rebel Alliance Leader Outlines His Cause," *New York Times*, April 20, 1988, A3.

15. See Jeri Laber and Barnett Rubin, "'A Whole Nation Is Dying': Unnoticed by the World, Soviets Are Systematically Destroying Afghanistan," *St. Louis Post-Dispatch*, February 1, 1985, 3B; Lucy Komisar, "No One Wins or Loses: Why?" *The*

Blade: Toledo, Ohio, January 3, 1988, page unknown, Human Rights Watch: Helsinki Collection, Series IX: Washington, D.C., Office Files, Box 1, Columbia University Rare Book and Manuscript Library (hereafter HRW Collection); Christina Dameyer, "In Afghanistan, Soviets Find Replacing Islam with Communism Isn't Easy," *Christian Science Monitor*, August 6, 1985, 11; James Rupert, "Soviets Try to Reshape Afghan Culture," *Washington Post*, January 13, 1986," A18.

16. Barnett R. Rubin, "Human Rights in an Afghan Peace Settlement, A Proposal for a Report by Human Rights Watch," December 30, 1987, HRW Collection, Series I: Jeri Laber Files, Box 1; "Afghanistan: Five Years After the Soviet Invasion," HRW Collection, Series I: Jeri Laber Files, Box 1; "Public Themes on Afghanistan," U.S. Dept. of State, September 1987, HRW Collection, Series I: Jeri Laber Files, Box 5; Report on human rights violations in Afghanistan by the Swedish journalist Börje Almqvist, HRW Collection, Series I: Jeri Laber Files, Box 6; United States Department of State, Bureau of Public Affairs, "Afghanistan: Seven Years of Soviet Occupation," Special Report No. 155, December 1986, HRW Collection, Series I: Jeri Laber Files, Box 7. For the history of Helsinki Watch and its role in the Cold War, see Snyder, *Human Rights Activism*.

17. Mamdani, *Good Muslim, Bad Muslim*, 119; Eqbal Ahmad, "Genesis of International Terrorism," *Dawn*, October 5, 2001, http://www.hartford-hwp.com/archives /27d/083.html (accessed April 13, 2010); Cullen Murphy, "The Gold Standard: The Quest for the Holy Grail of Equivalence," *Atlantic Monthly* (January 2002), http:// www.theatlantic.com/past/issues/2002/01/murphy.htm (accessed April 13, 2010).

18. Rashid, *Taliban*, 13, 18; Michael J. Sullivan III, *American Adventurism Abroad: Invasions, Interventions, and Regime Changes Since World War II*, rev. ed. (Malden, MA: Blackwell, 2008), 187, 190; Kolhatkar and Ingalls, *Bleeding Afghanistan*, 8; Rashid, *Taliban*, 18; Coll, *Ghost Wars*, 65.

19. Mamdani, *Good Muslim, Bad Muslim*, 125–26.

20. Kolhatkar and Ingalls, *Bleeding Afghanistan,* xiv, 9; Mamdani, *Good Muslim, Bad Muslim*, 144; Sullivan, *American Adventurism Abroad*, 188

21. Mamdani, *Good Muslim, Bad Muslim*, 143.

22. Revolutionary Association of the Women of Afghanistan, "A Short Biography of Martyred Meena, Founding Leader of RAWA," http://www.rawa.org/meena.html (accessed December 6, 2007); Anne E. Brodsky, *With All Our Strength: The Revolutionary Association of the Women of Afghanistan* (New York: Routledge, 2003), 90–92; Melody Ermachild Chavis, *Meena: Heroine of Afghanistan* (New York: St. Martin's, 2003), 139–57.

23. For a detailed description of Rabbani's troubles, see Amin Saikal, "The Rabbani Government, 1992–1996," in *Fundamentalism Reborn?* ed. Maley, 29–42.

24. Pakistan aided Hekmatyar, the Saudis backed Pashtun leader Abdul-Rab al-Rasul Sayyaf, and the Iranians supported Shi'a factions. Anwar-ul-haq Ahady, "Saudi Arabia, Iran and the Conflict in Afghanistan," in *Fundamentalism Reborn?* ed. Maley, 117–34; Mamdani, *Good Muslim, Bad Muslim*, 149–63.

25. Rashid, *Taliban*, 22–23.

26. Ibid., 25; Nancy Hatch Dupree, "Afghan Women Under the Taliban," in *Fundamentalism Reborn?* ed. Maley, 145.

27. John Burns and Steve Levine, "How Afghans' Stern Rulers Took Hold," *New York Times*, December 11, 1996, A6.

28. Rashid, *Taliban*, 114–15; Taliban decree by General Presidency of Amir Bil Maruf, Kabul, December 1996, appendix 1, in Rashid, *Taliban*, 219.

29. Rashid, *Taliban*, 115–16.

30. Roy Gutman, *How We Missed the Story: Osama bin Laden, the Taliban, and the Hijacking of Afghanistan* (Washington, D.C.: United States Institute for Peace, 2008), 221–36.

31. For firsthand accounts of the changes in women's status under the Taliban, see "Sulima" and "Hala," *Behind the Burqa: Our Life in Afghanistan and How We Escaped to Freedom*, as told to Batya Swift Yasgur (Hoboken, NJ: Wiley, 2002).

32. Rashid, *Taliban*, 106; Dupree, "Afghan Women," 145, 148, 154.

33. Taliban decree by the General Presidency of Amir Bil Maruf and Nai Az Munkar (Religious Police), Kabul, November 1996, appendix 1, in Rashid, *Taliban*, 217–18.

34. Rashid, *Taliban*, 105, 113; Dupree, "Afghan Women," 145; "Rules of Work for the State Hospitals and Private Clinics Based on Islamic Sharia Principles," Ministry of Health, on Behalf of Amir ul Momineen Mullah Mohammed Omar, Kabul, November 1996, appendix 1, in Rashid, *Taliban*, 218.

35. *Search for Freedom*, directed by Munizae Jahangir (2003; Women Make Movies, 2003), DVD.

36. See Sally Armstrong, *Veiled Threat: The Hidden Power of the Women of Afghanistan* (New York: Four Walls Eight Windows, 2002), 49–55; Isabelle Delloye, *Women of Afghanistan*, trans. Marjolijn de Jager (St. Paul, MN: Ruminator Books, 2003); Hafizullah Emadi, *Repression, Resistance, and Women in Afghanistan* (Westport, CT: Praeger, 2002); Elaheh Rostami-Povey, *Afghan Women: Identity & Invasion* (London: Zed, 2007), 1–39; Mary Smith, *Before the Taliban: Living with War, Hoping for Peace* (Fife, UK: IYNX Publishing, 2002); Rosemarie Skaine, *The Women of Afghanistan Under the Taliban* (Jefferson, NC: McFarland, 2002).

37. Rashid, *Taliban*, 110.

38. Bunch and Reilly, *Demanding Accountability*, 10–13. The Global Campaign was cosponsored by the CWGL, Asian Women's Human Rights Council, Austrian Women's Human Rights Working Group, Feminist International Radio Endeavor (FIRE), Human Rights Watch Women's Project, International Women's Tribune Centre (IWTC), ISIS International, the United Nations Development Fund for Women (UNIFEM), Women in Law and Development in Africa (WiLDAF), and Women Living Under Muslim Laws (WLUML). See also Garner, *Gender & Foreign Policy*, 109–12.

39. Garner, *Gender & Foreign Policy*, 84, 106–9.

40. Ibid., 110.

41. United Nations General Assembly, "Vienna Declaration and Programme of Action," July 12, 1993, A/CONF.157/23, Sec. 1, para. 18; Sec. II, paras. 36–37, http://www.unhchr.ch/huridocda/huridocda.nsf/(Symbol)/A.CONF.157.23.En (accessed October 8, 2008).

42. Ibid., Sec. II, para. 38.

43. "Iranian Women Hear Cries of Their Afghan Sisters," *Middle East Times*, November 1, 1998, reproduced on the website for the Nonviolent Radical Party, Transnational and Transparty (NRPTT), http://www.radicalparty.org/en/content/iranian -women-hear-cries-their-afghan-sisters (accessed June 1, 2015).

44. For detailed records on the Beijing conference and feminists' lobbying activities during the preparatory period, see the IWTC Collection, accession numbers 95S-69, 96S-34, and 00S-8.

45. WLUML, *Dossier 17*, June 1997, 103, WLUML Records.

46. WLUML, *Dossier 17*, 94–122; WLUML, *Dossier 18*, October 1997, 126–28, WLUML Records; WLUML, *Dossier 19*, February 1998, 125–26, WLUML Records; WLUML, *Dossier 21*, February 1999, 126–29, 160, WLUML Records.

47. WLUML, *Dossier 19*, 156–57. See also WLUML, *Dossier 18*, 155; WLUML, *Dossier 21*, 126–29, 163; Moghadam, *Globalizing Women*, 157.

48. Afkhami interview with author.

49. See SIGI Records; Afkhami interview with author; Moghadam, *Globalizing Women*, 166.

50. *SIGI News* 4, no. 1 (Winter/Spring 1996): 3, SIGI Records, Box PUB16; Public Schedules for the First Lady, October 21, 1996, Records of the First Lady's Office, FOIA 2006-0198-F (segment 1), Box 11, William J. Clinton Presidential Library, Little Rock, AR (hereafter First Lady's Office (seg. 1)).

51. SIGI-sponsored events include an NGO consultation meeting with the CSW in New York in March 1994; a conference in Athens on refugee women in September 1994; the conference "Religion, Culture, and Women's Human Rights in the Muslim World," in Washington, D.C., in September 1994; a conference on women's integration in commerce and industry in October 1994; a meeting with the CSW in New York in March 1995; the conference "Beijing and Beyond" in Washington, D.C., in May 1996; a conference titled "Rights of Passage" held in Washington, D.C., in September 1997; a panel presentation at the Middle Eastern Studies Association in November 1997; a symposium at Stanford in November 1997; a conference in Jordan on eliminating violence against women in Muslim societies in September 1998; and participation in an expert group meeting on violence against women and girls in October 1998. See SIGI Records, Boxes CONF1-CONF8.

52. Afkhami, *Faith and Freedom*; Mahnaz Afkhami and Erika Friedl, eds., *Muslim Women and the Politics of Participation: Implementing the Beijing Platform* (Syracuse, NY: Syracuse University Press, 1997).

53. Mahnaz Afkhami and Haleh Vaziri, *Claiming Our Rights: A Manual for Women's Human Rights Education in Muslim Societies* (Bethesda, MD: Sisterhood Is Global Institute, 1996).

54. Moghadam, *Globalizing Women*, 160.

55. Afkhami interview with author; *Claiming Our Rights* records, SIGI Records, Boxes PUB1–PUB10. By 1999, over two thousand people had participated in workshops based on the manual. Moghadam, *Globalizing Women*, 158.

56. Peter B. Levy, *Encyclopedia of the Clinton Presidency* (Westport, CT: Greenwood, 2002), 371; Virginia Sapiro and David T. Canon, "Race, Gender, and the Clinton Presidency," in *The Clinton Legacy*, ed. Colin Campbell and Bert A. Rockman (New York: Chatham House, 2000), 169, 175–76, 179–80, 194. Clinton again received the majority of women's votes when he ran for reelection in 1996.

57. Levy, *Encyclopedia of Clinton Presidency*, 372; Sapiro and Canon, "Race, Gender, and Clinton," 180, 185, 194–95; Barbara Sinclair, "The President as Legislative Leader," in *The Clinton Legacy*, ed. Campbell and Rockman, 77; Bill Clinton, *My Life* (New York: Alfred A. Knopf, 2004), 229–30, 273, 481–82, 490, 620, 880–90, 945; President's Interagency Council on Women, *Update to America's Commitment: Federal Programs Benefiting Women and New Initiatives as Follow-Up to the UN Fourth World Conference on Women*, April 1998 Supplement, 16 pages, http://secretary.state.gov /www/picw/archives/may1997_report/1998_april_supplement.html   (accessed April 29, 2010). I abbreviate Bill Clinton's name as "B. Clinton" to avoid confusion with works authored by Hillary Rodham Clinton, whom I abbreviate as "HRC."

58. Sapiro and Canon, "Race, Gender, and Clinton," 191–92; B. Clinton, *My Life*, 482, 499, 547–49, 555–56; Levy, *Encyclopedia of Clinton Presidency*, 372; Myra G. Gutin, "Hillary's Choices: The First Ladyship of Hillary Rodham Clinton and the Future of the Office," in *The Presidential Companion: Readings on the First Ladies*, ed. Robert P. Watson and Anthony J. Eksterowicz (Columbia: University of South Carolina Press, 2003), 279–80; Glenn Hastedt, "First Ladies and U.S. Foreign Policy," in *The Presidential Companion*, ed. Watson and Eksterowicz, 204, 206.

59. Garner, *Gender & Foreign Policy*, 100.

60. Warren Christopher, *In the Stream of History: Shaping Foreign Policy for a New Era* (Stanford, CA: Stanford University Press, 1998), 62.

61. Warren Christopher, "Democracy and Human Rights: Where America Stands," address at the World Conference on Human Rights, Vienna, Austria, June 14, 1993, Warren Christopher Papers, 1927–2011, Box 8, Hoover Institution Archives, Stanford University (hereafter Christopher Papers). See also Christopher, *In the Stream of History*, 66, 71.

62. Shattuck, "Violations of Women's Human Rights."

63. Ibid.

64. Sapiro and Canon, "Race, Gender, and Clinton," 194. See also Garner, *Gender & Foreign Policy*, 7–9; Butterfield, *U.S. Development Aid*, 270–72; Bill Clinton, "Re-

marks by the President at Human Rights Day Event," December 10, 1996, President's Interagency Council on Women, http://secretary.state.gov/www/picw/archives /961210.html (accessed April 29, 2010); B. Clinton, *My Life*, 671; PICW, *Update*, 8; Thomas W. Lippman, *Madeleine Albright and the New American Diplomacy* (Boulder, CO: Westview, 2000), 301; Levy, *Encyclopedia of Clinton Presidency*, 372; Bill Clinton, "Remarks by the President and the First Lady on International Women's Day, the White House," March 11, 1998, Records of the First Lady's Office, FOIA 2006-0198-F OPEN (segment 4), Box 11, William J. Clinton Presidential Library, Little Rock, AR (hereafter First Lady's Office (seg. 4)).

65. The President's Interagency Council on Women, memo announcing creation of the President's Interagency Council on Women, October 25, 1995, President's Interagency Council on Women Collection, 2006-0198-F OPEN (segment 3), Box 1, William J. Clinton Presidential Library, Little Rock, AR (hereafter PICW Records); List of PICW members, December 1998, PICW Records, Box 1; PICW Council Member Biographical Information, PICW Records, Box 1; Loar ADST oral history, 136–47.

66. Loar ADST oral history, 151.

67. Ibid., 152; President's Interagency Council on Women, *PICW 1995–2000: A Five-Year Report*, PICW Records, Box 3.

68. Loar ADST oral history, 156.

69. "History of the Department of State During the Clinton Presidency (1993–2001)," U.S. Department of State, Office of the Historian, archived website, http://2001 -2009.state.gov/r/pa/ho/pubs/c6059.htm (accessed April 30, 2010).

70. Garner, *Gender & Foreign Policy*, 100.

71. "History of the Department of State During the Clinton Presidency."

72. Garner, *Gender & Foreign Policy*, 113, 116.

73. Undersecretary for Global Affairs organizational chart, in Office of the Secretary, Administrative Support, Procedures, and Staffing, *1996 Secretarial Transition Background Materials,* November 1996, p. 56 of 124, Case No. F-2006-00896, Doc. No. C18598843, Department of State, FOIA Reading Room, http://foia.state.gov (accessed March 26, 2016); Loar ADST oral history, 157; Garner, *Gender & Foreign Policy*, 7.

74. Theresa Loar, oral history interview with author, Washington, D.C., June 30, 2011.

75. Loar ADST oral history, 159; Garner, *Gender & Foreign Policy*, 116, 148.

76. President's Interagency Council on Women, *America's Commitment: Women 2000: A Five-Year Review of Federal Programs Benefiting Women and New Initiatives as a Follow-up to the UN Fourth World Conference on Women*, January 5, 2000, PICW Records, Box 5; Loar ADST oral history, 181–96, 198–205; Garner, *Gender & Foreign Policy*, 10.

77. Hillary Rodham Clinton, *Living History* (New York: Scribner's, 2003), 298–308.

78. HRC, *Remarks Fourth World Conference on Women*, 6.

79. HRC, *Living History*, 299.

80. Gutin, "Hillary's Choices," 281; Levy, *Encyclopedia of Clinton Presidency*, 372; Hastedt, "First Ladies and Foreign Policy," 199; HRC, *Remarks Fourth World Conference on Women*, 1–7. Hillary also addressed the NGO Forum, World Health Organization Colloquium, and United Nations Development Fund for Women panel discussion while in Beijing. HRC, *Remarks Fourth World Conference on Women*, 9–29.

81. "Mrs. Clinton's Unwavering Words," *New York Times*, September 6, 1995, 24; HRC, *Living History*, 306. See also note from Congressman Bill Richardson to Hillary Rodham Clinton, enclosing *Congressional Record—House* from September 6, 1996, First Lady's Office (seg. 4), Box 14.

82. B. Clinton, *My Life*, 671.

83. See Levy, *Encyclopedia of Clinton Presidency*, 372–73; Sapiro and Canon, "Race, Gender, and Clinton," 189; David M. O'Brien, "Judicial Legacies: The Clinton Presidency and the Courts," in *The Clinton Legacy*, ed. Campbell and Rockman, 98.

84. HRC, *Living History*, 393; Albright, *Madam Secretary*, 280; John F. Harris, *The Survivor: Bill Clinton in the White House* (New York: Random House, 2005), 253–54.

85. B. Clinton, "Remarks Human Rights Day."

86. Rashid, *Taliban*, 178; Doc. No. 7: U.S. Embassy (Islamabad), Cable, "Meeting with the Taliban in Kandahar: More Questions than Answers," February 15, 1995, Confidential, 7 pp., Doc. No. 8: U.S. Embassy (Islamabad), Cable, "Finally, a Talkative Talib: Origins and Membership of the Religious Students' Movement," February 20, 1995, Confidential, 15 pp., and Doc. No. 15: U.S. Embassy (Islamabad), Cable, "A/S Raphel Discusses Afghanistan," April 22, 1996, Confidential, 7 pp., in *The September 11th Sourcebooks, Vol. VII: The Taliban File*, ed. Sajit Gandhi, National Security Archive Electronic Briefing Book No. 97 (September 11, 2003), http://www.gwu.edu/~nsarchiv/NSAEBB/NSAEBB97/index.htm (accessed February 28, 2010); "The Taliban Get a Polite Welcome from U.S.," *Economist*, October 5, 1995, http://130.183.89/magazine/oct96/taliban.html (accessed February 16, 2009).

87. Doc. No. 6: U.S. Embassy (Islamabad), Cable, "The Taliban: What We've Heard," January 26, 1995, Confidential, 10 pp., Doc. No. 17: U.S. Department of State, Cable, "Dealing with the Taliban in Kabul," September 28, 1996, Confidential, 6 pp., and Doc. No. 19: U.S. Embassy (Islamabad), Cable, "Ambassador Meets Taliban: We Are the People," November 12, 1996, Confidential 17 pp., in *The September 11th Sourcebooks, Vol. VII*; Gutman, *We Missed the Story*, 77.

88. Christopher spent the fall of 1996 dealing with the expansion of NATO and resulting tensions with Russia, the escalating crisis in Israeli-Palestinian relations, the ongoing conflict in Bosnia, U.S. airstrikes against Iraq, a diplomatic visit to China, and the secretary's first visit to Africa. Warren Christopher, Miscellaneous Speeches, 1996, Christopher Papers, Box 9; Daily Schedules, June–December 1996, Christopher Papers, Box 13; Timelines, Oral History Interviews, Briefing Materials, Christopher Papers, Box 14; U.S. Secretary of State Speeches/Testimonies—1996, Index of "Briefings and Statements," DOSFAN, Electronic Research Collection, archived web-

site, last modified June 10, 1999, http://dosfan.lib.uic.edu/ERC/briefing/dossec/1996
/index.html (accessed May 8, 2015).

89. Loar ADST oral history, 163. See also Loar ADST oral history, 164, 166; Association of American Rhodes Scholars, "Lee Coldren, 17 May 1943 to 29 July 2012," Scholars in the News—Obituaries, http://www.americanrhodes.org/news-obituaries
-690.html (accessed May 11, 2015).

90. Loar interview with author; Ralph H. Magnus, "Afghanistan in 1996: Year of the Taliban," *Asian Survey* 37, no. 2 (February 1997): 116; Kolhatkar and Ingalls, *Bleeding Afghanistan*, 24–25; Joel Mowbray, *Dangerous Diplomacy: How the State Department Threatens America's Security* (Washington, D.C.: Regnery Publishing, 2003), 64. The Taliban failed to capture the northern part of the country, which was defended by a group of mostly former mujahideen known as the "Northern Alliance." See Ahady, "Saudi Arabia, Iran and the Conflict in Afghanistan," 117–34.

91. Mowbray, *Dangerous Diplomacy*, 66–67.

92. Official Informal—Briefing Paper on UNDCP Afghan Projects for the Major Donors Meeting in Stockholm, from Secretary of State to U.S. Embassy in Islamabad, December 3, 1996, Case Number 4-2010-00045, Doc. No. C17615740, Department of State, FOIA Reading Room, http://foia.state.gov (accessed December 19, 2014); Confidential: The Taliban and Narcotics, from American Consul in Peshawar to Secretary of State, October 24, 1996, Case No. F-2010-00045 Doc. No. C17615738, Department of State, FOIA Reading Room, http://foia.state.gov (accessed December 19, 2014).

93. Doc. 17: "Dealing with the Taliban in Kabul"; Magnus, "Afghanistan in 1996," 116; Mackenzie, "United States and Taliban," 96.

94. Mowbray, *Dangerous Diplomacy*, 66.

95. Doc. No. 14: U.S. Embassy (Islamabad), Cable, "Senator Brown and Congressman Wilson Discuss Afghanistan with Pakistani Officials," April 14, 1996, Confidential, 4 pp., in *The September 11th Sourcebooks, Vol. VII*; Doc. 15: "A/S Raphel Discusses Afghanistan." For a discussion of U.S. reliance upon Pakistan during the Soviet-Afghan War, see Mamdani, *Good Muslim, Bad Muslim*, 119–77; Coll, *Ghost Wars*. For a discussion of Pakistan's support of the Taliban, see Rashid, *Taliban*, 183–95; Ahmed Rashid, "Pakistan and the Taliban," *Fundamentalism Reborn?* ed. Maley, 72–89; Barbara Elias, ed., *Pakistan: "The Taliban's Godfather?"* National Security Archive Electronic Briefing Book No. 227 (August 14, 2007), http://www.gwu.edu
/~nsarchiv/NSAEBB/NSAEBB227/index.htm (accessed February 28, 2010).

96. Mowbray, *Dangerous Diplomacy*, 68; Kenneth Freed, "Odd Partners in UNO's Afghan Project: War and Turmoil in Afghanistan," *Omaha World Herald*, October 26, 1997, 1A (accessed via LexisNexis Academic on April 28, 2010); Mackenzie, "United States and Taliban," 98–99. See also Unclassified: Caspian Energy Report for Congress, from Secretary of State to CIS Collective and OPEC Collective, May 3, 1997, Case No. F-2005-03603, Doc. No. C05276906, Department of State, FOIA Reading Room, http://foia.state.gov (accessed March 26, 2015).

97. Barnett R. Rubin, "U.S. Policy in Afghanistan," Council on Foreign Relations, *Muslim Politics Report*, no. 11 (January–February 1997): 6.

98. Mackenzie, "United States and Taliban," 97. See also Ahady, "Saudi Arabia, Iran and the Conflict in Afghanistan," 132.

99. Mowbray, *Dangerous Diplomacy*, 69; Mackenzie, "United States and Taliban," 98. Khalilzad served as Bush's ambassador to Afghanistan, ambassador to Iraq, and ultimately U.S. ambassador to the United Nations.

100. Zalmay Khalilzad, "Afghanistan: Time to Reengage," *Washington Post*, October 7, 1996, A21; Mowbray, *Dangerous Diplomacy*, 69–70.

101. Kolhatkar and Ingalls, *Bleeding Afghanistan*, 26; Elaine Sciolino, "State Dept. Becomes Cooler to the New Rulers of Kabul," *New York Times*, October 23, 1996, A14; Confidential: A/S Raphel's Meeting with President Niyazov, from U.S. Embassy in Ashgabat to U.S. Embassy in Riyadh, U.S. Consul in Karachi, U.S. Consul in Peshawar, U.S. Embassy in Islamabad, CIS Collective, and Secretary of State, May 14, 1996, Case No. M-2011-26453, Doc. No. C05118354, Department of State, FOIA Reading Room, http://foia.state.gov (accessed March 26, 2015).

102. Mackenzie, "United States and Taliban," 98–99.

103. Mowbray, *Dangerous Diplomacy*, 61; Mackenzie, "United States and Taliban," 97.

104. Glyn Davies, *U.S. Department of State Daily Press Briefing #156*, September 27, 1996, http://www.hri.org/news/usa/std/1996/96-09-27.std.html (accessed April 28, 2010). See also Kolhatkar and Ingalls, *Bleeding Afghanistan*, 25; Mowbray, *Dangerous Diplomacy*, 62.

105. Rashid, *Taliban*, 116; Magnus, "Afghanistan in 1996," 115; Anwar Faruqi, "Militants' Victory in Afghanistan Provokes Strange Responses," Associated Press Worldstream news wire service, October 1, 1996 (accessed through LexisNexis Academic on April 28, 2010).

106. Kathy Gannon, "Rebels Use Fear, Punishment to Impose Strict Islamic Law," Associated Press international news wire service, October 1, 1996 (accessed via LexisNexis Academic on April 28, 2010).

107. Ibid.

108. See Anwar Faruqi, "U.N. Agency Urges Tolerance by Taliban," United Press International news wire service, October 1, 1996 (accessed via LexisNexis Academic on April 28, 2010); Sarah Horner, "Taliban Asks for Diplomatic Recognition," United Press International news wire service, October 1, 1996 (accessed via LexisNexis Academic on April 28, 2010); "The Road to Koranistan," *Economist*, October 5, 1996, 21; Rod Nordland, "The Islamic Nightmare," *Newsweek*, October 14, 1996, 51; John Jennings, "The Taleban [*sic*] and Foggy Bottom," *Washington Times*, October 25, 1996, A23; "The Taliban's War on Women," *New York Times*, November 5, 1997, A1; John F. Burns, "New Afghan Rulers Impose Harsh Mores of the Islamic Code," *New York Times*, October 1, 1996, http://www.nytimes.com/1996/10/01/world/new-afghan-rulers-impose-harsh-mores-of-the-islamic-code.html (accessed May 14, 2008); John F. Burns, "Afghanistan's Professional Class Flees Rule by Ultra-Strict Clerics,"

New York Times, October 7, 1996, http://www.nytimes.com/1996/10/07/world /afghanistan-s-professional-class-flees-rule-by-ultra-strict-clerics.html?pagewanted =all&src=pm (accessed May 14, 2008); Elaine Sciolino, "The Many Faces of Islamic Law," *New York Times*, October 13, 1996, http://www.nytimes.com/1996/10/13 /weekinreview/the-many-faces-of-islamic-law.html (accessed May 13, 2008); John F. Burns, "Walled In, Shrouded and Angry in Afghanistan," *New York Times*, October 4, 1996, http://www.nytimes.com/1996/10/04/world/walled-in-shrouded-and-angry-in -afghanistan.html (accessed May 13, 2008); Christiane Amanpour, "Tyranny of the Taliban," *Time*, October 13, 1997, http://www.time.com/time/printout/0,8116,987161,00 .html (accessed May 9, 2008).

109. Jennings, "Taleban and Foggy Bottom," A23.

110. Faruqi, "UN Agency Urges Tolerance."

111. Kolhatkar and Ingalls, *Bleeding Afghanistan*, 28; Mackenzie, "United States and Taliban," 101; "Afghanistan, September 1996," SIGI Alerts, SIGI Records, Box PF8; WLUML, *Dossier 17*, 94–122.

112. Moghadam, *Globalizing Women*, 12–13.

113. Sciolino, "State Department Becomes Cooler," A14. Clinton had a 22- to 27-point lead over his opponent in polls among women voters. Susan Page, "Vote '96: The Gender Gap: Clinton Camp Mobilizing to Keep Women's Vote," *USA Today*, June 10, 1996, 1A (accessed via LexisNexis Academic on April 28, 2010).

114. Loar ADST oral history, 161–62.

115. Loar interview with author.

116. Loar ADST oral history, 164; The White House, "R. Nicholas Burns, Former Under Secretary, Political Affairs, U.S. Department of State," President George W. Bush, archived website, http://georgewbush-whitehouse.archives.gov/government /nburns-bio.html (accessed May 10, 2015).

117. Loar ADST oral history, 164.

118. Ibid., 165; White House, "R. Nicholas Burns"; John F. Burns, "Afghanistan Reels Back into View," *New York Times*, October 6, 1996, http://www.nytimes.com /1996/10/06/weekinreview/afghanistan-reels-back-into-view.html (accessed May 27, 2012); Transcript: State Department Briefing, October 4, 1996, State Department Daily Press Briefings, http://usembassy-israel.org.il/publish/press/state/archive /october/sd1_10-8.htm (accessed May 12, 2015). See also U.S. State Department Daily Press Briefings—1996, Index of "Briefings and Statements," DOSFAN, Electronic Research Collection, archived website, last modified May 19, 1999, http://dosfan.lib.uic .edu/ERC/briefing/daily_briefings/1996/ (accessed May 11, 2015); 1997 Press Briefings, U.S. Department of State archived website, http://secretary.state.gov/www /briefings/1997_index.html (accessed May 11, 2015).

119. Loar ADST oral history, 167.

120. Ibid., 166.

121. Cable from Secretary of State to American Embassy in Islamabad re: Afghanistan: Response to the Taliban Letter to the Secretary, December 10, 1996, Osama bin

Laden Collection, 2006-0228-F OPEN (segment 1), Box 14, William J. Clinton Presidential Library, Little Rock, AR (hereafter OBL Collection).

122. Secret: Afghanistan: UN Meeting Backs Holl and UN Peace Efforts; GA Resolution and Afghan Credentials, from SA Robin L. Raphel to the Acting Secretary, November 20, 1996, Case No. F-2012-28302, Doc. No. C05169003, Department of State, FOIA Reading Room, http://foia.state.gov (accessed March 26, 2015).

123. Loar ADST oral history, 165; Loar interview with author. See also memo from Theresa Loar to Hillary Rodham Clinton re: Update on Women's Human Rights, October 30, 1996, PICW Records, Box 2.

124. Loar interview with author.

125. Mackenzie, "United States and Taliban," 90, 101.

126. Loar ADST oral history, 170.

127. Mackenzie, "United States and Taliban," 101.

128. Madeleine Albright, "Secretary of State Madeleine K. Albright and First Lady Hillary Rodham Clinton: Remarks at Special Program in Honor of International Women's Day," Dean Acheson Auditorium, Department of State, Washington, DC, March 12, 1997, as released by the Office of the Spokesman, U.S. Department of State, http://secretary.state.gov/www/statements/970312.html (accessed December 4, 2009).

129. HRC, "Remarks Women's Day"; HRC, *Living History*, 393.

130. Mowbray, *Dangerous Diplomacy*, 73.

131. Loar interview with author.

132. PICW, *America's Commitment*, 155.

133. Madeleine Albright, "Secretary of State Madeleine K. Albright and Pakistani Foreign Minister Gohar Ayub Khan: Joint Press Available Following Signing Ceremony, Ministry of Foreign Affairs, Islamabad Pakistan," November 18, 1997, as released by the Office of the Spokesman, U.S. Department of State, provided to the author by Roy Gutman; Albright, *Madam Secretary*, 462.

134. Albright, *Madam Secretary*, 464; Rashid, *Taliban*, 180; Lippman, *Madeleine Albright and the New American Diplomacy*, 302–3.

135. Albright, *Madam Secretary*, 462; Ian Brodie, "Albright Attacks Taleban [sic] Oppression of Women," *The Times* (London), November 19, 1997, 17.

136. Thomas W. Lippman, "U.S. Plans More Active S. Asia Role: Albright's Trip Signals New Interest in Region," *Washington Post*, November 19, 1997, A26.

137. For examples of ongoing public conversations about Muslim women in the 1990s, see "The Taliban Government of Afghanistan Is Waging a War upon Its Women," *Philly Talk Radio Online*, fall 1998, http://www.phillytalkradioonline.com/comment/afghanwomen.html (accessed February 1, 2010); Ann Louise Bardach, "Tearing Off the Veil," *Vanity Fair* (August 1993): 122–27, 154–58, General Collections, Adams Building, Library of Congress, Washington, D.C.; Jean Sasson, *Princess: The True Story of Life Behind the Veil in Saudi Arabia* (New York: William and Morrow, 1992); *NBC Nightly News*, April 23, 1991, Television Archive, DVD; *CBS Evening News*, May 5, 1996, Television Archive, DVD. Scholarly publications included Afkhami

and Friedl, eds., *Muslim Women and the Politics of Participation*; Ahmed, *Women and Gender in Islam*; Geraldine Brooks, *Nine Parts of Desire: The Hidden World of Islamic Women* (New York: Anchor, 1995); Lila Abu-Lughod, *Remaking Women: Feminism and Modernity in the Middle East* (Princeton, NJ: Princeton University Press, 1998); Afkhami, *Faith and Freedom*; Mona AlMunajjed, *Women in Saudi Arabia Today* (New York: St. Martin's, 1997); Margot Badran, *Feminists, Islam, and Nation: Gender and the Making of Modern Egypt* (Princeton, NJ: Princeton University Press, 1995); Beth Baron, *The Women's Awakening in Egypt: Culture, Society, and the Press* (New Haven, CT: Yale University Press, 1994); Valentine Moghadam, *Modernizing Women: Gender and Social Change in the Middle East* (Boulder, CO: Lynne Rienner, 1993); Valentine Moghadam, ed., *Gender and National Identity: Women and Politics in Muslim Societies* (Atlantic Highlands, NJ: Zed, 1994); Valentine Moghadam, *Organizing Women: Formal and Informal Women's Groups in the Middle East* (New York: Berg, 1997). For memoirs and novels by Muslim women, see Afkhami, *Women in Exile*; Aman, as told to Virginia Lee Barnes and Janice Boddy, *Aman: The Story of a Somali Girl* (New York: Vintage Books, 1995); Cherry Mosteshar, *Unveiled: One Woman's Nightmare in Iran* (New York: St. Martin's, 1996); Hanan al-Shaykh, *Beirut Blues* (New York: Anchor Books, 1996); Hanan al-Shaykh, *I Sweep the Sun off Rooftops*, trans. Catherine Cobham (New York: Doubleday, 1998); Nina Bouraoui, *Forbidden Vision* (Barrytown, NY: Station Hill, 1995); Ahdaf Soueif, *In the Eye of the Sun* (New York: Pantheon, 1992); Nawal el Saadawi, *The Innocence of the Devil* (Berkeley: University of California Press, 1994); Nahid Rachlin, *The Heart's Desire* (San Francisco: City Lights, 1995); Nahid Rachlin, *Veils: Short Stories* (San Francisco: City Lights, 1992).

138. See Feminist Majority, "History of the Feminist Majority Foundation," http://www.feminist.org/welcome/chronology/timeline.asp (accessed April 21, 2010); interview of Feminist Majority president Eleanor Smeal by journalist Roy Gutman, Arlington, VA, July 1, 2004, typewritten transcript provided to the author by Roy Gutman, 1.

139. Smeal interview, 2, 14.

140. Margaret Cavin, "Evening Gowns to Burqas: The Propaganda of Fame," in *Readings in Propaganda and Persuasion: New and Classic Essays*, ed. Garth S. Jowett and Victoria O'Donnell (Thousand Oaks, CA: Sage, 2006), 155.

141. Cavin, "Evening Gowns to Burqas," 263–64, 273.

142. Ibid., 278; Smeal interview, 7. Smeal also went on the *Today Show* to ask Americans to buy handicrafts made by Afghan women through the FMF to support the anti-Taliban campaign. She claimed that she sold $66,000 through that one appearance.

143. Rashid, *Taliban*, 182; Smeal interview, 5.

144. Cavin, "Evening Gowns to Burqas," 268; interview of Mavis Leno by journalist Roy Gutman, May 2, 2004, typewritten transcript provided to author by Roy Gutman, 6; Margaret Carlson, "All Wrapped Up with Nowhere to Go," *Time* 153, no. 14 (April 12, 1999): 8; FMF Press Release, "Hollywood Mobilized for Afghan Women,"

Feminist News, March 31, 1999, http://feminist.org/news/newsbyte/uswirestory.asp
?id=2146 (accessed April 30, 2010). See also Cavin, "Evening Gowns to Burqas," 270–71;
Smeal interview, 6.

145. Handwritten note from Theresa Loar to Melanne Verveer on Feminist Majority Foundation "Eleven & a Half Million Waiting to Be Freed" event announcement,
February 1, 1999, First Lady's Office (seg. 4), Box 22.

146. Gutman, *We Missed the Story*, 174; Carlson, "Wrapped Up," 8.

147. For example, see FMF, "Hollywood Mobilized."

148. Cavin, "Evening Gowns to Burqas," 279–80. According to Smeal, *George*
magazine declared the campaign against "gender apartheid" the number one cause
for celebrities in 1999. Smeal interview, 6. Members of the public also contacted their
political representatives and members of the Clinton administration to urge non-
recognition and to express their outrage over the Taliban's abuse of women. See William J. vanden Heuvel of the Franklin & Eleanor Roosevelt Institute to Warren
Christopher, October 3, 1996, Christopher Papers, Box 23; Linda [no last name] of Mo-
zark Productions to Bill Clinton re: FMF & Afghan Women, July 14, 1999, with handwritten notes by Bill Clinton, First Lady's Office (seg. 4), Box 1; fax cover sheet from
Jennifer Jackman of the Feminist Majority to Ann Lewis, June 22, 1999, First Lady's
Office (seg. 4), Box 1.

149. Freed, "Odd Partners," 1A; Mackenzie, "United States and Afghanistan," 98;
Mowbray, *Dangerous Diplomacy*, 70–72.

150. Feminist Majority, "History of FMF."

151. Cavin, "Evenin Gowns to Burqas," 265; Smeal interview, 6.

152. Mowbray, *Dangerous Diplomacy*, 73; Mackenzie, "United States and Taliban," 102; Helen Laville, "Gender Apartheid? American Women and Women's Rights
in American Foreign Policy," in *The US Public and American Foreign Policy*, ed. Andrew Johnstone and Helen Laville (New York: Routledge, 2010), 155; Cavin, "Evening
Gowns to Burqas," 265.

153. Afkhami interview with author.

154. *SIGI News* 4, no. 2 (Summer 1996): 6, SIGI Records, Box PUB17; Loar interview with author. The SIGI members who attended were Mahnaz Afkhami, Shaha
Alireza, Boutheina Cheriet, Munira Fakhro, Fatima Mernissi, and Yasmeen Mur-
shed. U.S. officials present included Albright; Elaine Shocus, Albright's chief of staff;
Melanne Verveer, the First Lady's deputy chief of staff; Theresa Loar of the President's
Interagency Council on Women; and Suzanne Tarr-Whelan, the U.S. representative to
the UN Commission on the Status of Women.

155. Afkhami interview with author.

156. Loar interview with author.

157. *SIGI News* 4, no. 2 (Summer 1996): 6.

158. According to the available records, Afkhami continued to be invited to the
White House as late as December 2000. See President's List, List of Invited Guests,
Appointees Ceremony, Tuesday, December 19, 2000, PICW Records, Box 3.

159. Feminist Majority Foundation, FMF Press Release, "Maloney and Rohrabacher Plan Trip to Investigate Afghani Abuses," *Feminist News*, October 31, 1997, http://69.20.36.10/news/newsbyte/uswirestory.asp?id=2619 (accessed June 1, 2014).

160. Afkhami interview with author; Loar interview with author.

161. See Records on Sima Wali, 1987–2001, SIGI Records, Box M6; Records on Afghan women's human rights, 1996–2001, SIGI Records, Box GEO1-GEO2; Records on the Revolutionary Association of the Women of Afghanistan, SIGI Records, Box ORG9; Records on the Afghan Women's Council, Afghan Women's Counseling and Integration Community Support Organization, and Women's Task Force of the Afghanistan Reconstruction Support Committee, SIGI Records, Box ORG1.

162. Even though the FMF met with Afghan Americans and sent some representatives to Pakistan to visit refugee camps, Muslim feminists often critiqued its approach. Cavin, "Evening Gowns to Burqas," 273; Khan, "Between Here and There"; Laville, "Gender Apartheid," 156–70; Leno interview, 2; Smeal interview, 23–24.

163. Loar interview with author.

164. Ibid. For other another instance when the Taliban protested foreign criticisms about human rights in Afghanistan, see "Iranian Women Hear Cries of Afghan Sisters."

165. Confidential: Afghanistan: Meeting with the Taliban, from the Secretary of State to the U.S. Embassy in Islamabad, drafted by Sheldon Rapoport and approved and classified by Karl "Rick" Inderfurth, December 8, 1997, Case No. F-2010-02445, Doc. No. C05259861, Department of State, FOIA Reading Room, http://foia.state.gov (accessed December 19, 2014).

166. Gutman, *We Missed the Story*, 113.

167. Department of State, "Women and Girls in Afghanistan," Fact Sheet released by the Senior Coordinator for International Women's Issues, March 19, 1998, http://www.state.gov/www/global/womens/fs_980310_women_afghan.html (accessed December 4, 2009); PICW, *Update*, 14–15.

168. Mackenzie, "United States and Taliban," 103. The closure also had to do with demonstrations outside the embassy by the FMF and other groups. Smeal interview, 4.

169. Theresa Loar, "Statement on Women in Afghanistan at a Mock Hearing Before Senator Diane Feinstein," Washington, DC, March 2, 1998, as released by the Office for International Women's Issues, U.S. Department of State, http://www.state.gov/www/policy_remarks/1998/980302_loar_afgh.html (accessed December 4, 2009).

170. H. Con. Res. 336, Condemning the Taliban and Supporting a Broad Based Government in Afghanistan, 105th Cong., 2nd Sess. (1998), https://www.govtrack.us/congress/bills/105/hconres336/text (accessed June 2, 2014); S. Res. 68, Expressing the Sense of the Senate Regarding the Treatment of Women and Girls by the Taliban in Afghanistan, 106th Cong., 1st Sess. (1999), https://www.govtrack.us/congress/bills/106/sres68/text (accessed June 2, 2014); FMF, "Maloney and Rohrabacher Trip"; Loar interview with author.

171. Garner, *Gender & Foreign Policy*, 105.

172. B. Clinton, "Remarks on International Women's Day."

173. Press Briefing by Secretary of State Madeleine Albright and National Security Advisor Sandy Berger, White House, The Briefing Room, August 20, 1998, OBL Collection, Box 3. See also Confidential: Afghanistan: Bin Laden Reportedly in Jalalabad, from American Embassy in Islamabad to Secretary of State, October 14, 1996, Case No. F-2005-05447, Doc. No. C18596673, Department of State, FOIA Reading Room, http://foia.state.gov (accessed March 26, 2015).

174. See Hillary Rodham Clinton, "Remarks at the United Jewish Appeal Lion of Judah Conference," Washington, DC, September 14, 1998, First Lady's Office (seg. 4), Box 11; Hillary Rodham Clinton, United Nations International Women's Day Speech on Women's Rights, New York, March 4, 1999, http://clinton2.nara.gov/WH/EOP/First_Lady/html/generalspeeches/1999/19990304.html (accessed May 18, 2015); memo from Theresa Loar of PICW to Ambassador Wendy Sherman and Under Secretary Frank Loy, March 26, 1999, First Lady's Office (seg. 4), Box 22; Confidential: Afghanistan: Potential Incentives for the Taliban, drafted by T. Hushek, May 13, 1999, Case No. F-2006-02981, Doc. No. C18601077, Department of State, FOIA Reading Room, http://foia.state.gov (accessed December 19, 2014); Secret: A New Bin Laden Strategy, Action Memorandum from SA Karl F. Inderfurth, NEA Martin Indy, and S/CT Michael Sheehan, Acting, to the Secretary [Albright], May 15, 1999, Case No. F-2006-02981, Doc. No. C18601075, Department of State, FOIA Reading Room, http://foia.state.gov (accessed March 26, 2015); Unclassified NSC/RMO Profile Memo from Shoukria Haidar to Bill Clinton re: State Fwds Translation of Ltrs & Documents re: Women's Rights in Afghanistan/Taliban & Bin Laden, August 20, 1999, OBL Collection, Box 8; Taliban Executive Order: Qs & As, no date [likely July 1999], OBL Collection, Box 3; PICW, *America's Commitment*; *Celebrating America's Commitment to Women*, March 30, 2000, Dept. of State program pamphlet, PICW Records, Box 5; Madeleine K. Albright, "Remarks at Special Session of the United Nations General Assembly on Women 2000: Beijing Plus Five," June 8, 2000, New York, PICW Records, Box 6; Afghanistan: Statement by A/S Inderfurth Before the SFRC Subcommittee on the Near East and South Asia, July 20, 2000, from Secretary of State to All South Asia Collective, July 20, 2000, Case No. F-2011-03409, Doc. No. C17641420, Department of State, FOIA Reading Room, http://foia.state.gov (accessed December 19, 2014); Secret: Searching for the Taliban's Hidden Message, from American Embassy in Islamabad to Secretary of State, September 19, 2000, Case No. F-2011-03409, Doc. No. C17641503, Department of State, FOIA Reading Room, http://foia.state.gov (accessed December 19, 2014); Secret: Discussions on Usama bin Laden with Taleban Deputy Foreign Minister Jalil, from Secretary of State to American Embassy in Islamabad, November 9, 2000, Case No. F-2011-03409, Doc. No. C17641598, Department of State, FOIA Reading Room, http://foia.state.gov (accessed December 19, 2014); Secret: A/S Inderfurth Advises Ambassador Lodhi on U.S. Concerns with Taliban During November 16 Meeting, from Secretary of State to American Em-

bassy in Islamabad, November 20, 2000, Case No. F-2011-03409, Doc. No. C17641622, Department of State, FOIA Reading Room, http://foia.state.gov (accessed December 19, 2014); Beijing+5 Background, Talking Points, "Treatment of Women in Afghanistan," undated [but prior to Beijing+5 conference held in June 2000], First Lady's Office (seg. 4), Box 4; Loar ADST oral history, 170, 174.

175. Taliban Executive Order: Qs & As; President William J. Clinton, Executive Order 13129, July 4, 1999, http://fas.org/irp/offdocs/eo/eo-13129.htm (accessed May 12, 2015); Ambassador Karl F. Inderfurth, interviewed by Charles Stuart Kennedy, initial interview date April 27, 2001, Association for Diplomatic Studies and Training, Foreign Affairs Oral History Project, 83, http://www.adst.org (accessed December 18, 2014).

176. It was the FMF's first and only meeting with President Clinton. Gutman, *We Missed the Story*, 176. The FMF only met Albright once, in 2000. Smeal interview, 11, 14; Leno interview, 3.

177. Taliban Executive Order: Qs & As; Inderfurth ADST oral history, 83.

178. Loar interview with author; Loar ADST oral history, 171, 174.

179. Secretary of State Madeleine K. Albright and First Lady Hillary Rodham Clinton, Media Roundtable, Washington, DC, March 11, 1998, as released by the Office of the Spokesman, U.S. Department of State, First Lady's Office (seg. 4), Box 11.

180. Taliban Executive Order: Qs & As.

181. Inderfurth ADST oral history, 83.

182. Rashid, *Taliban*, 177.

183. After the 1998 embassy bombings, Taliban representatives reached out to the United States via back channels and appeared willing to negotiate about Osama bin Laden. See Classified: Afghanistan: Taliban's Mullah Omar's 8/22 Contact with State Department, from Secretary of State to American Embassy in Islamabad, August 23, 1998, Case No. F-2006-02981, Doc. No. C05252376, Department of State, FOIA Reading Room, http://foia.state.gov (accessed March 26, 2015). It is unclear whether such overtures were sincere. However, in their attempts to contact the United States, Taliban representatives expressed concern that the United States would still deny them recognition because of Afghan women's status, and they expressed continued unwillingness to change their policies on women. See Unclassified NSC/RMO Profile to David Walters, from Sandy Berger, re: Taliban Approach to David Walters re: Usama bin Laden, with attachments, August 18, 1999, OBL Collection, Box 8; Confidential: Taliban Representatives Bring Nothing New to Meeting with A/S Inderfurth and SC/T Coordinator Sheehan, from Secretary of State to American Embassy in Islamabad, July 10, 2000, State Case No. F-2011-03409, Doc. No. C1764, Department of State, FOIA Reading Room, http://foia.state.gov (accessed December 19, 2014); Secret: A Taliban Bid to Relieve Themselves of bin Laden? American Embassy in Islamabad to Secretary of State, September 15, 2000, Case No. F-2011-03409, Doc. No. C17641491, Department of State, FOIA Reading Room, http://foia.state.gov (accessed December 19, 2014); Secret: Taliban [redacted] Insists They Want to Find a Way out of UBL

Morass, from American Embassy in Islamabad to Secretary of State, November 2, 2000, Case No. F-2011-03409, Doc. No. C17641574, Department of State, FOIA Reading Room, http://foia.state.gov (accessed December 19, 2014); Searching for the Taliban's Hidden Message.

Chapter 7

1. George W. Bush, "Remarks on Signing the Afghan Women and Children Relief Act of 2001," December 12, 2001, American Presidency Project, ed. Gerhard Peters and John T. Woolley, http://www.presidency.ucsb.edu/ws/index.php?pid=73497&st=&st1 (accessed October 29, 2007).

2. NOW, "The Truth About George," Women's Rights, http://web.archive.org/web/20060112021709/http://www.thetruthaboutgeorge.com/women/index.html (accessed January 19, 2013); Michaele L. Ferguson and Lori J. Marso, "Introduction: Feminism, Gender, and Security in the Bush Presidency," in *W Stands for Women*, ed. Ferguson and Marso, 8; Faludi, *Terror Dream*, 33.

3. See George W. Bush, "Women's History Month, 2001: A Proclamation," March 2, 2001, http://georgewbush-whitehouse.archives.gov/news/releases/2001/03/20010302-2.html (accessed December 20, 2012); George W. Bush, "Women's Equality Day, 2001: A Proclamation," August 24, 2001, http://georgewbush-whitehouse.archives.gov/news/releases/2001/08/20010824-1.html (accessed February 7, 2013); Michaele L. Ferguson, "Feminism and Security Rhetoric in the Post–September 11 Bush Administration," in *W Stands for Women*, ed. Ferguson and Marso, 196.

4. Ferguson and Marso, "Introduction," 2. These appointees included Condoleezza Rice, Christine Todd Whitman, and longtime advisor Karen Hughes.

5. Ferguson and Marso, "Introduction," 1.

6. Laville, "Gender Apartheid?" 160; Faludi, *Terror Dream*, 49.

7. Eleanor Smeal, quoted in Faludi, *Terror Dream*, 50. Italics in the original. See also Lacayo, "About Face for Afghan Women."

8. Smeal interview, 13–14, 18; Gutman, *We Missed the Story*, 176; Laville, "Gender Apartheid," 157, 160; FMF Press Release, "Congressional Testimony of E. Smeal on the Plight of Afghan Women Before the Joint Hearing of the Subcommittee on International Organizations and Terrorism and the Subcommittee on Near Eastern and South Asia Affairs of the Committee on Foreign Relations U.S. Senate," October 10, 2001, http://www.feminist.org/news/pressstory.asp?id=5861 (accessed September 10, 2010).

9. For feminist criticisms of the FMF, see Iris Marion Young, "The Logic of Masculinist Protection: Reflections on the Current Security State," in *W Stands for Women*, ed. Ferguson and Marso, 117–18; Lori J. Marso, "Feminism and the Complications of Freeing the Women of Afghanistan and Iraq," in *W Stands for Women*, ed. Ferguson and Marso, 226; Laville, "Gender Apartheid?" 149–75; Laila al-Marayati and Semeen Issa, "An Identity Reduced to a Burka," *Los Angeles Times*, January 20, 2002, http://articles.latimes.com/2002/jan/20/opinion/op-almarayatiissa (accessed

March 8, 2013); Sonali Kolhatkar, "'Saving' Afghan Women," Znet free update, May 9, 2002, Revolutionary Association of the Women of Afghanistan (RAWA), http://www .rawa.org/znet.htm (accessed January 8, 2013); Hirschkind and Mahmood, "Feminism, the Taliban, Counter-Insurgency," 339–54.

10. Email from Afifa Dirana Arsanios to Greta Hofmann Nemiroff, enclosing a letter from the SIGI membership to the SIGI leadership, July 19, 2000, SIGI Records, Box GHN1; email from Isel Rivero to Greta Hofmann Nemiroff, August 7, 2000, SIGI Records, Box GHN1; fax from Greta Hofmann Nemiroff to Robin Morgan, enclosing letter from Robin Morgan to Mahnaz Afkhami, March 31, 1999, SIGI Records, Box GHN1; email from Greta Hofmann Nemiroff to Robin Morgan, November 22, 2000, SIGI Records, Box GHN1; email from Robin Morgan to Maria Suarez, August 14, 2000, attached to email from Maria Suarez to Robin Morgan, August 18, 2000, SIGI Records, Box GHN1; email from Greta Hofmann Nemiroff to Mashuda Khatun Shefali, May 25, 2000, SIGI Records, Box GHN1; email from Mashuda Khatun Shefali to Greta Hofmann Nemiroff, May 27, 2000, SIGI Records, Box GHN1.

11. Email from Robin Morgan to Greta Hofmann Nemiroff, November 22, 2000, SIGI Records, Box GHN1.

12. Email, Arsanios to Nemiroff, July 19, 2000, SIGI Records, Box GHN1; email from Greta Hofmann Nemiroff to Afifa Dirana Arsanios, July 19, 2000, SIGI Records, Box GHN1; email from Rivero to Nemiroff, August 7, 2000, SIGI Records, Box GHN1; email from Greta Hofmann Nemiroff to Rakhee Goyal, January 20, 2000, enclosing email from Rakhee Goyal to Greta Hofmann Nemiroff, January 18, 2000, SIGI Records, Box GHN1; fax from Nemiroff to Morgan, March 31, 1999, SIGI Records, Box GHN1; open letter from Greta Hofmann Nemiroff and Robin Morgan to SIGI Membership ("All"), date unknown [sometime after June 2000], SIGI Records, Box GHN1. Nemiroff and Morgan criticized Afkhami's leadership and SIGI's focus on Muslim women at the June 2000 general meeting in New York City, which Afkhami did not attend. They also sent an open letter to SIGI's membership afterward reiterating those criticisms in response to an email Afkhami had sent to some members defending her record as the organization's president. From the record, it appears as though Morgan in particular nursed personal grievances. She complained that SIGI's website did not sufficiently recognize the contributions of SIGI's members during the years before Afkhami took over the organization, particularly Morgan's own role as SIGI's founder. Morgan stated in emails exchanged with Nemiroff and Afkhami that her role as SIGI founder had been downplayed both on the website and in SIGI's operations. Morgan appears to have resented the fact that Afkhami's name was most prominently associated with the organization rather than her own.

13. Email, Arsanios to Nemiroff, July 19, 2000, SIGI Records, Box GHN1; email, Nemiroff to Arsanios, July 19, 2000, SIGI Records, Box GHN1.

14. Email from Robin Morgan to Greta Hofmann Nemiroff, September 15, 2000, SIGI Records, Box GHN1. Fatima Mernissi left SIGI to become a board member of WLP. The email from Morgan to Nemiroff about SIGI defections to WLP also indicates

that the pair encouraged, and sometimes pushed, members sympathetic to Afkhami to leave SIGI.

15. SIGI did try to resurrect itself as a social networking site for feminists, www .globalsister.org, in 2010, but that did not last long.

16. Sue Pleming, "Afghan Women Take Fight for Rights to U.S. Congress," Afghanistan News Center, December 14, 2001, www.afghanistannewscenter.com/news /2001/december/dec14s2001.html (accessed October 4, 2012).

17. Ibid.

18. Sonali Kolhatkar, "The Impact of U.S. Intervention on Afghan Women's Rights," *Berkeley Women's Law Journal* 17, no. 2 (2002): 22–23.

19. Christine McCarthy McMorris, "Bush and the Burqa," *Religion in the News* 5, no. 1 (Spring 2002), http://www.trincoll.edu/depts/csrpl/rinvol5no1/Bush%20burqa .htm (accessed February 7, 2013).

20. For descriptions of media coverage of Afghan women in the fall of 2001, see McMorris, "Bush and the Burqa"; Carol A. Stabile and Deepa Kumar, "Unveiling Imperialism: Media, Gender, and the War on Afghanistan," *Media, Culture and Society* 27, no. 5 (2005): 771–72.

21. McMorris, "Bush and the Burqa"; Rosenberg, "Rescuing Women and Children," 457.

22. See, for example, McMorris, "Bush and the Burqa"; Brown, "Any Day Now"; Howlett, "Afghan Women Fight Oppression"; Lacayo, "About Face for Afghan Women"; Peterson, "For Many Afghan Women, Bare Faces and Lives Resumed"; Latifa, written in collaboration with Shekeba Hachemi, *My Forbidden Face: Growing Up Under the Taliban: A Young Woman's Story*, trans. Linda Coverdale (New York: Hyperion, 2001).

23. Laura Bush, "Radio Address."

24. Bush, "Remarks on Signing Relief Act"; Rosenberg, "Rescuing Women and Children," 456.

25. George W. Bush, State of the Union Address, January 29, 2002, http:// georgewbush-whitehouse.archives.gov/news/releases/2002/01/20020129-11.html (accessed February 6, 2013).

26. Loar interview with author.

27. Colin Powell and Paula Dobriansky, "Remarks at a Conference on Women in Afghanistan," Eisenhower Executive Office Building, Washington, D.C., November 19, 2001, http://2001-2009.state.gov/g/wi/7250.htm (accessed May 27, 2010).

28. Colin L. Powell, "Remarks at Reception to Mark International Women's Day," Benjamin Franklin Room, Department of State, Washington, D.C., March 7, 2002, http://2001-2009.state.gov/secretary/former/powell/remarks/2002/8691.htm (accessed February 21, 2013).

29. Powell and Dobriansky, "Remarks at Conference."

30. George W. Bush, "America's Responsibility, America's Mission," September 17, 2002, in *The Imperial Tense: Prospects and Problems of American Empire*, ed. Andrew J. Bacevich (Chicago: Ivan R. Dee, 2003), 7.

31. Immerman, *Empire for Liberty*, 5.

32. Bureau of Democracy, Human Rights, and Labor, "Report on the Taliban's War Against Women," U.S. State Department, November 17, 2001, released in four parts at http://2001-2009.state.gov/g/drl/rls/6183.htm; http://2001-2009.state.gov/g /drl/rls/6185.htm; http://2001-2009.state.gov/g/drl/rls/6186.htm; and http://2001-2009 .state.gov/g/drl/rls/6190.htm (accessed May 27, 2010).

33. Powell, "International Women's Day." Minister Samar resigned in the summer of 2002 because she received death threats.

34. Powell and Dobriansky, "Remarks at Conference."

35. Office of International Women's Issues, U.S. Department of State, U.S. Support for Afghan Women, Children, and Refugees, June 22, 2004, http://2001-2009 .state.gov/g/wi/rls/33787.htm (accessed June 1, 2014).

36. For a list of Bush administration statements on women's human rights' centrality to its foreign policies, see my bibliography for this book located at http://www .kellyjshannon.com. See also archived U.S. Department of State website for 2001–9, Office of Women's Issues, Focus on Afghanistan, http://2001-2009.state.gov/g/wi /c6486.htm (accessed February 7, 2013).

37. For some examples, see Faludi, *Terror Dream*, 51–57; Marso, "Feminism and the Complications of Freeing the Women of Afghanistan and Iraq," 226–29; Stabile and Kumar, "Unveiling Imperialism," 765–82; Jefferson, "Out Go the Taliban, But Will Afghan Women Be Excluded Again?"; Shahnaz Khan, "Afghan Women: The Limits of Colonial Rescue," in *Feminism and War: Confronting U.S. Imperialism*, ed. Robin L. Riley, Chandra Talpade Mohanty, and Minnie Bruce Pratt (London: Zed, 2008), 161–78; Berenice Malka Fisher, "'Freedom for Women': Stories of Baghdad and New York," in *Feminism and War*, ed. Riley, Mohanty, and Pratt, 207–15; Dan De Luce, "U.S. Success in Afghanistan Questioned by Experts," WeNews, *WomensEnews* .org, October 4, 2004, http://womensenews.org/story/the-world/041004/us-success -afghanistan-questioned-experts#.UT5btOiaTZ1 (accessed February 1, 2013); Sonali Kolhatkar, "Afghan Women: Enduring American 'Freedom,'" *Foreign Policy in Focus*, Global Affairs Commentary, November 14, 2002, http://www.fpif.org /commentary/2002/0211afwomen_body.html (accessed October 29, 2007); *Lifting the Veil/Afghanistan Unveiled*, directed by Hugh Thompson, aired on CNN in August and September 2007 (Sharmeen Obaid Films, 2008), DVD; Jenna Pickett, "The Bush Administration and Afghan Women," Presidential Fellows Program Blog, Center for the Study of the Presidency and Congress, March 20, 2012, http://presidentialfellows .wordpress.com/2012/03/20/the-bush-administration-and-afghan-women (accessed February 1, 2013); Joan Smith, "Bush Fails Women in Afghanistan," *Common Dreams*, originally published in *Seattle Post-Intelligencer*, June 14, 2006, http://www .commondreams.org/views06/0614-27.htm (accessed October 29, 2007).

38. See Ferguson, "Feminism and Security Rhetoric," 192; Maureen Dowd, "Cleopatra and Osama," *New York Times*, November 18, 2001, http://www.nytimes .com/2001/11/18/opinion/18DOWD.html (accessed February 8, 2013); Kim Grady,

quoted in McMorris, "Bush and the Burqa"; Dina Rabadi, "U.S. Drags Feet on Ratifying UN Treaty on Women's Rights," Women's World, The Crisis: Open Forum, reprinted from *Chicago Tribune*, June 13, 2004, http://www.wworld.org/crisis/crisis.asp?ID=443 (accessed February 1, 2013).

39. Mary Hawkesworth, "Feminists Versus Feminization: Confronting the War Logics of the George W. Bush Administration," in *W Stands for Women*, ed. Ferguson and Marso, 176.

40. See Marso, "Feminism and the Complications of Freeing the Women of Afghanistan and Iraq," 222; Cooke, "Saving Brown Women," 469.

41. Ann Russo, "The Feminist Majority Foundation's Campaign to Stop Gender Apartheid: The Intersections of Feminism and Imperialism in the United States," *International Feminist Journal of Politics* 8, no. 4 (December 2006): 559.

42. Rosenberg, "Rescuing Women and Children," 459.

43. See Lila Abu-Lughod, "Do Muslim Women Really Need Saving? Anthropological Reflections on Cultural Relativism and Its Others," *American Anthropologist* 104, no. 3 (September 2002): 783–90; K. J. Ayotte and M. Hussain, "Securing Afghan Women: Neocolonialism, Epistemic Violence, and the Rhetoric of the Veil," *NWSA Journal* 17, no. 3 (2005): 112–33; Huibin Amelia Chew, "What's Left? After 'Imperial Feminist' Hijackings," in *Feminism and War*, ed. Riley, Mohanty, and Pratt, 75–90; Jennifer L. Fluri, "'Rallying Public Opinion' and Other Misuses of Feminism," in *Feminism and War*, ed. Riley, Mohanty, and Pratt, 143–57; Krista Hunt, "The Strategic Co-optation of Women's Rights: Discourse in the 'War on Terrorism,'" *International Feminist Journal of Politics* 4, no. 1 (2002): 116–21; Stabile and Kumar, "Unveiling Imperialism," 765–82; Katherine Viner, "Feminism as Imperialism: George Bush Is Not the First Empire-Builder to Wage War in the Name of Women," *Common Dreams*, originally published in *Guardian/UK*, September 21, 2002, http://www.commondreams.org/views02/0923-07.htm (accessed February 21, 2013).

44. Rosemarie Skaine, *Women of Afghanistan in the Post-Taliban Era: How Lives Have Changed and Where They Stand Today* (Jefferson, NC: McFarland, 2008), 8.

45. Ibid., 15.

46. Bette Dam, "The Misunderstanding of Hamid Karzai," *Foreign Policy*, October 3, 2014, http://foreignpolicy.com/2014/10/03/the-misunderstanding-of-hamid-karzai (accessed February 1, 2016).

47. Islamic Republic of Afghanistan, Constitution of Afghanistan, ratified January 26, 2004, Chapter One, Article Three, http://www.afghanembassy.com.pl/afg/images/pliki/TheConstitution.pdf (accessed February 2, 2016); Meghan Hallock, "A Policy of Mediocrity: A Review of United States Policy Concerning the Women of Afghanistan," *William & Mary Journal of Women and the Law* 11, no. 3 (2005): 501.

48. Kolhatkar, "Impact of U.S. Intervention," 13–18, 21; Rostami-Povey, *Afghan Women*, 74; Hayat Alvi, "Women in Afghanistan: A Human Rights Tragedy a Decade after September 11," November 12, 2012, *RAWA News*, http://www.rawa.org/temp/runews/2012/11/12/women-in-afghanistan-a-human-rights-tragedy-a-decade-after

-september-11.html (accessed February 2, 2016); Dam, "Misunderstanding Karzai"; Hallock, "Policy of Mediocrity," 83, 493.

49. Skaine, *Women of Afghanistan*, 18–22.

50. Ibid., 8.

51. Rostami-Povey, *Afghan Women*, 74–75, 80–94, 132–34; Skaine, *Women of Afghanistan*, 10–11; Stabile and Kumar, "Unveiling Imperialism," 775–77.

52. Skaine, *Women of Afghanistan*, 3; Kolhatkar, "Impact of U.S. Intervention," 19–20.

53. Skaine, *Women of Afghanistan*, 15–16.

54. Kolhatkar, "Impact of U.S. Intervention," 14; Skaine, *Women of Afghanistan*, 22–25.

55. Paul Richter, "U.S. Failed to Track Spending on Aid for Afghan Women, Auditor Finds," *Los Angeles Times*, December 29, 2014, http://www.latimes.com/world /afghanistan-pakistan/la-fg-afghan-women-20141230-story.html (accessed October 28, 2015).

56. Ferguson, "Feminism and Security Rhetoric," 192–93.

57. George W. Bush, "Outline for the Future of Iraq," Carlisle, PA, May 24, 2004, Presidential Rhetoric, http://www.presidentialrhetoric.com/speeches/05.24.04.html (accessed October 8, 2009).

58. Condoleezza Rice, "Remarks at the American University in Cairo," June 20, 2005, http://2001-2009.state.gov/secretary/rm/2005/48328.htm (accessed May 27, 2010); Allison Stevens, "In Rice's Speech Listeners Hear Rights, Rhetoric," *Women's E-news*, June 24, 2005, http://womensenews.org/story/the-world/050624/rices-speech -listeners-hear-rights-rhetoric (accessed May 27, 2010); Condoleezza Rice, "Joint Press Availability with Saudi Foreign Minister Saud Al-Faisal," Riyadh, Saudi Arabia, June 20, 2005, http://2001-2009.state.gov/secretary/rm/2005/48390.htm (accessed May 27, 2010).

59. Jonathan Karl, "Karen of Arabia: I, Mom Meets the Imams," *Saudi-US Relations Information Service*, October 23, 2005, http://www.saudi-us-relations.org /articles/2005/ioi/051023-hughes-karl.html (accessed May 27, 2010).

60. Ferguson and Marso, "Introduction," 2; "In Egypt, Laura Bush Urges Equality for Women," MSNBC, May 24, 2005, http://www.msnbc.msn.com/id/7918891 (accessed May 27, 2010).

61. Condoleezza Rice, *No Higher Honor: A Memoir of My Years in Washington* (New York: Crown, 2011), 379.

62. See Ed Bradley, "Women Speak Out in Saudi Arabia," *60 Minutes*, CBS News, March 23, 2005, http://www.cbsnews.com/news/women-speak-out-in-saudi-arabia/2 (accessed April 3, 2012); "Women in Saudi Arabia: UnShackling Themselves," *Economist*, May 17, 2014, http://www.economist.com/news/middle-east-and-africa/21602249 -saudi-women-are-gaining-ground-slowly-unshackling-themselves (accessed June 5, 2014); Adam Coogle, "The Limits of Reform in Saudi Arabia," Human Rights Watch, October 13, 2013, http://www.hrw.org/news/2013/10/13/limits-reform-saudi-arabia

(accessed June 5, 2014); "Women in Saudi Arabia to Vote and Run in Elections," BBC News, September 25, 2011, http://www.bbc.com/news/world-us-canada-15052030 (accessed June 5, 2014).

63. See "Woman to Woman in Afghanistan's Villages," *News Tribune*, April 27, 2012, http://www.thenewstribune.com/2012/04/27/v-printerfriendly/2122896/woman -to-woman-in-afghanistans.html (accessed March 12, 2013); Defense Critical Language/Culture Program, *Afghan Women: A Guide to Understanding an Afghan Woman's Role in Her Society* (Missoula, MT: Maureen & Mike Mansfield Center at the University of Montana, 2011).

64. Shirin Tahir-Kheli was born in India before its independence from Britain. The region of her birth is today part of Pakistan, but it was India at the time.

65. Shirin Tahir-Kheli, oral history interview with author, December 22, 2011, Bala Cynwyd, PA; Biography of Shirin Tahir-Kheli, Department of State, http://www .state.gov/outofdate/bios/56878.htm (accessed December 2, 2011).

66. Tahir-Kheli interview with author.

67. Ibid.

68. George W. Bush, "Speech to the Organisation for Economic Co-Operation and Development (OECD)," June 13, 2008, Paris: http://www.oecd.org/document/50/ 0,3343,en_2649_201185_40835506_1_1_1_1,00.html (accessed June 15, 2008).

69. Women's Initiative, George W. Bush Institute, http://www.bushcenter.org /bush-institute/womens-initiative (accessed March 12, 2013).

70. Amanda Terkel, "George W. Bush Warns Against Withdrawal from Afghan-istan: 'Women Would Suffer' (Video)," *Huffington Post*, April 1, 2011, http://www .huffingtonpost.com/2011/04/01/bush-withdrawal-afghanistan-women-suffer_n _843537.html (accessed April 2, 2011).

71. William I. Hitchcock, "Human Rights and the Laws of War: The Geneva Conven-tions of 1949," in *The Human Rights Revolution*, ed. Iriye, Goedde, and Hitchcock, 93–112.

72. For a sampling of memoirs and novels by Muslim women that were popular in the United States after 9/11, see my bibliography for this book located at http://www .kellyjshannon.com.

73. See *Osama*, directed by Siddiq Barnak (2003; Metro-Goldwyn-Mayer, 2004), DVD; *Baran*, directed by Majid Majidi (2001; Miramax, 2002), DVD; *Kandahar*, di-rected by Mohsen Makhmalbaf (2001; New Yorker Video, 2003), DVD; *Offside*, directed by Jafar Panahi (2006; Sony, 2006), DVD; *No One Knows About Persian Cats*, directed by Bahman Ghobadi (2009; MPI Home Video, 2011), DVD; *Circumstance*, directed by Maryam Keshavarz (2011; Lionsgate, 2011), DVD; *A Separation*, directed by Asghar Farhadi (2011; Sony, 2012), DVD; *Caramel*, directed by Nadine Labaki (2007; Lions-gate, 2008), DVD. For a sampling of scholarship, see my bibliography for this book located at http://www.kellyjshannon.com.

74. Lorraine Ali, "A Magazine of Their Own," *Newsweek*, May 27, 2002, 62; "Islamic Horizons," ISNA, http://www.isna.net/islamic-horizons.html (accessed March 14, 2013). ISNA elected its first female president in 2006.

75. See Asra Nomani, "Shaking Up Islam in America," *Time*, September 13, 2004, http://www.time.com/time/printout/0,8816,995073,00.html (accessed May 9, 2008); Jeff Chu and Nadia Mustafa, "Her Turn to Pray," *Time*, March 21, 2005, http://www.time.com/time/printout/0,8816,1039716,00.html (accessed May 9, 2008); Laurie Goodstein, "Stereotyping Rankles Silent, Secular Majority of American Muslims," *New York Times*, December 23, 2001, http://www.nytimes.com/2001/12/23/us /stereotyping-rankles-silent-secular-majority-of-american-muslims.html (accessed May 14, 2008); Andrea Elliott, "From Head Scarf to Army Cap, Making a New Life," *New York Times*, December 15, 2006, http://www.nytimes.com/2006/12/15/nyregion /15muslim.html?pagewanted=all&_r=0 (accessed May 14, 2008); Patricia Leigh Brown, "For the Muslim Prom Queen, There Are No Kings Allowed," *New York Times*, June 9, 2003, http://www.nytimes.com/2003/06/09/us/for-the-muslim-prom-queen -there-are-no-kings-allowed.html?pagewanted=all&src=pm (accessed May 14, 2008); Hanan Al Shayk, "My Mother, the Muslim," *Newsweek*, January 7, 2002, http://www .thedailybeast.com/newsweek/2002/01/07/my-mother-the-muslim.html (accessed May 14, 2008); Shireen Khan, "Being American—And Muslim," *Time*, April 4, 2008, http://www.time.com/time/nation/article/0,8599,1728061,00.html (accessed May 19, 2008); Lorraine Ali, "Reform: Not Ignorant, Not Helpless," *Newsweek*, December 12, 2005 (accessed via LexisNexis Academic on May 14, 2008); Asra Nomani, *Standing Alone in Mecca: An American Woman's Struggle for the Soul of Islam* (New York: HarperCollins, 2005).

76. Barack Obama, "Text: Obama's Speech in Cairo," *New York Times*, June 4, 2009, http://www.nytimes.com/2009/06/04/us/politics/04obama.text.html?pagewanted =all&_r=0 (accessed June 5, 2009).

77. "Biography: Melanne Verveer," U.S. Department of State, http://www.state /gov/r/pa/ei/biog/122075.htm (accessed November 12, 2009); Office of Global Women's Issues, U.S. Department of State, http://www.state.gov/s/gwi (accessed November 12, 2009).

78. Hillary Rodham Clinton, "Remarks at No Limits Public Policy Conference Luncheon," U.S. Department of State, November 6, 2009, http://www.state.gov/secretary /rm/2009a/11/131615.htm (accessed December 5, 2009); "Women's Empowerment Central to U.S. Foreign Policy," DipNote, U.S. Department of State Official Blog, October 1, 2009, http://blogs.state.gov/index.php/entries/womens_empowerment/ (accessed December 5, 2009).

79. Gayle Tzemach Lemmon, "The Hillary Doctrine," *Newsweek*, March 6, 2011, http://www.newsweek.com/2011/03/06/the-hillary-doctrine (accessed March 8, 2011).

80. Clinton and Verveer's programs included the Iraqi Women's Democracy Initiative; Secretary's War Widows Initiative; Small Grants Initiative; an anti-FGM initiative in Egypt; courses on women's entrepreneurship in Egypt; Advancing Women Villagers' Political and Economic Rights Initiative in Egypt; the Leading Women Program in Palestine; Combating GBV (gender-based violence) initiative in Pakistan; and Building Political Leadership Among Women program in Bangladesh. See

Programming in the Near East and North Africa, U.S. Department of State, Office of Global Women's Issues, http://www.state.gov/s/gwi/programs/region/nea/index.htm (accessed March 10, 2013); Policy and Programs, U.S. Department of State, Office of Global Women's Issues, http://www.state.gov/s/gwi/programs/index.htm (accessed March 10, 2013); Programs by Region, U.S. Department of State, Office of Global Women's Issues, http://www.state.gov/s/gwi/programs/region/index.htm (accessed March 10, 2013); Programming in South and Central Asia, U.S. Department of State, Office of Global Women's Issues, http://www.state.gov/s/gwi/programs/region/sca/index.htm (accessed March 10, 2013); Global Women's Issues Remarks, Testimony, and Releases, U.S. Department of State, http://www.state.gov/s/gwi/rls/index.htm (accessed March 10, 2013).

81. Afkhami interview with author.

82. Dexter Filkins, "Afghan Women Protest New Law on Home Life," *New York Times*, April 15, 2009, http://www.nytimes.com/2009/04/16/world/asia/16afghan.html?emc=eta1&_r=0 (accessed April 16, 2009); Rady Ananda, "Afghan Women Protest Marital Rape Law; Men Spit and Stone Them," *RAWA News*, http://www.rawa.org/temp/runews/2009/04/16/afghan-women-protest-marital-rape-law-men-spit-and-stone-them.html (accessed March 13, 2013).

83. Hillary Rodham Clinton, quoted in Matthias Gebauer and Shoib Najafizada, "Legalized Oppression of Women: Western Outrage over Discriminatory Afghan Law," *Der Spiegel Online*, April 3, 2009, http://www.spiegel.de/international/world/legalized-oppression-of-women-western-outrage-over-discriminatory-afghan-law-a-617276.html (accessed March 13, 2013).

84. White House, Office of the Press Secretary, News Conference by President Obama, Palaiz de la Musique et Des Congres, Strasbourg, France, April 4, 2009, http://www.whitehouse.gov/the-press-office/news-conference-president-obama-4042009 (accessed April 16, 2009).

85. Hillary Rodham Clinton, *Hard Choices* (New York: Simon and Schuster, 2014), 152–53. For a sampling of global public outcry, see mattbastard, "Obama on Afghan Marital Rape Law: Fighting Terror Trumps Women's Rights," bastard.logic (blog), April 4, 2009, http://bastardlogic.wordpress.com/2009/04/04/obama-afghanistan-women (accessed March 13, 2013); Philip N. Cohen, "Throwing Stones at Afghanistan's Marital Rape Law," *Huffington Post*, April 19, 2009, http://www.huffingtonpost.com/philip-n-cohen/throwing-stones-at-afghan_b_188646.html (accessed March 13, 2013); "Karzai: Afghanistan to Review Criticized Sharia Law," *CNN.com*, April 4, 2009, http://www.cnn.com/2009/WORLD/asiapcf/04/04/afghanistan.womens.rights/index.html (accessed March 13, 2013); Megan Carpentier, "Foreign Policy Fail: U.S.-Backed Afghan Government Passes Pro-Rape Law to Win Election," *Jezebel*, March 31, 2009, http://jezebel.com/5192134/us+backed-afghan-government-passes-pro+rape-law-to-win-election (accessed March 13, 2013); Heather, "More Feminist Perspectives on the Afghan 'Marital Rape' Law," Phem, April 10, 2009, http://www.phem.org/2009/04/new-perspectives-transnational-feminist.html (accessed March 13, 2013).

86. Rajiv Chandrasekaran, "In Afghanistan, U.S. Shifts Strategy on Women's Rights as It Eyes Wider Priorities," *Washington Post*, March 5, 2011, http://www .washingtonpost.com/world/in-afghanistan-us-shifts-strategy-on-womens-rights-as -it-eyes-wider-priorities/2011/03/02/ABkxMAO_story.html (accessed March 13, 2013); Terkel, "Bush Warns Against Withdrawal."

87. Aryn Baker, "Afghan Women and the Return of the Taliban," *Time*, August 9, 2010, 3, 20–27. While the official publication date of this issue was August 9, it began appearing on newsstands and other news outlets began reporting on its cover story as early as the last week of July 2010.

88. Ibid., cover and 3, 20–27.

89. Rod Nordlund, "Portrait of Pain Ignites Debate over Afghan War," *New York Times*, August 4, 2010, http://www.nytimes.com/2010/08/05/world/asia/05afghan .html?emc=eta1 (accessed August 5, 2010).

90. "Interview with Speaker Pelosi," *This Week with Christiane Amanpour*, ABC News Video, August 1, 2010, http://abcnews.go.com/ThisWeek/video/interview-speaker -pelosi-christiane-amanpour-this-week-afghanistan-midterm-elections-politics -11299153 (accessed August 12, 2010); Alessandra Stanley, "A TV Host Challenges Guest. That's News," *New York Times*, August 1, 2010, http://www.nytimes.com/2010/08 /02/arts/television/02watch.html?emc=eta1 (accessed August 2, 2010); "'This Week' Transcript: Pelosi and Gates," ABC *This Week*, August 1, 2010, http://abcnews.go.com /ThisWeek/week-transcript-pelosi-gates/story?id=11298444 (accessed March 13, 2013).

91. See Yifat Susskind, "Obama Backpedals on Empty Promises to Afghan Women," *Common Dreams*, June 23, 2011, https://www.commondreams.org/view /2011/06/23-10 (accessed March 1, 2013); Valerie Hudson and Patricia Leidl, "Betrayed," *Foreign Policy*, May 10, 2010, http://www.foreignpolicy.com/articles/2010/05 /07/the_us_is_abandoning_afghanistan_s_ women (accessed March 1, 2013); Ananda, "Afghan Women Protest Marital Rape Law"; Gayle Tzemach Lemmon, "Don't Abandon Us, Obama," *Daily Beast*, November 11, 2009, http://www.thedailybeast.com /blogs-and-stories/2009-11-11/in-security-crisis-afghan-women-leaders-demand -support.html (accessed December 19, 2009); Scott Levi, "The Long, Long Struggle for Women's Rights in Afghanistan," *Origins* 1, no. 12 (September 2009), http://ehistory .osu.edu/osu/origins/article.cfm?articleid=30 (accessed September 28, 2009); Nicholas D. Kristof and Sheryl WuDunn, "The Women's Crusade," Special Issue: Saving the World's Women, *New York Times Magazine*, August 17, 2009, http://www.nytimes .com/2009/08/23/magazine/23Women-t.html (accessed December 5, 2009; Dexter Filkins, "A Schoolbus for Shamsia," Special Issue: Saving the World's Women, *New York Times Magazine*, August 17, 2009, http://www.nytimes.com/2009/08/23/magazine /23school-t.html (accessed December 5, 2009).

92. Michael Gerson, "An Afghan Feminism," *The Washington Post*, July 10, 2009, http://www.washingtonpost.com/wp-dyn/content/article/2009-07-10/opinions /36851937_1_afghan-women-afghan-parliament-president-hamid-karzai (accessed December 19, 2009).

93. Department of State, 2001 Report on U.S. Assistance for Afghan Women, http://2002-2009-usawc.state.gov/news/c7542.htm (accessed June 1, 2014).

94. France banned the wearing of the Islamic veil in public schools and other venues in 2004 and completely banned the wearing of the face veil in 2010. Although the debates and ultimate adoption of these policies had much to do with French immigration issues and a crisis in French national identity, they also reflected French concern about Muslim women's human rights. For an excellent scholarly study of the French headscarf controversy, see Scott, *Politics of the Veil.*

95. Ferguson, "Feminism and Security Rhetoric," 215n13.

96. Rosenberg, "Rescuing Women and Children," 462, 465.

97. For a sampling of ongoing problems faced by women in the Islamic world, see Mona Eltahawy, "Why Do They Hate Us?" *Foreign Policy*, The Sex Issue (May/June 2012): 64–70.

98. Melanne Verveer, "Why Women Are a Foreign Policy Issue," *Foreign Policy*, The Sex Issue (May/June 2012): 90–91.

Index

Islamabad, 139–40, 141
Islam and FGM, relationship between:
asylum and, 122; *Hosken Report* and,
104–5; infibulation and, 101; lack of, 99;
Muslim arguments in favor of, 102, 108–9,
222n53; NGOs and, 108–9; relationship
between, perception of, 112–13, 117; U.S.
public perception of, 98–103, 104; virginity
and, 102, 112
Islamic Horizons, 172
Islamic Republic. *See* Iran; Iranian Revolu-
tion; Khomeini, Sayyed Ruhollah Musavi
Islamic Revolution. *See* Iranian Revolution
Islamic Society of North America, 172
Islamic State. *See* ISIS
"Islamization," 45, 47
Islamophobia: 9/11 and, 172–75; Iranian
Revolution and, 9–10, 18, 33–34, 55–56; as
racism, 186n33. *See also* Orientalism
Israel, 31, 39, 46

Jalal, Massouda, 167
Jarmakani, Amira, 19
jihad, 39, 47
Jim Crow, 91, 92, 95
Jordan, 170
Jury, Allan, 144

Kabul, 21, 125, 127, 139, 152
Kandahar, 127
Karzai, Hamid, 167, 175
Kassindja, Fauziya, 121, 122, 123
Kazakhstan, 140
Keddie, Nikki, 51
Kenya, 153
Khalilzad, Zalmay, 140–41
Khan, Amanullah, 21
Khartoum, 106
Khomeini, Sayyed Ruhollah Musavi: gender
policies of, 18, 29–32, 41, 42–43; news
media reporting on, 17, 30, 31, 32, 42; rise
to power of, 24, 27, 28, 40, 45; women's
support for, 62–66
Kirkpatrick, Jeane, 30
Koran: FGM and, 100, 102, 108, 112; women's
rights and, 64, 70, 72, 90, 202n81
Kuwait, 46, 79, 92, 94, 169, 170

language, 102
Larry King Live, 163

law: child abuse law, 117–18; family law, 26,
47, 62, 71, 72–73, 134, 175; about FGM,
114–20; gender equality, 67; public/private
divide and, 61; religious freedom, 117;
rights revolution and, 23; U.S. asylum
courts, 97; veiling and, 43; women's
freedom of movement and, 37, 43, 84, 85,
89–90. *See also* law, international; Shari'a
law, international: Clinton administration
and, 135, 147; feminist NGOs and, 69–70,
131, 133; FGM and, 117; Geneva Accords,
80, 171; transnational human rights
movement and, 23–24, 147; women's rights
in, 60–61, 131, 145, 147, 178. *See also*
CEDAW; United Nations
Law & Order, 98–99, 123, 217n1
Lebanon, 39–40
Ledeen, Michael, 31
Leno, Mavis, 149–50
liberals, American, 29–30. *See also* Democratic Party
Libya, 40
Lippman, Thomas, 147–48
literacy, 62, 106, 173
Loar, Theresa: Clinton State Department
reorganization and, 136, 137, 139, 143–47;
FGM and, 119; meeting of, with Taliban,
152; on non-recognition of Taliban, 153;
SIGI and, 151. *See also* OIWI; PICW;
SCIWI
lobbying: by feminist NGOs, 3, 6, 11, 74, 106,
130–31, 132; for non-recognition of
Taliban, 151–52, 156; by oil companies,
155
Long Ships, The, 22
Los Angeles Times, 149

madrassas, 129
Maeena, Khalid al-, 89
Mahmoody, Betty, 37–38, 55–56
Majlis, 25, 26
Malaysia, 46
Marie Claire, 123
marriage/divorce: adultery, 48, 71, 73, 96,
158; extramarital sex, 102; FGM and, 105,
121; marital rape, 175; polygamy, 21, 26,
29, 33, 62; women's equality in, 21, 26, 29,
209n79. *See also* families
McAlister, Melani, 9, 111
medical care, 135, 152, 158, 165

Soviet-Afghan War: consequences of, 128–30,
139; Soviet invasion during, 127–28; U.S.
intervention in, 40, 47, 128–29, 139; U.S.
policy goals during, 39, 42
Soviet Union. *See* Cold War; Soviet-Afghan
War
Spivak, Gayatri, 2, 166
Sri Lanka, 71, 73
Steinem, Gloria, 33, 94, 106, 110, 162
stoning, 48, 71, 73
Sudan, 45, 101, 190n30
Sunni Islam, 79, 127. *See also* Islam
Sweden, 116
Switzerland, 116
Syria, 174, 179

Tabriz, 32
Tahir-Kheli, Shirin, 170
Taines, Wendy, 85
Talbott, Strobe, 87–88
Taliban, 1–2, 15, 125–57, 181n5; anti-FGM
activism and, 123–24; Clinton administration, gender mainstreaming of, and,
133–38; feminist NGO response to, 131–32;
fundamentalism of, vs. Iran, 141, 142; name
of, 127; political recognition of, 11, 132, 136,
147, 148–56; rise to power of, 129–30;
Soviet-Afghan War and, 127–29; as terrorist
organization, 160; U.S. airstrikes against,
156; U.S. negotiation with, 175–76, 243n183;
U.S. support for, 138–41; women, violence
against, by, 176. *See also* Afghanistan
Tanzania, 153
technology, 68, 148
Tehran: veiling in, 21, 25, 28–29, 34–35;
women's protests in, 29, 32–33, 34–35
television, 23, 33, 130
terrorism: cause of, 40; by al Qaeda, 40, 153;
Taliban and, 140, 158, 160; U.S. withdrawal from Afghanistan and, 171
theocracy, 24, 30, 127
This Week with Christiane Amanpour, 176–77
Thomas, Marlo, 33
Time: on Afghanistan withdrawal, 176–77; on
FGM, 114; on Iranian Revolution, 17, 33;
on Saudi Arabia, 87–88
Togo, 122
transnational feminism, 5, 24, 104, 126, 154,
203n4. *See also* Decade for Women;
feminism/feminists

transnational human rights movement. *See*
Decade for Women; rights, universal;
women's rights
Treloar, Theresa Lynn, 88–89
Tribunal on Reproductive Rights in
Amsterdam, 71–72
Tucker, Judith, 52
Turkey, 21, 22, 39
Turkmenistan, 140, 141
Twain, Mark, 20

UDHR, 23, 58, 60, 63, 69, 80
UN Decade for Women. *See* Decade for
Women
UNICEF, 105, 145, 156
UNIFEM (United Nations Development
Fund for Women), 59, 145, 156
United Arab Emirates, 153
United Kingdom, 116
United Nations: Afghanistan's seat at, 145;
charter of, 23, 58, 80; FGM and, 103, 105,
106, 109, 118; first Gulf War and, 94;
lobbying of, 131, 132. *See also* Decade
for Women
United Nations Development Fund for
Women (UNIFEM), 59, 145, 156
United States: exceptionalism of, 164, 166,
178; global mission of, 100, 110, 120, 124,
146–47, 155; Iran and, hostility between,
34; as non-Muslim country, 12–13;
Pakistan and, alliance between, 147; Saudi
Arabia and, alliance between, 92, 99, 142.
See also foreign aid; U.S. Congress; U.S.
foreign policy; U.S. State Department;
values, American
Universal Declaration of Human Rights.
See UDHR
University of Nebraska, 150
Unocal, 140–41, 143, 147, 150, 152, 155
UN Refugee Agency (UNHCR), 154
U.S. Agency for International Development,
39, 115, 118, 120, 135, 154, 165
USAID. *See* United States Agency for
International Development
U.S. Congress: FGM and, 99, 106, 114–20;
women's rights, salience of, for, 118
U.S. Department of Defense, 82, 86
U.S. foreign policy: toward Egypt, 46; as
imperialistic, 45; Islamophobia and,
55–56; profit motive of, 150–51; Reagan

Acknowledgments

Like all books, this one could not have been written and published without input and support from so many people; it really takes a village. I am indebted to all of them. They have provided me with encouraging words, constructive criticism, research funding, inspiring ideas, and information. My book is much stronger because of others' feedback and assistance; its weaknesses are my own. I have so many people to thank. First and foremost, thank you to Peter Agree, my editor, for believing in this book and getting it published, and to the entire University of Pennsylvania Press team. I cannot express the depth of my gratitude to you.

I received generous support from several institutions and organizations that allowed me to complete this project: the History Department, College of Arts and Letters, and Peace, Justice, and Human Rights (PJHR) Initiative at Florida Atlantic University; the College of Arts and Sciences at the University of Alaska Anchorage; the Department of History, College of Liberal Arts, Center for the Study of Force and Diplomacy (CENFAD), and Center for the Humanities (CHAT) at Temple University; and the Society for Historians of American Foreign Relations (SHAFR). My colleagues and friends at many institutions also provided me with a scholarly community, helpful advice, and invaluable support, especially: Michael McGandy; Pamela Haag for her keen editorial skills and enthusiasm; Steve Engle, Ben Lowe, Mark Rose, Patty Kollander, Carla Calarge, and Lauren Guilmette; Ray Ball (who kept me sane and is the best writing buddy out there), Ian Hartman, and Paul Dunscomb; Lisa Jarvinen; Will Hitchcock, Todd Shepard, Harvey Neptune, and David Watt; and my Temple writing group, Michele Louro (who let me obsess), Kate Scott, Abby Perkiss, Cathy Dignaz, Holger Löwendorf, Ben

Brandenberg, Matt Johnson, and Wendy Wong. I would also like to thank my anonymous readers for pushing me to make this book much stronger, and Andy Rotter and Brad Simpson for believing in this project, reading multiple drafts, and helping me make it the best I could. You rock. I could not have done this without you. If I left anyone out, please forgive me and accept my thanks for your help.

I have had the opportunity to learn from an incredibly gifted community of scholars. My greatest debt is to my mentor, Richard Immerman. The amount of time and energy he invested in me and in this project is incalculable (and the number of emails I've sent him over the years asking for advice and the number of drafts of my chapters he has read are too numerous to count). He has been my greatest champion, and it is his scholarly example I strive to follow. Richard, I can't express how much your mentorship and friendship means to me. Thank you so much. To my other teachers and mentors I also owe a debt of gratitude: Frank Costigliola, Beth Bailey, David Farber, Petra Goedde, Firoozeh Kashani-Sabet, and the residents of Swift Hall at Vassar. You have made me a better historian in so many ways. I hope this book makes you proud. Last, thank you to all of the audience members and participants at various conferences and workshops where I presented portions of this project, especially SHAFR members, for your critical feedback and helpful research leads.

Thank you, too, to the army of archivists and librarians who helped me use archival collections, provided research leads, came to the rescue when microfilm machines malfunctioned, and reminded me to take lunch breaks. Aisha Shaheed from Women Living Under Muslim Laws was kind enough to send me copies of over two decades' worth of WLUML's dossiers and publications. Roy Gutman generously shared with me transcripts of interviews he conducted with FMF leaders and pointed me toward key documents. Just when I was about to give up on finding a recording of the *Law & Order* episode discussed in Chapter 5, Kenneth Pybus shared his copy with me. Caleb Mayo and Gabriel Tigerman also shared their expertise of the U.S. entertainment industry. And I am very grateful to Mahnaz Afkhami, Shirin Tahir-Kheli, and Theresa Loar, all of whom were kind enough to let me interview them.

Finally, to my friends and family outside of academia, thank you for your guidance and support. I am grateful for the girls' outings, the telephone marathons, and friends forcing me to have a social life. Thank you for appreciating my passion for history while reminding me that there is a larger world